The Secrets of Solomon's Temple

Kevin L. Gest

LEWIS

Wisdom is Supreme

"Blessed is the man who finds wisdom, the man who gains understanding...Get wisdom, get understanding...Wisdom is supreme; therefore get wisdom. Though it cost all you have, get understanding."

from Proverbs 3 and 4

To
Lois, Emma, Matthew and Alexander — and my mother.

First published 2007

ISBN (10) 0 85318 256 6
ISBN (13) 978 0 85318 256 6

Published by Lewis

an imprint of Ian Allan Publishing Ltd, Hersham, Surrey KT12 4RG.
Printed in England by Ian Allan Printing Ltd, Hersham, Surrey KT12 4RG.

Code:0611/B3

Contents

Acknowledgements

T he preparation of this book has resulted in much reading on matters that were originally unfamiliar to me, travelling to other lands and investigating history in a way that I had not previously contemplated. It involved locking myself away with a computer, and making endless drawings on graph paper to either prove or investigate various criteria. All this was over several years, during which time I put my family at inconvenience on many occasions. I can only thank them for their patience and understanding whilst I indulged my fascination for what I discovered.

To the members of St Cecilia Lodge 1636 I convey my gratitude for the many hours they endured listening to talks and lectures from me over a ten year period, as I explained what I had discovered and gauged their reaction to the findings. In particular I would like to thank a good friend, and a surveyor by profession, W. Bro Mike Oulten, who listened attentively to my ramblings at other times and encouraged me to keep looking; and Mike yet again in company with W. Bro Ron Cuff OBE, both of whom felt that I should record my findings in anticipation that they would be of interest and value to others. It was their encouragement that inspired the writing of this book. Coupled with this I would also like to thank the Provincial Grand Master for the Masonic Province of Sussex for permitting me to take and use a number of photographs of the Sussex Masonic Temple that are used in this work. I also thank W. Bro Reg Barrow, curator of the Sussex Masonic Museum, who was very patient in commenting on some of my observations, little knowing where it would end.

Needless to say, the publication of any book involves many people. I can only thank the many staff at Ian Allan–Lewis Masonic Books, for their assistance, and in particular the guidance and encouragement I received from Peter Waller in the early stages of the writing, Nick Grant for his patience with the illustrations and corrections, and Martin Faulks for his guidance on marketing issues.

I also thank the wonderful team of staff and librarians in the Masonic Museum and Library at Freemasons' Hall in London, who so often sought out long-forgotten documents at my request or guided me to information I might never have contemplated. I would also like to thank the librarians and other staff who assisted me at The British Library in London, RIBA - The Royal Institute of British Architects, Royal Astronomical Society, London; Royal Observatory Greenwich, Sussex Reference Library, City of Brighton Central Library; the staff at the Egyptian Government Tourism Department in London, the City of Westminster Reference Library, London, The Jewish Museum, Camden, London, and other sources of information and reference which are too many to name individually.

My thanks also go to Crichton Miller for use of images he created relating to the use of the Celtic Cross; to Dr Robert Lomas for his encouragement and permission to use material he developed in respect of the *Megalithic Yard* and the works of William Preston; Paul Bush and the Dean of Peterborough Cathedral for their permission to use information and drawings previously produced about the cathedral – and again others too numerous to mention individually.

Special note: In this book I have made reference to the works of Mr George Lesser and his investigation through the 1960s of the use of sacred geometry in the construction of various cathedrals across Europe, and in particular, Chartres Cathedral. Efforts have been made to locate the publishers of his works, Tiranti, to gain approval to use certain illustrations, but to no avail. It seems that the Tiranti publishing enterprise was sold in the 1970s and attempts to locate who then owned the previous published works lists have resulted in silence. I therefore apologise in advance for any inconvenience the subsequent use of such material may cause them.

Every effort has been made to track down all copyright holders and obtain copyright clearance but in the event of any omission please contact the author via the Publisher so that any necessary correction can be made in future impressions of the book.

The Opening –
Sun rise, an inspiration

It was still dark. Except for the sound of my own breathing, no other noise broke the silence of the night. The embers of the fire glowed a deep red. The air was so still that the smoke from a smouldering, partly burnt log rose vertically and mingled with the haze of the Milky Way as if the misty texture above had been created solely by it.

I clambered out of my sleeping bag. Moving quietly around the camp fire so as not to disturb my colleague, I placed some small logs on the fire to keep it going. On, too, went a small billycan of water, enough to make one large mug of hot coffee.

I had woken quite normally and felt that dawn couldn't be too far away. Our wind-up watches had stopped some days previously and we had no idea what man-contrived hour we were living in. Way out of range of radio stations we had, for the previous week, resorted to rising with the sun and ceasing the labours of the day when the Sun was just setting. With coffee in hand I moved away from the now blazing fire and perched myself on the front of the old Volkswagen. Before going into the outback of Australia I had been advised to take one of three types of vehicle: a four-wheel-drive; a locally manufactured car – a Holden – spares were easy to come by; an air-cooled Volkswagen – no water hoses or radiator to worry about. The old Volkswagen was all I could afford.

Sitting in the Kimberley Ranges of North West Australia, the stars in the sky above had a clarity that was rare. The nearest big town, radiating intrusive light from car headlamps, advertising signs and street lamps, was about 400 hundred miles away. The Southern Cross stood out amongst the constellations, whilst Orion, which I referred to as 'my old chum' because it was one of the first major star groups I had learned to recognise, rolled across the sky in the north. In the months I had been in the bush I had come to realise that I was looking at the heavens as hundreds of generations before me must have done. The stars, many more than one could see near a city, stood out with a bright crispness, whilst the background of deep space was as black as one could imagine. I had even seen an abundance of shooting stars, something one hardly knew existed when one was in a city environment.

Although I hadn't realised it as I perched on the front of the Volkswagen with my coffee, I was facing towards the east. By the time most of the coffee had been drunk, the first glow of dawn was breaking on the horizon. It wasn't the first dawn I had witnessed, but I watched in awe as the daily drama unfolded. The stars in the east began to fade as the light from the Sun took precedence. As the fiery yellow ball appeared over the horizon an unexpected and comforting warmth hit me full in the face. The air, which had been completely still, suddenly and gently rushed towards the brightened horizon as if the Sun was a vast magnet attracting it. A kookaburra cackled in the distance. There was a soft rustling noise from the long white grass that surrounded us as the tops of the stems brushed gently against each other in the slight movement of the air. A flock of parrots, grey and pink in colour – Galahs – flew almost overhead, wheeled and circled, then swooped to the ground several hundred yards away. The air also held a slight aroma of eucalyptus and dried grass where previously there had been nothing except the crispness of the night air and the slight fragrance of instant coffee rising from the mug cupped in my hands.

Although I had watched dawn breaking many times before, on that particular morning my senses seemed to find an extra affinity with the world around me. I was filled with an inner peace and tranquillity, a feeling of being completely at one with my surroundings, totally in tune with the world – with nature – and my part in it. It was so good to be alive – to feel alive.

That *alive* feeling left its mark. Even today, many years later, I can close my eyes and be transported back to that morning and experience it all: the light, the warmth, the movement of the air, even the smell of the world mingled with the coffee. It was a spiritual experience I will never forget.

Many years later my attention was particularly drawn to the rising Sun and its influence on the people of ancient civilisations. It took very little research to realise that such civilisations worshipped the event as the basis of life itself and that the impact it had many generations ago was still to be felt today. It turned up in the most unexpected of places.

Freemasonry was one of them.

Chapter 1
Why the Sun?

Solomon, King of Israel in the Old Testament of the Bible, is a character well known to the followers of the three primary western religions of Christianity, Islam and Judaism. He lives on through reference to Solomon's Temple in Jerusalem and for his perceived wisdom. He was clearly an accomplished leader, builder and diplomat. And, if tradition is taken to its logical conclusion, he was clearly a man of considerable charm and presence – which is perhaps epitomised by his relationship with the Queen of Sheba. His leadership is demonstrated in numerous acts, perhaps the most significant being that related to the building and furnishing of the first Temple in Jerusalem. Reading between the lines of the biblical text, his reign coincided with a period of stability for the worshippers of *Yahweh,* a people whose ancestors had for several previous generations roamed the Sinai peninsula after their exodus from Egypt and been involved in battles to secure their promised land. With that stability must also have come a period of relative wealth, as evidenced by descriptions of the opulent furnishings of the Temple.

As a consequence of his links to the first Jerusalem Temple, and his purported wisdom, we are led to believe that *Solomon* was his name. But suppose it wasn't his name. Suppose it was a word that described his role and position. Suppose it was a word which described what he did, his job. Thus, if the name of the Temple was a reflection of the title of his role or position, then that could change our understanding about the meaning and purpose to which the temple served. It could describe what the temple was for, or what it was dedicated to, rather than who it was named after. His supposed wisdom may have then been a reflection of the skills and knowledge he had acquired in relation to his function instead of implying that he was a person of superior intellect, or that he had highly developed powers of reasoning.

The ramifications of such a revelation would be far reaching.

Despite the fact that I had, over several years, held executive office in business as well as in a number of social organisations and committees, there was nothing I had experienced in life that had quite prepared me for Freemasonry. My first impressions were of an organisation whose practices were, at best, obtuse. Yet at the same time there is a dignity and grandeur to the proceedings that comes from a very old and established tradition. I realised later that this grandeur was enhanced by the decor of the room that the Lodge, of which I was a member, used for its meetings.

Some years after my initiation, that room, together with its design and decor, became a focus of my attention. It was to result in a fascination that led me on a journey of discovery which changed my understanding and perceptions of the historical setting of certain events associated with the major orthodox religions, in ways I had never anticipated.

The subject of Freemasonry is one that has, at various times in the past few hundred years, attracted a mixture of public excitement and hysteria. There are families where membership of this very old fraternal society has existed for generations, fathers initiating sons, and later grandsons, with great pride. There are others that regard it as an organisation that perpetrates evil and anti-religious sentiments; a secret society wherein the members are engaged in plots to destabilise and overthrow government; a body of men which is involved in ensuring that its members are promoted to high office in local government, institutions or major corporations, in preference to any other person of similar ability. Yet, repeated investigations by government officials and respected individuals, who had not been freemasons but had conducted research into its history and structure, have concluded that such fears are unfounded. Instead they report that it is a highly moral and intellectual organisation which in the past has been an instigator, motivator and sponsor of significant charitable and scientific undertakings, a role which it still continues.

Freemasonry is a male-dominated organisation, although, since the early years of the 20th century, female participants have enjoyed their own Lodge structure in the United Kingdom, operating in a manner commensurate with that of their male counterparts. Men join Freemasonry at a variety of stages in their lives, from twenty-one years of age upwards. They come from a variety of socio-economic backgrounds, remain members for a variety of reasons but obviously would not do so unless they gained some inner satisfaction from their membership. The typical period of membership is in excess of 25 years. Most join in middle age, whilst those who join at a young age are likely to be regular supporting members for over 40 or 50 years. There are those who resign from membership and do so for equally varied reasons.

Freemasonry is a global organisation that, if properly regulated, complies with and is accepted under the constitution of the United Grand Lodge of England (UGLE). The UGL of England traces its beginnings to the year 1717 when a small group of lodges based in London met together and formed the Grand Lodge of England, the forerunner of the governing body that exists today. However, Masonic lodges have existed for much longer. In Scotland for instance, there are lodges known to have existed in Edinburgh in the 15th century. The oldest known Lodge in England for which records survive is the Lodge of Antiquity No 2 – Minute Books are available from 1736 but others are known to have been available from 1721, and have since been mislaid. The oldest minute books held at the Library of Freemasons Hall in London are for a meeting of a lodge that met in a public house known as the Swan and Rummer, and date from 1725. However, Elias Ashmole recorded in his diary that he was initiated as a Speculative Mason at Warrington in 1646, some 70 years before the formation of the Grand Lodge of England.

There have, in the past, been many eminent writers and researchers who believed that the origins of Freemasonry were derived from the sacred knowledge retained by the priests of Ancient Egypt; that it transferred to the civilisations of Greece and Rome before coming to Britain with the Roman legions two thousand years ago.

Typical Lodge meetings consist of enacting a series of short plays that contain a moral message and encourage personal insight and understanding. All of this is contained in a complicated story involving the building of King Solomon's Temple.

Featuring in the Old Testament books of Chronicles and Kings, Solomon's Temple has an aura of having been something special, an aura which has withstood the passing of time. There are numerous written works devoted solely to the subject of the Temple, along with a variety of images and models made over the centuries in attempts to convey what it may have looked like. Despite this, Solomon's Temple has proven to be something of an enigma. Some archaeologists and academics have questioned whether it ever existed at all.

In the introduction to his ground-breaking book *A Test of Time,* Dr David Rohl reflects on a thesis presented by Professor Thomas L. Thompson of Copenhagen University, whom Dr Rohl cites as 'one of the leading authorities on matters biblical'. Dr Rohl comments on Professor Thompson's opinion as follows:

'...he is basically saying that the Old Testament stories are a fictional composition written in the second century BC and that, as a result, it would be a 'complete waste of time' (in his words) for anyone to attempt to confirm those stories through archaeology.'[1]

Indeed, the basis of Dr Rohl's book stems from concern about the significant gap between what biblical text tells us happened some three to four thousand years ago and the ability of the archaeological community to substantiate it through field evidence, despite 150 years of excavations in Egypt, Israel and surrounding territories. Dr Rohl goes on to make a most interesting observation as a consequence of this lack of evidence:

'....we are left with one fundamental problem for those who would advocate using the Bible as a source of history; archaeological excavations in Egypt and the LEVANT, on-going for the best part of the last two centuries, have produced no tangible evidence to demonstrate the historical veracity of the early biblical narratives. Direct material support for the traditional history of the Israelite nation as handed down in the books of Genesis, Exodus, Joshua, Judges, Samuel, Kings and Chronicles, is virtually non-existent. It is as if the Israelites simply picked up their belongings, left Egypt in the reign of Rameses II (thirteenth century BC) and walked into Sinai to miraculously disappear from history for around four hundred years before resurfacing in the campaign inscriptions of the ninth century kings of Assyria. Where did they go? According to the Bible, they went to settle in Palestine where they were to eventually forge nationhood under the charismatic kings of the United Monarchy Period – Saul, David and Solomon. But virtually nothing resembling this epic adventure is to be found in the archaeological record of

Palestine. For that matter, their centuries long Sojourn in the land of the pharaohs has also left absolutely no trace in the Nile valley or its delta.'[2]

Dr Rohl goes on to add:

'......it is essential to find archaeological evidence which shows that the events recorded in the Old Testament actually happened and that characters such as Joseph, Moses, Saul, David and Solomon really walked this Earth some three to four thousand years ago.'[3]

Clearly if there is doubt that *Moses, David, Saul and Solomon* really walked this Earth, then, by definition, there has to be some doubt as to whether the Temple attributed to Solomon was ever built. Alternatively, a temple, which later would be regarded with some renown, may have been built, but not by Solomon, yet attributed to him through the Old Testament text. There have been those who have suggested that the Temple wasn't actually built in Jerusalem but that it was part of a complex, attributed to Solomon, which has been excavated at Megiddo. But even Solomon's connection with these excavations is doubted. Again quoting from Dr Rohl:

'Monumental structures once attributed to the building activities of Solomon in the cities of Megiddo, Gezer and Hazor have been shown over the years to date from various archaeological periods spanning centuries. The 'Solomonic Gate' at Megiddo is no longer dated to the time of Solomon – yet the modern tourist sign erected in front of it continues to inform visitors that they are standing before a gate "from the time of Solomon".'[4]

The problem of the existence of Solomon is even further confounded. Dr Rohl notes that Solomon was not his name at birth, but a name attributed to him some time after his death. So, if there was no one by the name of King Solomon, then who was the person that was subsequently given this name? And, why was his name changed?

It is assumed that the era which we refer to as being that covered by the reign of Solomon was one in which his kingdom enjoyed a prolonged period of peace. Hence, it has been argued, that his name is derived from the Hebrew word *shalom* meaning *peace*.[5] There are other researchers who have different interpretations for the origins of his name, a subject which we will come to in due course.

So, there is potentially a problem. Based on the earlier comments from Professor Thompson, and enlarged on by Dr Rohl, the archaeological community leaves us with a dilemma:

- We have a race of people who form the pivotal focus of much of western religion, but have seemingly left little or no archaeological evidence for their early existence in Palestine, the Sinai or Egypt.

- We appear to have no evidence for the existence of a group of kings, Saul, David and Solomon, whose written commentary in the Old Testament is the source of considerable inspiration to thousands of people every day.

- It is questionable whether a building that forms the centrepiece of one of the oldest surviving fraternal organisations in the world, Freemasonry, has ever existed.

- It is doubted if the name attributed to the person revered for his wisdom and building enterprise, Solomon, was actually his real name.

What are we to make of all this?

There are possible answers to the problems caused by the missing evidence noted earlier, as Dr Rohl so ably demonstrates in his book. This he does through re-examination of some of the archaeological evidence and artefacts that have been recovered but considered in a different context by the archaeological community.

This, though, still leaves us with a number of unanswered questions especially relating to Solomon and the connection with Freemasonry. If there is no evidence to support the existence of a man named Solomon, then how does he, and the Temple which is attributed to him, come to be connected with Freemasonry?

There was no overt reference in my family to membership of Freemasonry in the paternal line of my ancestry, but my maternal line was very different. When I was in my early teenage years my grandmother encouraged me to join if the opportunity presented itself. She had come from a fairly large family that grew up in the early years of the twentieth century. Most of her brothers had been members of the fraternity and several of her sisters married men who were Masons, or went on to join, being encouraged by their family tradition. Thus it was that, having been duly programmed by my grandmother, when an opportunity arose for me to join as I approached middle age, I too was initiated into this ancient institution.

A few years after my initiation we had a lecture in our Lodge, the first for many years. It was what is known as a Prestonian Lecture, so named after one of the great Masonic historians and recorders – William Preston. William Preston is particularly remembered for a work entitled *Illustrations of Masonry*, first published in 1772, which is a reference work often quoted in respect of early recorded Masonic sources. A Prestonian lecture is one, so we are informed, founded on well-structured research. The title of the lecture we received that evening was *The History of Freemasonry in England*. The subject matter caught my attention and I looked forward to the proceedings, hoping to gain an insight into a history which, at that time, was still largely unknown to me. I listened intently. I was less than enthusiastic about the conclusions. These stated that:

- there was no history of Freemasonry in England prior to 1717, the year the Grand Lodge of England was formed by four London-based lodges.
- whilst some members believed that Freemasonry held some great secret, many had looked and come to the conclusion that there is nothing there.
- Freemasonry had been formed solely as a gentleman's club and has always remained as such to this day.

For reasons which I cannot explain, a complete disbelief in those conclusions grew in me over the following months. Maybe I had wanted something more mysterious to be revealed, and it wasn't. I felt there had to be something else. So much so, that I spent the next couple of years reading a vast range of books on Masonic history. Whilst they imparted a great deal of information they didn't answer a number of key issues that had arisen in my mind. Many of the authoritative books on Masonry had been written some decades previously and were often based on research conducted in the late 19th century. Most dealt with the history of the institution, speculated on its origins and/or from where certain practices and elements of our ceremonies, had been derived. At the end of this brief period of reading and research a number of other questions had been raised in my mind:

1. The United Grand Lodge of England, in a video recording produced and made available for anyone to purchase who had an interest in Freemasonry, noted that our ceremonies revolve around a complicated tale involving King Solomon's Temple.
   a. Why, I wondered, should this building, briefly mentioned in the Old Testament of the Bible, be such a focus of attention?
   b. Was there something about this building that was not immediately obvious?
   c. Why would a so-called gentleman's club be interested in such an obscure religious building of antiquity? It was difficult to imagine that someone, at some time in the past few hundred years, had suddenly been swept along on a wave of enlightened imagination, had thought it a good idea to include it in Masonic ceremonies, and had done so.
   d. Was there, I wondered, something about Solomon's Temple which was not immediately obvious as implied or conveyed by traditional religious teaching?

2. At the commencement of one of the Masonic ceremonies it is pointed out that Freemasonry is *a peculiar system of morality, veiled in allegory.* I thought I knew what an allegory was but I still looked up the word in an Oxford Dictionary to ensure I had a correct interpretation. The definition stated was:

Why the Sun?

'narrative describing one subject under the guise of another'[6]

In other words an allegory is one thing masquerading or presented as something else; a truth or reality which is covered over or hidden from obvious view, such as in a story. So within our ceremonies there is a blatant statement that beneath the outer shell of Freemasonry there is something which is hidden and not immediately obvious. This, I reasoned, is hardly in accordance with the Prestonian lecture conclusions, that *there is nothing there.*

3. My instincts kept directing me back to the reference about a *peculiar system of morality.* At face value this is a highly respectable ideal, to encourage honesty and integrity in all the things one does in life. Morality is a code by which one should live one's life and regulate one's actions. It is, therefore, a code which governs life and gives it order. It is a code by which civilised peoples should conduct their affairs and relate to each other. I began to wonder why the word *peculiar* should be used. I persuaded myself that perhaps the reference to a *peculiar system of morality* could refer to some other *code* which, in an orderly fashion, influences our life.

4. I developed a fascination with the year in which four lodges, based in London, met together to create a single administrative body to govern their proceedings – The Grand Lodge of England. The year in question was 1717. This number is so often casually written down as a footnote of Masonic history – a passing point of reference and nothing more. But this number – 1717 – is very symmetrical. Why did the four London-based lodges come together in this particular year and not a year earlier in 1716, or a year later in 1718? For some time I began to believe that I was reading too much into something which was, after all, simply a number to define a year. But I was well aware that nothing in Freemasonry is quite that simple, everything is there for a purpose. The symmetry of the numbers nagged at me, but several years were to pass before an unexpected answer presented itself.

When one first joins a Masonic Lodge one is accepted into what is known as *The Craft*. The Craft Lodges in Freemasonry comprise three levels of attainment known as degrees. These degrees are called:

Entered Apprentice; signifying, as with the trades of old, a person who knows nothing of the skills of the trade they are joining and who is at the starting point of their learning process; their name has been entered into the register to show that they have been accepted as suitable for training, in exactly the same manner as in the Guild system of old.

Fellow of the Craft; signifying that the basic skill, understanding and knowledge of the trade has been achieved.

Master Mason; to signify that one has now achieved a thorough understanding of the skills of the industry and is a Master of one's trade.

Today these three levels of attainment relate more to a symbolic understanding rather than the actual knowledge associated with the trade of shaping and fashioning stone. Each degree has a very specific ceremony that every freemason is expected to complete. These ceremonies are all committed to memory and are passed on from one generation of freemasons to the next, word perfect, rather as the oral traditions of ancient civilisations and the operative masons of old would have been.

Like nearly all societies and clubs, the administration of each Lodge is undertaken by members nominated and elected to perform specific tasks, such as Secretary, Treasurer, Charity Steward and Almoner. There are three key offices in each Lodge. They are known as the Master, rather like the Chairman of any social organisation, and the Senior and Junior Wardens whose role is akin to being *chairmen in training*. There is a group of other officers of the Lodge, usually ranked in seniority, that participate in and perform the ceremonies. As one progresses through each office so one becomes responsible for the performance of a specific part in each ceremony, a part that must be committed to memory in both words and actions.

The room in which my Lodge would meet in Sussex, England, was referred to as a Masonic Temple. Other rooms used by lodges in other geographic locations, were often referred to as Lodge Rooms, which implied that there was a difference. Why, I wondered, was there a difference? The reasons I discovered later.

A new town – a new temple

The Sussex Temple is unique and the building that houses it has been granted Listed Building status. This means that it is regarded as a building of special architectural or historic significance and its character should be preserved. It wasn't always a Masonic building. It had originally been built in the 1820s and was later used as the residence of a family prominent in the local brewing business. In the late 18th century a small fishing village situated on the south coast of England, a village named Brighthelmstone, received a very rude awakening. The Prince Regent, son of King George III and later to be crowned King George IV, acquired a farmhouse close to the sea and set about transforming it into a palace. Fascinated by the designs of the East, recognising that at that time the British Empire was expanding its influence in territories such as India, the architecture of the palace reflected his interest. Architecturally, it would not have been out of place if it had been built by a Maharaja. But, in this small seaside fishing village it caused quite a stir. Today, with an interior restored to its former glory, it is known as the Brighton Pavilion, an outstanding tourist attraction in the resort of Brighton. Needless to say, the advent of the new palace resulted in the once small fishing village being rapidly transformed into a fashionable town adorned with spectacular terraced homes reflecting the Georgian architecture of the era in which they were built. It was during this period of the urban expansion of Brighthelmstone, that the former Prince Regent, King George IV, became a Freemason and later, Grand Master.

As the town of Brighton expanded over the next few decades and its population grew, it became an obvious destination for a new invention – the railway, which added greatly to the prosperity of the town. It was against this background of the development of the town, that, in the mid-1800s, Sussex freemasons started to seek a site where they could establish a permanent home. A meeting of Sussex freemasons was held in Brighton Town Hall in 1858 and although various sites were examined, and several more meetings of Sussex freemasons followed, in 1893 the then Provincial Grand Master lamented that for various reasons none of the plans had come to fruition. Just a few years later, in 1897, the former house owned by the brewing family and an adjacent piece of vacant land, both of which are just a few minutes' walk from Brighton railway station, came into the possession of Sussex freemasons and provided the permanent Masonic home they had long been seeking. In the same year the foundation stone was laid for the former residence to become a Masonic Club which, on the completion of its conversion, boasted a snooker room, committee rooms and small rooms where Lodges could practise their ceremonies.

It wasn't until 1928 that the Sussex Masonic Temple was built into the complex that exists today. One of the reasons for the delay in building the Temple was the intervention of the First World War – the Great War of 1914-1918 – after which, because of the colossal human carnage on the battlefields of Europe, there was a considerable shortage of skilled craftsmen. This skills shortage impeded the opportunity for, and the speed of, construction.

Thus it was that the Foundation Stone was laid on 26th June 1919 by the Provincial Grand Master for Sussex, The Duke of Richmond. It was dedicated nine years later on 20th July 1928 by Lord Ampthill.

As I was investigating the background of these developments and explained my findings to a Lodge colleague – a well-respected local surveyor – he came to the conclusion that a design concept for the Temple had probably already been agreed by the mid-1800s. The concept probably dictated specific inclusions and the resultant size and space needed; what had been sought, after the meeting in Brighton Town Hall in 1858, was a location where it could be built. The former home of the brewer, together with the vacant land adjacent to it, provided an ideal location. And, as it was a town that had enjoyed royal patronage and attracted many residents of political influence with social rank and fortune, no expense was to be spared in its execution. The Sussex Masonic Temple was obviously intended to be something special. Indeed, we get a clear hint of this in the proceedings following the dedication ceremony. In proposing the toast of the 'Sussex Masonic Temple', Right Worshipful Brother Sir Alfred Robbins finished with these words:

'I have had the opportunity of looking over the building, and I have never seen one better planned for the use to which it has been put. I am satisfied that our children and our children's children, will in time to come, look back

*to the event of that day and say that in those days there were Masons who
believed thoroughly in the great principles of the Craft, and because of that
belief had striven to erect a building worthy in every way of the traditions of
the Craft and worthy of the high position to which Masonry had attained.* [7]

These words alone make it clear that this was indeed viewed as a very special
building.

Something *special* is what it has turned out to be, as we will see in the following
pages. By one of those strange coincidences that sometimes occur, the Lodge into
which I was initiated had met in rooms in the Royal Pavilion for most of the early
years of its existence before moving to the Sussex Masonic Temple not long after
the building had been completed.

The unusual decor raised questions

Although I have visited other Masonic complexes or places where lodges hold
their meetings, both in Britain and overseas, I have yet to find any that compare in
ornate decoration with that in which my own Lodge meets. It is simply yet
effectively decorated: the walls are wood panelled; there is unobtrusive diffused
lighting which gives an even illumination around the room, provided discreetly
from behind a pelmet enriched with a floral decoration; key furnishings are made
from wood that was lavishly carved by unrecorded hands of great skill and care,
many decades ago. In the central area of the otherwise wooden floor there is an inset
with a black and white chequered pavement encased by a tessellated border. In the
centre of the floor there are two circles of different sizes, one inside the other, the
smaller of which contains the letter 'G' painted in gold. But the dominant feature of
the room is an enormous and beautifully decorated zodiac on the ceiling. Measuring
some 40 feet (12.5m) in diameter, its effect is overwhelming when first viewed. At
equally spaced intervals around the circumference of the zodiac there are twelve
small panels which display a pictorial representation of each zodiac sign – every one
hand-painted by an unknown artist. Within the circle described by the zodiac the
ceiling rises to form a painted dome, the dome of the sky, again hand-painted in a
light pastel blue and complete with stars and a symbol of the Sun. The whole domed
ceiling hangs directly above the chequered pavement. It is obvious that no expense
had been spared when it had been originally installed. Clearly this room was
regarded as having considerable importance to have had such care and attention
directed to it.

Why the Sun?

During the first 10 years of my Masonic career, I had visited this room on many occasions and its setting became such a familiar backdrop to our proceedings that I didn't give the decor another thought. But, as we entered an era of being far more open about the Masonic movement after many years of being regarded with suspicion and lambasted with unfounded accusations about being a secret society, a social event was held in this Masonic complex to which wives and partners were invited. A special exhibition explaining some of our history was mounted in the main temple. Thus it was that as my wife entered the door of the Temple, so she was immediately struck by the dominance of the zodiac. She turned to me and asked why it was there. I was somewhat embarrassed to have to admit that I didn't know. A similar question arose about the tessellated pavement and again I had to admit to a complete lack of understanding as to its purpose. Other questions followed about the decoration and size of various objects and each time my embarrassment at not having a satisfactory answer grew more acute. At the end of that evening I realised that I had been so involved with getting my part in the ceremonies right, that I had not taken due stock of what was around me, what it was there for, why it was there or what it meant. This was something I clearly needed to correct.

Every Lodge holds what are known as *Lodge Instruction* evenings at which ceremonies are rehearsed and some of the lesser known facts about Freemasonry are meant to be conveyed. Having been a regular attendee at such evenings I was somewhat surprised at not having been acquainted with the reason and meaning of the temple fixtures. I asked the elders of our Lodge why the zodiac was there. I was amazed to find that none of them knew. A couple of members of very long standing commented that our Deputy Provincial Grand Master, a very senior office in Sussex-based Freemasonry, had once been heard to remark that he too had often wondered at its significance. I asked the curator of the Temple for his opinion, and he commented that he didn't know either. With these responses I realised that if it did have any significance at the time it had been installed, then that understanding had been lost to the current generation of freemasons. This point was further demonstrated when the curator added the comment: 'If you ever find out then please let me know. It is one of the first questions I am asked whenever I take visitors into the temple.' I was later to realise that the curator was very knowledgeable on the subject of Masonic history, so that comment implied that finding someone who knew what the zodiac was about, was most unlikely. If I was to find the answer then I needed to research it myself.

From this experience with our Masonic elders, I soon came to the conclusion that we were committing considerable effort into learning and perfecting our ceremonies but devoted no time at all to understanding what we were doing – or why we were doing it. If that same situation was common to other lodges then, as an entire organisation, we were in serious danger of losing any vestige of understanding about the basis of our ancient institution and, in consequence, we would end up as a society which was an empty shell devoid of meaning. When I voiced this opinion to some of the senior Masons in the Sussex area they acknowledged that we may have already reached such a situation. These negative comments only served to encourage me to find answers.

The *Quest* for understanding

There are those who believe that Freemasonry is a secret society, that it is the harbinger of some great secret. The official view, as I stated earlier, is that Freemasonry is little more than a gentleman's club.

As any Freemason will confirm, the ceremonies in the three Craft degrees use language which is somewhat arcane, together with complex actions, some of which can be uncomfortable to perform and, it could be argued, are deliberately designed to be so. Yet, when these ceremonies are performed well they convey a dignity and grandeur seldom experienced today in other walks of life. These ceremonies are absolutely unique. Thus, any freemason reading this book will understand my view when I state that I came to the conclusion that any individual, or group of people, who had deliberately sat down at a table, several hundred years ago, and contrived our organisation, our ceremonies – both in rhetoric and actions, the structure, offices, regalia and furnishings, solely for the purpose of creating a gentleman's club, would, without doubt, have been suffering from a serious mental disorder.

Despite the many authoritative books which pointed out and explained the origin and symbolic meaning behind certain aspects of our ceremonies, there was no explanation of a number of points that began to intrigue me. Amongst these was the way in which the Sun features in our ceremonies, pointing out:

- that the Sun rises in the east.
- that there is a duty to mark the setting Sun.
- that there is a duty to mark the Sun at its meridian – the highest point that the Sun reaches in the sky, the point we call midday.
- that the Earth constantly revolves on its axis in its orbit around the Sun.

There are other references to the Sun in addition to those mentioned above; even the symbol the Grand Master shows as part of his insignia, is that of the Sun. Why, I wondered, do we do this? Why is there all this reference to the Sun? Why would a gentleman's club need to point these things out?

Missing images

The Sussex Masonic Temple has another attribute, that of providing a museum and display centre of items of past Masonic memorabilia. This includes a number of aprons and other pictorial imagery that was part of the regalia of Freemasonry in the 18th and 19th centuries. What is striking is that a lot of that imagery contains a symbol of the *Sun, Moon and stars* as well as pictorial illustrations of biblical reference; Jacob's Ladder, connecting Earth with Heaven, is particularly well represented. Today, the regalia of Freemasonry is mass-produced by a few specialist suppliers and purchased by members as needed subject to one's progress and position. But in the 18th and 19th centuries everything was hand-made, especially the aprons, some of which display wonderful pictorial imagery, delicately embroidered with considerable skill. Today we purchase regalia with each new position of advancement. In earlier centuries members would have added new imagery to their existing regalia to indicate their position within the Lodge structure. Thus, in the past the imagery would have indicated knowledge and understanding, whereas today the regalia is more simply styled, devoid of elaborate imagery and more indicative of hierarchy and the length of membership. What, I wondered, had happened to cause this change? Why had the Sun, the Moon, the stars and biblical imagery suddenly ceased to be fashionable in Masonic regalia?

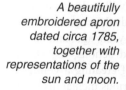

A beautifully embroidered apron dated circa 1785, together with representations of the sun and moon.

The Lodge into which I was initiated is, by modern standards, of long standing, having been founded in 1876. Originally, to have been accepted as a member one needed to have been a musician, or associated with music in some way, such as a church organist. This musical connection resulted in the Lodge being named after the patron saint of music – Saint Cecilia. At the time the Lodge was founded a banner was made that would have been displayed whenever the Lodge was assembled. This banner measured some six feet long by five feet wide, and had been delicately embroidered with silk threads to display a wonderful image of this renowned lady saint. Also embroidered on the banner were geometric images, similar symbols being prominent on other memorabilia of the 19th century, including the symbol of the pentagram. After some 75 years of faithful service, during which it had been repaired several times, the original banner was declared to be beyond further repair and was donated to the Sussex Masonic Museum. Another banner was made, similar in every respect to the original but with one major revision – the pentagram was omitted. In the same era, there had been two ornate lamps, carefully fabricated out of wrought iron, which illuminated the main entrance of the Sussex Masonic Temple. One had a geometric symbol of *Solomon's Seal* and the other was fashioned with a pentagram. In an age of senseless vandalism these lamps became the subject of persistent damage, during which on one occasion the lamp showing the pentagram was wrenched from the wall. When it was replaced the pentagram was removed and the replacement lamp was fashioned with yet another *Solomon's Seal*. Sadly, both lamps have since been removed. Why had the hitherto highly respected geometric pattern of the pentagram, an example of which sits prominently and proudly in the main steps of Freemasons' Hall in London, the home of the United Grand Lodge of England, the governing body of Freemasonry, dramatically fallen from favour? These were questions to which there was no immediate answer.

Mystical images

There was something else about the Sussex Temple which was intriguing. Just as the step to the main entrance of Freemasons' Hall in London shows a representation of a pentagram, the main step of the Sussex complex displays an altogether different pattern: sections of circles encompassed by an outer circle.

Yet again I approached the Sussex Masonic elders and enquired about what it meant. There were jibes about it being a secret sign, the symbolism of which they could not possibly divulge. It was obvious from their demeanour that they had no more of an idea about its relevance than they did about the zodiac. This pattern went on my list as another item to investigate.

The quest begins – thanks to the BBC

I resolved to find answers to the questions that had come into sharp focus. As my quest began, so several events occurred in my life in a short period of time that, with the value of hindsight, had a considerable influence on my line of enquiry. It turned out to be a course of enquiry which led me down a path of discovery and enlightenment, bringing me into contact with individuals of stature, taking me to distant places I would otherwise only have dreamed of visiting.

At first I had been unsure where to start. It hadn't taken long before I came to the conclusion that if I went down a traditional path of investigation, I would end up with a traditional answer. I had to try and approach any investigation into the subject of the zodiac, pavement, pentagram and symbol in the front step of the Sussex Temple from an entirely different angle using sources other than traditional Masonic works. I reasoned that if I still ended up with a traditional answer then I would be satisfied.

As I pondered the question about what sources I might use, several weeks passed. One evening I was driving near London Gatwick Airport and listening to a programme on the car radio broadcast by the BBC.[6] On this particular programme, listeners were encouraged to write to the presenter seeking answers to questions that puzzled them. Several such questions were then dealt with on one particular evening each week, in a segment known as 'Answers Please'. Thus it was that, on the occasion when I was listening near Gatwick Airport, we heard how a listener had written into the programme presenter noting that he/she had read that there were a number of discrepancies between biblical statements and their relationship to historical events. The listener asked if the programme could throw more light on this subject, and verify if this was true. To obtain answers, the BBC presenter made what appeared to be a live contact with the Vatican in Rome, spoke to a Vatican librarian and posed the question from the listener. The librarian agreed that there were a number of statements of events that did not fit with what we now know to have been the real chronology based on timelines produced from surviving historical records. One observation in particular, which I will paraphrase, stuck in my mind. It went along the following lines:

> *'For instance'*, noted the librarian, *'we refer to Jesus of Nazareth, implying that he came from a town of that name. The Roman authorities were very particular and meticulous about their record keeping. A lot of documents from that time have survived. We have not been able to locate any map for that area, or surviving document for that era, that shows a place called Nazareth. Our investigations show that no such place of that name existed prior to about 600 AD. So this poses us with a problem with the reference to the term – Jesus of Nazareth.'*

That simple statement provided me with the possible key I had been looking for. It seemed logical to take a closer look at the archaeological and historical setting and background to Solomon's Temple rather than merely relying on biblical text and *faith* as directed by the Church. I soon came to realise that there was a considerable difference between my understanding, based on what I had been taught at school and through religious indoctrination, and what had apparently happened based on historical records. In particular it is what has been left out, deliberately or otherwise, that distorts the imagery. It is what we are *not* told that colours our perceptions. When one is aware of the intervening facts a new angle on events is presented.

The Zodiac and the Pavement – another look

When we mention the term *zodiac* we may instinctively be inclined to think of it as an astrological tool used for fortune telling. It isn't surprising. Today there is hardly a magazine or newspaper in the western world that doesn't feature a horoscope, produced by astrologers, providing a forecast about events which may or may not occur in one's life; predictions relate to one's date of birth, which in turn is assigned to a specific sign of the zodiac.

Astrology is an ancient science derived thousands of years ago from the study of the movement of the heavens. It was the science of predicting where certain stars or planets would be at certain times on specific days. It was the forerunner of the science we know today as astronomy. And it was still a significant scientific force as recently as the 19th century, although it had started to give way to the more specific science of astronomy that developed in the 18th century.

It was possible, it seemed, that there was some logic to the zodiac surrounding the star-studded dome of the ceiling I so frequently saw in the Sussex Masonic Temple. Keeping in mind that if my assumptions were correct and that a design for the Sussex Temple had been created before the mid-19th century, then it would have been in an era when there would still have been considerable understanding about the former influence of astrology. Thus, I reasoned, the zodiac probably related to the astrology of star and planet location rather than fortune telling. If this was so, was there a message hidden in it?

The pavement was a different story. Not only did it prove to be more down to earth but, was inextricably linked to the zodiac.

I have previously stated that the pavement has a chequered area of black and white tiles encased within a tessellated border. There are ten tiles across the width and twenty-two along the length. This seemed an extremely odd ratio yet the pavement offered a visual proportion that appeared to naturally fit with the size of the room, the decor and the zodiac above. It made one wonder which had come first, the room – and then the pavement designed to fit in it, or whether the design of the dome of the ceiling had influenced the size of the room and then the pavement had again been proportioned to fit. I will, in due course, demonstrate that the three elements are linked by concepts developed by ancient civilisations to ensure harmony of form.

But, before I reached that stage, something else happened.

Why the Sun?

As news of my interest in certain aspects of the Sussex Temple became known, so a brother from another Lodge directed my attention to *The Lectures of the Three Degrees*. These *Lectures*, sadly, are seldom referred to or mentioned in lodges today, but they provided a useful point of reference. Quite where or when these lectures originated is unknown but early records of them seem to stem from William Preston's system of lectures first published in 1772. In the *Lectures* the Pavement is described as follows:

> *The Mosaic Pavement may justly be deemed the beautiful flooring of a Freemason's Lodge, by reason of its being variegated and tessellated... As the steps of man are trod in the various and uncertain incidents in life, and his days are variegated and chequered by a strange and contrariety of events, his passage through this existence, though sometimes attended by prosperous circumstances, is often beset by a multitude of evils; hence is our Lodge furnished with the Mosaic work to point out the uncertainty of all things here on earth. Today we may travel in prosperity; tomorrow we may totter on the uneven paths of weakness, temptation and adversity. Then while such emblems are before us, we are morally instructed not to boast of anything, but to give heed to our ways, to walk uprightly and with humility before God, there being no station in life in which pride can with stability be founded.*

Thus is the moral tone of the chequered area of the pavement stated, its object clearly defined. We are told that it is to remind us of the opposite fortunes we may experience in our passage through life. Just as day is light and night is dark, there is happiness and sadness; life and death; good health and ill health; financial well-being and poverty; likewise that there are those who have an abundance of all things at their command whilst there are many who are at the very lowest ebbs of life's misfortunes and to whom we should provide some assistance – we each, we all, have a charitable responsibility.

More just and moral lessons are difficult to envisage and yet so simply illustrated. This though raises specific questions:

- how did all this start?
- where did the idea of using these simple methods of moral illustration commence?
- where and how did the black and white chequered floor originate?

We are also presented with an allegorical interpretation of our surroundings. On the one hand it is a nicely designed floor on which we are invited to walk, yet on the other hand it contains a hidden symbolism – a message emphasising morality in its widest context.

When it comes to the tessellated border the *Lectures* continue:
'*The indented or Tessellated Border refers us to the planets which, in*

their various revolutions form a beautiful border or skirtwork round that grand luminary, the Sun...'

The Sun again!

From the observations made in the *Lectures* it appeared that the dome, as a symbol of the sky, represented Heaven whilst the pavement was a reflection of our life on Earth. It did not, however, explain why there should be any mention of the planets, or why specific attention was drawn to them. I had observed that the majority of Lodge rooms had a chequered pavement, but they didn't all have a tessellated border, so for them such *planetary* symbolism was lost. I became aware that some lodges in the north of England met in rooms which had a painted ceiling with stars affixed, but these were few and far between. None that I was aware of displayed the zodiac.

As the months passed, I regularly entered the Masonic Temple for our Lodge meetings, with the zodiac and the pavement in full view. Having developed an interest in their imagery I felt as if a hidden force was drawing me into them, telling me to keep looking. I was looking but I could not see whatever it was that was there to see. The only answer that seemed appropriate was the one widely accepted amongst freemasons that has already been mentioned, as a lesson in morality – that the pavement symbolises and represents the experience of life on Earth with its pattern of opposites, under the canopy of Heaven. It was an answer, but my instincts kept telling me there were more revelations to come.

Through my years of involvement with this ancient institution I knew that everything in Freemasonry was there for a purpose, be it a movement in a ceremony or a symbol. This reinforced in my mind that there had to be a specific purpose in the design. As I have previously stated, the number of tiles in the chequered pavement counted 22 along the length and 10 across the width. Neither number appeared to correlate with anything I knew. The total of 22 x 10 = 220 made even less sense.

Still I could not help feeling that there was something about the pavement that my instincts were trying to draw my attention to. As I had noticed that the pavement seemed to fit so well with the proportions of the Sussex Temple, with the overall length closely matching the diameter of the zodiac above it, I asked the curator if there were any surviving architectural plans of the complex, complete with dimensions, I could refer to. He was not aware of any detailed documents but he did provide me with a copy of a document, originally produced in the early 1920s, which showed a couple of key dimensions. These noted that the temple was 58 feet long and 40 feet wide. I now wanted to know how big the pavement was. It seemed that the only way I was going to find out was to measure it.

During this period a task had regularly fallen to me as part of our meetings. In the second degree ceremony there is a reference to the skill of the early stone masons. It is noted that at this level the individual will have acquired and demonstrated considerable skill in shaping and carving shapes or patterns in stone they were allocated to work with. In addition a tale is told about building a part of King Solomon's Temple against a backdrop of wars between the biblical Ephraimites and Gileadites. Some of the components of the Temple are referred to with measurements in cubits. This same unit of measure can be found in the Old Testament books of Kings and Chronicles. It was also a unit of measure used by the ancient Egyptians. I had noticed, by their reaction, that candidates had no idea about how big a cubit was, so without interfering with the contents of the tale, I would first introduce the candidate to the fact that a cubit was measured as the length from the point of the elbow to the tip of the middle finger of an outstretched hand, approximately 18 inches in length in imperial measure or just under half a metre in metric measurement.

Thus it was that after one such meeting I took a tape to measure the pavement. To save time, I had decided to measure one tile and then multiply this by the number of tiles in the length and breadth. The tessellated border appeared to be of an even width all around so I only had to measure one border and apply the dimension to the total perimeter. I realised that the temple complex had been built in an era when the standard unit of measure in Britain would have been in imperial feet and inches, not metric. Nevertheless, I made certain that my measuring tape had both units of measure marked on it. The tiles measured exactly eighteen inches square and the border was of the same dimension, eighteen inches wide. Eighteen inches – the representative length of a cubit. As I stood looking at the pavement it was immediately obvious that 22 tiles long could be interpreted as 22 cubits. But the border meant I could add one cubit around the sides. So, instead of being 22 x 10, it now measured 24 cubits x 12 cubits. The perimeter was not 1,296 inches, 108 feet or 33 metres, it was 72 cubits. This was to be my first breakthrough. It was much later that I discovered possible relationships that dictated this dimension.

Later still I was even more excited to discover that there was indeed an exact proportional relationship between the pavement and dome above.

The more I probed, the more questions were raised – the more answers were needed. But so far there were no answers. The quest to find those answers became increasingly compelling and I realised that I needed to progress them in a structured manner. It proved to be a revealing journey into the world of understanding as it was in ancient times and with no small measure of mystery attached.

I obviously needed to know more, to learn more – and understand.

Conclusion

Although Freemasonry is presented as a gentleman's club, it is clear that its ceremonies and procedures are vested in antiquity. The link between this ancient institution and Solomon's Temple was particularly obscure. It seemed possible that the zodiac, pavement and decor of the Masonic Temple in Sussex reflect that antiquity with origins and reasons that had long been forgotten.

Furthermore, in an effort to uncover answers, it appeared impractical to rely solely on biblical text, religious faith and conventional opinion but dictated a need to explore other sources of information. In particular I needed to find out more about:

- The possible origins of Freemasonry
- the Masonic connection with astrology/astronomy
- the influence of the pentagram
- the apparent harmonious visual relationships between the Sussex Temple zodiac and the pavement
- the meaning of the symbol in the front step

[1] *A Test of Time* – David Rohl
[2] *A Test of Time* – David Rohl
[3] *A Test of Time* – David Rohl
[4] *A Test of Time* – David Rohl
[5] The Pocket Oxford Dictionary – Oxford University Press
[6] From a document provided by W. Bro R. Barrows, curator of the Sussex Masonic Temple
[7] BBC Radio 2, Drive Time hosted by John Dunn, 5.00 pm – 7.00 pm; Tuesday evening sessions contained an 'Answers Please' segment.

Chapter 2
The Rise of the Sun

As we go about our lives in the 21st century western world to which we are now accustomed, most of us have little understanding or empathy for the world our ancestors knew, how they lived, how they survived, their beliefs, their fears, their hopes and dreams. It is, however, a sobering thought that every one of us alive today has a chain of ancestors that extends back to the dawn of man's first existence – a chain of beings who were born, learned how to survive in the environment in which they lived, partnered with another being and begat children, then died – a process which has continued for tens of thousands of years. We, today, are merely passing links in that chain of human development which, we trust, will extend far into the future.

Today we can look at a calendar and note how many days of summer may be left in the year. In the dark and cold days of winter we can take comfort in the knowledge that spring should be just around the corner. For our ancestors, who did not have the advantage of a clock, calendar, diary or networked computer schedule to identify exactly where they were in the passage of time, life would have been less certain. It is difficult to comprehend that tens of thousands of years ago, someone, somewhere must have recognised that at various intervals of days the Sun moved higher in the sky during what we call summer and that as it did so the air around them grew warmer. They must have recognised that as the air grew warmer so the flowers and trees came into bloom and that food, and the variety of it, became easier to find.

Imagine one of our ancient ancestors, thousands of years ago, maybe even tens of thousands of years ago, perhaps sitting round a fire in a cave one evening together with others from his/her tribe, suddenly saying to the others:

Have you noticed that when that big ball of light comes up over the trees it makes the darkness go away; that it is in a slightly different place when the air is warm by comparison with when the air is cold? Have you noticed that when that other ball of lesser light is in the sky when it is dark, sometimes it is like a whole round stone but at other dark periods it has bits missing, and that it then grows to a full round stone again? I wonder how that happens?

Someone, somewhere, at sometime noticed these things. Someone, somewhere at sometime began a process of dedicated observation. Someone, somewhere at sometime began to observe the detail of the cosmos, of the natural world around them and then how certain patterns of the cosmos influenced the natural world. Someone, somewhere at sometime noticed that by careful observation the patterns of the cosmos and nature were so regular that they could be predicted. Someone, somewhere at sometime put in place a mechanism for recording those observations and studying the patterns and understanding what they meant. Someone, somewhere at sometime evolved and directed a method of passing on that information from one generation to the next – a form of ancient university – with, no doubt, each generation adding to the accumulation of knowledge and understanding in an era long before writing and books had been invented.

Imagine too the debates and discussions which must have ensued, perhaps over days, months and even generations, as our ancestors sought to come to grips with understanding the information they were gathering – what the logic of the scenario implied. Consider the hours and days of torment and debate, discussion and information gathering needed to consider just the process of answering questions like:

What is the Sun?
Why is it warm?
How does it hang in the sky?
How does it move across the sky from one side to the other?
How does it get hotter and colder?What is happening that results in it moving higher in the sky at some times of the year by comparison with other times?
What makes the cycle repeat itself, day after day, year after year?

Because we are the beneficiaries of these thousands of generations of accumulated understanding, we take the knowledge for granted. As we probe the universe with the advantages of sophisticated electronic devices, satellites and radio telescopes, with dedicated teams of scientists pooled together to ensure results, we believe that we, in our generation, are making great progress. The achievements of our ancestors required even greater dedication, because of the limitation on what their eyes could see, and the primitive nature of their measuring and evaluating tools. What they achieved was perhaps even more remarkable than anything we have, or are doing, in our era.

Sadly, within the period of the 20th century, a microdot of time in the span of human understanding, we began to distance ourselves from that accumulated knowledge. The basis and origins of that knowledge are in danger of being lost, or treated with disdain.

Quite where or how the whole process of understanding the mechanics of the cosmos started is lost in the mists of time. Much of today's global understanding has been influenced by the development of western civilisation. This in turn, because of geographical proximity, draws much of its knowledge from the earlier civilising developments associated with the Greek and Roman eras. The part played by other peoples in other parts of the world was largely ignored. In recent years there has been a growing recognition that the same celestial processes attributed to the Mediterranean and Middle Eastern civilisations were being observed and recorded in India and China a very long time ago. Whether peoples in those areas were the first to discover how the celestial process worked and transferred that knowledge to the civilisations of Asia Minor, or the other way round, is unclear. However it happened, it certainly had to have been many generations ago.

Academics tell us that the Sun was the first deity. It was worshipped by the Maya, Ancient Egyptians and Babylonians. In the case of the Ancient Egyptians, the Sun god Ra can be traced back at least 5,000 years to around 3,000 BCE. Today in India there is a Maharani whose family claim 5,000 years of continuous descent from the Sun god. For a Sun god to have been a major deity, and with human form from 5,000 years ago, implies that the civilisations that existed at that time probably already had an advanced understanding of the significance of the fiery orb, based on information passed down to them from hundreds of generations prior to that. Greek philosophers, visiting Egypt in ancient times, record that the Egyptians had shown them records of astronomical data that went back a very long time.

It probably would not have taken more than a couple of generations of dedicated monitoring from a single location, such as from the top of a hill with a clear view to the horizon, to have realised that the Sun rose in a slightly different place on the horizon each day. These early *sky watchers* would have noted that the Sun moved to two extreme positions in its travel – positions which we refer to as the Summer Solstice and the Winter Solstice – and then repeated the cycle. They would have noticed that as the Sun moved north from its position at the Winter Solstice, so it climbed higher in the sky to that position which we call midday; that as it climbed higher in the sky so the air grew warmer as the season progressed from winter to summer. They would have noted that there was a point in the transit of the Sun along the horizon – a central point – which the Sun passed through on its way to bringing summer to winter, and winter to summer, and that on the two days in the annual cycle when this happened the length of the day and night were equal. We call these points the Spring Equinox and the Autumn Equinox. It would soon have been realised that the cycle had a high degree of predictability, being repeated after 366 sunrises.

It probably would not have taken more than a couple of generations of dedicated monitoring from the same single location to observe the cycles of the Moon; that every 30 sunrises the Moon passed through a process of being a full circle of light, diminishing to nothing and then gradually growing again to become the full circle. It would not have taken a lot of additional observation to note that from the time when the first slivers of light appeared after it had diminished, what today we call a *new moon,* that it again completed its cycle on the twenty-eighth day; and that the natural world was also influenced by similar cycles, such as female menstruation.

It would not have taken too much further evaluation to have recognised that on a sunny day a dark projection – a shadow – would be created by an upright object, such as a tree and that the shadow moved around the base of the object as the day progressed and grew longer and shorter depending on the cycle of the Sun. Watching and recording the movement of the shadow ultimately enabled a prediction of time and season; such timings were totally aligned with the movement of the Sun along the horizon and its height in the sky at midday.

Of course, this knowledge would have brought with it new questions, such as, where did the Sun go when it went below the horizon at night?

Predicting the seasons and the time of the year would have helped enormously in the transition from a nomadic hunter-gatherer existence to one of settlement, domestication of certain animals, food and crop management. With the passing of time it would have influenced clothing, adaptation of hunting weapons and the development of permanent styles of shelter.

In amongst all this would have come a study of the night sky and with it a realisation that some stars moved across the heavens in the same plane as the Sun and Moon – these stars would be later called planets. Groups of stars, or those which formed patterns which reminded our ancestors of something in their customs, mythology or what they had seen, were given names – they became the constellations. Our ancestors would have noticed that some planets moved across the sky faster than others, whilst some were so slow their movement was difficult to detect. Imagine the intellect, debate and logical reasoning which these ancestors must have embarked on to reach the conclusion that the one travelling fastest must have been travelling around a smaller circle, or orbit, by comparison with the others. And what were they travelling or circling around? The Earth? The Sun? Something else? The logic may also have extended to suggesting that the planets were all the same size and travelling at the same speed. This would lead to a further logical conclusion that if they were travelling around the Earth then the one travelling the fastest must have been the closest. By definition the one travelling the slowest must be furthest away. We know today that these conclusions would have been incorrect but they would have seemed very logical a few thousand years ago. Imagine too the realisation of the enormity of the act of creation as they recognised the vast distance from us that the circles created by the paths of the planets indicated. These must have been truly mind-numbing revelations.

Precession of the Equinox

There were other implications associated with the movement of the Sun that would have taken much longer to understand, like the phenomenon known as Precession of the Equinox. Unlike the cycles of the Sun, rising above the horizon at dawn 366 times in a calendar year, or the Moon with its 30-day and 28-day cycles, or the annual movement of the Sun through the equinoxes and solstices, precession takes around 26,000 years to complete just one cycle.

Through the study of the stars at night and the endless cycle of the apparent movement of the Sun along the horizon and its elevation in the sky, together with the monitoring of the solstices and the equinoxes, our astronomer ancestors would have observed this other phenomenon of celestial mechanics. They would have noticed that at dawn after intervals of 30 days, the same time interval as a cycle of the Moon, the Sun would rise into one of the 12 constellations or patterns of stars which line the path that the Sun travels – the ecliptic. The Sun then passes across a particular constellation as the 30-day period progresses and crosses all 12 constellations in the year. It would not have taken a huge jump to connect the passage of the seasons to the movement of the Sun along the horizon at dawn – the four seasons equating with the four quarters created by the annual cycle of the Earth's passage around the Sun. Whilst it is speculation, it is possible to imagine that noting the three primary positions of the Sun on the horizon as being significant they chose to divide each of the quarters of the seasonal cycles into three sections and from that named the 12 constellations into which the Sun rose on its apparent annual journey. However it happened, 12 constellations were defined and named. Each was allocated approximately 30 degrees of a circle. These 12 constellations became known as the Great Belt or Great Circle – better known to most people today as the signs of the zodiac. On the morning of the Spring Equinox, as the Sun crosses the horizon it does so into one of the twelve constellations of the zodiac that line the path that the Sun, the Moon and the planets travel.

Precession is caused by a slight wobble in the Earth's axis. This wobble causes a very gradual rolling action that in turn results in a very slow rotation of the axis. As a consequence the horizon gradually moves forwards relative to the path the Sun travels, taking, it is estimated, 25,920 years for the axis to complete one full rotation. The visible effect is that the Sun appears to rise into one of the 12 constellations at dawn on the morning of the Spring Equinox and then, over the period of the next 2,160 years, it very slowly moves across that constellation and into each other constellation in turn. So 5,000 years ago the Sun rose into the constellation of Taurus on the Spring Equinox. Today it rises into the Constellation of Pisces and in between these epochs was the constellation of Aries, the prominent constellation at the time of Solomon.

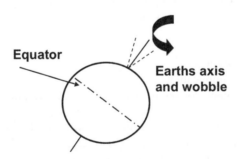

In the scriptures there is mention of *killing the fatted calf.* Some writers have suggested that it is an indication that the event the scriptures refer to occurred in the era when the prominent constellation was Taurus – the bull. Later we find references to rams and sheep supposedly signifying the era of Aries – the ram. There has also been much speculation that reference to fishes within Christianity over much of the past 2,000 years, indicates the current precessional era of Pisces – the fish. There are those who believe that year 1 (1 CE / 1 AD) of the Christian era, the nominal start of our current western calendar systems, marked the time when the precessional era of Aries was finally closed and the new era of Pisces commenced.

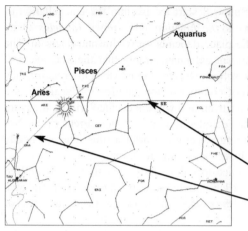

The sky at dawn in Jerusalem on the morning of the Spring Equinox 1000 BCE, the epoch in which Solomon's Temple was built. The sun is just on the horizon and rising into the constellation of Aries. (sky background printed from Skyglobe software)

The horizon

The ecliptic – the path the sun follows.

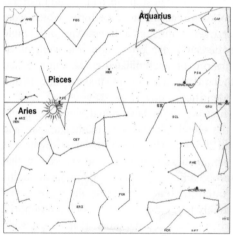

The sky at dawn in Jerusalem on the morning of the Spring Equinox in 1 CE, the era in which the Christ child is believed to have been born heralding the start of Christianity. The sun is just on the horizon and rising into the leading edge of the constellation of Pisces. (sky background printed from Skyglobe software)

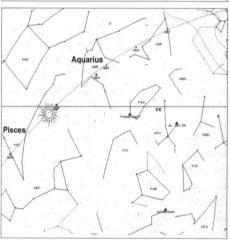

The sky at dawn in Jerusalem on the morning of the Spring Equinox 2000 CE. Three thousand years after the epoch in which Solomon's Temple was built, the sun rises into the closing phase of the constellation of Pisces. The precessional age is moving towards the cusp of Aquarius – the dawning of the age of Aquarius. The precessional rotation of the Earth is approx 14 degrees every one thousand years. (sky background printed from Skyglobe software)

The Rise of the Sun

In the not too distant future the Sun will start to rise into the constellation of Aquarius so immortalised by reference to *the dawning of the age of Aquarius*. Quite when this change is predicted to take place depends on whom one refers to. The Maya of South America, in their ancient calendars, imply that the new age will commence in 2012. When I raised the subject with the Greenwich Observatory, they suggested that the new age would not commence for another 350 years. It is a question of where one starts measuring from and what is decided will be the point in the sky, perhaps a single star, that denotes the end of the current cycle. Not withstanding these differences one thing is certain – after a time lapse of nearly 2,160 years, our precessional age of Pisces is coming to its end.

It would have probably taken our ancestors thousands of years to have noticed that the Sun travelled across one constellation before moving into the next, and then the next, and that it was yet another of the cycles which had been created as part of the governance of the cosmos.

The knowledge and discovery of this process of celestial mechanics demonstrates the incredible ability of our ancestors to keep records, in some form, which were passed from one generation to another over many generations. Any one single generation would probably not have detected the precessional movement. It probably needed some 5,000 years or more of accumulated understanding and observation together with some form of record against which to make a comparison, before the phenomenon was positively identified.

According to surviving records, the first person to have noted, understood and explained the precessional cycle was the Greek philosopher, mathematician and astronomer Hipparchus. He did so around 245 BCE. This doesn't mean to say he was the first, only that he is the first for whom there is evidence in records of that understanding. The Babylonians and Mesopotamians also knew and understood this celestial process. However, keeping in mind the time it takes for the precessional movement to be noticeable, it is highly likely that the process was being monitored thousands of years prior to Hipparchus being awarded the glory. If my suggestion that it would probably have taken some 5,000 years of observation to understand the mechanics of precession, not to mention any time lapse earlier during which someone observed that the phenomenon occurred, then we are projecting back to the sixth or seventh millennium BCE – 9,000 years ago.

Some of the information gathered and interpreted by our ancestors was not always welcome. The Ancient Greek astronomer Anaxagoras is recorded as having declared to the ruling hierarchy of the day that in his opinion the Moon was probably a lump of rock orbiting the Earth, and that it was probably about the size of one of the Greek islands. He declared his theory around 480 BCE. His insight cost him dear. He was accused of irreligious activity and cast into exile.

What is also understood is that as a consequence of the Sun being the first deity it would also have been logical for the early priesthoods to have become the custodians of knowledge and formulate methods of conveying that knowledge from generation to generation in much the same way as the primary religions still operate today. Graham Hancock, in his best-selling book *Fingerprints of the Gods*, points out that a priesthood devoted to studying and recording the movement of the Sun, and other astronomical relationships, existed for possibly thousands of years at Heliopolis in Egypt, and that this priesthood amassed a considerable amount of data and understanding. Other authors have noted, mostly out of speculation, that it was probable that the ruling priesthoods of antiquity, realising the importance of ensuring their accumulated knowledge was transmitted to future generations, and that it required a higher than normal intellect to understand, explain and continue the research, would seek out young boys who showed intelligence and cultivate them for a life as astronomer-priests. Some writers have even gone so far as to suggest that priests would seek out women as partners who also showed a high degree of intelligence, and have children by them, in anticipation that children resulting from the relationship might prove sufficiently intelligent that the information could be passed on within a family line. This would, of course, have been an early attempt at genetic manipulation. If this were true it would suggest that our ancestors had at least a basic understanding of the natural world and selection process, which extended beyond just a study of the sky. It is interesting to note that sections of the Old Testament are a record of just such priestly family lines. This includes David. We read of *David's line* – his descendants. Prior to David's line there is another such priestly line mentioned in the Bible. It comprises the descendants of Moses' brother Aaron – the priesthood known as the Levites. There are places in the world where this type of regime is perpetuated even today. In India, the Brahmin caste is the highest of the caste grades and is akin to a priesthood from which the ruling elite have traditionally evolved. It is also interesting to note that the seven-branch candlestick of the Israelites, the menorah, which is believed to have had its origins around the time of Moses, relates specifically to the planets – Mercury, Venus, Mars, Jupiter, Saturn, plus the Sun and Moon. Moses, who, we are told, laid the foundations of the Israelite traditions, is believed to have lived around 1400 BCE, which means that considerable astronomical knowledge must have been well established by that time, being conveyed from generation to generation, through the priestly line.

Stonehenge on Salisbury Plain is known as a solar marker and calendar. Tradition has it that it was probably built by the Druids who were the prevailing priesthood and custodians of knowledge of their era, in Britain and much of western Europe. Although the Druidic connection appears in some 20th century literature, English Heritage, which is responsible for the site, now suggests it was built by three separate cultures. The construction of Stonehenge, according to English Heritage, is dated to around 2100 BCE. But prior to the erection of this highly complex and accurate solar clock, the construction methodology of which still baffles archaeologists and mesmerises those who visit it, another henge had been constructed on the same site. This earlier construction was made with wooden poles instead of large stone slabs. It may well have been a temporary prototype, easy to construct, to prove the science before a much more elaborate and permanent structure built in stone was attempted. Holes cut into the ground and which originally housed the wooden posts were discovered by John Aubrey around 1666 and, quite naturally, are now referred to as 'the Aubrey holes'. Using carbon dating techniques these holes, and therefore the wooden poles mounted in them, have been dated to 3,100 BCE. This implies that the *Wooden Henge* was used for a period of 1,000 years between its construction and that of the one that remains, made from stone. It has to be further argued that the *Wooden Henge* was an attempt, which probably succeeded, to build what today we would recognise as a piece of scientific apparatus that would enable the monitoring of known data as it then existed. It would have enabled the priesthood to continue to build on that understanding as the apparatus enabled them to observe and monitor celestial activity against a known installation. Assuming it was used regularly for observations, then the data collected from it needed to be understood and transmitted across many generations before the stone structure was attempted.

When we relate this to the account of Anaxagoras and his attempt at estimating the size of the Moon, and the construction of the *Wooden Henge* on Salisbury Plain, then they are both indications that an understanding, interest and study of the universe had been undertaken for some considerable period in earlier antiquity. If we assume 1,000 years of watching and recording prior to building the *Wooden Henge,* we now have a time lapse which takes us back to 4,000 BCE.

The world is dotted with the remains of solar observatories of differing ingenuity, with many having originated from the era prior to 2,500 BCE. Thus, it is quite likely that someone recorded the details of the Precession of the Equinox well before the time of Hipparchus. The records either haven't survived or we just haven't found them yet.

How big is the ball?

Along with recording the celestial spheres and their movements it is also obvious that early civilisations would have wrestled with trying to understand what the world itself was. Standing at any point on land, or indeed a shoreline, one's line of sight ceases at the horizon. Yet, if you walk towards the horizon all you discover is that the horizon has moved away from where you first saw it. What you can see is another distant horizon. This phenomenon must have caused great debate in early civilisations as they sought to understand that the reason the horizon kept moving away was because of the curvature of the Earth's surface – that the Earth is a very large ball. Once that had been realised the next problem to solve would have been to define just how big the ball is.

Just as Hipparchus was the first person for whom we have surviving records to show that he understood the principles of precession, so the Greek philosopher Eratosthenes was the first person recorded as having measured the circumference of our planet.

Eratosthenes had a job that offered him many opportunities. He was in charge of the great library that used to exist in Alexandria. This library, history tells us, held many records of considerable antiquity. Eratosthenes was therefore in a position to have unrestricted access to them. Tradition has it that amongst the prized collection of materials were documents that Alexander the Great, after whom Alexandria is named, had recovered or collected whilst he was conquering parts of India. Included in those documents, it is believed, was reference to the fact that the Earth is a sphere.

Eratosthenes was well acquainted with trigonometry and geometry. He also knew that due south of Alexandria, some 5,000 *stadia* away (430 miles or 720km) and situated on the banks of the River Nile, was the town of Syrene, known to us today as Aswan. In the town there was a well, where, when the Sun was directly overhead at midday on the day of the Summer Solstice, it shone directly down on the waters below. It was the only time of the year this could happen. It was also known that on the same day and at the same time, a vertical object raised in Syrene, such as a stick or obelisk, did not cast a shadow. Back in Alexandria on the same day of the year, Eratosthenes noted that by placing a stick vertically in the ground it cast a short shadow. He measured the length of the shadow and through his knowledge of geometry he was able to define the angle of the Sun relative to that at Syrene. It was 7.2 degrees. He obviously knew that if the Earth was a sphere it could also be defined by a circle of 360 degrees. So, dividing 360 degrees by 7.2 told him that the distance from Syrene to Alexandria was one fiftieth of the distance around the full circle – the Earth.

360/7.2 = 50.

Thus, multiplying the 5,000 stadia by 50 gave him the length of the polar circumference of the Earth:

430 miles x 50 = 21,500 miles (rounded)
720km   x 50 = 36,000km (rounded)

Eratosthenes's results were remarkably accurate when compared with satellite measurements of modern technology. The sheer enormity of the size of the Earth must have been stunning to a civilisation where the majority of people travelled only a few miles from their place of birth, whilst the most learned, like Eratosthenes, may have travelled but a few hundred miles.

It just so happens that, as a consequence of Eratosthenes' stick producing a shadow with an angular relationship of 7.2 degrees, the length of the shadow on the day of the Summer Solstice when measured in Alexandria is always one eighth of the length of the stick.

Assume the length of a stick of 64 units.

64 x sin 7.2 degrees = 64 x 0.125 = 8.

According to two other philosophers, Cleomedes and Posidonius, Eratosthenes wrote several books and produced maps of the then known world. Sadly, none of these have survived into our current era. Cleomedes and Posidonius apparently had access to some of the originals and from their descriptions it seems that the Eratosthenes maps revealed a territorial knowledge of the land masses from Scandinavia through North Africa, Sinai and the Red Sea, and from Britain through Asia Minor. Following his calculation for the size of the globe he must have realised that vast and undiscovered lands would exist beyond the then known world.

The fact that the Earth is a sphere seems to have been well understood in ancient times. It is even noted in the Old Testament. In Isaiah 40:22 the text reads:

The Rise of the Sun

He [God] sits enthroned above the circle of the Earth.

The Earth as a sphere, and its measurement, seem to have been understood well before Eratosthenes recorded his experiment. Several investigators and writers have pointed out that there are links between the dimensions of the Great Pyramid of Giza and a range of geophysical attributes, including the diameter and circumference of the Earth. Again, noting that archaeologists and historians tell us that the pyramids on the Giza plateau were built around 2,500 BCE, it suggests that this knowledge had been accumulated well before that time.

The Egyptian priests were considered so advanced in their understanding of geometry and its practical application that many Greek philosophers visited Egypt in the hope of gaining an insight into this accumulated knowledge. Plato and Pythagoras were amongst them. On the basis of the old adage that *knowledge is power*, it may well have been that those Greek sages that visited Egypt were not provided with access to the full secrets of Egyptian understanding but merely given a few fundamental insights into the basic knowledge. Progressively over several centuries and generations, the Greeks then built on that basic information and have been acclaimed in history for providing us with much of the geometrical knowledge we have today.

There is even a well-founded suggestion that the Egyptian Royal Cubit of 20.63 Imperial inches is derived from, and related to, the circumference of the Earth and easily replicated through knowledge of the pentagram. We will return to the geometry of this suggestion in another chapter.

Over the past century, many researchers have delved into the mysterious dimensions of the pyramids of Giza, and, whilst some of the esoteric characteristics claimed for them may be wide of the mark, the fact remains that they appear to have been designed on sound geometric principles, and many of those principles relate to the circle of the Earth. By definition, therefore, it is highly likely that the size of the Earth had been estimated well before 2,500 BCE, over two thousand years prior to Eratosthenes being awarded the glory.

Today, we have an Earth measure

Most people today, if asked to point out the diameter of the Earth, would do so by referring to the equatorial circumference. To the philosophers and men of science in ancient times it was the polar diameter and circumference that was the basis from which the size of the Earth was calculated, as we have seen above with the experiment devised by Eratosthenes. Today we have a unit of measure, adopted by many countries as their standard, which is also derived from measuring the circumference of the Earth. It is the Metric measure – the metre.

The word *metre* is taken from the French spelling, but its root is from the Greek word *metron* which means 'measure'. In 1791, the French Academy of Sciences set about establishing a standard unit of measure. Several approaches to this problem were considered. The approach that was finally agreed to have been most favourable was to measure the distance of the quadrant of the circumference of the Earth, along a median that passed through Paris from the North Pole to the Equator and use a 1/10,000,000th part of it to create the standard. This approach was agreed by the French Government in 1793. Over the next few years, astronomers and scientists conducted their survey and in 1799 the standard was set using a series of bars made from platinum. Alas, it was discovered that a minor error in calculations had resulted in the defined standard being short by 0.0002 metres, or 1/5th of a millimetre. Thus, based on this original French method of defining the metre, the polar-equator distance can be defined as 10,000,000 metres. The entire polar circumference of the Earth would therefore be 40,000,000 metres, less 4/5th of a millimetre.

The key point though is that the method of measurement was by reference to the polar meridian, measuring the distance of the Earth's quadrant from pole to equator, the fourth part of a circle, and multiplying the result by four to obtain the overall circumference of the planet. The records suggest that this is exactly the same method used by the philosophers and priests of ancient times.

One other fact of interest relates to Freemasonry. The Academy of Sciences was founded in France in 1660. This was almost exactly the same time as the founding of the Royal Society in London. Both organisations had a similar objective – the research and promotion of science.

The Royal Society traces its origins to the 1640s, when a group of philosophers met to discuss ideas presented by Sir Francis Bacon. This group has become known as the *Invisible College.* These were the years of the Commonwealth (Republican) government of Oliver Cromwell. With the restoration of the monarchy in 1660, and the return to England of Charles II, the Royal Society as such was formed. The primary motivator was Sir Robert Moray, who was a close confidant of Charles II and initiated as a freemason. Moray gathered together a group of men, versed in aspects of science. Of the twelve men present at the inaugural meeting, eleven, it is alleged, were freemasons, and the twelfth was sympathetic to the ideals of this ancient institution. Thus, it could be claimed that the renowned Royal Society was founded by freemasons.[1]

The Shadow

Just as Eratosthenes used the shadow of a stick to be able to calculate the circumference of the globe, so the civilisation that we know as Ancient Egypt used another form of stick, the obelisk, for its study of celestial mechanics. Two of the most renowned obelisks, considered to be of great antiquity, were taken from Egypt in the 19th century as European nations embarked on their period of Empire building. One is known as Cleopatra's Needle that was removed from Alexandria and taken to London in 1877 by a Freemason, Sir James Erasmus Wilson, and erected beside the River Thames a year later, with great Masonic ceremony. It is believed to have originally been erected in Heliopolis, but moved to Alexandria by the Romans.

The second obelisk stands in Place de la Concorde, Paris, being one of a pair from the Luxor Temple.

The shape of the obelisk was ideal for monitoring purposes – yet another example of a piece of early scientific apparatus. Being capped with a pyramidion, the obelisk rose to a point. Thus, the shadow cast on the ground provided a clearly defined point as a marker. In addition, if one was standing regularly at a fixed location around the base of the obelisk, the pointed top could be used as a reference marker for studying the movement of the planets and other stars in the heavens. It was a highly innovative tool. It may well have evolved from an earlier use of a stick, or a spear that had been stuck in the ground, point uppermost. Nevertheless, its origins appear to extend back to an era beyond 2,500 BCE.

Such a device would have been useful to a builder. Let us imagine that there was an instruction that a new building must have a true east-west orientation. The true east- west alignment would be determined at sunrise on the day of the Spring or Autumn Equinox. So, by placing a device with a pointed top in the centre of the area of ground due to be the building site, and aligning a second pointed object with the first, and with the place on the eastern horizon where the Sun first appeared, one would have a true east- west alignment. If one then bisected that line of orientation at right angles, one would also have a true north-south alignment. The true cardinal points of the Earth would be established simply by using two pointed markers aligned to sunrise at the time of the equinox and a line drawn at 90 degrees to that east-west alignment. Two spears, a length of cord or material and a stake hammered into the ground provided a *compass*.

The same result could be achieved using the shadow cast by the Sun at its meridian, that is, when the Sun is at its highest in the sky – what we call midday. If, for several weeks and days prior to the Spring Equinox, the shadow of the Sun was marked on the ground between mid-morning and mid-afternoon there would be various 'V' shaped patterns on the ground which became more discernible as the Sun rose higher in the sky with each passing day. From day to day these patterns would vary little, but over a period of about one month there would be a noticeable difference, especially if one was living in the Middle East. By drawing a line through the base of the 'V' shape to the base of the marker pole or obelisk, the true north-south alignment would be determined. If that line was bisected then the true east-west alignment could be determined. The advantage of *marking the sun at its meridian* would be that the *compass* could be set at any time of the year.

There would be yet a further advantage to *marking the sun at its meridian.* If an inerasable line was installed in the ground along the line of the shadow cast by the obelisk or marker post, then by marking the position of the shadow every day it would enable a check to be made on the progress of the seasons. Religious festivals could be *marked.* Keeping in mind that knowledge about the working of the world, the macro-cosmos, was likely to be retained within the priesthood of a religious community, then ensuring the accurate *marking of the sun at its meridian* would have been deemed a responsible task. It would have enabled a cross-reference by day with phases of the Moon by night. Within the priesthood, the Sun would have ruled the day, whilst the Moon would have ruled the night.

Let us now imagine that a semi-circle was drawn around the base of obelisk or marker post, to the north of the post, so that the shadow cast by the marker crossed that semi-circle a short time after sunrise and until sunset. Let us further imagine that, around the edge of the semi-circle, marks were made at 15° intervals from the line which represented midday, then a rudimentary sun-clock would be established, because, as mentioned earlier, a 15° rotation of the Earth represents what today we call one hour. Six 15° sectors, on either side of the midday shadow, would have created a shadow clock marking the hours that we now know as 6 o'clock in the morning until 6 o'clock in the afternoon. There would, therefore, have been 12 segment marks on the semi-circle. Needless to mention, a full circle, with the second semicircle being to the south of the post, would have added a further 12 segments, making 24 segments in all, thus marking and defining the 24 hours of the rotation of the Earth.

Heliocentric v Geocentric

Today, almost every schoolchild in the western world knows that the Earth orbits the Sun. But acceptance of this concept was not easily won.

As we have previously noted, Eratosthenes was the first recorded person we know of who proved that the Earth was a ball, and measured it. But this didn't answer one basic question. Did the planets, the stars and the Sun and Moon travel around the Earth in a geocentric universe, or did the Earth travel around the Sun in a heliocentric universe? Science and astronomical observations suggested that the Earth orbited the Sun. The scriptures stated that God had made Earth first, and the firmament with the Sun, Moon and stars, afterwards. Therefore, the view of the religious community was that the Earth had to be the centre of creation and the centre of the universe around which everything else was built.

This perspective fuelled a debate which continued for centuries, even before the advent of the Christian era. In the early days of the Roman Church it was decreed that the geocentric universe was the correct system and that to postulate anything else was heresy. And that is the way the church in Rome treated the matter until the late 19th century. As a consequence, this enforced doctrine became the established belief in Western Europe for around 1,500 years. It was from within the Catholic Church itself that seeds of change were eventually to originate. In the 15th century, a Catholic bishop was quietly making discoveries that were to change our accepted understanding.

Copernicus lived between 1473 and 1543, and was acknowledged in his lifetime as a notable astronomer and theologian. By 1507, after some years of careful observations, he understood that the Earth was not flat but spherical and, more importantly, that it orbited the Sun as did the planets. The Earth, it seemed, was somehow interwoven with them. He developed this thesis until in 1513 he privately circulated a paper to a few close friends, explaining his theories. Copernicus was not daft. He knew that the Catholic hierarchy of the day would have branded him a lunatic and a heretic if he had formally tried to publish his ideas at that time. Eventually Copernicus' theory was published in 1543 in his book entitled *De revolutionibus orbium coelestrium, The Revolutions of the Celestial Spheres*. Later branded by the Vatican as 'Copernican Theory', it was frowned on by the Church, so much so that the book was placed on the 'forbidden' list in 1616 and not removed from it until 1853.

Not only did Copernicus' idea upset many of the accepted philosophies then standing, together with those who supported them, but the Church decided that uttering such ideas was an act of heresy and the perpetrator could be put to death or thrown into jail.

And that is what happened to another renowned scientist and astronomer, Galileo Galilei. Galileo was born in 1564, just twenty-one years after the publication of Copernicus' theories. Through his own astronomical studies he began to realise the truth of Copernicus' work and he began to teach the related ideas. The Church was not pleased. Galileo was arrested on a charge of heresy. It is reported that Galileo was tortured for his view and only escaped being put to death by finally admitting that he was wrong. But not, it is recorded, before crying out under torture '...but they move', a reference to his own observations of the movement of stars and planets in their various orbits. For holding Copernican views Galileo was subjected to internal exile and lived the last eight years of his life under house arrest until his death in 1642. Others would continue to explore Copernican theory until eventually it was recognised that Copernicus and Galileo had both been right; the Earth was round and it did orbit the Sun. Copernicus and Galileo had, by scientific deduction, shown the heliocentric universe to be reality. Scientific and religious beliefs were now in serious conflict.

Although 2,000 years apart, the consequences suffered by Galileo were similar to Anaxagoras. The religious establishments clearly had some difficulty coming to terms with new scientific discoveries once they had decided on, and set, the philosophy of their religious dogma.

As mentioned earlier, the seven-branched candle holder used by the Israelites, the menorah, was directly related to the planets that were known to them at that time. There was one holder for each of the Sun, Moon, Mercury, Venus, Mars, Jupiter and Saturn. Of them all, Saturn was regarded as the most significant. It was believed that Heaven, where God the creator resided, was just beyond the orbit of Saturn. Thus, the planet and its orbit were the closest point one could imagine to the source of divine creation.

Three thousand five hundred years ago our ancestors thought that Saturn was the furthest planet away from the Earth. The next planet in our solar system, and the third largest, is Uranus. It was discovered by William Herschel in 1781. Neptune, the next planet, was discovered in 1846. In 1930 a further orbiting mass was discovered, defined as a planet and given the name Pluto. Seventy-five years later, the advances in astronomy resulted in the definition of a planet changing and Pluto was demoted. Bearing in mind that Saturn was an established component of Israelite understanding, emanating from the time of Moses, and that Moses lived around 1,400 BCE, then some 3,100 years at least had elapsed from the establishment of Israelite religious doctrine to the discovery that there were other planets in our solar system. This single discovery would have done much to undermine the core religious philosophy which then existed, bringing science and religion into more conflict.

Numbers, Arithmetic and the macro-cosmos

Needless to say, if our ancestors had an ability to estimate the size of the globe on which we live, then they must have had an understanding of basic arithmetic.

There is a widely held view amongst many academics that the origins of mathematics started with the Babylonians sometime around 2,000 BCE. Numbers were used well before that time as a method of quantifying and measuring. One only has to look to the pyramids of Giza to see this. The pyramids were supposedly built around 2,500 BCE, five hundred years before the development of Babylonian arithmetic. Mathematics is really the use of numbers or groups of numbers to solve problems against predefined rules, such as multiplication, division, squaring, calculus.

Quite likely it would have been the early merchants that developed the basic understanding. If they had bought 200 goats for a specific price, they would have wanted to know how much that was for each goat. If they were going to sell the goats they would have wanted to know how much profit they were making on their investment, otherwise why do it? Later it is probable that government administration developed mathematics further with the desire for the collection of taxes. But according to historians it was not until around 500 BCE that the Greeks began to build on the mathematical principles that the Babylonians had developed.

Yet again, however, we see that our ancestors had a good understanding of numbers probably 5,000 years ago, or more.

Researchers tell us that long before they evolved principles of mathematics, our ancestors developed an interest in numbers and their relationship with the natural world. They discovered that the most common numbers in nature were 3, 5 and 7.

The number 3, for example, can be related to the movement of the Sun and its 3 primary positions: the Equinox, Summer and Winter Solstices. The number 5 occurs frequently in plant forms with the number of petals on flowers. As already mentioned, 7 was the number of known celestial spheres in ancient times.

We also learn that ancient civilisations were interested in number patterns and events which inspired those number patterns. So number patterns like:

     12121212121212

or

     666666666

or

     318318318

were held in particular reverence.

Our ancestors would also add and subtract numbers to have greater significance and symbolism. Take for example the *mysterious* number 9. If you take the answer of any multiple of 9 and add together the digits in the answer, it will always add up to 9. For example:

$$2 \times 9 = 18 \qquad 1 + 8 = 9$$
$$8 \times 9 = 72 \qquad 7 + 2 = 9$$
$$24 \times 9 = 216 \qquad 2 + 1 + 6 = 9$$

$32 \times 9 = 288 \qquad 2 + 8 + 8 = 18 \qquad 1 + 8 = 9$

$237 \times 9 = 2133 \qquad 2 + 1 + 3 + 3 = 9$

Then there was the order of numbers. Take as an example the first three digits in the numbering system, 1, 2 and 3. These numbers have a special quality:

$1 + 2 + 3 = 6$

$1 \times 2 \times 3 = 6$

The number 6 was highly revered. The scriptures record that God created Heaven and Earth in 6 days. It was therefore a powerful symbolic number. The number 7 had equal symbolic power because the scriptures record that on the seventh day God rested.

Just as the pattern of numbers held certain symbolism, so too did the geometry of the natural world. Take for example the number 5.

The above picture is of the flower of the blackberry bush. It looks identical to the pattern which we know as the pentagram with its five petals spread out in similar geometric pattern. The same applies to many flowers, as can be seen below.

It is not difficult, therefore, to understand how our ancestors would have seen a relationship between arithmetic, geometry and the natural world. They were all bound together in the macro-cosmos.

Numbers were, apparently, used for other symbolic purposes. The people of ancient times did not have a concept of the numeral that we know as '0' or zero. For generations, what we know as zero was an indication that *nothing was there.* So the number 10 could also be defined as 1. The number 1 was seen as the start of the counting process, it had *unity* with the deity and as such came to represent the deity. As 1 (one) is an odd number, and because of its links to the deity, all odd numbers were regarded as lucky. This tradition holds true even today in Islamic culture. The number 20 could also be interpreted as 2, the concept of duality, of Heaven and Earth.

The Origins of Geometry

It is believed that it was from the study of the heavens that the basis of geometry was derived:

- That the 366 sunrises in the solar year became the basis of the 360-degree circle. In the Babylonian era the basis of counting was 60. When the Sun reaches the extremities of its Winter and Summer Solstice passage, its movement would have been hardly detectable using the basic, though normally effective, apparatus that the ancients had at their disposal. The Sun would have been seen to dwell at the ends of its travel for a few days. A three-day dwelling period at each end of the travel would have seemed reasonable. Therefore, 360 would not have been an unrealistic choice for defining the length of a cycle, and therefore a circle. It would have been seen to be a logical number easily divided into smaller parts, based on the number 60. By ignoring the residual six days of sunrises, leaving 360, it was an ideal number to fit in with the Babylonian counting system and geometry. 360 divided by 2, half, would be 180; divided by 3 is 120; divided by 4 is 90; divided by 5 is 72; divided by 6 is 60. The number 60 is easily divided into two parts of 30; 60 divided by 3 is 20; 60 divided by 4 is 15; 60 divided by 5 is 12. In geometric terms, by segmenting the number pattern, or the circumference of a circle, it is a convenient way of producing small angles, without the need for sophisticated instrumentation. One just had to remember a few basic principles relating to a circle.
- The lunar cycle of 30 days became the basis of the religious calendar. 360 days divided by 30 = 12. This would have a relationship with the Great Circle, also known as the Great Belt – the zodiac and the twelve constellations the Sun would enter during the annual solar cycle.
- The solar cycle became the civil calendar. The scriptures tell us that the world was created in 6 days with the seventh being a day of rest. The week was therefore defined as 7 days from very early times. Because God had created Heaven and Earth and then rested on the seventh day, the number

7 came to be regarded as something special – a highly revered number. A week of 7 days divided into the number of days in a solar cycle, is 52, and $5 + 2 = 7$.

- The number 72 fitted closely with the allotted lifespan of man – three score years and ten. But it also had another significance. The rotation of the Earth's axis during the Precession of the Equinox is 1 degree every 72 years. So, in a typical human lifetime the Earth's precessional rotation would have advanced one degree. This was the number I had found in the Brighton Masonic Temple pavement directly beneath the canopy of the zodiac.

- To measure the passage of time, a clock – a shadow clock, perhaps based on an obelisk – might have a circle drawn around the base of a vertical pole. The position of the Sun at its meridian, midday, the highest point in the sky the Sun reaches on any specific day, could be marked with a straight line from the centre of the base of the obelisk, or pole. From this, the circle could be divided in half. Each half could be easily divided to provide 4 segments each of 45 degrees. It is then easy to divide each segment of 45 degrees into three equal parts. This would result in each semi-circle having 12 segments. Therefore, the full circle would have 24 equal segments. Each segment would therefore be 15 degrees. As mentioned earlier, the Earth rotates 15 degrees in a time period which we define as an *hour* in our modern units of time. The Earth rotates 15 degrees of its daily 360-degree cycle in one hour and completes one full rotation in 24 x 15 degree segments – 24 hours. Once again we can see the influence of the ancients in our current measurement of time; 60 minutes = 1 hour; 60 seconds = 1 minute.

- The number 15 has one other symbolic characteristic. The lunar cycle is 30 days and the Moon is full on the 15th day of each new cycle, marked from when the first sliver of light would be seen – the new Moon.

From the above it will be noted how, through observing the rhythm of the solar system and the resultant effect on the macro-cosmos, these influences would be interwoven with the principles of geometry. Foremost in their observation of the heavens were the Mesopotamians, credited with naming the twelve constellations of the zodiac. Thus, by around 2,000 BCE they had a reasonable understanding of geometry. Whilst Pythagoras' Theorem defines a means of finding the length of the hypotenuse of a right-angled triangle using the sum of the squares on the other two sides, it was a process that the Babylonians were also aware of. Pythagoras packaged it in a way that we could easily understand and gained immortality in so doing, but the Babylonians, who already knew this process, passed into obscurity. An ancient clay tablet from Babylon clearly demonstrates their understanding. It was the Greek philosophers and mathematicians who ultimately received much of the credit for geometric discovery, but in many respects they were building on groundwork by the Babylonians and Egyptians.

Conclusion

Knowledge about the Sun, its rising and setting, progress of the seasons and precession of the equinox, were attributes well understood by our recent ancestors. They had learned to use the shadow cast by the Sun to measure the circumference of the Earth with a high degree of accuracy. It is also clear that they had a thorough understanding of cycles of the Moon.

These they clearly saw as the guiding lights in their lives such that they became the heart of their religious belief systems.

All the knowledge our ancestors possessed about the natural world was the type of knowledge needed to enable the operative stone masons to perform their building tasks. One could now understand why it appeared in Masonic ceremonies as a legacy of those bygone eras.

Designing a building in sympathy with the forces of creation, with the macro-cosmos, was something different. That clearly required specialist knowledge. What was that knowledge?

[1] *The Invisible College* – Robert Lomas

Chapter 3
Secret knowledge – Sacred wisdom

*'.....Seest thou the fountain of instructions that takes its rise from wisdom?
......What use is there in knowing the causes of the manner of the sun's
motion, for example, and the rest of the heavenly bodies, or in having studied
the theorems of geometry or logic, and each of the other branches of
study?.....For treating of the description of the celestial objects, about the
form of the universe, and the revolution of the heavens, and the motion of the
stars, leading the soul nearer to the creative power, it teaches to quickness in
perceiving the seasons of the year, the changes of the air, and the appearance
of the stars; since also navigation and husbandry derive from this much
benefit, as architecture and building from geometry. This branch of learning,
too, makes the soul in the highest degree observant, capable of perceiving the
true and detecting the false, of discovering correspondences and
proportions, so as to hunt out for similarity in things dissimilar; and
conducts us to the discovery of length without breadth, and superficial extent
without thickness, and an indivisible point, and transports to intellectual
objects from those of sense.'*

from Sacred Texts[1]

Well before the development of sophisticated arithmetic compilations, geometry
was an important tool for solving the types of problems that today we solve easily
as a consequence of our mathematical understanding. It was realised by our
ancestors that three geometric figures – the square, circle and the triangle – formed
the foundation of nearly all their particular problem solving. The circle was the most
revered of all the geometric symbols, being a line which had no definable beginning
and therefore no end, and as such represented infinity. The centre of the circle was
the most revered point, being that from which every part of the circumference was
equidistant, the centre of creation and therefore infinite in its power. In addition the
easiest of the three symbols to construct was the circle. A peg could be hammered
into the ground, a length of cord or material loosely tied to the stake at one end and
a stick at the other, and then whilst holding the cord or material taut, one could
scratch a circle in the ground by walking around the stake. However it was derived,
the circumference of the circle could then be used to establish the four faces of a
square.

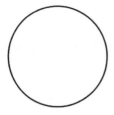
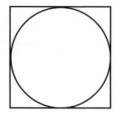

The principles of geometry were recorded in a series of *theorems* expounded by the Greek mathematician Euclid around 300 BCE. One of the first principles he alludes to is a process of dividing a straight line into two equal parts. This is done by taking the line, AB, and drawing two circles of equal diameter, one circle at each end of the line, so that they overlap.

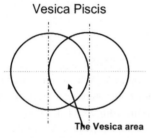

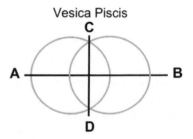

Drawing a vertical line between the points C & D will bisect the line AB into two equal lengths.

This concept can be taken one stage further when the circles, both of equal diameter, are drawn such that the circumference of one circle touches the centre of the other circle. This geometric pattern was well known to the ancients and has been passed down to us with the title *Vesica Piscis*. The resultant area where the two circles overlap is known as the *Vesica*. It produces some interesting characteristics. For example, it is possible from this use of the two circles to determine an angle of 30° and 60°. This is shown in the diagram below through the points where the 60° is defined by the points ACB. The bold line at an angle represents the hypotenuse of a right angle triangle, CBA. Thus, the opposite angle, BAC, is 30°. By turning this simple relationship into a rectangle (as shown by the dotted lines) and bisecting the angles with a pair of compasses, it is possible to create the angles 15°, 30°, 45°, 60°, 75° and 90°. Thus, with a simple pair of compasses and a straight edge, eg 24 inch gauge, our ancestors were able to determine the primary geometric angles regularly used.

Vesica Piscis

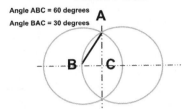

This simple geometric structure immediately lends itself to the construction of another important figure – the equilateral triangle.

Vesica Piscis

Equilateral Triangle from circles in Vesica Piscis

So, our ancestors, through their knowledge of geometry, were able to produce, with considerable accuracy, the three most common geometric forms in their construction armoury – the circle, the square and the equilateral triangle – the latter two being derived from the basic form – the circle. Thus, the circle became a highly regarded geometric device. But, more importantly, it was the point at the centre of the circle which was most revered, for no circle could be constructed without it. And, as the circle became the form for the origins of so much other geometry, which in turn provided the basis for the construction of many of the temples, palaces and significant buildings of ancient times, so this point within the circle was seen as the centre from which all creation emanated. One can imagine how, through their knowledge of the interlinked macro-cosmos, and a belief that God had designed and implemented every last element of it himself, our ancestors believed that He must have used the same geometric principles. So, too, it can be imagined that the centre of the circle, infinite in the wisdom and knowledge that could be derived from it, was revered as God himself.

The vesica, or central area of the interlocked circles, was treated not only with reverence but as a sacred entity. It was an area from which so much else, geometrically, could be created. With their knowledge of the macro-cosmos, it was not lost on our ancestors that the shape was not dissimilar to that of the female vulva, the origins of intelligent form – the origins of all of us. It thus represented the geometry of life. As time has passed it has acquired other meanings. As an example – the central area is also shaped like an eye and has thus come to mean *shared vision* or *common ground.* In the Vatican bookshop, a postcard is available which shows the Seal of Cardinal Antonio Correr (1431-1445) who was the Bishop of Bologna between 1407 and 1412. The shape is unmistakably that of the vesica. Within the vesica the illustration shows a group of people in prayer, whilst a further image of a man, probably representing Jesus Christ, ascends to Heaven, the latter being depicted as a five-pointed star. The *common ground* of the Christian belief. The seal demonstrates the symbolic significance with which the shape of the Vesica was held. Even today, church choristers and those associated with church music will be very familiar with the symbol as it forms the basis of the medals they receive as a demonstration of their proficiency.

Knowledge of the practical potential of Vesica Piscis would have been of considerable use to builders in ancient times, enabling devices for measuring 30°, 60° and 90° angles to be evolved on site, rather than carrying cumbersome devices with them from one place to another. In the Cairo Museum there is a wonderful display of builders' squares, found on archaeological sites in Egypt, which have been dated to around 2,500 BCE. Whether or not they were created using the geometric principles of Vesica Piscis is a matter of pure speculation. Nevertheless, a method for the creation of such tools was clearly understood in those times.

Many of the floor plans for the construction of churches and major monuments have been derived from the principles of Vesica Piscis.

Edward Condor, a former Master of the Mason's Company in London, in his book entitled *The Hole Craft & Fellowship of Masonry, With a Chronicle of the History of the Worshipful Company of Masons of the City of London* makes the following observation:

> *'... about the 12th century, we can easily imagine how the construction of the equilateral triangle ... must have struck the early Christian architect, and given him, by the intersection of the two circumferences, a new model for the arch......'*

The arch he refers to we now know as the *Gothic* arch, a feature of the great cathedrals of Europe that were built in the 12th and 13th centuries. Most sources of information note the fine examples to be found in Canterbury, and in Chartres Cathedrals. The Gothic style is believed to have originated with the building of the cathedral dedicated to St Denis, in what today are the northern suburbs of Paris. This concept was first used in England in the rebuilding of Canterbury Cathedral after the original building had been destroyed by fire.

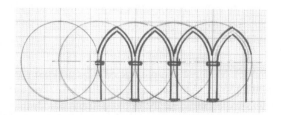 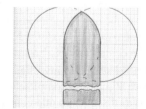

Indeed, this design concept is alluded to in Peterborough Cathedral, which is situated about thirty miles north of the university city of Cambridge, England where internal walls are adorned with carvings which show a series of interlinked arches derived from the Vesica Piscis form. It is almost as if the medieval builders were leaving a record that the principle of the interlocked circles provided the basis of the cathedral's design and construction. We will return to the geometry of Peterborough Cathedral again in another chapter.

The above figure shows part of the southern wall inside Peterborough Cathedral. The Vesica Piscis link is clearly defined.

Yet further evidence can be seen in Lincoln Cathedral, which is situated on the central east coast of England. This cathedral supports two wonderful rose windows: one facing the north and the other the south. Both windows are circular but two vesicas can clearly be seen depicted in the lead-work.

Other geometric symbols can also be developed from the interlinked circles. Amongst these was one closely associated with King Solomon that, at different times, has been referred to as *Solomon's Seal,* the six-pointed Star of David. The pentagram is also sometimes referred to as *Solomon's Seal.* Because of its significance, will come back to *Solomon's Seal* in another chapter.

Although it is a geometric process hardly spoken about in the 21st century, Vesica Piscis is still in use today. It can often be seen displayed as a Christian symbol.

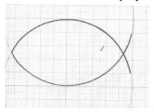

Until I started to investigate the Sussex Masonic Temple, the concept and term of Vesica Piscis was completely unknown to me. Yet it was to yield a surprise. For, as we will discover in due course, it was to feature directly in the design of both the Sussex Masonic Temple and Solomon's Temple.

The Chain

Vesica Piscis also enables another geometric potential, that of a chain. By drawing a line from the top of the vertical axis of one of the circles to the bottom of the vertical axis of the adjacent circle, the line will cross the centre of the vesica. An additional circle added such that its circumference sits on the centre point will create a chain effect, based on half radii. Obviously such an effect could be obtained on a horizontal or vertical plane. This chain effect was, apparently, regarded as a lucky symbol by the ancient Egyptians, as a consequence of which, four such interlocking circles were chosen to become the symbol used by a prestigious motor vehicle manufacturer based in Germany.

Vesica Piscis into a chain

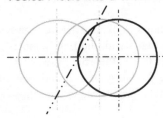

The circle's constant – squaring the circle

The ancients realised that there had to be a relationship between the circumference of a circle and the diameter, the ratio that today we know as *pi (π)*. The Egyptians are known to have settled on a ratio of 3:1, a ratio that is found in relation to the pillars of Solomon's Temple:

> *He cast two Bronze pillars, each eighteen cubits high and twelve cubits around by line.*   *1 Kings 7:15*

On the basis of the 3:1 ratio, a measurement of twelve as a circumference would give a diameter of four. This ratio is expounded in a Masonic ceremony where, in relation to the pillars, it is stated :

> *....the circumference was twelve cubits and the diameter four.*

The Egyptians knew, however, that the exact ratio was a little more than the precise number 3. In their attempt to discover the exact ratio the Egyptians sought a square whose side dimension gave an area equivalent to that of a specific circle. This was known as *squaring the circle*. It was discovered that a circle with a diameter of 9 units (9 cubits) produced the same equivalent area as a square where the sides measured 8 units (8 cubits). Nine divided by eight (9/8) equals 1.125. This is believed to have given them the ratio constant of 3.125. This is remarkably close to the value regularly used today of 3.142, a variance of just 0.5%. Measuring 3⅛ (three and one eighth) was not easy, but measuring 12½ (12.5) was. And 12.5 is a very close equivalent of the value of 4 x π (pi).

The value of Phi

There was yet another numerical relationship which seemed to be of particular interest to our ancestors. Just as the numbers 3, 5 and 7 were seen as the most common in nature, so too, it was realised, was the value Phi, and Phi could also be interpreted geometrically. Whereas most arithmetic or geometric characters have a single definable number, Phi has two numerical values, 1.618 and 0.618, which, for convenience, is written simply as 1.6 or 0.6. Phi has also become known as the Golden Ratio – or Divine Proportion. It is one of those fascinating geometric characteristics that, again, is hardly ever mentioned today, yet our ancestors used this ratio in the building of many of the great and surviving structures of antiquity, like the Parthenon in Athens, which later generations have come to revere. The proportional relationships employed create an effect which dictates that a structure is visually in harmony.

To understand this we should look at what has come to be called the Fibonnaci series. In simple terms this starts with the first numbers in our counting system, 0, 1 and 2. If we add together 0 + 1, then the answer is 1. If we now add 1 + 1, the answer is 2. If we now take the latest total, 2, and add it to the previous total, 1, we get 3. If we continue with this format we get the following series of totals:

0 + 1 = 1	8 + 5 = 13
1 + 1 = 2	13 + 8 = 21
2 + 1 = 3	21 + 13 = 34
3 + 2 = 5	34 + 21 = 55 and so on.
5 + 3 = 8	

In the Fibonnaci series we find that if we take any two adjacent totals and divide one by the other then the result is very close to the value of Phi.

$$13/8 \; = 1.625 \; (1.6) \qquad 8/13 \; = \; 0.615$$
$$55/34 = \; 1.6176 \qquad 34/55 \; = \; 0.618181818181818181818181818...$$

We find that once we have passed the first few totals, the arithmetic results in the totals oscillate around the figures of 1.618 and 0.618, but always begin with 1.6 and 0.6. Thus, these two numbers, 1.6 and 0.6, have become synonymous with representing Phi.

If we look at the first two columns of numbers in the summations above and draw rectangles with those ratios, then we have what is known as the Golden Proportion.

The Golden Proportion based on 21 + 13

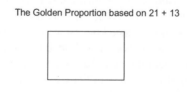

The Golden Proportion, also known as Divine Proportion, features in the geometric construction of some of the great cathedrals of Europe. And, as we will see, it turns up in the most unexpected of places.

Phi is a characteristic found extensively in ratios associated with the structure of the human body, such as in the relationship of the distance between the centre of the eyes and the width of the head, and the distance from the elbow to the wrist as a ratio of the length of an arm measured from the shoulder to the elbow. The most commonly referred to is the position of the navel relative to the height of a person. If you measure the height of a person, then measure the distance from the top of the head to the navel and then the position of their navel from the soles of the feet, which is equivalent of the navel relative to the ground, and divide the distance from feet to navel by the distance from the navel to the top of the head, the result is Phi, 1.618 (1.6). The spiral of a sea snail's shell also has the ratio of Phi. Pythagoras is attributed with having discovered this connection in nature with all the things we find pleasing to the eye. When it comes to human beauty the same ratios are found: for example, the width of the nose as a ratio of the width of the mouth. This is suggested by extensive work on defining what we find as beautiful in the human face by a facial surgeon based in the United States of America.[1]

Generally speaking, a structure which has been built based on the concept of Phi has proportions which are symmetrical and pleasing to the eye, in the same way that many attributes of nature are equally pleasing. Being related to nature it was therefore seen as being the proportion favoured by the *creator*, and as such was a divine creation – hence the expression Divine Proportion.

Geometrically the ratio can be drawn as follows:

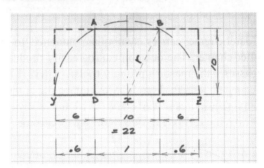

From this it will be seen that a square of any size can be turned into a rectangle of Golden Proportion with the above square ABCD becoming the rectangles defined by the baseline DZ or CY. There are sections of the great European cathedrals where one can clearly see how the constructing masons would have used this type of geometry to provide a building of *divine proportion*.

This aspect of the value of Phi has other geometric connections which we will come to in due course.

The Mason's secret square

Amongst this general geometry there was another *secret* that masons of old understood and used. It is variously known as the *secret cut, sacred cut* or *secret square*. Because it is so allied to the work of the masons, I have come to call it *the Mason's secret square*.

The following picture is of a window in a church in Lewes, the county town of East Sussex. The church traces its history to the era just after the Norman Conquest and was therefore built in the same period as many of the great cathedrals of Europe. Inside it features the pointed Gothic arch construction not only typical of the time but inherent in the geometric process of Vesica Piscis. This type of design is not unusual and can be found in many churches and prominent buildings.

The octagonal outer frame carries symbolism attached to it which will be mentioned in another chapter. The octagon can be easily produced using a square and a pair of compasses – the mason's primary tools.

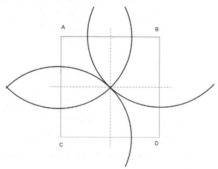

The process starts by drawing a square. Then from each of the corners A, B, C and D an arc is drawn which passes through the centre of the square and bisects the outer edge. The octagon can then be drawn as shown.

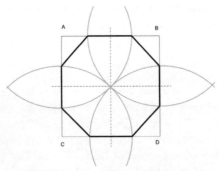

By drawing vertical and horizontal lines through the points where the edges of the octagon meet, or where the arcs cut the outer square, so an inner *secret* square is revealed.

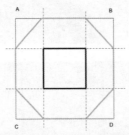

Returning to the church window in Lewes, it appears to have been constructed by first creating an outer square that has determined the overall size. Circles in Vesica Piscis have determined the height and width of the quatrefoil cross in the centre.

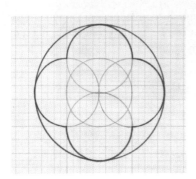

The entire layout would have been achieved with the aid of a pair of compasses, a straight edge, such as a square, and a working knowledge of the secrets of *sacred geometry*.

A square around the central circle of the Vesica Piscis has set the inner points of the quatrefoil, whilst *the Mason's secret square*, derived from the original outer square and octagon, has set the thickness for the relief around the pattern set by the Vesica circles. It is as if in the construction of this medieval church, the builders were recording the geometric principles which governed its setting out and construction.

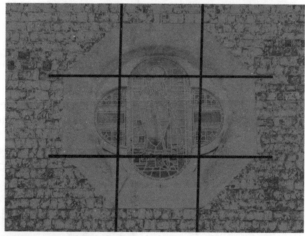

The secret square – and the number 12

The geometry that is the basis of creating the secret square has another use which links the number eight with the number twelve. By drawing a circle inside the original outer square, and then four other circles of the same diameter with their centres at the midpoint along each side of the square, the petal shape shown below is derived. At the point where each curve of the petal touches the inner circle and the vertical and horizontal axis, the spacing represents one equi-spaced 12th point around the inner circle. In other words, it is a way of creating 12 equi-spaced points on the circumference of a circle.

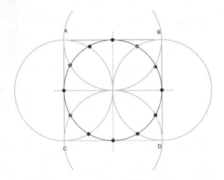

There are many fine stained glass Rose Windows in great cathedrals and churches that are based on the number 12, and, being circular, required a method of ensuring equal balance. One such example can be found in the cathedral at St Denis, just to the north of Paris. There are several wonderful circular stained glass windows, but

perhaps the most unexpected is the one which faces the west and depicts the 12 signs of the zodiac.

The outer rim has 24 triangular segments depicting the cycle of the Earth in one day, and the 15° spacing that represents one hour.

Sacred Geometry – a mason's secret

Through my introduction to this arena of geometry, its association with the macro-cosmos and its use in the design and construction of sacred buildings, I was made aware that this entire genre of geometric form, and its use, had at sometime in the past become known as *sacred geometry*. It was easy to understand how the masons of ancient times would have been expected to understand that knowledge – it was essential for their craft. In fact, in nearly all freemasons' lodges a letter 'G' is positioned close to the centre of the room being used. Historical documents, and research by others, indicates that this letter 'G' denotes *geometry*. It dawned on me that in ancient times this was knowledge to be jealously guarded. It was the type of information which demanded that it was passed on only within the craft as each craftsman demonstrated that he had fully understood, and could demonstrate, a proficiency of understanding and reproduction at each new level of knowledge attainment. To ensure that this information remained a *craft secret* draconian punishments were meterd out to offenders who violated the code of honour they swore to obey – not to disclose such secrets to anyone who was not entitled to know them. This helped to ensure confidentiality of valuable trade secrets. Thus, each new level of proficiency demanded a demonstration of recognition, so that others of similar or superior knowledge had a means of knowing that an individual had, indeed, achieved a certain level of understanding and acceptance within the craft. Today, in various areas of professional attainment, certificates are issued by regulated examining bodies, and the production of a certificate to a prospective employer serves to demonstrate a level of proficiency in understanding in a profession, both in theory and practice. Today's examination procedures are, therefore, merely an extension of the type of advancement processes evolved by craft fraternities like the masons.

The ancient memory of the Sun and Moon lives on

Within the Communion service of the Anglican Church there is a segment known as the *Nicene Creed*. It is a statement that the congregation utter aloud, reaffirming their individual and collective commitment to their religion. Like, no doubt, many other frequent attendees at church services, I routinely joined in this reaffirmation. So it was, that one Sunday morning our then vicar, as part of his sermon, spoke about the *Nicene Creed*. He pointed out that we were reaffirming a commitment set out by bishops at the Council of Nicaea in the fourth century. He marvelled at the many generations who had, since that time, faithfully made that reaffirmation so that we were receiving it as it was originally scribed.

This event occurred during a period when, in an effort to understand more about our ancestors, I was reading a lot about ancient history, and kept finding references and cross-comparisons between ancient religions and their connections with the prominent western religions that exist today. Almost by chance, I stumbled into a genre of books that looked at religion in an historical context, rather than statements of faith, and questioned the interpretations that, in the past, Church dogma and rhetoric had both reinforced and expounded as an absolute truth. These books opened up a whole new world to me, and provided answers to many aspects of religion that I felt had not been successfully addressed through my own religious practices.

I do not intend to dwell here on a detailed review of such material other than to note that the Sun, the Moon and the macro-cosmos were key components of all the early religions, even passing into the symbolism of Christianity. What did become of interest to me was that, as the doctrine of Christianity spread through Europe, so other religious beliefs were swept away before it under a heading of *paganism*. To obliterate any record of these religions, pagan sacred sites were often absorbed into Christendom by, perhaps, a church being built on the site; pagan festivals were absorbed into the Christian religion and 'rebranded'. These include:

- 25th December, previously a date associated with the Winter Solstice and celebrated as the rebirth of the Sun. It became the primary festival for the followers of *Sol Invictus*, the Roman Sun god.

- Twelfth Night, as in the 12 days of Christmas, was a Druidic festival. It was a point where the Sun could be positively measured moving northwards after dwelling at its most southerly point, the Winter Solstice. Twelfth Night was also celebrated as a festival for the rebirth of the Sun, which would soon bring warmth, light and abundance back to the Earth, banishing the cold, dark days of winter. It was a festive time in Celtic Europe when, prior to the arrival of Christianity, trees and bushes would be decorated as part of an encouragement for the rebirth of the natural world. In Christianity it became the celebrated date when the three wise men supposedly arrived in Bethlehem in search of the new king, bearing with them gifts of gold, frankincense and myrrh. It later became the feast day of St John, celebrated on 6th January.

Interestingly, there have, over the centuries, been many Masonic *feast days* that were celebrated on 6th January. This makes a direct connection again between Masonic ceremony and the Sun: whether intentional or by accident, the link was there.

The legacy of Sun and Moon worship is still a feature of our lives. The memory lives on in our calendar through the names of the days of the week. All the days of the week are named after gods associated with the planets. Saturday, for instance, was the Saturn god's day. Saturn was a key feature of the early Israelite religion and it is noted that this is the day that those of the Jewish faith celebrate as their Sabbath. The Norsemen and Vikings, who had invaded the northern part of Britain, left a memory of their gods through Woden, Thor and Freyja, which had direct connections with the macro-cosmos. Most parts of Britain were obviously influenced by the French language following the Norman Conquest. With a strong Latin influence derived from the Romans, that legacy can be found in the names of other days of the week, which were named after the Roman gods. So the full list runs like this:

Saturday was the Saturn god's day.
Sunday was for the Sun god.
Monday was for the Moon god –   Lundi links with lunar
Tuesday was for the Mars god –   Mardi
Wednesday is for the Mercury god – Mercredi and Woden
Thursday was for the Jupiter god – Jeudi and Thor
Friday was for the Venus god –   Vendredi and Freyja

The religious festival of Easter was derived from the pagan festival of Eastre. This festival celebrated the arrival of spring, a time of rebirth and renewal. There does not appear to have been a precise day to define when this festival was celebrated. This changed when it was absorbed by the Christian Church as a date to remember the crucifixion. The early Church, through the Council of Nicaea around 325 CE, fixed the celebration day to being the first Sunday after the first Full Moon that occurs on or after the Vernal (Spring) Equinox. This practice still holds today, some 1,700 years after it was first defined. The date for Easter is fixed by the transit of celestial orbs of the Sun and the Moon. The Solar (Sun) Calendar had, by Roman times, become the calendar by which civil events and administration were governed. Religious institutions still used the Lunar (Moon) Calendar. The Roman Emperor Constantine had convened the Council of Nicaea. Although he championed the establishment of Christian acceptance, he still held to a belief in the Roman gods of that time, and in particular, worship of the Sun god, *Sol Invictus*. By setting the festival day as a Sunday (the Sun god's day) Constantine was therefore appeasing his god, formalising the festival of Eastre, and bringing together the civil and lunar calendars. In many respects, this was a master-stroke of diplomacy.

At the time when the Council of Nicaea met in 325 CE, the civil calendar in use was one devised by Julius Caesar. This calendar remained in operation across Europe until the 16th century. It had certain weaknesses, as a consequence of which key dates had drifted so that, for example, the Spring Equinox, which we know as 21st March, had drifted in time by about ten days. By the 16th century, the Catholic Church was having a great deal of difficulty constantly trying to tie together the date as defined by the calendar with traditional events defined from solar and lunar observation. During the reign of Pope Gregory a new calendar was devised, the Gregorian Calendar, which we still use today for secular purposes. It first came into being in 1582 and its use gradually spread through all the countries over which the Catholic Church then held political sway. It was nearly 200 years later, in 1752, that the calendar was adopted in England, and thereby its colonies, especially America. To make up the days' difference that had accumulated in the Julian Calendar, some realignment was necessary. In England this was done in the month of September when Wednesday 2nd September was followed by Thursday 14th September. This caused considerable outrage, especially between landowners and their tenants, when the latter, on paying their rents, believed they were being cheated out of ten days of payments for days that did not exist.

The structure of the Gregorian Calendar, as we all know, dictates that there are some months with 28 days, some with 30 days and others with 31. And then, of course, there are the leap years, which inflate the month of February to 29 days. Thus, it was with some surprise that I came across a reference to the fact that since the early days of the foundation of the United Nations, a proposal has apparently been outstanding for a new global calendar system. It has, apparently, been suggested that this new calendar would have 12 months each of 28 days, almost an echo of the religious lunar calendars of ancient times, plus a further month to be installed between the current months of June and July, to mop up the surplus days.

12 months of 28 days = 336 days

365 days – 336 days = 29 days and 30 in a leap year.

And what name has been suggested for this new month? ... Sol, the Sun, again.

As previously mentioned, the early Christian religion absorbed previous pagan sacred sites by building a church on the same ground. Nearly all churches are named after a saint. The Catholic Church had implemented a structure where a specific feast day was allotted in the calendar as celebration of a particular saint. So the feast day for St George, as an example, is 23rd April. It was a common practice to build a church with an orientation not just on an east-west axis, but more accurately aligned to the point on the eastern horizon where the Sun rose on the day of the festival associated with the saint to whom the church was dedicated. So, a church dedicated to St George would be oriented to that point on the horizon where the Sun rose on 23rd April. Also of note is that the altar was invariably placed in the east so that the first of the Sun's rays of the day should illuminate it. It is for this reason that a large window was usually installed at the eastern end of a church.

This orientation process needed to be thoroughly understood by the masons undertaking the building work. Within their repertoire of skills was a need for not only the methods and tricks of the trade associated with fashioning stone but the knowledge associated with the principles of celestial mechanics and geometry.

Theoretical principles are fine but they are of no value unless they are put to practical use. Putting them to practical use demands the development of apparatus, instruments and repeatable procedures to ensure consistency of results. Realising that our ancestors did not have the advantage of tables of logarithms and trigonometry, then any apparatus they developed had, of necessity, to be simple to use and make. The question is, did our ancestors have instruments that enabled such sophisticated measurements? The answer is most probably yes. Surprisingly a simple device may have come in a form that most people in the western world will recognise, although in an entirely different context.

The Celtic Cross

The cross that we have known as part of the iconography of Christianity represents the device on which Jesus was crucified and symbolises the pain and suffering that accompanied the event. However, for the first few centuries after the events in Jerusalem two thousand years ago, the symbol of the cross was not identified with the fledgling Christian religion, especially as we have come to know it through the Latin Cross, with its long upright post and shorter cross arm.

The original symbol was the fish or Ichthys (Greek word for fish) symbol which, according to tradition, the early Christians used as a secret means of identification in an era when they were persecuted by the Roman authorities. The persecution only stopped with the Declaration of Milan in 313 CE, which effectively made the Roman Empire a secular province.

The symbol of the cross has its origins in more ancient times. There are many theologians who identify the first mention of a cross as being in the Old Testament, with reference to Adam and Eve and the Garden of Eden. Genesis, chapter 2 verse 10 reads:

> 'A river watering the garden flowed from Eden, and from there it divided; it had four headstreams.'

The four headstreams are believed to be a reference to the four cardinal points of north, south, east and west, which created a symbol of a cross. As a consequence of this it was not unusual for gardens to be set out with paths that crossed at right angles in the centre to create four separate areas of cultivation, a pattern that became known as a quadrangle.

In pre-Christian times, there was a symbol of a circle, bisected with a cross, which represented the Sun, the resultant image being known as the sun-wheel, whilst the circle on its own represented the Moon.

The Roman Emperor, Constantine, encouraged the adoption of Christianity as a single religion to unite the Empire, from which came the Council of Nicaea in 345 CE. He supposedly had a dream in which he saw a symbol of a cross and encouraged it to be adopted. It became known as the labarum. Constantine also worshipped *Sol Invictus* – the Sun god. As a result, the Labarum is a symbol that has been shunned over the years by those of more devout worship, who, because of its origins, consider it to be a pagan symbol representing the Sun god and the sun-wheel.

The Labarum   The Ankh – *key of life*

Amongst the first forms of cross used was the *Ankh*, an Egyptian hieroglyphic meaning *life*. Today it is often referred to as the *key of life*.

These points, and many others, came to my attention when I took a deeper interest in the Celtic Cross. Several times during the course of my research, I came across references suggesting that the design of the Celtic Cross was based on ancient wisdom. Various writers suggested that the arms of the cross represent the four cardinal points of north, south, east and west, whilst the circle represents the circle of the Earth or the circle of the horizon. Despite various enquiries over several years, finding evidence to support these statements proved to be fruitless.

In recent centuries, the Celtic Cross has come to be associated with the earliest days of Christianity in the British Isles. It is believed to have been derived from the era when Celtic Christianity dominated religious beliefs in Britain prior to the departure of the Roman Legions from British shores around 450 CE. Celtic Christianity existed for several hundred years before St Augustine arrived in England in 597 CE, bringing with him the doctrine of the Church of Rome. The Roman form of Christianity that arrived in England spread north and west from Kent, where St Augustine had established his initial base. The dominant Celtic version had spread through Ireland, Wales, the North, West and Southwest of England and Southern Scotland. Amongst the most famous centres for the development of Celtic Christianity were those on the island of Iona, just off the Scottish west coast, where St Columba established a monastery and, later, Lindisfarne, also known as Holy Island, on the coast of Northeast England, in what is now the county of Northumberland.

In Margam Park, just outside of the South Wales town of Port Talbot, there stands a wonderful example of a Celtic Cross. Hoary with age, nobody is sure quite how old it really is. Unlike the plain four-arm crosses regularly found in Christianity, Celtic Crosses are usually embellished with interwoven patterns said to represent the vine of life. Some, like that in the picture below, seem to indicate ornate studs which symbolically fix the circular head to the arm and upright of the conventional cross, whilst the large stud in the centre is more redolent of an axle or pivot.

In *The Holy Kingdom*, Adrian Gilbert, together with Alan Wilson and Baram Blackett, investigates possible connections between the Celtic Welsh kings and the legends of King Arthur. They also explore legends that the biblical Joseph of Arimathea visited South Wales shortly after the crucifixion of Jesus Christ in Jerusalem. It is believed that Llantwit Major, a small community on the coast of Cardiff Bay not far from Margam, was the site of a monastery developed shortly after the visit of Joseph of Arimathea. At a small church at Llantwit Major, Adrian Gilbert noted the remains of another Celtic Cross which he assessed as being of great antiquity. It may even have been associated with that early monastery. If that was indeed the case, then it would imply that the Celtic Cross existed in the early years of the first centuries of the Christian era. It is a design which was relatively unique to the area dominated by the Celtic Christian tradition and as such would imply that the original concept of the design must have existed prior to the arrival of Christianity in Britain. So, how was this relatively unique design arrived at?

A Celtic Cross on the Estate of the Earls of Spencer, Northamptonshire, England.
Photograph taken by and reproduced by kind permission of Crichton Miller.

It is interesting to see that the Vine of Life carved on the shaft resembles the interlocked circles of Vesica Piscis with another two circles at the base of the shaft. Intertwined serpents are engraved on the circular head, and there are markers at the ends of the cross arm.

The problem is that nobody knows for certain where the design of the Celtic Cross originated. There is a view that it emanated from the 8th or 9th centuries and that it was brought together as a combination of Christian symbolism and the pagan symbols for the Sun, which was a circle inscribed with a cross – the sun-wheel – and the Moon, which was a circle. Peoples that we now refer to as the Celts, and who are frequently defined as having been pagans, lived in the British Isles for several thousand years prior to the Roman occupation. Paganism is sometimes viewed as devil worship, but that is a terminology promulgated by the early Christian bishops who wanted everyone to believe what they preached; anyone who had a contrary belief was branded as being in league with the devil or practising witchcraft. A pagan is someone who does not follow what we are encouraged to accept as established religious beliefs and may believe not in one god but several. Worshipping the Sun and the Moon would have been natural to someone prior to the spread of the Christian doctrine.

In addition to the Celtic Cross, there are other examples of pagan and Christian symbols being brought together. Much of early Christian iconography showed it. The Roman Emperor, Constantine, was, as mentioned earlier, responsible for turning the Romans to the Christian belief as a way of unifying his empire. Although accepting the symbol of the cross, he also believed in the cult of *Sol Invictus*, worship of the Sun god. As a consequence, we are told, he merged the two so that Christ is seen in crucifixion iconography as being on a four-armed cross, with the halo of the Sun god sitting behind his head.[2] It is imagery that has been continued down the centuries and implies a subtle reference to a continuation of the Sun god influence.

From the above, it is not difficult to understand how the Celtic Cross was later to be regarded as the combined symbolism of the Celts and the early Christians: the cross of Christianity superimposed on the disc of the Sun. In many respects it was a perfect harmonisation of Christian and Celtic imagery.

This raises questions as to why the pagan symbol for the Sun was a circle embossed with a cross? The priesthood of the Celts were what we have come to know as the Druids. The Druids were well known for their understanding of the macro-cosmos and had a very advanced knowledge of the way in which the celestial spheres and the heavens worked. In many respects, their knowledge was feared by the Romans who eventually suppressed them, so that they were forced to retreat to the island of Anglesey, off the northwest coast of Wales. Here, the Druid priests were finally defeated and slaughtered by the armies of Rome. With their passing went the knowledge that they had inherited from hundreds of generations of their forefathers. Despite this, it is possible to evolve a scenario that may well have been the origins.

Let us imagine that the Druidic priests had wanted to monitor the annual progression of the Sun. A point of reference would be along the horizon and from a vantage point such as the top of a hill or an open plain, the horizon would have encircled them. It would be logical to replicate the circle of the horizon conveniently on the ground – a stone circle, perhaps. To monitor the heavens consistently over a long period of time demanded standing in the same spot to have the same point of reference. This dictated finding the centre of the circle. By monitoring the shadow at midday and sun-rise on the day of the equinox, and producing from them lines going north-south and east-west, so the centre could be established: a circle divided by a cross. The lines of the cross may have been visible by day, having perhaps been scratched into the ground, using something like an antler, but watching the Moon by night would result in the lines being invisible. So a circle with a cross would symbolise the Sun and one without a cross would symbolise the Moon. This is, of course, speculation.

Sadly, many rulers in history, through ignorance, or as a futile demonstration of power, have destroyed records and traces of knowledge that hundreds of generations of our ancestors had carefully collated and passed on to subsequent generations. Is it possible that, with the destruction of the Druids by the Romans, the understanding of the origins of the Celtic Cross passed with them? Without positive evidence, academics and researchers have only been able to take informed guesses throughout the 20th century. But that may now change thanks to an invention by Crichton E. M. Miller, around the start of the 21st century.

Crichton Miller is a keen sailor and well qualified in navigation. He developed an interest in trying to understand how our ancestors of millennia past were able to navigate vast seas long before the development of the sophisticated processes that have evolved in the past 500 years. We know, for example, that groups of Vikings sailed from Norway to Iceland and Greenland over 1,000 years ago. In pits beside the pyramids at Giza, archaeologists discovered several large ships that had been deliberately buried. Originally it was thought that they might have been used for funerary processions or localised navigation on the River Nile, but examination by marine architects showed that they were designed for more distant seafaring and were capable of coping with deep sea swells and waves. Those boats were built over 4,000 years ago. It is known, too, that the Phoenicians, contemporary with the era of King Solomon, sailed to Cornwall in Britain to acquire tin, which they then traded around the Mediterranean and Middle East. That was over 3,000 years ago. In addition, it is known that in the era of King Solomon, ships set sail from Red Sea ports and traded goods in India. All of this dictated that knowledge of some form of navigational instrument, or other methodology, was needed.

After several years of investigation, Crichton Miller found that he had developed a simple instrument comprising a staff and cross arm which resembled a cross. A plumb line and a circular plate, with markings to represent the 360 degrees of a circle, were attached to the cross. What he realised he had evolved was a representation of a traditional Celtic Cross. Having arrived at this position he tried to further his development through contact with the academic community but found a complete lack of interest. So, to give the device credence and prominence, he patented it – globally – under UK Patent Application GB 2 344 654 A. It is a beautifully simple device which can be used to measure, amongst many things, the altitude of the Sun, Moon, stars and constellations of the zodiac; the vertical alignment of a building or standing stones such as those at Stonehenge; the horizontal alignment of courses of stone blocks used in the walls of a palace or temple; the angular alignment of a pyramid, – and latitude. By monitoring the shadow of the staff when the Sun is at its meridian, midday, and drawing a north-

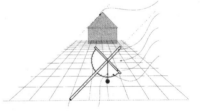

The above illustrations have been reproduced by kind permission of Crichton Miller and were first used as illustrations in his book 'The Golden Thread of Time'. They show how an instrument, based on the concept that we know as the Celtic Cross, could be used for surveying and horizontal alignment, vertical and angular alignment, and astronomical measurement.

south line along the orientation of the shadow, or by placing the staff horizontally on it, the plate on which the angles have been marked immediately becomes a compass. In short, it is an easily portable surveying tool, sextant, compass, astronomical instrument for monitoring celestial movement – all in one.

Since producing his fascinating book, *The Golden Thread of Time*, Crichton Miller has gone on to show how longitude could have been measured with reasonable accuracy, using the same device. In more modern times this was not possible with any accuracy until John Harrison invented his maritime clocks in the 18th century. In so doing Harrison changed the face of navigation and established Greenwich as a global meridian for the measurement of time. Crichton Miller reports that as his device and patent have become more widely known so an increasing number of academics, particularly from the USA, have been taking greater interest in his development and its uses. He also points out that an ancient device known as an astrolabe, used for celestial measurement throughout the Middle Ages, and with its origins established at well in excess of 2,000 years ago, has physical characteristics which resemble the head of a Celtic Cross.

Adrian Gilbert, who was previously mentioned, has written several books on the subject of ancient knowledge and esoteric wisdom. In his book *Signs in the Sky* he noted that the term *serpent* was frequently used in ancient times to define a shadow cast by the Sun. I couldn't help remembering that the Celtic Cross in Northamptonshire (see photo) shows an image of intertwined serpents on the circular head. This would make sense if the cross was used for measurements using the shadow of the Sun, and a shadow was regarded in ancient times as a serpent.

In the book of Exodus we read how, when Moses returned to Egypt, he addressed the Pharaoh and requested the release of all the Israelites from bondage. During that meeting, he and the priests of Egypt entered into a contest to see who would cast the biggest serpent. Moses won. We are told in Exodus that they threw down their rods and they became serpents.

> *When Pharaoh shall speak unto you, saying, Shew a miracle for you: then thou shalt say unto Aaron, Take thy rod, and cast it before Pharaoh, and it shall become a serpent... And Moses and Aaron went in unto Pharaoh, and they did so... : and Aaron cast down his rod before Pharaoh, and before his servants, and it became a serpent... Each one threw down his staff... But Aaron's staff swallowed up their staffs.* Exodus 7:9 - 12

> *And the LORD said unto Moses, make thee a fiery serpent, and set it upon a pole... And Moses made a serpent of brass, and put it upon a pole...* Numbers 21:8 - 9

In the above text from Exodus one can imagine that Pharaoh may well have wanted Moses to prove who he was, what his credentials were for making such demands in the interests of the Israelites. A demonstration of methods of measurement and geometry related to the macro-cosmos, derived from the shadow of the Sun, or the other characteristics of the Celtic Cross arrangement, would demonstrate that he was no ordinary peasant who had just wandered in out of the desert, but was highly educated in the wisdom of the type reserved for the selected few in the hierarchy – the type of information that might be passed on to a Prince and Ruler in Egypt.

The second quotation from Numbers is even more intriguing, especially the reference to a *fiery serpent*. If the allegory of the serpent is that it was a shadow, then the making and placing of a special metal device on a pole may well have been a reference to a graduated marker for measuring angles, together with a plumb line, as Crichton Miller evolved. Keeping in mind that Moses was brought up as a Prince in Egypt and had been educated in all the knowledge of the priests, it may have been that the wisdom of Moses was more developed than that of the priests brought to confront him.

Crichton Miller cites several places where the symbol of a cross could have been used by our ancestors in the layout of henges and other ancient sites, for recording and monitoring the movement of the Sun and Moon. Amongst these are earthworks at Pickaway County, Ohio, USA.[3] These are believed to have been constructed before the pyramids of Giza, that is at least 4,500 years ago. He cites yet another near the Tygart River, also in Ohio, which has all the appearance of the Celtic Cross.[4] Then there is yet another known as Callanish, on the Isle of Lewis in the Outer Hebrides in Scotland.[5]

The link between Moses and Aaron's Staff, the Celtic Cross and its origin is, of course, a theory. Perhaps some might consider it an outlandish theory. But, when Frank Whittle invented the jet engine, he started from a position of harbouring an outlandish theory. Yet, the theory seems to make sense, especially when we note that some modern academics consider that the Celtic Cross *was brought together as a*

The above photograph shows Crichton Miller holding a hand-held measuring device resembling a working Celtic Cross whilst observing the rising sun at the time of the Summer Solstice. The wheel is marked with angles to 360 degrees, is weighted to ensure vertical alignment and rotates about the central pivot; markers in the ends of the cross arm enable alignment. The angle is read through a hole in the shaft of the cross at the bottom of the wheel.

combination of Christian symbolism and the pagan symbols which signified the Moon and the Sun, pagan symbols that were well defined before the arrival of organised Christianity in Britain. We should also remind ourselves that, in the early years of the establishment of the Christian religion in Britain, many pagan sites and symbols were absorbed by the Church as a means of 'Christianising' them, to eliminate what the Church saw as the demons of the past. Much of that pagan symbolism was already very old, well established and understood. Within the priesthood it may have been known of for a thousand years or more. Is it possible that in their attempt to 'Christianise' a previous instrument of paganism, the early Roman Church preserved it?

Crichton Miller's observations about the development and use of the Celtic Cross are based on many years of research, observation and experimentation. He started out trying to resolve a problem related to navigation in ancient times and reconstructed a device with considerable similarities to the Celtic Cross. He has gone on to demonstrate the versatility of the device as an instrument for measuring and monitoring – a device entirely in keeping with the principles of ancient knowledge about the macro-cosmos.

So, what relevance does this have to my quest in respect of Solomon's Temple? It demonstrates that a device, normally attributed to having been derived from Christian beliefs

- may have had its origins thousands of years prior to the events which allegedly took place in Jerusalem 2,000 years ago;
- may have been used in the construction, siting and setting out of henges, stone circles, and other ancient monuments,
- was a device for monitoring the seasons by the passage of the Sun and Moon.

Far from being solely a symbol of religious belief it may well have been a practical tool used in the setting out, and construction, of an important building such as Solomon's Temple. It would, therefore, have been recognised and used by the masons of that era.

Conclusion

What I realised from my research was that there was a relationship between an understanding of early astronomy, as our ancient ancestors would have known it, and geometry; that they would have recognised a connection between geometry and nature so that the whole were seen as interwoven in the macro-cosmos; that there were so many areas where one aspect of the study of the macro-cosmos overlapped the other that it would be seen as the creative work of a great and divine architect, the Architect of the Universe, or the Geometrician of the Universe.

It also demonstrated how our ancestors could have a knowledge of the movement of the heavens, the rising and setting of the Sun and precessional rotation of the Earth, and how to use that understanding for the alignment and setting out of structures, or the geometric design of an important building.

It also became apparent that all of this information was protected, and conveyed from one generation to the next, through a priesthood who were, invariably, the educated elite of a society or civilisation. It was therefore logical that for the building of any major structure, the stonemasons involved needed to know and understand that same knowledge, otherwise implementation of the plan may not have resulted in a structure that met the requirements. It was also likely that the knowledge was imparted gradually as a mason demonstrated sufficient skill in working with stone, an understanding of the knowledge that had already been imparted to them, and that they were able to use that knowledge and keep it to themselves by not imparting it to others who were not qualified to know or use it.

From these conclusions I decided that I needed to understand more about how some of this information may have become associated with Freemasonry and why certain geometric characters seemed to have such prominence.

[1] From Sacred Texts Chapter XI.—The Mystical Meanings in the Proportions of Numbers, Geometrical Ratios, and Music.
www.sacred-texts.com/chr/ecf/002/0020401.htm
[2] Dr Stephen Marqardt, as shown in a BBC-TV programme on beauty hosted by John Cleese.
[3] See, *The Hiram Key*, Christopher Knight and Robert Lomas
[4] *The Golden Thread of Time*, Crichton Miller
[5] *The Golden Thread of Time*, Crichton Miller
[6] *The Golden Thread of Time*, Crichton Miller

Chapter 4
The Secret of Solomon's Seal

The Hexagram and the Pentagram

The hexagram and the pentagram are both referred to as *Solomon's Seal.* How, I wondered, could that be? How could they both be Solomon's Seal?

In the past, the pentagram has had clear links with Masonic symbolism. The hexagram still features. It is the symbol cast in a medal that, when worn in Masonic ceremonies, serves as an indication to other brethren that the wearer is an initiated member of the Royal Arch degree of Freemasonry, a degree which completes the education of a Master Mason. The Masonic medal shows the hexagram symbol encased in an outer circle.

The hexagram symbol has been accorded several titles, such as the *Star of David* or *Magan David,* in addition to *Solomon's Seal.* Sometimes the triangles that are at the core of the symbol are intertwined and sometimes they are not. Sometimes they are shown with an outer circle encompassing them, and sometimes they are without.

The pentagram is also referred to by variant names, such as *pentalpha, pentangle* or *pentacle.* Just like the hexagram, it is sometimes shown with the core elements intertwined and sometimes not. Sometimes it is encompassed by a circle, and sometimes without. And to add to its mystery there are times when it can be seen with a circle inscribed in its centre so that its circumference just touches a pentagon which will be visible in the middle of the pentagram.

There must, I assumed, be a reason for these differences – which meant trying to find the origins of both.

Hexagram – Early origins

There is a tradition that suggests that use of the hexagram extended back, many centuries before Solomon, to ancient Mesopotamia, and that it was absorbed across different cultures. The Encyclopaedia Judaica notes that by the Iron Age, examples could be found from India to Britain. At certain times in antiquity, it was used in its two separate component parts; with the triangle pointing upwards it represented the male sex, and when pointing down, it represented the female. When overlapped it is thought the resultant image created by the two triangles implied harmony. During my background investigation into this symbol, I found a passing reference to the fact that the symbol had been found embroidered into clothing worn by Hebrew descendants. Anthropologists apparently considered it merely decorative. With the implication of the male/female representation and a conjoined suggestion of harmony, I couldn't help wondering if, when embroidered on clothing, it symbolised that the wearer was *married.* I had no proof of such an assertion and I had not found any other references to such an idea. It just seemed to be a logical conclusion. Then, by chance, I was flicking through a book I had picked up in a library, when a page fell open and my eyes were drawn to the following sentence:

> *The Hexad is also the symbol of marriage, because it is formed by the union of two triangles, one masculine and the other feminine.*[1]

The book I had stumbled on was first published in 1928. What struck me was the positive and unequivocal nature of the statement implying that at some time this must have been a more widely accepted connotation. I could not help wondering why this function of the triangles in the hexagram was not more widely commented on. Maybe it is because the symbol has been completely overshadowed by the events that affected the Jewish peoples through the 1930s and 1940s, and the subsequent links to the formation of the state of Israel.

There is a belief, originating from ancient times, that the hexagram was regarded as a symbol that, because of its six points, defines the creation of the universe: a creation which extends north, south, east, west, up and down. It was also apparently linked with ancient principles of Earth measurement[2] whilst, from the Indian subcontinent, we learn that it represents the united shields of the gods Vishnu and Shiva.[3] By the Middle Ages it was to be found in Christian churches and cathedrals and widely used in Muslim countries during the same period.

References to a link between the hexagram and *magic* abound, as a consequence of which it was also viewed as being a symbol which attracted good luck. There are also many references that suggest the symbol was widely used by alchemists, with one triangle representing *fire* and the other *water.* This apparently symbolised the harmonisation of opposites.

The Star of David as a symbol of the Jewish peoples

Quite how or why the symbol of the hexagram came to have such a definitive link with Judaism is unknown. There are tantalising clues and there is considerable mythology, but no more so than can be attributed to the cross as a symbol of Christianity.

The hexagram has had periodic associations with the Jews since the Middle Ages. In 1354, Charles IV apparently granted the Prague community permission to have their own flag on which the hexagram was depicted. From there its use spread through Austria, Southern Germany and Holland. Again in Prague, in 1492 the hexagram was identified as a printers sign.

Several sources noted that at various times through that epoch Jews were expected to wear a badge which enabled them to be identified. This was because the Catholic

Church held the Jews responsible for the death of Jesus Christ by not calling for his release when Pontius Pilate provided an opportunity for him to be freed in Jerusalem just prior to the crucifixion. As a result, and recognising that the Catholic Church held spiritual and political sway over most of Europe during the Middle Ages, Jews were excluded from carrying on trade and from holding administrative office in government. The wearing of the hexagram symbol suggests that the political climate of the day clearly associated a link between Judaism and the hexagram. Through the 20th century, and into the 21st, the hexagram has become unmistakably linked with the Jews, perhaps as a consequence of the Nazis demanding the same use and identification process as was used in the Middle Ages as a prelude to the subsequent holocaust.

King Solomon's Temple was built around 950 BCE, but, it appears, that the first definable connection with ancient Israel, derives from a seal which was, according to tradition, used in the 6th century BCE, apparently as a Seal of Jerusalem[4]. Encyclopaedia Judaica notes that the *"oldest undisputed example is on a seal from 7th century BCE found in Sidon"*. That was some three to four hundred years after the era attributed to Solomon. There is a tradition that the symbol appeared on a ring that Solomon wore, but despite this fable appearing in a number of references that I consulted, it was nearly always referred to as a *tradition,* with no supporting facts to verify authenticity. There is even a tradition that the hexagram as the *Star of David* came about because King David had a shield that had the emblem emblazoned on it, whilst another interpretation of the tradition records that the shield itself was shaped in the form of the hexagram.

Whilst the symbol of the cross appeared prominently on Christian churches from the early years of the formation of that religion, the hexagram was not used in that way by the Jewish peoples. Although it appeared in buildings associated with other religions, the hexagram was not featured in synagogues as a matter of routine decoration. A positive identification with the Jews was the presentation of the symbol on the wall of a synagogue in Capernaum around 200 BCE. This was some 500 years before the cohesive formulation of Christianity, as we have come to know it today, was agreed at the Council of Nicaea in 325 CE. But, this link does not mean that it was used exclusively by the Jews. As mentioned earlier, it was a symbol which was indicative of good luck and harmony, and was used by different cultures. Prior to the Christian era it was not a symbol exclusively used by, or connected with, Judaism.

Despite periodic historical records that show the symbol being used in a Jewish connection, its direct and universal association with the Jews is fairly recent.

According to various accounts, in the 17th century there was a boundary which separated the Jewish quarter of Vienna from the Christian area. The boundary line was apparently marked by boundary stones, on one side of which appeared the hexagram and on the other a symbol of the cross. This idea may have been borrowed from the Venetians who had used a similar designation in a part of their city in the late Middle Ages. Indeed, in Venice it seems that a chain was placed across passageways at night in the area where the Jews lived, to further symbolise that it was a protected quarter. The word *ghetto* is derived from an Italian word *ghetto/gheto* meaning 'slag', the waste metal produced by metal foundries and casting. The areas in Venice where this type of work was undertaken became known as ghettos. It was to one of these areas that the Jewish population of the city was centred and became a protected and segregated area within the Venetian Republic in 1516. In Prague there had been a use of the symbol to define the Jewish people from the 14th century, and it is believed that it is from those beginnings that use of the hexagram gradually spread across Europe to become the cohesive symbol of recognition we know today.

It seems that by the 17th century, groups of Jews were dispersed across Europe and began looking for a symbol that would define their religious unity in the same way that Christianity was symbolised by the cross. The hexagram seemed to fit the bill. However, its widespread acceptance seems to have originated between 1822 and the 1840's when it was used by the Rothchild family in their coat of arms, noting that they were connected with the Habsbergs and the Austrian Emperor[5]. It wasn't until 1897 that the symbol was, apparently, officially defined as the global emblem of the Jewish community. Today, the hexagram sits prominently on the flag of modern Israel, an unambiguous symbol of that nation.

Inconclusive evidence

The foregoing comments are a distillation of the information I gathered in respect of the hexagram symbol, although they are not intended to be a definitive thesis. There are hundreds of sources, references and internet websites one can consult, but irrespective of the source the same type of information comes up time and again. This rather implies that it is all that is known about the symbol.

From these observations, it will be noted that there is no conclusive evidence to link the hexagram, *Star of David,* with the entire Jewish peoples until the 19th century, although there are periodic and localised connections, such as that from 600 BCE and a wall frieze in 200 BCE. There are more positive connections from the period defined as the Middle Ages, but that is some 2,000 years after the Solomon era. There appears to be no definitive connection with King Solomon, the person with whom the term *Solomon's Seal* is so positively identified. This suggested to me that if there was a positive link then there had to have been some other dimension to the symbol, a dimension which was not common knowledge, perhaps the type of *secret* information retained by priesthoods such as the Levites.

What is more, the hexagram symbol can be found in many Christian churches and cathedrals built in medieval times. It was an era when the foundations of the Church were rock solid. There was literally only one religion tolerated throughout Europe, the doctrine of the Roman Church. I could not image that an alchemical symbol or one indicative of magic, paganism, or lucky charms, all of which might have been viewed as connection with evil, could be displayed in buildings that were of religious significance. One of the most prominent hexagrams I found in a cathedral in England can be seen in Chichester Cathedral where it is a significant feature of the northern aspect. What is more, it is encased within a circular rim, exactly as in the medal which is an emblem of Royal Arch Freemasonry.

Fig 3.1 The above picture is of the hexagram in the north wall of Chichester Cathedral. This cathedral was built between 1075 and 1108.

Fig 3.2 The above image is from a church at Jarrow, just outside Newcastle in the north east of England. This part of the church is all that remains of a once thriving monastic enclave where the Venerable Bede (672-735 CE) lived most of his life. The symbol is encased in a circular rim.

Fig 3.3 The above image is of a stained glass window in the south side of the Cathedral of Notre Dame, Paris. Building commenced in 1163. The hexagram is encased within a circle.

The Secrets of Solomon's Temple

Some 400 miles to the north of Chichester is the town of Jarrow, now largely absorbed into the city of Newcastle. Although in a slightly different representation, the same hexagram symbol is to be found in a church nearby. The church is believed to have been part of a complex emanating from the years immediately after the merger with the Catholic Church of the former Celtic Christian Church. This merger was agreed at the Synod of Whitby in 664 CE. The section of church is all that remains of an impressive monastery which once occupied the site. It was the monastery where the Venerable Bede, who recorded one of the earliest histories of England, spent most of his life. Bede also had a fascination for Solomon's Temple, a matter we will again turn to in due course. Bede never travelled more than a few miles from the Jarrow monastery, which suggests that for him to have taken such an interest in the Solomonic Jerusalem Temple there had to have been some tradition which existed at that time, that had resulted in its stature being transmitted to an outpost of the Christian world, and have been of such a nature that Bede regarded it as worthy of devotion.

A few hundred miles to the south of Chichester is Paris, home to one of the most famous cathedrals in the world – the cathedral of Notre Dame. Originally commenced in the 12th century, it was almost destroyed during the French Revolution. This cathedral is striking in its geometric symbolism and its links with the macro-cosmos. A number of stained glass windows allude to the principles of *sacred geometry* and the mason's art; yet, hundreds of people visit it, admire its proportions and decor but have no understanding of the symbolism around them. A beautiful stained glass window in the south face of the cathedral, the face presented to the Sun for much of the day, depicts the sign of the hexagram.

Noting the hexagram's widespread use, it was evident that the connection with the hexagram had to have some other significance in addition to a connection with the Jewish people. It appeared to have a strong connection with Christianity from early times but was prolifically used by the Church based in Rome.

I couldn't help believing that there had to be something else about this symbol which was regarded as special by virtue of the fact that it had crossed continents over a period of perhaps 1,500 years after the rule of Solomon, to eventually adorn some of the great cathedrals of Europe, cathedrals built by the masons in medieval times.

The distinctive pattern of the symbol, and the way in which it was used in the churches and cathedrals, suggested the link was geometric – but how? – and why? The masons of old who had built those churches and cathedrals had an obvious appreciation of geometry. And we know that geometry is a key feature of Freemasonry. Was there, I wondered, a link between the two that might provide a clue to the mystery of *Solomon's Seal*? Possibly.

But, before I came to a conclusion I had to understand where the other *Solomon's Seal* – the pentagram – fitted into the scenario.

Pentagram

Like the hexagram, the origins of the pentagram lie in the mists of time, long before the Solomonic period. The symbol is also referred to as a *pentalpha, pentangle* or *pentacle.*

Some of the earliest archaeological discoveries that reveal the use of a pentagram figure have been found in the area of the Middle East known as ancient Mesopotamia, much of which is now part of modern Iraq. Some of the artefacts that have been recovered and show this symbol have been dated to around 3,000 BCE, some 2,000 years before the epoch of David and Solomon. Other artefacts showing the pentagram symbol have been discovered by archaeologists in what had been the ancient city of Babylon, and dated to around 900 BCE – the Solomonic period. The pentagram also appears on statues associated with Ancient Egypt. During the period of the Roman Empire, the pentagram was apparently used as a symbol to represent the building trades, one of which was obviously that of the masons.

The symbolism attached to the use of the Pentagram, appears to have varied depending on the culture in which it was used. In the past it has symbolised the five elements of, Earth, Fire, Water, Air and Ether, with Ether being associated with the spirit. It is also seen as representing the five senses of, sight, hearing, smell, touch and taste.

According to some researchers, the use of the pentagram dates back to at least the epoch of a ruler in Mesopotamia named Uruk IV, around 3,500 BCE. At that time the pentagram apparently symbolised 'heavenly quarter' or 'direction'.[5] Through this we can see that an early symbolic definition provided a link with astronomy. This may be significant because the pentagram is often connected with the planet Venus. This connection seems to emanate from an esoteric astrological belief which suggested that various conjunctions of that planet with the Sun will result in observing 5 distinct patterns, each of 8 years duration, which describe the pentagram pattern in the sky over a period of 40 years (5 x 8 = 40). This pattern was, apparently, so regular that the 40-year cycle became a stellar clock for ancient peoples who had noted that the planet returned to exactly the same relative position in the sky at the end of each 40-year cycle. This astronomically linked pattern is referred to in a number of books. One of the most interesting of such books, which explores the passage of Venus, its possible link with the pentagram and the influence it had over ancient peoples, is entitled *Uriel's Machine*, written by two English freemasons, Christopher Knight and Robert Lomas. They were exploring links between certain Masonic ceremonies, the Book of Enoch and the 40-year cycle of Venus. In the process of their investigations they made a number of discoveries, including a possible link between the cycles of the planet, the *Groove Ware people* of antiquity, and Newgrange – a large circular building in Ireland which has been dated to around the same era as Stonehenge. Knight and Lomas later put forward a theory that reference in the *Bible* to various periods of '40 days and 40 nights' derives from an allusion to the cyclical passage of Venus[6] as it was understood by ancient civilisations.

Although modern astronomers deride this ancient concept of the cyclical passage of Venus, it still held sway until very recent times. A graphical representation of the passage of Venus over the 40-year period, which clearly shows an unmistakable pentagram pattern, is illustrated in a book by the Scottish astronomer, James Ferguson (1710-1776). Ferguson, who was substantially self-taught in various science disciplines, is described in reference sources as having been 'an enthusiastic experimental philosopher, mechanist and astronomer'. He is attributed as the writer of one of the first popular text books on astronomy, first published in 1756. Ferguson paid particular attention to the passage of Venus and produced a number of diagrams which illustrate a geometric association with orbits of planets.

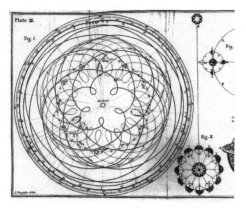

This diagram shows the pattern the planet Venus describes in the sky as it orbits the Sun, as observed from Earth. It was produced by the astronomer James Ferguson in a book entitled 'Astronomy explained upon Sir Isaac Newton's principles, and made easy to those who have not studied Mathematics', published in 1756. Reproduced by kind permission and assistance of the Royal Astronomical Society.

There were Masonic researchers, mostly from the late Victorian and early Edwardian eras, who presented a hypothesis that the origin of some of the ceremonial content, and other material used in Freemasonry, is derived from what, in ancient times, were regarded as the 'mystery schools'. These were a form of secret society that, it appears, harboured knowledge about various subjects, including astronomy, alchemy, arithmetic, the macro-cosmos and geometry, and passed this information on to their adepts, many of whom were individually selected. One such school in ancient Greece, was that of the Pythagoreans, an apparent secret society that used the pentagram as a symbol of recognition. Some of the knowledge these ancient adepts are credited with having access to does seem to have found its way into the Masonic psyche of the 19th and early 20th centuries, and there is mention of it in the 18th century. In the absence of any direct evidence that could be established to verify a link with the 'mystery schools' and, in particular, that associated with Pythagoras, I could only conclude that this interpretation arose out of an education system which developed in private boarding schools like Eton and Harrow, which championed an understanding of classical history together with the social inspiration fostered by the Renaissance and interest in languages such as Latin and Greek. It would have been these private boarding schools that educated many of the senior freemasons of the Victorian and Edwardian eras, pre-university or prior to their purchasing commissions in the colonial and military services that then existed. As such, it is easy to understand how they might trace the content of certain Masonic ceremonies and symbols to a direct line of descent from the classical era of Greece and Rome.

As previously mentioned, the Church based in Rome 'christianised' sites and practices which it deemed to be pagan by building a church on a sacred site or subsuming pagan symbolism. This was an attempt on the part of the Church to eradicate what it considered to be evil practices. Instead of eradicating them, the Church unwittingly preserved many of them. So, it will not be a surprise to learn that the pentagram also has religious overtones, including connections with Christianity, where the five points of the symbol represent the five wounds of Christ during the crucifixion; head wounds caused by the crown of thorns, nails through the hands and feet. The symbolism of the number 5 is most often recorded in architecture by the pentagon, from which the pentagram can be defined. A fine example can be found in the church attached to St John's College of Cambridge University. It is interesting to note how the symbol is also contained within the geometric forms of an equilateral triangle and a circle.

A website which provides a number of interesting observations about connections with Freemasonry, and comments on the pentagram, is that operated by the Grand Lodge of British Columbia and Yukon. It makes the point that despite the pentagram being illustrated on a number of Masonic artefacts, it is not mentioned in, and does not have any connection with, any Masonic ceremony or lecture. My own experience only endorses those sentiments. However, it does not answer the points noted earlier, that the pentagram symbol sits prominently in the front step of Freemasons' Hall in London, or that it featured in the external lamps on the Masonic Centre in Brighton. In one of the Masonic ceremonies, it is suggested that all freemasons should study what have become known as the Seven Liberal Arts and Sciences – grammar, rhetoric, arithmetic, music, logic, astronomy and geometry. With geometry comprising a key component of Masonic understanding, the only conclusion one can derive is that the geometric proportions of the pentagram may have as much to do with its presence in Freemasonry as anything esoteric. This is the same conclusion I had arrived at for the hexagram. If that is so, then what are the characteristics that are of particular interest?

When the pentagram is encompassed by a circle, the resultant figure is defined as a *pentacle*. I couldn't help observing that both the hexagram and pentagram can sometimes be used on their own and, at other times, are defined within a circular outer rim. Could it be that when encompassed by the circle, they then became known as *Solomon's Seal?* If so, then it suggested that there was something about the circle that connected these geometric forms with King Solomon.

The Connection with Freemasonry

Having demonstrated proficiency in the first three degrees of Craft Freemasonry, one may be invited to join the next stage of one's Masonic progression. This is referred to amongst freemasons as Royal Arch Freemasonry, or simply as Chapter. The emblem of this degree is a hexagram encased by a circular outer rim. Within the centre of the hexagram is a further symbol, a pair of compasses supporting a representation of a globe and, yet again, an image of the Sun.

The description that explains the symbolism attached to this configuration notes that the hexagram is *a double triangle, sometimes called the Seal of Solomon.* Engraved on the emblem are two inscriptions, both in Latin. One inscription translates as 'Nothing is wanting but the Key'. Needless to point out, on seeing this for the first time as a new member of a Chapter, my mind immediately began asking:

What is it the Key to?

How is the Key used?

Where can I find this Key?

The other inscription translates as 'If thou canst comprehend these things, thou knowest enough'.

Enough about what?

What *things* are we expected to know about?

The description then goes on to a lengthy geometric explanation associated with Platonic theory and the Platonic solids: tetrahedron, octahedron, cube, icosahedron and dodecahedron. There is an explanation of a connection between the 1st Book of Euclid and the triangles, which is in such complex language that I doubt very many Masons have read, let alone understood, what is being conveyed to them. Although mentioning the five primary Platonic symmetrical solids, it ignores the one most revered by Pythagoras, the sphere, which he regarded as the most perfect.

Sphere

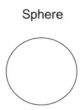

The Secret of Solomon's Seal

Triangle into Pyramid

Triangle into Tetrahedron

Triangle into Icosahedron

Pentagon into Dodecahedron

Irrespective of the explanation about the Chapter emblem, the description makes no further reference to the *Seal of Solomon*. By virtue that the term *Seal of Solomon* or *Solomon's Seal* has passed into use, it reaffirmed my belief that it was derived from practical geometric application. I wondered if it was in some way associated with *Solomon's Temple*. Somewhere in time it had to have acquired its title and it is so specifically linked to King Solomon that it is difficult to imagine that the title was dreamed up, many years ago, and associated with Solomon, just for the sake of giving it a name. What I had come to realise was that, in ancient times, people did things for a practical purpose. They did not have the luxury of using esoteric devices simply so that such titles could exist.

Because the hexagram and pentagram, along with King Solomon, feature extensively in Masonic symbolism and ceremonies, and some mythology surrounds all three, I set out to try and understand where the connection with King Solomon, and hence the Hebrews, might have originated. It was because of the possible connection with geometry, an obvious knowledge of the operative masons which features in Freemasonry, that it seemed worth while exploring this further.

A solution to the secret of Solomon's Seal

In an earlier chapter, I pointed out the geometric significance to the use of two overlapping circles, defined as Vesica Piscis. I also noted that this geometric structure has the additional capacity to enable the drawing of an equilateral triangle as a consequence of a 30° and 60° angular relationship when a line is drawn within the vesica. It is obvious that the symmetrical geometric relationship which resides within the vesica figure dictates that a *Star of David* can be accurately produced.

Vesica Pisces – Star of David

The above image could be reproduced using the
simple masons tools of a pair of compasses
and a straight edge, such as a square

What is more, the resultant geometric symbol can be fully enclosed by a circle which touches each of the outer points when the circle is drawn from the exact centre of the vesica. Indeed, the outer circle defines the consistency of form.

It therefore occurred to me that there was a simple explanation for the difference in terminology between when the equilateral triangles overlap, one on top of the other, as in figure above, by comparison with when the triangles are intertwined, as in the figure below.

Is this the secret of
Solomon's Seal?

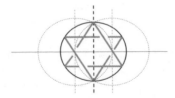

The interlocked triangles are indicative of the use
of the overlapping or interlocked circles derived
from Vesica Piscis.

The Secret of Solomon's Seal

In other words, the use of the *Solomon's Seal* is indicative of a knowledge of the geometric potential of Vesica Piscis. It is evidence of knowledge of the secrets of *sacred geometry*. It displays knowledge of some of the *mason's secrets*. It displays knowledge useful for setting out and planning some of the most significant buildings of antiquity. This would surely have been regarded as important information, not to be lost, but passed on from one generation to the next.

This is all very well for the *Star of David*, but what of the pentagram?

Searching through books on geometry, I found only one method of constructing a pentagram accurately that seemed to match. It involves the circle and the square.

To construct a pentagon or pentagram figure, first draw a circle, followed by a right angle square, the sides of which just touch the circumference of the circle. Note the point where the vertical axis passes through the centre and circumference of the circle (in the figure below this is the line CD). Construct a straight line (EF) from the point where the vertical axis passes through the circumference down to an opposite corner of the square. Place the point of a pair of compasses at the place where the line (EF) passes through the horizontal axis of the circle (line AB), and describe an arc or circle from the point where the line EF crosses the vertical axis CD through the horizontal axis AB.

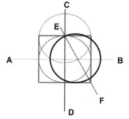

Pentagon basic geometry

Then place the point of the compasses at the point where the line EF and CD cross; extend the compasses to the point on the horizontal axis AB which has been made by the circle or arc described from the point CD; EF, and describe an arc to the circumference of the circle. The resultant cord represents the length of one side of a pentagon.

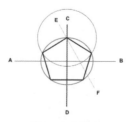

the pentagon

The Secrets of Solomon's Temple

Once the five points of the pentagon have been established on the circumference of the first construction circle, the pentagram symbol is easy to construct using a straight edge, such as a ruler, or builders' square.

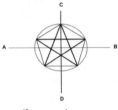

the pentagram

Having constructed a pentagram based on geometric principles, we find that the resultant symbol has certain interesting characteristics, as we can see in the diagram below.

the pentagram angles

- Each point on the outer circle where one of the 5 legs of the pentagram touch (A,B,C,D,E) has an angular separation of 72°.
- between each leg, e.g. AFB, is 144°, which is twice 72.
- The angle of each leg, for example CBD, is 36°, which is half of 72.

There are yet further interesting characteristics. There is a clear link with the Golden Ratio and the value of Phi. If one takes the length of the chord between the points AB, which also makes one side of the pentagon, as a ratio to the length of an arm of the pentagram, the value is 1.618 or 0.618.

Sometimes the pentagram symbol is illustrated with a circle drawn about the centre, and just touches the inside of the legs, or pentagon.

the pentagram and golden ratio

The diameter of the resultant circle is 0.6 of the radius of a circle drawn around the outer points, or the radius of the outer circle is 1.6 times that of the diameter of the inner circle, another direct link between the pentagram and the Golden Ratio, Phi, and its two values of 1.6 and 0.6.

The Golden Ratio also manifests itself in another way. If you take any straight arm of the pentagram and note the point at which the other lines cross it, then the shortest length of the arm is always 0.618 of the length of the arm.

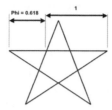

the pentagram and golden ratio - 2

If a triangle is drawn between the two points at the ends of the legs of the pentagram plus sides of the triangle, then the base has a ratio of 1 whilst the sides have a value of 1.618.

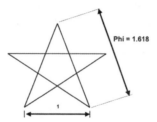

the pentagram and golden ratio - 3

The apex of the triangle will have an internal angle of 36° whilst the internal angles at the base will each be 72°.

The Hexagram/Pentagram link to units of measure

Earlier in this chapter I mentioned that there was the suggestion of a link between the hexagram and Earth measurements. Despite considerable searching I found nothing which provided any positive evidence to support such a claim. Rather unexpectedly, I did find one which makes such a connection with the pentagram.

Assuming traditional claims about Earth measurement are based on ancient practices, then the unit of measure may well have been the cubit. A particular unit of measure used in Ancient Egypt was known as the Royal Cubit, a measure which on the Imperial standard is 20.63 inches (525mm). I came across a paper which suggests that the Royal Cubit was based on the size of the Earth.

The argument set out in the paper[7] suggests that the Egyptian priests were seeking a means of producing a standard unit of measure. They had measured the circumference of the Earth and from that they had determined that one minute (1/60th of a degree) of latitude represented 6,046 feet. This dimension on its own would have been too large to handle as a standard measure. In modern times this is a distance of over one mile (5,280 feet). The writer notes that the latitude which served as the boundary between Upper and Lower Egypt was 29° 27', and was the division between the districts of Memphis, an Egyptian capital, and Medum. Therefore, a measure which related to this latitude would also serve to unite, symbolically, the two territories of Upper and Lower Egypt. As the unit of measuring circular angles was in sixtieths then, it is suggested, the priests took the 6,046ft measure, geometrically reduced it by the equivalent of the cosine of 29° 27' (0.8708) and divided the result by 60 and then 60 again. This would have resulted in a more manageable measure of 1.46246 feet or 17.5495 inches. Interestingly, this dimension of 17.5 inches is close to the normally accepted measure for the standard cubit of around 18 inches.

Using the geometric principles for constructing a pentagram, a circle of 17.5495 would be drawn and a square constructed around it. The horizontal axis was then divided by a line drawn from the top of the vertical axis to the bottom corner of the square around the circle. The length of the resultant line, BF in the following diagram, then equalled 20.63 inches, the recognised value of the Royal Cubit in standard Imperial measure. As will have been seen from the previous construction methodology for a pentagram/pentagon, if an arc is then described from point F, with a centre at B, then a pentagon can be inscribed inside the outer circle and the length of each side will also be 20.63 inches.

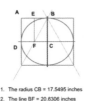

1. The radius CB = 17.5495 inches
2. The line BF = 20.6306 inches

Pentagram geometry and the Royal Cubit

Needless to say, if a pentagram was inscribed using the same points as for the pentagon, then the arms would produce a relationship with the Golden Ratio. The Royal Cubit would, therefore, have been in complete harmony with the macro-cosmos.

A Geometric discovery – Solomon's Seal and the pentagram

It was whilst I was reproducing some of these geometrical processes that I made a discovery. I found that the point on the horizontal axis, AB, used to provide the arc to the outer circle, and thereby defining the point of a leg of the pentagram, was very close to the side points of the circles which overlap in the vesica. When I first drew this on a sheet of A4 graph paper, the variance was noticeable but small. On a much larger scale it represented 12mm per metre, or a variance of just 1.2%. This inaccuracy only becomes distinguishable as the size of the geometric construction, and the resultant figure, increase.

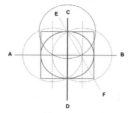

Vesica Pisces and the pentagram

One could, therefore, well image that the masons of old would have used this simple Vesica Piscis construction method for their designs and implementation. In most circumstances the variance would not be noticeable. This geometric construction would therefore be based on the same process used for constructing a hexagram. It is easy to understand how, and why, the term *Solomon's Seal* has come to be associated with both figures: the *Star of David* and the pentagram. Both, when intertwined, are derived from the intertwined circles – Vesica Piscis. It would have been a construction process simple to remember when working on a major construction site, such as a temple or cathedral. As such, it would have been included in the mason's secret of *Solomon's Seal*.

Solomon's Seal

At the time of writing this chapter, and despite making reference to numerous works by others, I have not encountered any previous suggestions that claim a vesica piscis solution as being a geometric definition of the term *Solomon's Seal* or how it can be applied to the hexagram or pentagram. I commend it to readers.

Having now established a possible credible explanation for the *Seal,* this then leaves still one question to be answered – why is it linked to King Solomon?

Conclusion

With respect to the hexagram, or *Star of David,* my investigations revealed that a definitive and global link of the hexagram with Judaism is as recent as the late 19th century – having grown in association progressively from about the 14th century. The suggestion is that the hexagram was an established and accepted symbol well before the Solomonic era. There are early Jewish associations with the symbol, but no more so than its use in other cultures as a symbol of good luck, or esoteric significance to represent harmony. It may have been used by the Hebrews in ancient times as a symbol of marriage but it is unclear if such symbolism extended back to the epoch of the charismatic monarchs – Saul, David and Solomon.

Archaeological discoveries in Mesopotamia trace the use of the pentagram symbol back to an era some 2,500 years prior to the building of Solomon's Temple. As well as being a clean geometric figure, with interesting angular characteristics, it has, in antiquity, been associated with the cycles of the planet Venus.

It is believed that the pentagram was a symbol of recognition for the adepts of a *mystery school* created by the Greek philosopher and mathematician Pythagoras. The teachings of Pythagoras appear to have been inculcated into Ancient Freemasonry. As reference to the pentagram symbol is not made in any Masonic ceremony or lecture, the presence of the pentagram in Masonic culture can be related, in part, to this ancient connection. This may explain the presentation of the symbol in the main steps of Freemasons Hall in London, home of the United Grand Lodge of England, although the official interpretation in Freemasonry is that it is a symbol of Friendship and a talisman of Harmony and Goodwill.

The connection of both the hexagram and pentagram symbols with the operative masons of ancient times is possible through the simple geometric construction that can be achieved, based on Vesica Piscis. When constructed using the principles defined as Vesica Piscis, they are directly linked to overlapping or intertwined circles. I submit to readers that it is when the symbols are produced in this manner and are enclosed within a circle that they both take on the form defined as *Solomon's Seal,* that the construction of *Solomon's Seal* was a secret of the operative mason's trade as a symbol of knowledge about Vesica Piscis, which was used in the design and setting out of certain buildings.

What I still needed to find was a reason why there is a reference to *Solomon* and where and how such a reference may have originated.

[1] Encyclopaedia Judaica
[2] *The Secret Teachings of All Ages* by Manley P. Hall p219
[3] *Ancient Freemasonry*, Frank Higgins p248
[4] *Ancient Freemasonry*, Frank Higgins, p133
[5] Encyclopaedia Judaica
[6] http://www.menorah.org/starofdavid.html
[7] Encyclopaedia Judaica
[8] website under the name 'Grand Lodge of British Columbia and Yukon' – http://freemasonry.bcy.ca/symbolism/pentagrams.html
[9] *The Book of Hiram* by Christopher Knight and Robert Lomas. Also see Uriels Machine by the same authors.
[10] From a paper published on the internet at http://www.sover.net/~rc/deep_secrets/cubit/index.html

Chapter 5
Pythagoras, mystery schools and freemasonry

ow was the information contained in ancient wisdom conveyed from one generation to the other? Part of the answer seems to relate to the 'mystery schools'.

In an earlier chapter I made reference to the mystery schools that are understood to have existed in Ancient Greece during the classical era. Amongst these was one attributed to Pythagoras, the philosopher and mathematician. Some of the knowledge attributed to this mystery school in particular has surfaced in Freemasonry.

According to traditional accounts, the mystery schools have a history possibly dating back to beyond 2,500 BCE. One was apparently related to Isis and Osiris, the premier deities of Ancient Egypt and from whom, tradition has it, the Egyptian empire was seeded. The main religions apparently had their own mystic teachings aside from the regulated doctrine. This mystical knowledge was imparted to selected individuals who were initiated into those secrets, usually with the first three levels of attainment being referred to as *three degrees*. This is the same practice as is found in Freemasonry even today.

It is well respected that knowledge about the macro-cosmos, the workings of nature, its cycles, and the celestial patterns, was the domain of a select group of people known as the priesthoods. These priesthoods not only understood the world around them and conducted investigations into matters about the way the world worked but they ensured that information and the cumulative knowledge then known to man was passed from one generation to the other. They were *Magi,* the custodians of knowledge and understanding, and it follows that the more senior one became within the hierarchy, so the understanding of any particular subject was likely to be more extensive, whilst the access to the knowledge of almost any known subject was broad.

In his book *Ancient Freemasonry,* Frank Higgins makes the following observation about such priesthoods and the process of initiation that surrounded them:

> *'The object of all the ancient ceremonies of initiation was purely and simply the preservation of the priestly caste. This particular division of society, endowed with leisure and the means for the pursuit of knowledge, discovered much, but discovered nothing which it might have freely imparted if it had seen fit to the great masses.'[1]*

As time passed, it is highly likely that these priesthoods became trapped in paradigms in which customs, dogma and perceptions were well established to a point where change was not tolerated or contemplated. The earlier reference to the experience of Anaxagoras and his estimates about the size of the Moon, serve to illustrate the point. Punishment was meted out to those who sought an alternative path or proposed solutions or propositions which did not fit with the established dogma. In Anaxagoras' case, the punishment was exile. It is, therefore, not difficult to understand that secretive societies may well have developed which explored new ideas and conveyed them to adepts, people who were willing to explore and promulgate new concepts.

The priesthoods of Ancient Egypt are credited with having a well-developed understanding of the macro-cosmos, geometry, astrology and the rules of basic numbering systems. Likewise the Druids of Britain are credited with the same knowledge. In some respects, Druidic understanding is believed to have been superior to that of the Egyptians. The terrain of Egypt dictated that the priests there had a deep understanding of the plants and animals appropriate to the warm, dry environment they inhabited; they learned how to build with mud, brick and stone because trees and wood were sparse. On the other hand the Druids were surrounded by forests which harboured a different set of animal life and a wealth of flora and fauna. Wood was in such abundance that it became the main building material. Both the Druids and Egyptians had one thing in common – their knowledge, understanding and study of the celestial movement. The Druids are believed to have later absorbed into their doctrine much of the philosophical understanding attributed to Pythagoras.

As time passed so the learned men of each culture became known as *sages* or *wise men; one of those who knows.* It was Pythagoras who apparently invented the terminology – *philosopher* – meaning *one who is attempting to find out.*[2]

According to tradition, Pythagoras was born in Sidon in Phoenicia. There is some doubt as to the exact year, but it is thought to have been around 580 BCE .[3] He is attributed as having become conversant with esoteric knowledge. According to tradition, having learned all he felt he could from the Greek philosophers of the day, he became an initiate of the Eleusinian mysteries; he went on to Egypt and was admitted to the Mysteries of Isis by the priests at Thebes; he was then initiated in the Mysteries of Adonis before passing into Mesopotamia and receiving the Mysteries of the Chaldeans; finally he ended up in Hindustan to learn from the priestly Brahmin caste.[4] With the value of so much that he had learned, he returned to the Mediterranean and established his school at Crotona in Southern Italy, where he initiated *Pythagorean* disciples, to whom he conveyed the secret knowledge he had gained in his travels.

I have already mentioned that the pentagram was apparently used as a symbol of recognition by the adepts of his school. It has been speculated that the reason he chose this symbol was because of its connection with the natural world, the macro-cosmos. Most people if asked to cut an apple in half will do so on a line through the sprig; that is, along the length of the apple as it would hang from a tree. If, however, an apple is cut in half through what might be deemed its equator, so the symbol of the pentagram will be revealed at the core. It would therefore have been very easy for an adept of the school to have demonstrated their connection without having to say or write anything. They could simply take an apple, cut it in half and reveal the symbol within.

Pythagoras apparently taught the alchemical wisdom of his day, along with geometry, music, arithmetic and astronomy. These four subjects form the basis of what, during the Renaissance, became known as the Liberal Arts and Sciences. The Liberal Arts and Sciences are attributed to the knowledge of the Masons, as recorded in a document held at the Bodleian Library in Oxford. In the early days of formalised academic education in what we know today as the Universities, study of the Liberal Arts and Sciences was the basis of the Master of Arts degree.

The key to Pythagorean counting was the number 10, which Pythagoras defined as the most perfect number, and infinite, a number that, of course, has a close association with the number of fingers or toes attributed to the human form.

Pythagorean teaching dismissed the first two numbers of the counting system, which Pythagoras called the *Monad* and *Duad*, as having no significance, but placed great store on the next two numbers, 3 and 4. These, when added to the first two result in the total 10 (1 + 2 + 3 + 4 = 10), the *Decad*. It is, apparently, from this Pythagorean terminology that today we use the term *Decade* to define a period of 10 years. Interestingly, there is a view that when two freemasons shake hands they are symbolising the Pythagorean *Decad*. The *Decad* can be divided into two equal portions of five, and thus, two hands coming together, each with five fingers, creates the *Decad*.[5]

Pythagoras is reputed to have placed great store by the number 3. According to Aristotle, *'the Pythagoreans say.... all things are defined by threes; for end and middle and beginning constitute the number of the all, and also the number of the triad'*.[6] It is interesting how this simple conjecture remains a common feature of our language today:

> *'everything goes in threes...'*
> *'a cold is three days coming, three days with you and three days going'*

Pythagoras also attributed certain symbolic significance to the prime numbers in the range 1 to 9. As an example consider the number 666. Pythagoras' system added the individual component numbers together and then added together the digits of the answer to reduce it to a single value within the range 1 to 9. Thus:

$$6 + 6 + 6 = 18$$
$$1 + 8 = 9$$

Pythagoras attributed the number 9 to symbolising man himself.

The table of Pythagorean numbers

No	Name	Pythagorean symbolic representation
1	Monad	Symbolises the father. It always remains in the same condition and separate from the multitude. A symbol of the mind, stable and pre-eminent; an hermaphrodite being male and female, odd and even because when it is added to an even number it makes one which is odd. A Monad added to another Monad creates the Duad.
2	Duad	Symbolises the mother of wisdom; the duality of heaven and earth.
3	Triad	Seen as the first number which is odd (Monad not always being seen as a number). Characterises friendship, peace, justice, prudence, piety, temperance and virtue.
4	Tetrad	Regarded as the most perfect number. Symbolic of the deity because it embodies the first four numbers. The number of the seasons. The middle of the week. The four elements: Air, Fire, Water, Earth. The four corners of the Earth: north, south, east and west. Characterises harmony, strength, virility.
5	Pentad	The number 10 divided into two equal parts. The sum of the first odd and even numbers $3 + 2 = 5$. This is one of two numbers which when multiplied by itself reproduces itself in the product. Characterises immortality, cordiality, providence, sound.
6	Hexad	Represents the creation of the world. The sum and product of the first three numbers $1 + 2 + 3 = 6$; $1 \times 2 \times 3 = 6$. The second number which when multiplied by itself reproduces itself in the product. The symbol of marriage as defined by the two overlapping triangles. Characterises harmony.
7	Heptad	Regarded as the number of religion, to reflect the seven celestial spheres and spirits (Earth omitted but including the Sun and Moon). Regarded as symbolic of life, as a child born after a 7-month gestation would normally live.
8	Ogdoad	Sacred symbol of the cube, which has eight corners. Special qualities note that 8 divided into 2 parts = 4; 4 divided into two parts = 2; 2 divided into two parts = 1, Monad (1-2-4-8-4-2-1). Characterises love, counsel, prudence, law.
9	Ennead	The first square of an odd number ($3 \times 3 = 9$). Regarded as the number of man because it takes nine months of gestation to receive life. Sometimes it was regarded as an evil number being an inverted 6. Characterises the ocean and horizon.
10	Decad	Regarded as the greatest of numbers. Represented in the tetractys (triangle of ten dots). Embodiment of all the previous numbers. The basis of arithmetic as it enabled counting using the human calculator – fingers.

The above table is paraphrased and edited from information provided in – 'The Secret Teachings of All Ages' by Manley P. Hall.

Pythagoras, mystery schools and freemasonry

Included in Pythagorean teaching was a system whereby certain words held a numerical significance which gave them a hidden meaning. Manley P. Hall notes that the first step in obtaining a numerical value for a word is to ensure that it is defined in its original language, and then goes on to add that this really works only with words derived from Greek or Hebrew. Indeed, Hall points out that both the Greeks and the Hebrew Qabbala used this system. He demonstrates that the word we know in English as *Jehovah* is synonymous with the *Demiurgus* of the Jews. When this word is translated back into Hebrew it is characterised by the following Hebrew letters:

Yod-He-Vau-He.

By then consulting a conversion table printed in Hall's book, the letters are allocated numbers. So, Demiurgus (Jehovah) becomes:

Yod-He-Vau-He.

10 + 5 + 6 + 5 = 26

Thus, to the derived word *Jehovah* is attributed the numerical value of 26. Taking the Pythagorean process to its conclusion by reducing this total to a single number, then $2 + 6 = 8$. From the above table it will be seen that the number 8 (Ogdoad) represents the sacred cube with its eight corners. However, the cube was also a symbolic representation of the world. Thus, we could interpret the word *Jehovah* as symbolising the world.

Manley Hall points out that:

'Old Testament words and names, therefore, must be translated back into the early Hebrew characters and New Testament words into the Greek.'

At the risk of being overtly controversial, what is being suggested here is that names and phrases of the Bible have a hidden *mystic* characteristic. In other words, the Bible contains a code, a code unlocked by applying the type of process typified by the Pythagorean doctrine!!

But it is for his geometric understanding that the name *Pythagoras* is most well known. Pythagoras' Theorem is taught to almost every schoolchild in the western world.

In a right angle triangle, the square of the hypotenuse is equal to the sum of the squares of the other two sides, i.e. $a^2 + b^2 = c^2$. This is demonstrated in a right-angle triangle with the proportions 3,4,5

e.g. $3^2 + 4^2 = x^2$ $\quad$ $9 + 16 = 25$ $\quad$ $\sqrt{25} = 5$

This theorem is shown diagrammatically as follows:

This symbol is attributed to Pythagoras in explaining the theorem. It is also known as Euclid's 47th proposition.

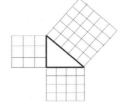

The above symbol is well known in Masonic lectures and is illustrated in certain emblems. In particular it features on a jewel worn by a former Master of the Lodge – yet again linking the ancient knowledge of Freemasonry with geometry.

I wondered how far back in time I needed to go to find a reference to Pythagoras in published Masonic materials. The earliest mention I could find in Masonic literature was in one of the most revered early works of the fraternity – *Illustrations of Masonry* by William Preston, published in 1795. An original and ancient copy of this rare and remarkable work was made available to me through my local connections, but I confess that the print style did not lend itself to easy reading. Fortunately, a well-published freemason, Robert Lomas, co-author of *The Hiram Key*, had produced an on-line version which was much easier to digest having been translated from the old English that was the common writing style when Preston compiled the original work, and provided the benefit of word search. Robert Lomas has very kindly given permission for extracts to be printed here. In respect of the history of Masonry in England, Preston wrote the following references to Pythagoras. In order that they are not taken out of context, a broad area of the text is reproduced.

First there is a reference to Pythagoras and the Druids:

The Druids, we are informed, retained among them many usages similar to those of masons; but of what they consisted, at this remote period we cannot with certainty discover. In conformity to the antient practices of the fraternity, we learn that they held their assemblies in woods and groves, and observed the most impenetrable secrecy in their principles and opinions; a circumstance we have reason to regret, as these, being known only to themselves, must have perished with them.

They were the priests of the Britons, Gauls, and other Celtic nations, and were divided into three classes: the bards, who were poets and musicians, formed the first class; the vates, who were priests and physiologists, composed the second class; and the third class consisted of the Druids, who added moral philosophy to the study of physiology.

As study and speculation were the favourite pursuits of those philosophers, it has been suggested that they chiefly derived their system of government from Pythagoras. Many of his tenets and doctrines seem to have been adopted by them. In their private retreats, they entered into a disquisition of the origin, laws, and properties of matter, the form and magnitude of the universe, and even ventured to explore the most sublime and hidden secrets of Nature. On these subjects they formed a variety of hypotheses, which they delivered to their disciples in verse, in order that they might be more easily retained in memory; and administered an oath not to commit them to writing.

There is a further reference, this time relating to confidentiality:

It is well known, that the usages and customs of masons have ever corresponded with those of the ancient Egyptians, to which they bear a near affinity. These philosophers, unwilling to expose their mysteries to vulgar eyes, concealed their particular tenets and principles of polity under hieroglyphical figures; and expressed their notions of government by signs and symbols, which they communicated to their Magi alone, who were bound by oath not to reveal them. Pythagoras seems to have established his system on a similar plan, and many orders of a more recent date have copied the example. Masonry, however, is not only the most ancient, but the most moral institution that ever subsisted; every character, figure, and emblem, depicted in a Lodge, has a moral tendency, and tends to inculcate the practice of virtue.

We then find a further reference that alludes to Pythagoras being initiated into the same knowledge that formed the philosophy of Masonry, and then a dissertation on the travels and knowledge gained by the Sage:

The records of the fraternity inform us, that Pythagoras was regularly initiated into masonry; *and being properly instructed in the mysteries of the Art, propagated the principles of the Order in other countries into which he travelled.*

Pythagoras lived at Samos, in the reign of Tarquin, the last king of the Romans, in the year of Rome 220; or, according to Livy, in the reign of Servius Tullius, in the year of the world 3472. He was the son of a sculptor, and was educated under one of the greatest men of his time, Therecydes of Syrus, who first taught the immortality of the soul. Upon the death of his patron, he determined to trace science to its source, and supply himself with fresh stores in every part of the world where these could be obtained. Animated by this desire of knowledge, he travelled into Egypt, and submitted to the tedious and discouraging course of preparatory discipline which was necessary to obtain the benefit of Egyptian initiation. When he had made himself a thorough master of all the sciences which were cultivated in the sacerdotal colleges of Thebes and Memphis, he pursued his travels through the east, conversing with the Magi and Indian Brachmans [Brahmins], and mixing their doctrines with those he had learnt in Egypt. He afterwards studied the laws of Minos at Crete, and those of Lycurgus at Sparta. Having spent the earlier part of his life in this useful manner, he returned to Samos well acquainted with every thing curious either in nature or art in foreign countries, improved with all the advantages proceeding from a regular and laborious course of learned education, and adorned with that knowledge of mankind which was necessary to gain the ascendant over them. Accustomed to freedom, he disliked the arbitrary of Samos, and retired to Crotona in Italy, where he opened a school of philosophy; and by the gravity and sanctity of his manners, the importance of his tenets, and the peculiarity of his institutions, soon spread his fame and influence over Italy and Greece. Among other projects which he used to create respect and gain credit to his assertion, he concealed himself in a cave, and caused it to be reported that he was dead. After some time he came abroad, and pretended that the intelligence which his friends gave him in his retreat, of the transactions of

Crotona, was collected during his stay in the other world among the shades of the departed. He formed his disciples, who came from all parts to put themselves under his direction, into a kind of republic, where none were admitted till a severe probation had sufficiently exercised their patience and docility. He afterwards divided them into the esoteric and exoteric classes: to the former he entrusted the more sublime and secret doctrines, to the latter the more simple and popular. This great man found himself able to unite the character of the legislator to that of the philosopher, and to rival Lycurgus and Orpheus in the one, Pherecydes and Thales in the other; following, in this particular, the patterns set him by the Egyptian priests, his instructors, who are not less celebrated for settling the civil than the religious (o)economy of their nation. In imitation of them, Pythagoras gave laws to the republic of Crotona, and brought the inhabitants from a state of luxury and dissoluteness, to be eminent for order and sobriety. While he lived, he was frequently consulted by the neighbouring republics, as the composer of their differences, and the reformer of their manners; and since his death (which happened about the fourth year of the 70th olympiad, in a tumult raised against him by one Cylon) the administration of their affairs has been generally intrusted to some of his disciples, among whom, to produce the authority of their master for any assertion, was sufficient to establish the truth of it without further inquiry.

The most celebrated of the philosophical notions of Pythagoras are those concerning the nature of the Deity, the transmigration of souls into different bodies (which he borrowed from the Brachmans [Brahmins]), and the system of the world. He was the first who took the name of philosopher; that is, a lover of wisdom. His system of morality was admirable. He made unity the principle of all things, and believed that between God and man there were various orders of spiritual beings, who administered to the divine will. He believed in the doctrine of the metempsychosis, or transmigration of souls; and held that God was diffused through all parts of the universe, like a kind of universal soul, pervading every particle of matter, and animating every living creature, from the most contemptible reptile to mankind themselves, who shared a larger portion of the divine spirit. The metempsychosis was founded on this maxim, that as the soul was of celestial origin, it could not be annihilated, and therefore, upon abandoning one body, necessarily removed into another, and frequently did penance for its former vicious inclinations, in the shape of a beast or an insect, before it appeared again in that of a human creature. He asserted, that he had a particular faculty given him by the gods, of remembering the various bodies his own soul had passed through, and confounded cavillers by referring them to his own experience. In his system of the world, the third doctrine which distinguishes his sect, was a supposition, that the sun was at rest in the centre, and that the earth, the moon, and the other planets moved round it in different orbits. He pretended to have great skill in the mysterious properties of numbers, and held that some particular ones contained a peculiar force and significance. He was a great geometrician, and admitted only those to the knowledge of his system, who had first undergone a probation of five years silence. To his discovery is attributed the 47th proposition of the first book of Euclid, which, in geometrical solutions and demonstrations of quantities, is of excellent use; and for which as Mr. Locke observes, in the joy of his heart, he is said to have sacrificed a hecatomb. His extraordinary desire of knowledge, and the pains he took to propagate his system, have justly transmitted his fame to posterity. The pupils who were initiated by him in the sciences and study of nature at the Crotonian school, brought all their goods into a common stock, contemned the pleasures of sense, abstaining from swearing, and eat nothing that had life. Steady to the tenets and principles which they had imbibed, they dispersed abroad, and taught the doctrines of their preceptor, in all the countries through which they travelled.[7]

Words in parentheses are the author's addition.

The United Grand Lodge of England was formed in 1813 by the merger of two Grand Lodges known separately as the Ancients and the Moderns. Thus, by virtue that it is referenced by Preston in his work of 1795, Pythagorean doctrine must have been a recognised feature of the fraternity well before that time. It explains why much of the Victorian and Edwardian literature produced on the history of Freemasonry, and some of its ceremonial attributes, espouses attitudes and reflections of Pythagorean doctrine, together with symbolism that was attached to it, including the use of the pentagram.

As with other subjects of my research, I had read widely on the subject of Pythagoras and felt I had a good understanding of his philosophy. I now knew enough without turning my enquiries into a thesis on the history of this very learned figure of history. There were a series of key elements that I had uncovered which had satisfied my interest, particularly how and why Pythagoras came to have such a close connection with Freemasonry. What it did not explain was how it found its way into the Order.

Conclusion

1 Recognising that, according to tradition, Pythagoras had gained his knowledge from his extensive travels and initiation in the esoteric understanding in the Eastern Mediterranean, Egypt, Mesopotamia, Persia and Northern India, the symbolism in numbers espoused by Pythagoras may well have been a common theme across the cultures. With such widespread use it is understandable how this knowledge would have permeated its way through subsequent ages.

2 The most perfect number defined by Pythagoras was the number ten, 10. It would be logical, therefore, to find this number in any designs based on Pythagorean doctrine.

3 The pentagram was the symbol of recognition for the initiates at the school in

Crotona. With Pythagorean doctrine being inculcated in Freemasonry it was logical that the symbol should make its presence in the fraternity.

Now the question that needed answering was — how were Pythagorean concepts used?

[1] *Ancient Freemasonry*, Frank Higgins, p248
[2] *The Secret Teaching of All Ages* – Manley P. Hall
[3] *Encyclopaedia Britannica*
[4] *Ancient Freemasonry*, Frank Higgins
[5] *The Secret Teaching of All Ages* – Manley P. Hall
[6] Aristotle – See – http://history.hanover.edu/texts/presoc/pythagor.htm
[7] An on-line version of *Illustrations of Masonry*, Book 4, Section 1, by William Preston, transcribed by Geraint and Robert Lomas and available at http://www.robertlomas.com/preston/padlock/book4/bk4sect1.html

Chapter 6
Ecclesiastical Influence –
Wonderful Masons

David died and Solomon assumed the throne of Israel. Based on the timelines associated with biblical chronology, the interval of time between Joseph being taken as a prisoner of the Midianites, through the slavery of the Israelites in Egypt, the Exodus, the conquest, the reign of Saul and David, to the era when Solomon came to power as the King of Israel, was an astonishing seven hundred years. The time lapse between the design and construction of the Ark of the Covenent and the building of the Temple in Jerusalem was nearly five hundred years. The Temple was built to house what was already an ancient relic.

The Temple – a lavish undertaking

On reading about the first Jerusalem Temple in the Old Testament one cannot help but be impressed by the lavish and ostentatious decoration detail that is recorded; the massive commitment in labour; and the effort that both Solomon and his friendly neighbour, Hiram, King of Tyre, expended in securing what were regarded as the right materials for the job and transporting them to the building site.

a. The decoration:

And Solomon overlaid the inside of the house with pure gold, and he drew chains of gold across, in front of the inner sanctuary, and overlaid it with gold.

1 Kings 6:21

And he overlaid the whole house with gold, until all the house was finished. Also the whole altar that belonged to the inner sanctuary he overlaid with gold.

1 Kings 6:22

He carved all the walls of the house round about with carved figures of cherubim and palm trees and open flowers, in the inner and outer rooms.

1 Kings 6:29

The floor of the house he overlaid with gold in the inner and outer rooms.

1 Kings 6:30

b. The commitment of labour and materials needed for the construction of this first Temple:

> *King Solomon raised a levy of forced labour out of all Israel; and the levy numbered thirty thousand men.*
>
> *1 Kings 5:13*

> *And he sent them to Lebanon, ten thousand a month in relays; they would be a month in Lebanon and two months at home; Adoniram was in charge of the levy.*
>
> *1 Kings 5:14*

> *Solomon also had seventy thousand burden-bearers and eighty thousand hewers of stone in the hill country,*
>
> *1 Kings 5:15*

> *besides Solomon's three thousand three hundred chief officers who were over the work, who had charge of the people who carried on the work.*
>
> *1 Kings 5:16*

c. The supply line of materials, much being shipped from Tyre:

> *My servants shall bring it down to the sea from Lebanon; and I will make it into rafts to go by sea to the place you direct, and I will have them broken up there, and you shall receive it; and you shall meet my wishes by providing food for my household.*
>
> *1 Kings 5:9*

> *So Hiram supplied Solomon with all the timber of cedar and cypress that he desired.*
>
> *1 Kings 5:10*

What is more, this massive commitment of labour and materials hardly seems justified when we consider that the overall dimensions of the Temple indicate that it was about the size of a typical church that can be found in many small towns and villages in England.

> *The house which King Solomon built for the Lord was sixty cubits long, twenty cubits wide, and thirty cubits high.*
>
> *1 Kings 6:2*

Assuming, for ease of conversion, that a cubit is 18 inches in Imperial measure or half a metre in metric measure, this building was about 90 ft (30m) long by 30 ft (10m) wide and 45 ft (15m) high. It would fit into the rear garden of numerous houses of every town in Britain. Yet, the Old Testament records that this small temple required 183,300 men to be involved in the construction, of which 150,000 men were employed to cut and haul the stone from the quarry to the place of the final building site.

It has been suggested in the past that this enormous use of manpower was needed mostly to construct a solid platform around the top of Mount Moriah as the foundation before the temple was built on it. Even making allowance for the preparation of the foundations, it seems to have been a very large work force. What is more, this army of conscripted construction labour does not seem to have been very efficient because the construction took years to complete.

> *And in the eleventh year, in the month of Bul, which is the eighth month, the house was finished in all its parts, and according to all its specifications. He was seven years in building it.*
>
> *1 Kings 6:38*

The number of labourers involved with this building project was almost on a par with the construction of the Great Pyramid of Giza, built around 1,500 years earlier than the first Jerusalem Temple. Estimates by Egyptologists suggest that the building of the Great Pyramid was undertaken by 100,000 men over a twenty year period.[1] In simple terms, if the pyramid builders had used the same numbers of men as were employed in building the Temple, they may have completed the construction in ten years. The sheer number of men involved suggests that the scale and complexity of the projects were similar.

Or, are we perhaps being told something else?

Take for example the number of people needed for the construction. We have noted above, that by any standards, huge numbers of workmen were involved.

If you add together the 30,000 who went to Tyre, 70,000 hewers of stone, 80,000 haulers, 3,300 overseers, and forget the noughts which identify the thousands, we have:

$$30 + 70 + 80 + 33 = 213,$$

and taking Pythagoras to his logical conclusion of reducing the answer to a single number, then we have $1 + 2 + 3 = 6$, the value for harmony.

The 30,000 that went to Tyre could be treated as 30, the number of days in the religious – lunar – calendar. Those associated with cutting and moving the stone was $70,000 + 80,000$ which can be reduced to 15, the angular rotation in degrees of the Earth that represents 1/24 part of a day; what today we term an hour. This number too can be reduced to 6, symbolising harmony. The 33 could represent the three primary positions of the Sun on the horizon – 3 as it moves north and 3 moving south, and can again be reduced to 6.

Nearly one and half millennia ago, a then unknown monk living in a relatively remote corner of the former Roman Empire took the same numbers, and many others associated with the temple, and gave them a symbolic interpretation. History knows him as the Venerable Bede.

Bede – the Tabernacle and the Temple

The idea of adding together numbers to create an altogether different symbolic allegory clearly became well established in religious circles. One of the most prominent examples relates to the Venerable Bede.

The Venerable Bede lived at the end of the 7th and into the early decades of the 8th century CE. He was born in 673 CE and died 735 CE. He has come to fame because of an exceptional collection of writings he left behind that were related entirely to the era of his life. He was a monk who lived around the time that the Celtic Christian Church, well established in the northern and western areas of Britain, and the Roman Catholic Church, which had established itself firmly in the southern and southeastern areas, merged at the Synod of Whitby in 664 CE. Bede is credited with having written a detailed account of the proceedings of the Synod even though it took place nine years before his birth.

Bede had been taken into the ecclesiastic and monastic community at a very young age. He devoted his life to it, never moving more than a mile or two from its walls. His connections with the world outside of this immediate monastic circle were therefore very limited, which makes his achievements, and his fame, all the more remarkable.

The Venerable Bede was born some 1,300 years ago, about 250 years after the Roman armies had left Britain. Many of the Roman customs would have still been functioning; houses and prominent buildings were still standing. Hadrian's Wall, just a few miles north of the monastery, probably still stood in its original condition. Folklore and tales about the Roman era probably abounded within communities. It was against this background that Bede wrote a history of the peoples of England as he then understood it, from that folklore and documents that he was able to secure. Bede's history is a work that is still referenced today.

Bede is credited with being the first known person to have used the AD calendar date concept, (Anno Domini – Latin, which means 'In the year of our Lord'). A monk by the name of Dionysius Exiguus devised the AD concept in the year 525 CE although it actually came into use in 532 CE to set year 1 AD, the origins of which is where and how the current year dating system is derived[2]. Bede was the first to use it as we know it today and devised the additional concept of BC (Before Christ) to define the period prior to 1 AD. Both of these designations remained prominent until the late 20th century when the letters CE came to prominence as a replacement for the AD reference along with BCE as an alternative for BC. The CE designation has several interpretations - in the Christian Era – in the Current Era – in the Common Era, whilst BCE is shorthand for Before the Christian Era. To put the period of Bede's life into context, he lived in the time prior to the invasions of northern England by the Vikings, and elsewhere along the east coast by the Jutes and Angles, all of whom intended conquest of England. Alfred the Great would not be king for another 150 years. It was some 400 years prior to the Norman Conquest and the death of King Harold at the Battle of Hastings. It was also around the time when the religion that we now know as Islam was first created.

As well as recording history, as he understood it, Bede developed an interest in the macro-cosmos including the passage and phases of the Moon. Perhaps this is not so surprising, these phases provided the basis of the lunar calendar which was at the heart of the timetable governing religious affairs and festivals. The AD dating system was based on just such lunar cycles and in particular a concept known as the 532 years Great Cycle. We know that in our current western calendar system, a date may occur on a Monday one year and move forward to the Tuesday in the next year, except, that is, in a leap year. So the day of the Summer Solstice, 21st June 2000 was on a Wednesday, whereas the same date in 2001 was on a Thursday. Throughout Bede's life, the Julian calendar was the one that operated all over Europe. It was replaced in 1582 by the Gregorian calendar. In the Julian calendar the solar cycle took 28 years before all the dates exactly repeated themselves on appropriate days. If the lunar cycle was used it took 19 years for the cycle to be repeated. Thus, for the lunar and the solar calendar cycles to coincide it took 19 x 28 = 532 years. This became known as the Great Cycle or the Great Paschal Period and was used for calculating the date of Easter. Bede, it would seem, fully understood the astronomical implications associated with this influence.

The monastery to which Bede was attached stood on the banks of the River Tyne, just east of the modern city of Newcastle. What at one time would have been open countryside, with the river yielding fish to supplement the diet, is today heavily industrialised with a river that, through the twentieth century, suffered the ravages of pollution. Where once Bede could have looked across the river at yet more open countryside and woodland, today his gaze would fall on a forest of oil storage tanks. The location beside the river proved to be ideal for Bede. He made a study of the rise and fall of the tides and is credited with discovering the connection of tidal movement with the phases of the Moon. He knew that the Earth was a sphere, understood the relationship of the seasons relative to the position of the Sun on the horizon, that it moved from the northern to the southern hemisphere and returned; he had an understanding of the relativity of the length of the shadows cast by the Sun and their relationship to the latitude position on the face of the planet.[3]

For one who did not travel further than the immediate surroundings of his monastery, Bede appears to have been remarkably well versed in the principles of ancient wisdom. Almost the only contact he had with the wider world was through letters and visits to the monastery by brother monks and dignitaries of the church, which implies that the only place that wisdom could have been encountered was within his monastic community. This seems to have included knowledge of Pythagorean principles and mysticism, because amongst Bede's writings which have survived are two intriguing works now known as *De Tabernacle* and *De Templo*. *De Templo* has been translated from the original Latin and is now available in a wonderful book with the title, *Bede: On the Temple*.[4] In this work Bede discusses various attributes of Solomon's Temple in what is regarded as an allegorical interpretation of both the Tabernacle and the Temple.[5] He treats the description, dimensions and furnishings as a comparative prophesy for the events that were later recorded as the central theme of Christianity.

In *De Templo* Bede makes frequent reference to *The Book of Paralipomenon* as a source of information. It is a book of scripture seldom mentioned today in regular sources of religious text. The Catholic Encyclopaedia describes this work as follows:

> 'Two books of the Bible containing a summary of sacred history from Adam to the end of the Captivity. The title Paralipomenon, books "of things passed over", which, from the Septuagint, passed into the old Latin Bible and thence into the Vulgate, is commonly taken to imply that they supplement the narrative of the Books of Kings (otherwise known as I-II Sam. and I-II Kings); ......In the Protestant, printed Hebrew, and many Catholic bibles, they are entitled Books of Chronicles.'[6]

So, based on the Catholic Encyclopaedia definition, Bede was reflecting text that today we find in the two Books of Chronicles.

In the Old Testament there are descriptions of aspects of the Temple which have numbers associated with them and Bede multiplies them together and assigns symbolic meaning to both the numbers and the totals.

For example, commenting on the height of the pillars at eighteen cubits each, he points out that $3 \times 6 = 18$, and notes that the 3 is a reference to faith based on the tradition of the Holy Trinity, whilst the 6 refers to works because, as the Old Testament book of Genesis states, the world was made in six days.[7] He points out that the number ten (10) conventionally intimated the 'hope of heavenly rewards'.[8] In the same section he notes that twenty (20) is 4×5; the 5 he asserts, relates to the five books attributed to Moses – the Mosaic law – whilst the 4 he attributes to the four Gospels.[9] Bede's work contains many such numerical manipulations. To do this means that somewhere in his monastic career he came into contact with a philosophy for taking biblical numbers, manipulating them and assigning a symbolic meaning or interpretation.

In the Old Testament we are told that Solomon's Temple had a main room called the Hall, and the Inner Sanctuary or Holy of Holies, whilst the Temple was approached through an outer courtyard. Bede notes that this is a copy of the concept used for the Tabernacle devised by Moses. The courtyard was where the mass of worshippers would assemble, and represented the multitude of the people; the Hall was where the *select*, priests and teachers, would assemble, and symbolised the Earth; whilst the Inner Sanctuary was entered only by the High Priest, and symbolised Heaven. Thus, in its simplistic form, the Temple building, with the two main rooms of the Hall and the Holy of Holies, was a symbolic representation of Heaven and Earth. The Inner Sanctuary was dimensionally a cube measuring 20 cubits x 20 cubits x 20 cubits. If the integers are multiplied together then the total is eight (8), and, as shown earlier, the number 8 symbolised the sacred cube. Thus, from Bede we can interpret the sacred cube as a symbolic reference to Heaven.

So, just how could Bede have come into contact with this knowledge in the first place? He provides us with an interesting answer. Section 3.3 in the translation of *De Templo* deals with the number of stonemasons, hewers of stone, quoted as involved with the building of the Temple. The text refers to the stonemasons as *latomi.* The Anglo-Saxon Dictionary defines the word *latomi* as *'A stone wright – a worker in stone – a mason'.*[10] The term *latomi* appears in a more recent document published by Kent Archaeological Society and referred to as *"Archaeologia Cantiana Vol. 58 - 1945 page 36, Recent Discoveries in the Archives of Canterbury Cathedral. A Note on the Craftsmen. By John H. Harvey"*. This document records the names of some of the key craftsmen associated with building works at Canterbury Cathedral in the 13th and 14th centuries. In this document a direct connection between the term *latomi* and *freemasons* is made:

> *'Probably the earthquake led to the stoppage of work on the new nave, which had been in progress since 1378. This, too, was taken in hand by Chillenden and carried to a triumphant conclusion; in the account for 1396/7 we see in brief the activity of a single year. The working staff comprised 20 freemasons (latomi) 3 setters (leggeres), and 4 labourers to assist them, all hired by the year at a total cost of £167 0s. 8d. This allowed for three unpaid holidays of a week each at Christmas, Easter, and Whitsun, as well as certain unpaid feast days. The current rates of pay would be approximately 3s. per week for freemasons, 2s. 6d. for setters, and 2s. for labourers, which would work out at rather less than 45 weeks' work in the year, or a total of some 30 unpaid festivals in addition to the three weeks' holidays. The masons were less fortunate than those employed on the King's works, where approximately half the 40 to 50 feast days in the year were paid.... '*[11]

The translation of Bede's *De Templo* and the *latomi* connection with the Temple, then states:

> *'These stonemasons, who figuratively represent the woodcutters, are the holy preachers who train the minds of the ignorant ... and strive to change them from the baseness and deformity in which they were born, and when they have been duly instructed, endeavour to render them fit to join the body of the faithful.'*[12]

From this, Bede is identifying the stonemasons as teachers, and to be a teacher requires that one has been taught and understands the significance of specific knowledge. The knowledge that was prevalent at that time was the same type of knowledge that I have termed *ancient knowledge,* which in more recent times has been known as the Seven Liberal Arts – grammar, rhetoric, music, logic, arithmetic, astronomy (astrology) and geometry. The Seven Liberal Arts were knowledge specifically attributed to the masons of old and transferred to Britain by stonemasons who came from France.

When the Romans left British shores some 250 years before Bede was born, construction of buildings reverted to the use of wood. The founder of the monastery at Jarrow was a nobleman named Benedict Biscop. He travelled widely and experienced life in monastic communities in Britain, France and Italy, and greatly admired the architecture and customs he encountered. He was, apparently, particularly impressed by the use of coloured glass in windows. Thus, when the building of the Jarrow monastery commenced, Biscop brought stonemasons and glaziers from France to erect the monastery buildings. Information presented by the Bede's World exhibition at Jarrow notes:

> *'At this time the Anglo-Saxon building tradition was to build in timber; the monasteries of St Peter's and St Paul's were amongst the first stone buildings in Northumbria since the days of the Roman Empire, and would have created an impressive statement in the landscape.'* [13]

The implication of this is that Benedict Biscop, who founded the monastery at Jarrow to which Bede was dedicated, brought stonemasons from France for the construction and that the *ancient knowledge* which was later known as the seven liberal arts, may well have been evident at Jarrow through those masons. So, is there any evidence that this might well have been the case? I suggest that there is.

Towards the end of the 19th century, Edward Condor became Master of the Mason's Company. He wrote a book entitled, *The Hole Craft and Fellowship of Masonry, with a Chronicle of the History of the Worshipful Company of Masons of the City of London.* In this book, Condor points out the link that inevitably existed between the masons of history and the ecclesiastical establishment. He notes:

> *'The masons at the cathedrals and other large ecclesiastical buildings were attached to the monastery, and often a technical school of masonry was founded by monks, who in teaching the craft would not forget the higher or symbolic meaning to be derived from the geometrical figures used in tracing sections... It was doubtless this geometrical knowledge which the early masons wished to keep a trade secret ... and by forming themselves into a brotherhood, they were enabled to accomplish this.'*

From this, we are given to understand that knowledge about the construction of substantial stone buildings was retained within the various monastic orders. A visit to the original site shows that the monks of the monastery at Jarrow, to which the Venerable Bede was attached, constructed very substantial quarters for themselves, together with an equally substantial church. Only a few ruins of the monastery now remain, whilst the eastern end of Bede's church has been integrated with a more recent church development. The original monastery was of cathedral proportions with massive stone walls, stairways, fire hearths, chimneys, doorways and windows – all of which required knowledge of the mason's craft to construct. Furthermore, this monastery was built several centuries prior to the subsequent great cathedrals in England, and the monasteries that were attached to them.

It is, therefore, possible that Bede encountered the mysticism and allegorical interpretation associated with numbers and geometric shape from the monks in charge of the building of the monastery, and he drew on that understanding when compiling his *De Templo*.

In the translation of *De Templo* we find an interesting description of the portico of Solomon's Temple. In section 6.2 it states:

> 'The portico in front of the nave of the house was twenty cubits long. It is obvious, therefore, that this portico was built on the east side of the temple. For the temple faced eastwards just as the tabernacle did, and had the vestibule door on the east opposite the temple door according to what Josephus the Jewish historian quite explicitly tells us so that the equinoctial sunrise could shed its rays directly on the ark of the covenant through the three doors, namely the portico, the temple and the oracle.' [14]

In his use of the term oracle Bede seems to be implying what is referred to elsewhere as the Inner sanctuary or Holy of Holies. Some other writers and model builders have interpreted the oracle to be a tower above the portico. The Catholic Encyclopaedia defines it as *"A Divine communication given at a special place through specially appointed persons; also the place itself"*. In respect of the Hebrews, the encyclopaedia then goes on to associate the word with the Ephod, which it describes as *"...a linen dress worn in ritual circumstances..."*. Throughout the related section in the encyclopaedia there is nothing to directly connect the word Oracle with the Holy of Holies of Solomon's Temple. We will return in due course to both the Oracle and the detail about the portico, mentioned above.

Ecclesiastical connections with masonry

Although the official line is that Freemasonry traces its origins to 1717, records exist that suggest that some form of organised structure existed at a much earlier date. Lists of previous Grand Masters of the Order date back to a time prior to the Norman Conquest. Most of these lists are derived from a work printed in 1795 entitled *Illustrations of Masonry* by William Preston. Preston notes that the principles of Masonry were known to the Druids and reintroduced to Britain by the Romans. Indeed, there is a stone that was unearthed in Chichester in the late 18th century which carries an inscription suggesting a connection with a fraternity of early masons. This stone was kept in trust by the Dukes of Richmond for many years on the Goodwood Estate, just outside of Chichester. In the 18th and 19th centuries various Dukes of Richmond had been either Grand Masters of the Order or held prominent positions of influence within it. Later, in the early years of the 20th century, they were the Provincial Grand Masters for the Masonic Province of Sussex, the county in which the stone was discovered.

The following is taken from the section of the *Illustrations of Masonry* that notes the *History of Masonry in England:* (Reproduced by courtesy of Robert Lomas.)

> *After the departure of the Romans from Britain, masonry made but a slow progress, and in a little time was almost totally neglected, on account of the*

irruptions of the Picts and Scots, which obliged the southern inhabitants of the island to solicit the assistance of the Saxons, to repel these invaders. As the Saxons increased, the native Britons sunk into obscurity, and ere long yielded the superiority to their protectors, who acknowledged their sovereignty and jurisdiction. These rough and ignorant heathens, despising every thing but war, soon put a finishing stroke to all the remains of ancient learning which had escaped the fury of the Picts and Scots. They continued their depredations with unrestrained rigour, till the arrival of some pious teachers from Wales and Scotland, when many of these savages being reconciled to Christianity, masonry got into repute, and lodges were again formed; but these being under the direction of foreigners, were seldom convened, and never attained to any degree of consideration or importance. Masonry continued in a declining state till the year 557, when Austin, with forty more monks, among whom the sciences had been preserved, came into England. Austin was commissioned by pope Gregory, to baptize Ethelbert king of Kent, who appointed him the first archbishop of Canterbury. This monk, and his associates, propagated the principles of christianity among the inhabitants of Britain, and by their influence, in little more than sixty years, all the kings of the heptarchy were converted. Masonry flourished under the patronage of Austin, and many foreigners came at this time into England, who introduced the Gothic style of building. Austin seems to have been a zealous encourager of architecture, for he appeared at the head of the fraternity in founding the old cathedral of Canterbury in 600, and the cathedral of Rochester in 602; St. Paul's, London, in 604; St. Peter's, Westminster, in 605; and many others. Several palaces and castles were built under his auspices, as well as other fortifications on the borders of the kingdom, by which means the number of masons in England was considerably increased.

Some expert brethren arrived from France in 680, and formed themselves into a lodge, under the direction of Bennet, abbot of Wirral, who was soon after appointed by Kenred, king of Mercia, inspector of the lodges, and general superintendant of the masons.

During the heptarchy, masonry continued in a low state; but in the year 856, it revived under the patronage of St. Swithin, who was employed by Ethelwolph, the Saxon king, to repair some pious houses; and from that time it gradually improved till the reign of Alfred, AD 872, when, in the person of that prince, it found a zealous protector.

Masonry has generally kept pace with the progress of learning; the patrons and encouragers of the latter having been most remarkable for cultivating and promoting the former. No prince studied more to polish and improve the understandings of his subjects than Alfred, and no one ever proved a better friend to masonry. By his indefatigable assiduity in the pursuit of knowledge, his example had powerful influence, and he speedily reformed the dissolute and barbarous manners of his people.[15]

Preston states that in 680 CE a group of masons were brought to England from France. This was the era in which Benedict Biscop commenced the building of the Jarrow monastery to which Bede was attached.

As can be seen, there are several references to monks, abbots and bishops in the period from the 6th century CE and there are still more in the period to the 14th century. The names include Bishop William de Wykeham who oversaw the building of Chichester Cathedral. In the period just after the Norman Conquest we find Gundulph, Bishop of Rochester, who not only oversaw the building of parts of Rochester Cathedral but who also built the Tower of London. The list of Grand Masters, or Patrons as they were apparently called until later times, starts with one *Austin the Monk*. And who was *Austin the Monk?* As we can see in the text by Preston, it turns out to be none other than St Augustine, the monk who, history tells us, brought Roman Christianity, the Roman Catholic Church, to England around 597 CE, converted King Ethelbert of Kent and his Queen to Christianity, commenced the building of the first Canterbury Cathedral, on which land the current cathedral stands, commenced and established the monastery of St Peter and St Paul in Canterbury, and in the process of all this became the first Roman Catholic Archbishop in England. The monastery to which Bede was connected was established in two conclaves, also known as St Peter's and St Paul's.

If Preston's assertions about the origins of Freemasonry are correct, and we consider the references to the term *latomi,* then it is clear that there was a very strong connection with the ecclesiastical establishment of earlier times. There are in Freemasonry certain elements of ceremonies that have a distinct appearance of ecclesiastical influence, an aspect of which, in the 20th century, various sections of the Church were critical. Yet it would appear that it is from the close association with the ecclesiastical establishment as former patrons of the craft that Freemasonry may well have inherited its outward appearance of ecclesiastical ritual. Edward Condor made this same point in his book *The Hole Craft and Fellowship of Masonry.* It was published in 1897.

It also adds weight to the suggestion that Bede would have encountered the symbolism of numbers as a consequence of an interaction with the building of the monastic community of which he was a part.

Sacred Geometry, *Ancient Wisdom* and the great Cathedrals of Europe

We have already noted that an understanding of geometry produces useful mathematical relationships, such as in the case of Vesica Piscis. This ancient geometric wisdom was also used for the plans of some of the great cathedrals of Europe, in what became known as the Gothic style. Probably the cathedral that is most admired and referred to is the great Gothic structure at Chartres, just southwest of Paris. It was one of the first four such cathedrals to be built in this new architectural style, the others being at Sens, Senlis and St Denis, just to the north of Paris.[16]

How the Gothic design originated has been the subject of much debate. It is now generally accepted that it derived from cultural influences experienced by the

Crusaders, and in particular, by the Knights Templar, during their period in the Middle East. One of their great supporters was a bishop who later became immortalised as St Bernard. He was probably not the originator of the design, but certainly championed its use.

The papal authority of the Roman Catholic Church dominated the whole of Europe in the era when the cathedrals were built. Inquisitions and persecutions dictated a strict observance of the religious doctrine the Church espoused. Along with that went philosophies about science and astronomy, the universal order and its relationship with the creation, the scriptures and concepts of Heaven and the afterlife. Progressive development slowed and Europe gradually sank into what has become known as the Dark Ages. By comparison, the Islamic world had become a progressive centre of enlightenment. Its understanding of geometry, numbers, arithmetic and shape grew, and this was reflected in the unique style of its architecture. The suggestion has been that masons associated with Islamic building principles were taken prisoner following various military actions and that they conveyed their knowledge to the invading crusader knights. Some were even shipped back to Europe to supervise the construction of particular buildings. From this, a new and enlightened use of geometry and proportion was evolved which led to the creation of the Gothic style. Thus, it can justifiably be said that the crusader knights, and in particular the Knights Templar, were influential in this architectural concept. The influence of the ancient use of geometry was not limited to the cathedrals built in France, evidence of such use can be found in English cathedrals as well.

Peterborough Cathedral

In England, Peterborough Cathedral shows evidence of how the masons of the medieval period used geometry to define the structure.

A small booklet on sale in the cathedral, titled *The Geometric Skeleton of Peterborough Cathedral,* illustrates how this was probably done. The booklet was compiled by Frederick Stallard, Canon Emeritus of Peterborough Cathedral, with the assistance of Paul Bush.

Many of the great cathedrals of Europe suffered damage by fire in the earlier medieval period: Chartres, Canterbury, Chichester and Lincoln were just a few of the casualties. Peterborough was another, having been gutted by fire in 1116. Fire is still a potential hazard for these wonderful buildings. Both York and Peterborough Cathedrals suffered similarly in the closing years of the 20th century, but thanks to the timely intervention and skill of dedicated firefighters and availability of modern fire appliances, the damage was contained and these ancient buildings were saved. If the incidents had occurred just a hundred years earlier they may well have been totally lost.

After the fire of 1116, rebuilding at Peterborough commenced. The result is substantially the structure we see today. Amongst its many attributes and, perhaps, its main claim to fame, is its use as the resting place for the body of Mary, Queen of Scots, immediately after her execution at the direction of Elizabeth I. Mary, Queen of Scots, was the mother of James I of England and VI of Scotland. Research in the late 20th century suggests that Freemasonry, as it is currently structured, follows principles set down in Scotland at the direction of James I (VI), known as the Shawe Statutes, so named after William Shawe who was directed by James to regularise Masonry in Scotland.

The work undertaken by Frederick Stallard and Paul Bush is praiseworthy in so far as the number of measurements that needed to be taken, plus drawings studied and made, would have been extensive and, no doubt, required no small measure of dedication over a prolonged period.

In short, Messrs Stallard and Bush came to the conclusion that the length of the cathedral was based on 10 squares, each with a side dimension of 39 feet, whilst the width across the transept was measured by 5 such squares. The total width of the nave is the equivalent of two 39-feet squares positioned side by side. A number of other key dimensions were based on multiples of 39 feet. The next key level of measurement is in squares of 78 feet, twice that of 39 feet, followed by the next level at 117 feet which is 3 times 39 feet, and then 156 feet. As a consequence of the use of this 39-feet dimension, most of the volume of the cathedral can also be defined in 39-feet cubes.

The measurement of 39 feet seemed to me to have been a strange choice for the medieval Master Masons in charge of the construction to have made. Why not round it up to 40 feet or down to 35 feet. Surely these would have been easier numbers to manage. There is a realistic problem with such speculation. What is now known as the Imperial unit of measure, feet and inches, was not formalised until around the reign of King Henry VIII, at least four hundred years after the rebuilding work at Peterborough was undertaken. A dimension of 39 feet is not something one just conjures out of the air. It had to have been derived somehow. I could find no evidence that any form of standard measuring device existed in those times which could be taken from one building site to another, other than the ancient measure of the cubit. The next prominent measure at Peterborough identified by Messrs Stallard and Bush was 78 feet. Interestingly, if we assume that one cubit is the equivalent of 18 Imperial inches, then 78 feet is the equivalent of 52 cubits. 52 corresponds with the number of weeks it takes the earth to orbit the sun one full cycle/circle. Was this coincidence? Somehow, I reasoned, the masons undertaking the work had to have had a method of determining measurements and standardising them for the project. That methodology would then have set the basis for the 39-feet measures that Messrs Stallard and Bush had uncovered. It took a lot of background reading before I was confident of a sustainable answer. When it came, the answer seemed obvious – it was connected with the Sun.

Sizing Peterborough Cathedral using the Sun – hypothesis

Through my research over the years, the range of material I had studied was immense, and the subject matter broad. I had spent a lot of time reading about the ancient monoliths such as Stonehenge and other similar ancient structures throughout the United Kingdom. This included those in the more northerly Scottish islands such as Orkney. The common factor between them was that they had all been constructed to denote key solar events, especially the equinoxes and solstices.

It was through this period that I encountered reference to investigations by one Professor Alexander Thom of Oxford University, who had commenced examination of such sites in the mid-1930s. He published most of his findings twenty years later, in the 1950s. From the detailed survey work he had undertaken he had reached the conclusion that the builders of these ancient monuments, some of which were dated to around 4,500 years old, had been built on a standard unit of measurement that he later termed a *Megalithic Yard (MY)*. He determined its length to be 2.72 feet or 2 feet 8.6 inches or 0.83 metres, just a few inches short of the modern Imperial yard. He also noted another measure, which he called a *Megalithic Rod (MR),* that he defined as being 2.5 times greater than the *Megalithic Yard.* The *Megalithic Yard* unit of measure seemed consistent in monuments as far apart as the Orkney Isles and the West of England. This clearly implied that these ancient peoples had a means of determining such a measure with some accuracy, as well as knowledge of geometry and astronomy. What Professor Thom was unable to determine was how it was done.

Fascinated by this mystery, and with wild dreams of solving it, I spent a lot of time thereafter trying to role-play the thinking of a person from 4,500 years ago, devising structures and poring over trigonometric tables, calculating angles and shadow lengths and monitoring the movement of the Sun using a computerised solar simulator, all with the objective of trying to find a repeatable solution – but to little avail.

It was then that two freemasons previously mentioned in this book, Robert Lomas and Christopher Knight, published their third book – *Uriel's Machine.* This book set out to investigate connections between certain Masonic ceremonies and the ancient religious text known as the Book of Enoch, and in particular a person referred to in the text as Uriel. In the past, Uriel has sometimes been presented as an angel or supernatural being. Lomas and Knight concluded that Uriel was probably a Druidic or Celtic priest, well versed in geometry, who understood many of the principles of the celestial mechanics of the Earth, and how that information could be used; and that Uriel taught others the secrets, who then transferred the knowledge to the Mediterranean civilisations who built on that understanding. The book concludes with an examination of the *Megalithic Yard.* Robert Lomas went one stage further and developed a method for reproducing it – using the Sun – and published the details on his internet website.

It was these same principles of measurement that I then applied to the geometry of Peterborough Cathedral. After several visits to the site, I came to the conclusion that the key measure was not the 39-feet dimension, but that of 78 feet.

Defining the 78 feet reference

In their booklet *The Geometric Skeleton of Peterborough Cathedral* Frederick Stallard and Paul Bush show some concise drawings to indicate the relationship between certain elements of the structure.

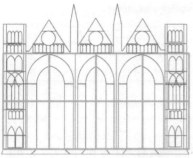
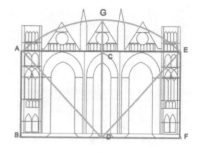

Reproduced from The Geometric Skeleton of Peterborough Cathedral.
Reproduced by kind permission of Paul Bush

In the text, they note how the front face is compiled of squares, each with a side dimension of 39 feet, how two resultant 78 feet squares determine the basic width, and how the resultant rectangular form determines the height of the triangular features above the main arches.

I felt there was a step before this. What is more, I felt that the guiding base of that step was built into the cathedral south wall – the representation of the pillars and arches that resulted in an illustration of Vesica Piscis.

It is also worth mentioning in passing that exactly the same pattern of vesica piscis can be found in the Knights Templar Round Church at the Temple, just off Fleet Street in London. It forms an entire gallery above the main body of the circular end to this famous church.

My conclusion was that when the layout of the cathedral was being considered, the front face started with three circles, each of 78 feet in diameter, connected in vesica form. This would result in the two outer circles defining the overall width and basic rectangular shape of the front façade, whilst the three centres of the circles define the vertical centres of the portal arches.

The Vesica basis of Peterborough

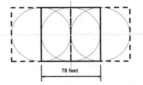

Using *the Mason's secret square*, previously mentioned, the 78 feet diameter circle and resultant square would be reduced to 39 feet. Three circles in vesica form, as with the 78 feet basis shown above, would set the position for the centre lines along which the supporting pillars would be constructed through the length of the Nave and Choir. Frederick Stallard and Paul Bush are quite right in their assessment that the length represents 10 squares of 39 feet diameter – 10 accords with Pythagoras' philosophy. The length and width could equally be defined by 5 squares of 78 feet. The value 5 was also a key value in Pythagoras' philosophy. The width of the transept is half the length of the cathedral. It would have been logical for the builder masons to reduce the size of the dimension by half using the *Mason's secret square* and then use the resultant size to determine the distance across the transept. It could also be used to set the vesica relationship that defined the line for the main support pillars. In addition, and based on the measurements I took at Peterborough, reducing the 39 feet square by half again, using the *Mason's secret square*, seems to define the spacing between the main support pillars along the length. Of course, I was able to reach these conclusions only as a consequence of the dedicated effort already made by Messrs Stallard and Bush.

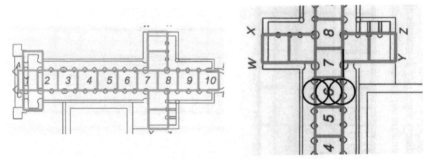

Reproduced by kind permission of Paul Bush. The Vesica Circles have been added by the author for illustration purposes.

Although these results were encouraging, they did not indicate how the 78 feet diameter, which I believe was the key dimension, might have evolved in the first place.

I couldn't help believing that somewhere in the design process, key symbolic numbers had been used by the Master Masons involved. I constructed a computer spreadsheet into which I fed all the key symbolic numbers I had encountered, and added, multiplied and divided them, looking for a result that came close. To my

astonishment, the key number which produced the closest result revealed itself to be 28.
78/28 = 2.785.

This result was so remarkably close to Professor Thom's measured value for the *Megalithic yard,* 2.83 feet, that I felt it couldn't be ignored. The variance is just 0.065 feet, which is just over 0.78 inches or 19.81mm. Over the full 78 feet dimension this would result in an accuracy of 2.3%. In a website produced as an appendix to *Uriel's Machine,* Lomas and Knight note that:

> *...the curious British measurement unit known as a 'rod' or a 'pole' is equal to 6 megalithic yards to an accuracy of one percent. There are 4 rods to a chain and 80 chains to a mile. Could it be that the modern mile of 1760 yards is actually based on the prehistoric measure of the Megalithic Yard?* [17]

Variances in the accuracy up to 3% would be well within the acceptable limits of error.

I could only conclude that at the time that Peterborough Cathedral was built, the masons of the medieval period used the same ancient method for determining their equivalent of what Professor Thom called a *Megalithic Yard* by using the shadow of the Sun. They then increased the length of the shadow 28 times to provide the comparative dimension of 78 feet, the number 28 being connected with the 28 days of light visible from the Moon which formed the basis of the lunar cycles used to regulate the Church proceedings. Thus, the same value of regulation was used to determine the outline of the structure and was linked directly to the macro-cosmos and God's creation as they understood it. Then, using the principles of *sacred geometry* – the *Mason's secret square* – they reduced or increased the 78-feet dimension, depending on their design needs. Hence the reason why the 39-feet squares identified by Messrs Stallard and Bush are so prominent.

All of this fits well with the evaluation work done by Frederick Stallard and Paul Bush. It approaches the dimensions from a different perspective and still arrives at the same relative values.

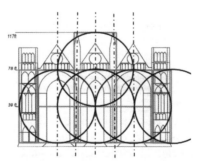

I hope Messrs Stallard and Bush will not mind too greatly if I superimpose an outline of the Vesica Piscis structure for the façade on a sketch they created and published in their booklet – *The Geometric Skeleton of Peterborough Cathedral.* In addition to the assessment made above, it seems to me that the overall width of the cathedral façade is based on three circles each of 78 feet diameter in Vesica Piscis, whilst two such circles in the vertical plane set the maximum height. This would accord with, and be symbolic of, the three positions of the Sun in the horizontal plane as it traverses the horizon, and with the Trinity, whilst two circles in the vertical plane would be symbolic of the duality of Heaven and Earth. The width from the centre of the circle to the centre of an adjoining vesica determined the width of the side towers, whilst the vertical centre lines running through the two vesicas in the horizontal plane determined the centre lines for the two pointed towers. The height of the two side towers appears to be 5 times the distance from the centre of a circle in the horizontal plane, to the centre of an adjacent vesica.

The sole purpose for my superficial investigation of Peterborough Cathedral was to try and determine if *sacred geometry* of the type well known in the ancient world, known to and used by the operative masons of the medieval period, seemed to be present in the design of this structure. The conclusion I reached was that it is.

I have subsequently provided this information to Paul Bush, co-author of the booklet *The Geometric Skeleton of Peterborough Cathedral*. He, together with the Dean of the Cathedral, has very kindly given permission for the selected sketches to be reproduced here.

As previously mentioned in passing, in their book *Uriel's Machine* Robert Lomas and Christopher Knight discovered a method of re-creating the *Megalithic Yard*. Robert Lomas has kindly provided further details about how this can be done. See Appendix 1.

Chartres

The town of Chartres is built on the side of a shallow valley through which a river runs. The cathedral sits prominently at the highest point above the valley. Most of the countryside that surrounds this valley is fairly flat. As a consequence of modern agricultural technique, what must, in ancient times, have been a substantial forest has given way to vast open fields. As a result, when one is approaching Chartres from almost any direction, the cathedral stands out in the landscape and can be seen from many miles away.

The present cathedral was built over a period of thirty years in the early 13th century after a fire completely ravaged an earlier cathedral, built on the same site in 1194. Substantial churches are believed to have been built on the site from the earliest days of the spread of Christianity, probably even before the collapse of the Roman Empire. It is revered, amongst its many qualities, as having escaped from many of the revolutions and destructive acts that have overtaken many of the other European cathedrals, in consequence of which, the guide books tell us that it serves today *'as an encyclopaedia of medieval life and faith'.*[18] Chartres achieved considerable wealth by being the custodian of an important Christian artefact that brought thousands of pilgrims flocking to the town. On public display in the northeast part of the cathedral, that artefact is known as the Santa Camisia, a piece of cloth presented to the Emperor Charlemagne in 876 CE from Constantinople, as having been the veil worn by Mary, mother of Jesus, at the time of Christ's birth.

Pilgrims later flocked to Chartres to view this relic and in consequence it became a very wealthy cathedral.

The cathedral is equally well known for a labyrinth built into the floor about halfway between the main doors at the front of the cathedral and the Nave. In reality the labyrinth does not appear to be in a position that is central between the Royal Portal and the transept. There has been considerable speculation as to what purpose it served. The generally accepted view is that pilgrims arrived at the cathedral, and then followed the labyrinth on their knees, reciting prayers until they reached the middle, as a spiritual awakening.

Although the interior of the cathedral is quite austere, with its walls blackened by the smoke and soot from burning candles over the centuries, the acoustics are remarkable, amplifying the singing of a congregation during a service with an unexpected clarity and resonance that sits easily on the ear. When a service has finished there is a gentle hum to the building at a pitch that is comforting and not the least bit intrusive, whilst shafts of sunlight through the stained glass windows to the south illuminate the interior with a delicately diffused light. The harmonious sounds and delicate natural light combine to create a feeling of calm.

At the eastern end, and around the Choir, is a very ornate screen, sculptured in stone, with panels depicting the most notable stories and events contained in the Bible. Even in the stonework above the doorways there are images depicting scenes associated with biblical text.

Chartres also became a major centre of learning, especially the study of subjects that later became known as the Seven Liberal Arts – arithmetic, geometry, astronomy, music, grammar, rhetoric and dialectic. The term *dialectic* is a slight variation on the usual reference of *logic*. It also boasts some the most remarkable stained glass windows in the world.

As a stalwart observer of the passage of the centuries, at the time of my last visit, large sections of this medieval cathedral were in obvious need of repair and restoration.

Chartres Cathedral has been the subject of considerable investigation over many decades. One such study was undertaken by George Lesser, an architect and member of the Royal Institute of British Architects (RIBA) in the mid-20th century. He conducted a wide examination of the use of geometry in the design of numerous churches and cathedrals across Europe, and published his findings in three volumes between 1957 and 1964.[19] Volume 3 deals almost exclusively with Chartres. Sadly Lesser died before he had the opportunity to see his final volume in print. Over many years, he devoted considerable time and effort to making site measurements as he explored how the masons of the medieval period set out the key structural positions. His resultant volumes contain many wonderful illustrations to substantiate his findings, and large fold-out diagrams to indicate the ground plane geometry.

In particular George Lesser noted the use of the octagram. It seemed to be present in many of the earlier cathedral designs. In particular I noted from his works that a number of structures conformed very closely to a scale dictated by two octagrams that touched.

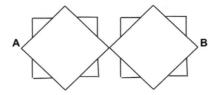

The outer edge of the horizontal octagrams set the width of the cathedral or church, whilst the ends A and B of the angled octagrams set the overall length.

When he reviewed the floor plan of Chartres, it revealed a series of squares, circles and octagrams that determined the key points.

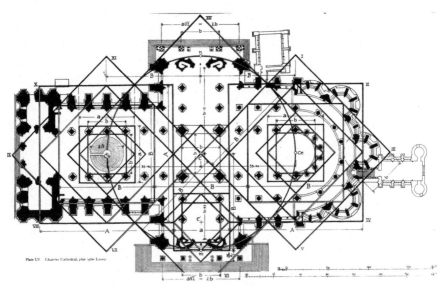

Plate LV. Chartres Cathedral, plan (after Lesser)

The main circle, at the centre of the structure, delineates the position of the labyrinth and the centre of the curved end of the Choir; they are both equi-spaced about the centre of the cathedral. This circle appears to be the governing factor. Not shown on this drawing by George Lesser is that two further circles of the same diameter as the one shown, and each drawn about the centre of the labyrinth and Choir, produces three circles in Vesica Pisces form, exactly as with the Peterborough Cathedral façade. And in the façade of Chartres Cathedral we find an image of the vesica. This then raises the question as to what dictated the diameter of the centre circle, because it is from that dimension that the proportion, at least in the length of the cathedral, seems to have been derived. Scaling plans, it seems to have been based on 12 squares of 12 cubits, or a circle 144 cubits in diameter or 72 cubits radius. This has relationships with the pentagram. Indeed, embossed at specific locations in the cathedral, one can find the image of the Star of David, the pentagram and, as previously mentioned, the vesica. But there may be another reason, which we will come to shortly.

The symbol of the vesica sits prominently above the main door of Chartres Cathedral, built in the 13th century. Within the vesica is an image of Jesus which underlines the reverence with which the symbol was regarded.

My last visit to Chartres was in mid-winter. When we first arrived it was a clear day with watery sunshine breaking through a cloud-studded sky. It was almost midday when, having entered by the west door and studied much of the interior, we exited via a door on the south side of the transept. It was clear from the shadows cast by the building that the orientation of the structure was not on the true east-west line found in many Christian churches, but oriented along a line with the eastern end pointing more in the direction of the northeast, at a compass bearing of just under 50 degrees. On returning home, I checked the compass bearing against solar angles for the solstices and equinoxes. I came to the conclusion that the orientation was in the direction of the first light of day at the time of the Summer Solstice, with the cathedral rotated around the centre of the transept.

On the subject of the orientation towards the Summer Solstice sunrise, there was more positive confirmation. In the library of the Royal Institute of British Architects I located a book titled *Chartres – Sacred Geometry, Sacred Space*. In it, the author, Gordon Strachan, confirms that the orientation is towards the Summer Solstice and draws comparisons with the layout of Stonehenge. He also notes that the cathedral is 37 Megalithic Rods wide across the transepts whilst the diameter of the Sarsen stone circle at Stonehenge measures 37 Megalithic Yards. This has close connections with my earlier views in respect of Peterborough Cathedral and I was particularly interested to note the reference to Megalithic Yard and Rod. Whilst Stonehenge is renowned for its solar alignment, it also has a certain axis which was

The west face of Chartres Cathedral

used for monitoring the Moon. The same appears to be the case with Chartres Cathedral. Gordon Strachan comments,

> *..its north and south spires, so different in styles and height, symbolize the Sun and Moon....Their two complementary cycles are ingeniously built into the fabric of the design in the form of two slightly different axes, which run the length of the building* [20]

One could only marvel at this hidden aspect of the design. As mentioned earlier, the Sun sets at the same geometric angle relative to true east as it has risen on that day. By virtue that the orientation was aligned to sunrise on the day of the Summer Solstice, then the western end would be aligned to sunset on the day of the Winter Solstice. Thus, at the Winter Solstice, which the early church selected as Christmas to overshadow the original pagan festive season, as the Sun moved around to the west and was fully in line with the centre of the western façade, so a broad beam of light would shine through the elongated window above the Royal Portal and along the centre of the cathedral. This would result in an illuminated pathway along the length of the Nave and Choir to an altar near the Ambulatory. The end of the Choir in the east is curved, as can be seen in the ground plan. As noted in the plan produced by George Lesser, the distances between the centre of the transept and the centre of the semi-circle at the end of the Choir, and the centre of the transept to the centre of the labyrinth, are equal. I could only visualise that on a bright clear evening, when the Sun was just sitting on the horizon, the shadow cast by the lower edge of the window corresponded with the top of the labyrinth whist the upper curve of the window corresponded with the curve of the screen at the end of the Choir. As the equinox is the centre point between the solstices, then on that day the bottom edge of the window corresponded with the centre of the labyrinth and the curved end of the beam of light would extend as far as the centre of the transept as the Sun passed around the west on the day of the equinox. At the time of the Summer Solstice the beam of light would shrink to touch the lower outer edge of the labyrinth. Thus, the diameter to the labyrinth would be a reflection of the Sun, and the ground plan of the cathedral would be reflection of a harmonious relationship with the natural rhythm of the cycles of the seasons, and thereby life, as created by the deity. This, I hasten to add, is only my speculation and I have found nothing, as yet, to substantiate it. I hope in due course to return on a suitable date to see if the theory is confirmed.

As we will see, a similar relationship of light and shadow also seems to have been incorporated in the design of Solomon's Temple, in which case Chartres Cathedral would also be a reflection of that same ancient knowledge.

Gordon Strachan also noted the harmonious tones that are created in the building and attributes this in part to the alignment of the two axes for the Sun and the Moon, which create a slight twist in the orientation of the structure. It is as if the building was tuned to give a controlled ambiance.

There is a view that the designers and builders of these magnificent cathedrals were attempting to re-create their perception of a space on Earth which was a reflection of the harmony of shape, form, light and sound that was likely in Heaven, thereby pleasing to, and at one with, the creator and Great Architect of the Universe.

Thus, in the fabric of Chartres Cathedral we find the same concepts of ancient wisdom and understanding that had been the domain of our more distant ancestors who had based much of their understanding on the natural environment and the macro-cosmos. Furthermore, Chartres was the primary centre of learning for the knowledge which is at the core of study that freemasons are encouraged to comprehend – the Seven Liberal Arts.

Barcelona

At the end of the 19th century, a young architect from the Catalan region of Spain and the city of Barcelona was making his way in the world, and a name for himself through his rather unusual designs. His name was Antonio Gaudi (1852-1926). One of Gaudi's greatest works was the design for a new church. Because a cathedral already exists in the city, the Gaudi design is known as a basilica – *Templo de la Sagrada Familia*. Gaudi was assigned the design work in 1884, following a dispute between the Catholic Church and the original architect appointed to the task. Gaudi started a completely new design and was associated with the project for some 40 years. Construction of this vast new basilica became a stop-start affair: there were financial difficulties, Gaudi's untimely death – killed in an accident with a street tram – and the Spanish Civil War. The latter brought a halt to the building work and resulted in the destruction of some of Gaudi's original drawings and models. One hundred years after Gaudi had created his original design the building of the basilica had made little progress. It was in the 1990s that a determined commitment to the task was finally agreed, and every effort is being made to ensure its completion in the first quarter of the 21st century.

I visited the building in the closing years of the 20th century. It was then still without a roof, but the main pillars were in place ready for it to be added. Beneath the main body of the structure, in an area compatible with the concept of a crypt, there was an exhibition of some of Gaudi's original concept drawings. There were models showing how some of the intricate decoration that adorn the outer façade was made. There was one small exhibit, not particularly distinguished, that most visitors passed with hardly a glance. I was almost guilty of the same attitude but as I passed so my eyes lighted on the word Chartres. This exhibit showed a number of the notes made by Gaudi, and in particular how he much admired the design of the Gothic cathedrals and had decided to create his own design based on the same concepts that had been used at Chartres nearly one thousand years earlier. As a result, the stonework around the main doors on either side of the church is festooned with elaborate images depicting biblical scenes, just as at Chartres. The purpose of some of the imagery is not immediately obvious. For example, beside a door on the south side is a plaque, carved in stone, which contains numbers in rows and columns. As I watched, hardly anyone gave them a second glance or commented on them. Yet, they contain a subtle message. When adding together the numbers in rows, columns or diagonally, the answer is always 33, the age at which, tradition has it, Jesus Christ was crucified. And Freemasonry has 33 degrees of attainment.

Also in the notes was a clear depiction of geometric proportion, and in particular with the Golden Ratio. He expressed that in the shape of the spirals used in stairways.

Although not completed during my visit, the outline of the east-facing wall was evident and in it was provision for very substantial windows of cathedral proportions. One could only imagine how the brilliant sunlight will flood into the cavernous interior. Whether the harmonious tone will be comparable with Chartres we will know only when the basilica *Sagrada Familia* is finally completed.

What Gaudi appears to have done, having recognised its value, is to reflect the same design parameters used by the medieval masons in a relatively modern structure that is a testimony to the wisdom, and oneness with the macro-cosmos, that our ancestors had achieved.

The connection with the Wardens

From this I concluded that the Master Masons of the medieval period still retained knowledge akin to that used by our ancient forebears about how to use the Sun, probably at the time of the equinox, to determine what to them was a standard unit of measure, a unit which they could easily replicate and retain by cutting a pole, or rod, to the length of the resultant shadow. This use of such a rod or pole to create a unit of measure in major construction projects would have been long before the standardised Imperial measure of a *rod* was conceived.

There are two senior offices within a Masonic Lodge whose task it remains to *mark the position of the Sun in the west* and to *mark the Sun at its meridian (midday)*. These two positions are known as the Senior Warden and Junior Warden. Coincidentally, the emblem of their respective offices is a pillar. These pillars vary somewhat subject to the interpretation of the Lodge. Generally speaking, they are made from a hard and durable wood and will each stand about a foot (0.3 metres) high. When the Lodge is conducting its business, the Junior Warden will lay his pillar horizontally, whilst that for the Senior Warden stands vertically. It stands to reason that if a pole, obelisk, pillar, or other similar device, were used to cast a shadow by which this unit of measurement could be derived, then two people, well versed in the knowledge, would need to work together. One would monitor the position of the Sun relative to the vertical pole, interpreted today in the role of the Senior Warden, whilst the other would have the task of marking the length of the shadow cast by the pole and thereby setting the unit of measure when instructed by the Senior Warden to do so. His role is reflected in the position we now know as the Junior Warden. Thus, these important duties, and the skill and knowledge attached to them, are remembered today. The vertical plane is that with which the Senior Warden worked, and is reflected by his pillar being placed erect when the Lodge is conducting its business, whilst the horizontal plane was that in which the Junior Warden worked and is reflected in his pillar being placed horizontally.

It also follows that, in addition to reconstructing the unit of measure, these two skilled masons could use the same technique on any day of the year when the Sun shone to determine the four cardinal points: north, south, east, west. This would enable the N-S and E-W axis radiating through a central point to be used for constructing a right-angle square, a tool that would be needed by the builders. And, keeping in mind that most early Christian churches were named after saints, and the centre line of the church would be aligned to that point on the horizon where the Sun rose on the feast day reserved for that saint, then the same marker and shadow procedure could be adopted for determining the line of orientation.

The pole or obelisk that the masons used in their work would probably have had the upper end shaped to a point which would enable more accurate marking. Sadly, in many lodges new innovative representations of these *poles* have crept in, some showing globes representing the Earth, whilst others display the characteristics of classical architectural columns such as Doric or Corinthian designs. It would seem that such designs may be misplaced and that an obelisk shape is probably more in keeping with the traditional furnishings of the Lodge room.

The two freemasons that we now call Senior and Junior Warden would have been very important individuals in the development of any building project in ancient times, hence their seniority today, closely connected to, and in support of, the Master of the Lodge.

Light instead of shadow

There are of course occasions when a beam of light would be equally as effective as a shadow.

As mentioned earlier, as part of my research I visited Egypt on three separate occasions, looking at the structure and design of temples and other aspects of their ancient civilisation.

My second visit to Egypt centred on Cairo, expressly for the purposes of seeing the Sphinx, the pyramids and the Egyptian Museum. I took the opportunity of several tours that were on offer. These included a visit to the stepped pyramid at Saqqara and the remains of the old capital at Memphis. There was yet one other tour I felt I couldn't pass up. It was to the ancient city of Alexandria. Included in the itinerary was a visit to a Coptic monastery, set at a desert oasis, about halfway between Cairo and our destination.

The Coptic monastery proved to be more interesting than I had expected. The complex had originally been founded in the early centuries of the Christian religion. We were met by a very congenial monk who had an impeccable knowledge of English. He acted as our guide, showing us where the monks ate, slept and entered periods of solitary contemplation which could last from a few days to several years.

Thus it was that we visited the main church late in the morning. The Sun was climbing to its zenith whilst its rays reflected off the desert sand with almost blinding brilliance. As we left our shoes outside, we could hear the intoning chant of a priest from within the church. It was obvious that a service or ceremony was in progress. As we entered, I felt uncomfortable that our tour party, about 12 people, was intruding on what was taking place. It wasn't just that we had walked in on the ceremony, but that we were invited to pass round the inside of the room and observe everything on display whilst the priest continued chanting and praying, without hesitation – unmoved by our arrival. The main room of the church was dimly lit by a single light bulb hanging in the centre of the room, directly above a lectern that the priest was using. The atmosphere was thick with a smoky haze from the burning of incense and candles. The smoke hung almost motionless in the air for want of a breeze that would disperse it. A small gathering of about eight people sat cross-legged on the floor in front of the priest. These people, we were told, came from a nearby village. They had with them a sick child. They had asked the priest to pray for the deliverance of the child. This only made me even more uncomfortable about our intrusion.

By the time of our arrival in the church, the priest, we were told, had been offering prayers for several hours. Despite our visit the priest continued chanting and reciting prayers, and whilst he did so the monk who was our guide explained that the priest would carry on his ritual for about two hours more, as he did at this time every day.

The main body of the church led off a corridor that provided the only entrance route. As everyone from our tour party filed around the church, I noticed that the only lighting in the corridor came from a small square opening set high in a wall at the furthest end of the corridor from the main door. Through this opening, the bright light of the Sun was concentrated into a narrow beam about nine inches square. The smoky atmosphere created by the burning incense and candles clearly delineated the shaft of light. This beam reflected on a white plastered wall directly opposite the position where the priest was standing. He could see it but his congregation had their backs to it. We spent some three-quarters of an hour in this part of the monastery complex and passed this wall on three separate occasions. I could not help noticing the way the beam of sunlight had moved down and across the wall as the Sun outside had moved higher in the sky whilst making its southerly transit. It became obvious to me that this was the clock that the priest used to time his daily ritual. Irrespective of the time of the year, the shaft of light would strike one edge of the white plastered section at the same time each day. Depending on the season the position would move up and down the wall corresponding with the position of the Sun above the horizon. As the two-hour period progressed and the Sun rose higher in the sky, so the beam of light would move down and diagonally across the plaster. When the shaft of light had moved off the plastered area, two hours had expired and the priest knew it was time to stop. It was a simple demonstration of the use of the Sun as a timepiece. I couldn't help but wonder how many tourists each year passed through that corridor and missed this link with an ancient but effective use of the Sun and the principles of celestial mechanics. It was a wonderful revelation. This was a working example of the simple, yet effective, technology of ancient times - an understanding we have almost forgotten about in our modern 21st century world – the use of the Sun as a timepiece.

Light – and the temple of Abu Simbel

It was on my first visit to Egypt that I made the journey from Aswan (Syrene) to Abu Simbel. Threatened by the rising waters of the River Nile and Lake Nasser after the completion of the Aswan Dam in the mid-20th century, this temple was seen as such an important artefact of ancient Egypt that it was cut, piece by piece, from the face of the cliff that originally housed it, and reassembled in a safer location above the waterline. I had watched documentaries and read magazines showing the engineering feats associated with the mammoth task of removal and reassembly.

As we walked down the dusty stone-strewn track that led to the complex, I was filled with excitement at the prospect of actually seeing and touching this ancient monolith. The excitement was more than justified. It was awe-inspiring. It was everything I had ever seen in pictures.

The temple of Abu Simbel was built by Ramesses II, also known as Ramesses the Great. In chapter 10, I refer to the subject of historical and biblical chronology. From the information gathered. I have produced a table which shows that Ramesses was contemporary with Rehoboam, the Israelite king who succeeded Solomon. Thus, the building of Abu Simbel was probably commenced about thirty to fifty years after Solomon's Temple was completed. Ramesses II has been identified in the chronology as the Pharaoh Shishak[21], who invaded Jerusalem during the reign of Solomon's son, Rehoboam, about twenty-five years after the Temple had been completed. Shishak/Ramesses the Great, made Jerusalem subservient to him and took away much of the Temple gold and silver in payment for not razing the city to the ground.[22] This triumphant venture by Ramesses II is recorded in the wall panels of Abu Simbel.

The entire façade of Abu Simbel is oriented to face the east. Cut into the cliff face is the entrance doorway to the temple. The doorway is flanked on either side by two massive statues of the pharaoh and his queen. Above the door is a hawk-headed statue of Ra Harakht complete with sun disc on his head. This is not surprising for this temple was supposedly dedicated in part to the Sun god, Amon-Ra, and featured what was called the *miracle of the Sun.*

Although the temple is some 125 feet (39 metres) wide by 210 feet (65 metres) long, the small doorway belies the magnificence of the interior. In fact, the doorway seems inappropriately small by comparison with the size of the statues that flank it and by the size of the cavern one enters with its massive supporting pillars. But, the doorway is deliberately small because it had a practical purpose.

Leaving the bright sunlight behind and entering the temple, it took some minutes before my eyes had fully adjusted to the relative darkness of the main chamber. Two rows of magnificently carved pillars, each in a representation of human form, and so large that a 6-foot-tall man is dwarfed by them, stand guard, watching all who pass beneath. At the rear of the main hall is a small doorway leading to the Holy of Holies, a small room wherein four compact statues are engraved in the end wall. The statues represent Amon-Ra – the Sun god, Rameses II, Harmakis – another name for the term Sphinx which in turn means 'Horus who is on the horizon', and Ptah – the god of darkness.

Around the time of the Spring Equinox when the Sun is travelling north along the horizon, for a short period at dawn a shaft of light penetrates the doorway in the façade, along the full length of the hall and between its guardian statutes, on into the Holy of Holies and illuminates on successive days, Amon-Ra, then Rameses II, followed by Harmakis. The alignment and size of the two doorways, plus the overall length of the hall and Holy of Holies, is such that the shaft of light is then extinguished before it reaches Ptah – the god of darkness. Obviously at the time of the Autumn Equinox when the Sun is moving along the horizon from the north and towards the south, so the order of the illumination process is reversed whilst Ptah remains in the dark.

As I left the dark of the hall and emerged into the bright sunlight outside, I noticed a shallow range of hills on the far horizon, on the opposite side of the River Nile - Lake Nasser. There was a clear path for the light of the dawn Sun to travel to the temple. From where I stood in front of the temple the top of the hills on the horizon seemed to be lower than the entrance doorway. In consequence, I mused, the light would be sloping uphill between the doorway and the Holy of Holies at the rear of the inner chamber. I re-entered the temple and, much to the amusement of other visitors, I fell to my knees and looked along the length of the stone temple floor. Sure enough, the temple had a slight uphill slope from the doorway in the façade towards the Holy of Holies, for optimum alignment. It was such a gentle slope that it was virtually impossible to detect it whilst walking around inside.

Once outside again, I accosted our guide to ask if there were special tours organised to witness the solar event for which the temple had been built. Alas, no. He went on to add that since the relocation of the temple it didn't work quite as well as it used to. The surveyors, he pointed out, with all the latest instrumentation and computer technology of the time, had made an error in the calculations and it wasn't quite so accurately aligned any more. This only served to increase my admiration for the masons of 3,000 years ago who had originally carved it, and the skills they had possessed.

Abu Simbel, Peterborough Cathedral or Chartres Cathedral, the men who created these excellent monuments were truly wonderful masons.

Conclusion
1. It seems that Pythagorean principles, which he no doubt taught in his mystery school together with the geometry for which he is also credited, were well known to at least some members of the ecclesiastic establishment during the early years of the spread of Roman-based Christianity in Europe.
2. The symbolism of number appears to have been well established, especially with Bede. His remote location would imply that such symbolic interpretations were well understood and accepted within the Church.
3. The ancient principles of geometry, including the use of the Vesica, was knowledge understood and practised by the operative masons that designed and built the great cathedrals of Europe.

With the above information now to hand, it seemed appropriate to test the design of the Masonic Temple in Sussex to see if the same principles were involved there. If so, it would imply that they remained an important component of Freemasonry until at least the end of the 19th century.

[1] *Fingerprints of the Gods* – Graham Hancock, Part VI, chapter 34
[2] Dionysius Exiguus at www.wikipedia.org
[3] Information available in displays at Bede's World, Jarrow and also on www.bedesworld.co.uk.
[4] Bede: *On the temple*. Translated by Sean Connolly and with an introduction by Jennifer O'Reilly. Published by Liverpool University Press 1995.
[5] Tomes, R. "Divided by a Common Scripture: Jewish and Christian Approaches to the Bible." http://www.art.man.ac.uk/RELTHEOL/JEWISH/TomesFT3.htm.
[6] The Catholic Encyclopaedia, Book of Paralipomenon

[7] Connolly, S. (1995) with an introduction by Jennifer O'Reilly. Bede: *On the Temple*, section 18.6.

[8] Bede section 22.3

[9] Bede section 2.3

[10] The anglo-Saxon Dictionary – online at http://dontgohere.nu/oe/as-bt/read.htm?page_nr=912

[11] Harvey, J. H. *Recent Discoveries in the Archives of Canterbury Cathedral* A Note on the Craftsmen--
www.kentarchaeology.org.uk/Research/Pub/ArchCant/Vol. 058%20-%201945/05/36.htm

[12] Bede section 3.3

[13] Information available in displays at Bede's World, Jarrow and also on www.bedesworld.co.uk.

[14] Connolly, S. (1995) with an introduction by Jennifer O'Reilly. Bede: *On the Temple*, section 6.2

[15] Preston, W. *Illustrations of Masonry* (online version), Book 4, History of Masonry in England, Sect. 2 - History of Masonry in England under St Austin, King Alfred, and Athelstane; and also under the Knights Templars. Transcribed by Geraint and Robert Lomas and available on line at http://www.robertlomas.com/preston/padlock/book4/index.html

[16] Chartres, *Sacred Geometry, Sacred Space* by Gordon Strachan

[17] Appendix to *Uriels Machine*, Lomas and Knight

[18] *Chartres Cathedral*, text Malcolm Miller – Pitkin Guides

[19] *Gothic Catherdals and Sacred Geometry* by George Lesser. Vol 1 1957, Vol 2 1957, Vol 3 1964

[20] *Chartres, Sacred Geometry, Sacred Space* by Gordon Strachan, page 12

[21] *A Test of Time* – Dr David Rohl

[22] Holy Bible, New International Version, 2 Chronicles 12

Chapter 7
Sacred knowledge resurfaces

*.....For treating of the description of the celestial objects, about the form of the universe, and the revolution of the heavens, and the motion of the stars, leading the soul nearer to the creative power, it teaches to quickness in perceiving the seasons of the year, the changes of the air, and the appearance of the stars; since also navigation and husbandry **derive from this much benefit, as architecture and building from geometry.***

Old Testament

The wisdom of the ages. I felt I had accumulated sufficient understanding to begin trying to resolve some of the aspects of the Brighton Temple, and Masonic Ceremonies, which had intrigued me and set me on the course of enquiry in the first place.

Vesica and the design

The basic design of the temple was the first to be easily solved. An old illustration from the 1920s provided a clue and, later, a copy of an architect's drawing confirmed that the length and width of the room was based on 3 circles, each of 40 feet diameter in Vesica Piscis form.

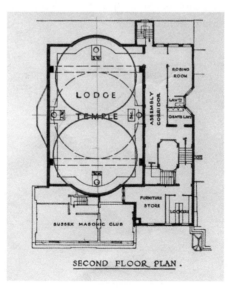

This quickly led to solving the puzzle about the pattern in the front door step. This too proved to be derived from Vesica Piscis.

The symbol on the front door step

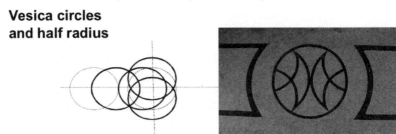

**Vesica circles
and half radius**

It was as if, in placing this design in the front step, and in a glass panel above the door, it was a pronouncement that on entering the building one was entering a place where there was an understanding of the principles of the interlocked circles, Vesica Piscis, and thereby of ancient geometry and wisdom.

It was not a misplaced idea. I have in an earlier chapter made reference to the black and white tiled floor and how, by taking a measure to it, I had discovered that it seemed to be based on the cubit measurement, and that it measured 12 cubits wide by 24 cubits long, resulting in the perimeter measuring 72 cubits.

The intertwined circles of 40 feet diameter in Vesica Piscis, used to define the width and length of the main temple, revealed a connection with the temple floor. Keeping in mind that the floor can also be interpreted as having a measurement in cubits, I discovered that by drawing the vesica based on 2 circles each of 40 cubits diameter, the largest rectangular area, created by two equal squares, that could be derived within the vesica, and remain in proportion with the room, was exactly that of the floor, 24 cubits long, 12 cubits wide.

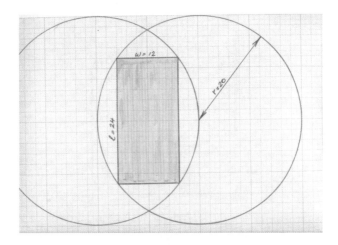

The zodiac

The zodiac which dominates the ceiling proved to have an interesting alignment which serves two purposes. First there is the alignment of the constellation of Aries which sits directly in front of the Master's chair, the chair of King Solomon. This is clearly a record to indicate the era in which events surrounding him took place.

The constellation of Aries sits directly above the chair of King Solomon

And secondly, in so doing it reminds us that the axis of the Earth has a slight wobble which results in the relative position of the belt sliding backwards by one constellation in about 2,160 years, a process known as Precession of the Equinox, which takes around 25,960 years to complete its passage through all 12 constellations. What is more, the chequered floor directly beneath it has a perimeter with a numerical value of 72. It takes 72 years for the effects of precession to advance the belt just one degree. If we take the 2,160 and drop the zero, we have 216, and this is the product of 6 x 6 x 6, i.e. 666.'

Six hundred, sixty and six

As we have noted:

1. In early religious organisations the number 6 was sacred because the Old Testament states that God had created the world in 6 days.
2. To the ancient philosophers the number 6 symbolised *harmony and beauty*, and was even associated with marriage.
3. The importance of the number 6 is represented in the Star of David, which is a 6-pointed star and was also considered a lucky talisman.
4. It was seen as the most pure number being both the product and sum of the first three, i.e. 1 + 2 + 3 = 6 and 1 x 2 x 3 = 6.

139

5. The number 6 also symbolised the Sun.
6. As we have seen there is a direct relationship between the number 666 and the Precession of the Equinox through the number 216(0) which is the product of 6 x 6 x 6. Precession can be observed over a long period of time by noting the progressively moving position of the presiding constellation at dawn on the morning of the Spring Equinox.

For many years this number, 666, has been associated with evil. It is implied that this association derives its origins from the Bible's Book of Revelation, where the number 666 is referred to as the number of the beast. The Book of Revelation text reads:

Here is wisdom. Let him that hath understanding count the number of the beast: for it is the number of man; and his number is six hundred, three score and six. Revelation 13:18

This connection with a beast was progressively challenged in the closing years of the 20th century as historians recognised that Jerusalem, 2000 years ago, was a city being occupied by an invading force – the Romans. It was a time when rebel inhabitants were engaged in what is best described as 'terrorist activity against Rome'. This insurrection grew in momentum through the decade of the 60s CE, until it was finally crushed by the Romans at Masada in 70 CE. It is speculated that the reference to 'the beast' was a code in use at that time, meaning Rome and its Emperor.

To me, the interesting line is *for it is the number of man.* The Old Testament states that the lifespan of man is three score years and ten. I wondered therefore if the reference to man was 66 + 6 = 72. So, in a man's lifetime, precession will advance the constellation belt by one degree.

The Romans treated these sacred numbers with the same reverence as the ancient peoples of Egypt, Babylon and Greece. In the Roman counting system the letter (I) counts as 1; the letter V as 5; the letter X as 10; the letter L as 50; the letter C as 100 and the letter D as 500. If you add together these numerical categories, or six number groups, the answer is 666.[2]

Another key number is 36, which is 6 x 6. Equally significant is the fact that if you take all the numbers in the sequence 1-36 and add them together the answer is 666.

The Book of Revelation is not the only one where there is mention of 666. When I processed a word search of an electronic copy of the Old Testament, I found a reference much earlier, in the Book of Ezra.

' and the children of Adonikam' six hundred, sixty and six.' Ezra 2:3

But perhaps most surprising of all is that my computer-based word search found the first reference to the number 666 in the Old Testament directly relates to the main personality attached to my enquiries: King Solomon.

'Now the weight of gold that came to Solomon in one year was Six hundred, three score, and six, talents of gold.' 1 Kings 10:14

Gold at that time, partly because of its colour, also symbolised the Sun. So we have two symbolic references to the Sun in one single passage of the Old Testament; gold and the number 6 x 6 x 6 = 216(0).

Whilst certain aspects of the number 6 were held in special reverence, there are other combinations which appear regularly in the Bible; for example, just as 6 x 6 x 6 = 216, and 36 is 6 x 6, so 72 is (6 x 6) + (6 x 6); 36 = (6 + 6 + 6) + (6 + 6 + 6); 12 = 6 + 6. All these numbers appear in the Brighton Temple.

Looking for Pythagoras

The temple connections didn't stop at the number 6. Around the walls is a pelmet, from behind which diffused subtle lighting is emitted. The pelmet is decorated with florets of nine petals. From the connection with Pythagoras, this is the symbol of man. Knowing that Pythagoras' teaching had been an element of Masonic life early in the 20th century, it suggested that there should be more such evidence. In particular I looked for evidence of two other numbers: the number 8 and the number 10.

Again, earlier in this book, I mentioned that the chequered floor of the temple was arranged with the area inside the border being 10 tiles across and 22 long. Here at least was one example where the number 10 existed. By drawing a line across the centre then, two rectangles of 10 cubits by 11 cubits resulted, which meant nothing. So, I decided to create squares 10 cubits x 10 cubits. I did this by taking the entire width of the inner pavement and then 5 cubits on either side of the centre line. To my amazement it produced the exact dimensions of the Golden Ratio.

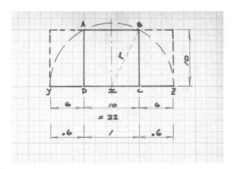

Indeed, in the graph above the arc clearly produces points Y & Z at a distance marginally larger than 6 to reflect 0.618. 10/6.18 = 1.618. And, there is harmony with the number 10 because there are 6 squares balancing either side of the central 10 squares.

Something I had not expected was also produced. By treating the size of the square as 1 unit instead of 10 units then I could also treat the 6 units on either size as 0.6 or the value of Phi = 0.618. And it didn't stop there, because

0.618 + 1 + 0.618 = 2.236 which is also = √5.

'G' is for Geometry

The research Lodge, Quatuor Coronati, and various books written by eminent freemasons, point out that the letter 'G' when displayed in a temple, does not mean God, as many prefer to imagine, but that it actually means Geometry. The centre of the Brighton Temple is dominated by two letter 'G's. One is in the light fitting above the centre of the pavement. This we can probably accept is a reference to the Grand Geometrician of the Universe. That in the centre of the pavement, probably refers to Geometry only, as we will see.

I have already mentioned that one of the most common symbols found in Freemasonry is the pentagram. It seemed logical to believe that somewhere in the room, a pentagram or pentagon was easily defined based on the pavement geometry. Images of the pentagram often feature a circle in the centre, and the fact that there are two circles in the centre of the pavement was not lost on me. Sure enough, a pentagram perfectly fitting with the outer of the two circles and the pavement dimensions, soon revealed itself.

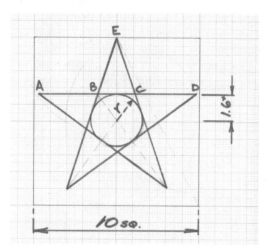

By linking the outer of the two pavement circles to the design of the pentagram, it seemed that all was complete. However, the purpose of the innermost circle was not yet defined; neither were the lozenge-shaped devices which link the two circles.

When first looking at this design one can easily draw the conclusion that it is a symbolic representation that the Grand Geometrician of the Universe is at the centre of all creation, *from whence all goodness flows*, and that the lozenge shapes are decorative arrowheads linking our material world (the pavement as mentioned earlier) with the grand design. But there are other possibilities:

1. There are eight lozenges. The number 8 was one I was looking for because in Pythagoras' philosophy it symbolised the sacred cube. The sacred cube symbolised the world. The Knights Templar are known to have revered the number 8 and its connection with the Holy Sepulchre, where, according to tradition, Christ was buried. By the time of the Knights Templar, the Christian doctrine was referring to Christ as 'the light of the world'. Further, in the Islamic Holy City of Mecca, the primary artefact of reverence and worship is a cube – the Kaaba.

2. In geometry there is a figure which can be constructed from a pentagon/pentagram called an icosahedron. This is a complicated structure which, when rotated, creates the same optical presentation as is evidenced by the lozenges.

3. That it is derived directly from natural phenomena associated with the Sun.

4. That the circles dictate further geometry which results in these patterns.

Further Possibility – Shadow alignment

We must remember that we look at the world in this new millennium with the benefit of the knowledge, experience and technology that we have today. When building a new and important structure, our ancestors in ancient times did not have sophisticated laser technology theodolites or digital imaging. Their theodolite was the Sun, and the shadow cast by it. It is well documented that early civilisations, and in particular the Egyptians, used shadow poles for this purpose. These shadow poles were in the shape of an obelisk. An obelisk usually has a pyramid-shaped top. The point at the top provided an excellent marker for the end of a shadow.

In the sketch below, imagine that the triangle ABC is one face of a pyramid. The Sun rising just above the horizon at dawn and illuminating the face pointing towards the Sun would result in the face ABC being in shadow, and the resultant shadow cast would be somewhat elongated, ADC. The shape DCBA is equivalent to the *lozenges* within the centre circles. The letter 'G' is also yellow – the colour of the Sun. Could this be to signify the important role of the Sun as used by our ancestors as they set about constructing new edifices?

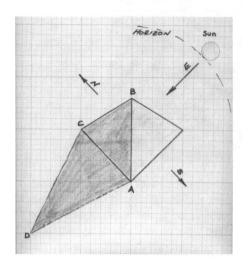

Consider the photograph of the circles above, again. There are eight such lozenges. Thus, the angular displacement between them, is 45 degrees (360/8=45). The lozenges do not start on the vertical or horizontal axis. They are offset by 22.5 degrees. This corresponds with the nominal angle of tilt in the Earth's axis. This could mean that the lozenges signify the eight major points on the horizon that would have been important to our ancient brethren; North, South, the eastern and western horizons at the times of the equinoxes and solstices- what today we call the tropics and the equator. They could further signify that the angular position relative to south, when the sun is at its meridian, would be the same when the sun rises on the horizon in the east , as it is to the angular position relative to south when it sets on the western horizon

As the Sun rises in the east ... as the Sun sets in the west ...
The Earth constantly revolving on its axis in its orbit around the Sun ...

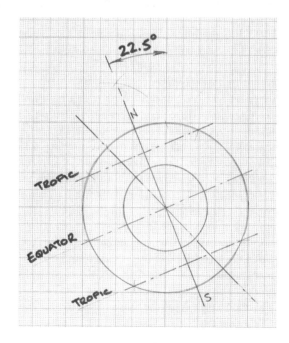

Sacred knowledge resurfaces

Almost as if drawing attention to the use of the shadow, the window grilles in the temple also show obelisks and semi-circular patterns that relate to the passage of the Sun across the horizon at both the solstices and the equinoxes.

The pointed vertical bars are of the same design as a classical obelisk. Furthermore, the centre for the scientific priesthood of ancient Egypt was supposedly based at Heliopolis near Giza. There were two obelisks at this location that were later moved to Alexandria by the Romans. One was dismantled in the 19th century and now now stands on the banks of the River Thames in London. We know it as Cleopatra's Needle. The installation on the Embankment was apparently conducted with full Masonic ceremony.

Further Possibility – Geometry based on the circles

With the larger of the two circles at the centre of the pavement at 1.5 cubits radius, a circle is drawn, and a pentagon constructed within it. A second circle is then drawn, also of 1.5 cubits diameter, so that it touches the base line of the pentagon at points A and B. A further pentagon is then constructed as a mirror of the first. Connecting the two pentagons as shown in the diagram below produces the same symbol as the lozenges at the centre of the circles. Keeping in mind that there is so much other geometry associated with the Temple, it seems highly likely that this geometric solution, again based on the number 5, is a particularly appropriate one. But there is one small variation. Two sides of a pentagon do not provide a 90° inside angle. However, all is not lost, as we will see.

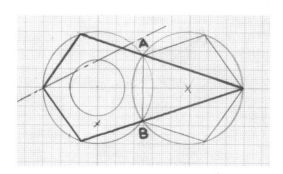

The Sacred Geometry of the Octagon and the Star of David

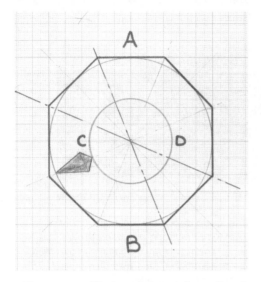

Sacred geometry appears in many religious buildings. A further example is the octagon. As with all such geometry it can be produced easily with the aid of a pair of compasses and a straight edge, such as a square.

The octagon illustrated above shows that the starting point is a circle, surrounded by a square. A line drawn between the opposite corners of the square, and passing through the centre of the circle, creates an angle of 45° relative to the vertical and horizontal axis. Bisecting this angle will create divisions of 22.5°, the angular displacement of the lozenges in the centre circles.

Octagonal geometry was an important sacred geometry used by the Knights Templar in the construction of their churches. They used this geometry to build churches which were round on the outside and with eight supporting pillars within, or octagonal in outer shape, of which many fine examples are still in use in Europe. This geometry was used in Templar holdings which are still in existence in Britain: at Rosslyn Chapel near Edinburgh, The Round Church in Cambridge, The Round Church in Northampton and the Round Church at the Inner Temple, just off Fleet Street, London. Where the church is round, the eight supporting pillars are also positioned on an inner circle whose diameter is related to the outer walls.

I took a steel measuring tape on a visit to the Round Church in Cambridge. My measurements suggested that the inner circle, which provided the centre line for the supporting pillars, was at a radius of 6 cubits, and the outer walls at 12 cubits, making an overall diameter of 24 cubits. Thus the inner circle is half the diameter of the outer.

This is exactly the geometric ratio of the two circles at the centre of the pavement in the Brighton Temple. From these two circles a six-pointed Star of David can be created, as an alternative method to the one previously shown using Vesica Piscis.

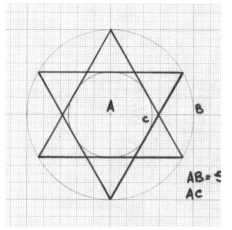

The radius AB creates the centre circle of 58" diameter, whilst radius AC creates the inner one of 29" diameter.

The sides of the triangles are at a tangent to the edge of the innermost circle, and create equilateral triangles.

Thus, we have a pentagram (5-pointed star) around the outer edge of the circles, enclosing a Star of David (6-pointed star) within them.

We must now refer back to the sacred geometry of the octagon. The sloping sides of an octagon have an inner angle of 135°, which means that, in the configuration shown in the earlier diagram where it is offset by 22.5°, the sloping sides are either 45° from the horizontal or vertical.

This combination of octagon, pentagram, and double circles, reveals one last geometric symbol in all its glory …

Square & Compasses from basic geometry

The symbol opposite is derived from the 10 cubit square around the centre of the pavement which also defines the value of Phi. The outer edge of the Compasses is the outer edge of the legs of the pentagram. The Square is derived from the lower sloping sides of the octagon. The inner edge of the leg of the Compasses corresponds with the angular relationship of the equilateral triangles (Star of David) based on two circles.

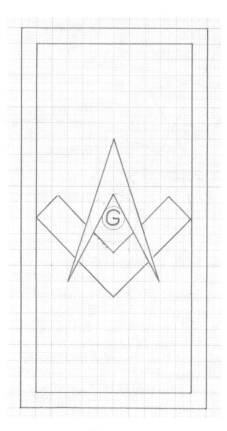

The above diagram shows the hidden design set against the pavement in the Brighton Masonic Temple. But that is not all there is. Let us again return to the two circles.

The Square and Compasses

The origin of the Masonic emblem of the Square and Compasses has been the subject of debate in Freemasonry for many years. There have even been suggestions that the symbol originated in China, thousands of years ago.

It was whilst watching a television documentary on the subject of war machines created by the Roman Army that a new possibility emerged.

There was a particularly large catapult, which had the ability to deliver a very large boulder against the city walls of a defending army. Part of the programme centred on reconstructing, and then demonstrating, a replica of such a device. This proved to be a major feat of engineering that included the use of substantial timber frames. To gain authenticity, those undertaking the reconstruction joined the timbers using joint methods typical of the period. They mentioned that in medieval France all the typical joints that a carpenter might encounter were given the names of birds. So, by remembering the names of birds and joints associated with them, all the carpenters of that trade knew what type of joint was being referred to. One can imagine a letter sent from one carpenter to another saying something like, '... and for the upper part of the structure use magpie joints'. Most people wouldn't have clue what that meant but it would have been a very effective coding system amongst carpenters of the period. The makers of the reconstruction model pointed out that such symbolism was used in other trades in the Guild system in France.

Having been able to easily construct a Square and Compasses emblem in the pavement geometry, it occurred to me that this Masonic emblem may well have been a means which enabled an operative mason of ancient times to demonstrate to others his knowledge of geometry, a knowledge of such significance that he would be seen as a master of his trade – a Master Mason.

With this thought in mind I spent several months looking at documents relating to the various Guilds that were available in London, but could find no supporting evidence to substantiate the theory. But then, if it was a trade secret it would not have been written down for all eyes to see. There is a sentence in Masonic ceremony where a candidate states that he:

>...*will not write those secrets, carve, mark or otherwise them delineate on anything...so that the secrets of a mason may be inadvertently revealed.*

Is it possible that the Square and Compasses emblem which so defines Freemasonry, could be viewed in the same manner as the motifs used by the French carpenters?

Geometric Constants in the Temple

Vesica Piscis has already been mentioned at some length. In addition to creating a rectangle of representative size equating to the dimensions of the floor, it enables the definition of certain mathematical constants, such as the values of:

$$\sqrt{2} = 1.414$$
$$\sqrt{3} = 1.732$$
$$\sqrt{5} = 2.236$$

Each of the above is a ratio of x:1.   (rounded to 3 places of decimals)

Finding $\sqrt{2} = 1.414$

As previously mentioned, the outer edge of the pavement of the Brighton Temple measures 24 cubits x 12 cubits. This means that the area of the pavement can be divided into squares each of 12 cubits. As each edge of each resultant square has sides that are equal, we can therefore consider each side to have a numerical value of 1.

Thus, the two squares (pavement) can be seen as a ratio of 1 wide to 2 long or (12 cubits + 12 cubits) long by 12 cubits wide.

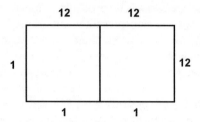

Let us say that in the Brighton Temple, each pavement square is 12 x 12

$$a^2 + b^2 = c^2 \quad 12^2 + 12^2 = c^2 \qquad\qquad so, c= \sqrt{144} + 144 = \sqrt{288} = 16.97$$

However, to return to the ratio of 1, we must divide by 12.

Therefore, $16.97 \div 12 = 1.414 = \sqrt{2}$

Producing $\sqrt{}$ - the pavement

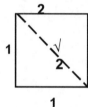

Finding $\sqrt{3} = 1.732$

We have already seen that the size of the Brighton temple is based on 3 circles in Vesica Piscis, where each circle is 40 feet in diameter. Thus, each circle has a radius of 20 feet.

We now create two circles in Vesica Piscis each representing 40 feet diameter or 20 feet radius.

Producing $\sqrt{3}$ in Vesica Piscis

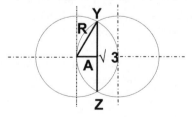

The angular line (R) represents the hypotenuse of a right-angle triangle. The horizontal line (A) is the base of a right-angled triangle. Because the hypotenuse (R) is drawn from the centre to the circumference of the circle, it has the length equal to the radius, 20.

The horizontal line between the circles is at a point which is half the radius. So, if the radius of a full circle is 20, then half the radius is 10.

Thus, the vertical side of the triangle is half the length of the solid vertical line (YZ):
So, by applying Pythagoras' theorem:

$a^2 + b^2 = c^2$ $10^2 + b^2 = 20^2$ so, $20^2 - 10^2 = b^2$ so, $400 - 100 = 300$

therefore, $b = \sqrt{300} = 17.32$

The vertical line (YZ) is twice the length of the triangle's vertical side.

Thus 17.32 x 2 = 34.64

However, it should be to a ratio of 1. We have a ratio of 20.
34. 64 ÷ 20 = 1.732 = $\sqrt{3}$.

Conclusion

The original creator(s) of the design of the Brighton Temple clearly possessed a most awe-inspiring knowledge of Sacred Geometry and it's effect on, or heritage within - Freemasonry. Somebody at sometime, had clearly gained wisdom and understood how it could be used. Much of it was presented as one thing, but revealed something else entirely – which is an allegory, and in Masonic ceremonies we are told *Freemasonry is a peculiar system of morality veiled in allegory.....*

a.   The zodiac is rotated so that the sign of Aries sits above the chair of king Solomon.

b.   The length of the temple is dictated by the width of the room, which is defined by the diameter of a circle.

c.   The tessellated floor size corresponds to the largest rectangle that can be made in a vesica.

d.   There are the mathematical constants $\sqrt{2}$ $\sqrt{3}$ $\sqrt{5}$.

e.   The ability to display the value of Phi = 1.618 and 0.618

f.   The presentation of a pentagram.

and many more items not immediately obvious.

I decided to assess if the Sussex Masonic Temple geometry might apply to Solomon's Temple, and thereby establish a positive link with Freemasonry. That dictated that I took a closer look at biblical texts, following through any links.

What I found was that when one views and investigates religion from an academic perspective rather than faith, a whole new range of possible explanations of biblical events begin to surface. These new explanations are only possible with the value of recent discoveries in science and archaeology that were not available to our forebears of one hundred years ago.

It is the biblical texts that I next turned my attention.

[1] *Fingerprints of the Gods* – Graham Hancock
[2] *Genisis* – David Wood

Chapter 8
Things may not be as we were taught

WARNING:
There are aspects of religion considered in this chapter that those of an intense religious conviction may be uncomfortable with.

Traditional education in the mid-20th century taught that organised civilisation started around 5,000 to 8,000 years ago, about 3,000 to 6,000 BCE. This is because decipherable documented history appeared to evolve from about that time. It was in this era, we are given to believe, that the ancient civilisations of Egypt, Sumer and Akkadia, began, the latter being in what later became known as Mesopotamia. From these beginnings, we were further led to believe, the domestication of animals commenced; plants were specifically selected, their seeds gathered and sown on specially prepared ground; it was the beginning of organised farming; it was, supposedly, the start of the epoch when settled and stable communities commenced and enabled the development of subsequent civilisations. Immediately prior to this initial period of settlement, our ancestors were supposed to have been little more than hunter-gatherers wandering the plains, were of minimum intelligence, and still wielded stone clubs. By the close of the 20th century the accumulated field evidence, and subsequent evaluation by archaeologists, had provided us with a very different perspective.

Recently discovered ancestor knowledge
Excavations at Çatal Höyük, in modern Turkey, show evidence of a very advanced community living in an early form of shallow multi-storey apartment blocks. Çatal Höyük was discovered in the 1950s and is thought to have been founded between 7,000 BCE and 8,000 BCE, some 4,000 to 5,000 years prior to the development of Ancient Egypt. There are some archaeologists who believe Çatal Höyük to have been the first city, from which our western civilisation originated. The inhabitants kept domesticated animals, grew selected crops, ground a species of primitive wheat into flour, had scrupulously clean accommodation lined with plaster that was ornately decorated and which was replaced about every six months. It is also believed that the religious cult of the Mother Goddess as a symbol of fertility and life may even have commenced in this area. For reasons which are still unclear the entire community appears to have deserted their relatively safe and secure collective. Where they went is also still a mystery.

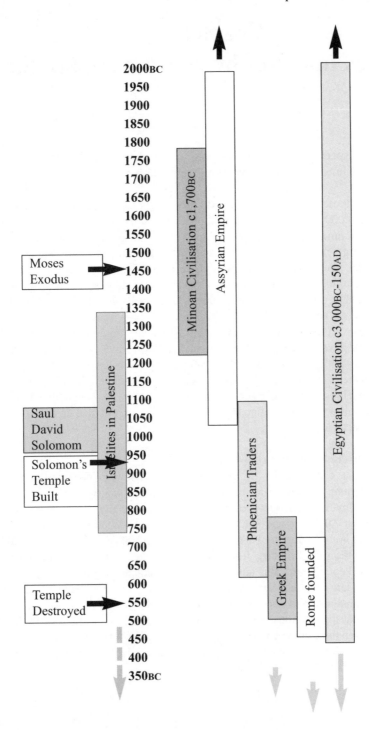

Things may not be as we were taught

Before the so-called Ancient Egyptian civilisation developed around 3,100 BCE another advanced group established themselves on the Mediterranean islands of Malta and Gozo. This culture built what are now regarded as the oldest free-standing stone structures in the known world. Long before the Egyptians began to develop their prowess in building with stone, the inhabitants of Malta and Gozo had built impressive temples out of large stone blocks. Even as early as 4,500 BCE they appear to have developed a concept of moving very large stones by manoeuvring them on specially carved stone balls, rather like large ball-bearings. This is a unique application which does not appear elsewhere. They had mastered the art of cutting and lifting large regular stone blocks and organising them into tight-fitting courses; they made circular protective walls and they carved delicate images into selected sections.

At Taxien, towards the southeast of Malta, one can still see carved in rocks, the outline of several animals that must have been common to the island several millennia ago, when the images were apparently created. Certain aspects of the temples had clear stellar alignments indicating that these people had knowledge of the movement of the heavens. The official archaeological view is that specific passages were oriented towards sunrise on the day of the Winter Solstice, which perhaps implies that they were following a tradition of celebrating the potential return of the warmth of the Sun and the new life it would bring – the repeating of nature's cycles exactly as the Celts and Druids are known to have done. Linked with these cycles, and from the discovery of carved figures of large voluptuous ladies, they also appear to have had a religious belief centred on the Mother Goddess as a symbol of fertility. And such was their skill and ability in working with stone that in some cases, perhaps for important ceremonial reasons, rather than building a square opening as a doorway using four pieces of manageable stone, as can often be seen in later temples in Egypt, they cut a hole for a doorway right through one large piece of rock, a feat of craftsmanship and accuracy which would challenge any modern highly trained stonemason, quite apart from the difficulty of transporting and managing the stone in the first place. Using what we are led to believe were relatively simple tools, they managed to drill holes in stone which possibly provided sockets for the fitting of wooden poles that might have acted as a gate or door. And, equally astounding amongst the relics that have been discovered was a large stone pot, with relatively thin walls and curved in the style that graced many later civilisations around the Mediterranean. By definition, this pot had to have been carved from one piece of stone. Whilst these impressive temples and their usages were probably at their peak around one thousand years before construction of the impressive pyramids of Giza was even commenced, their origins are believed to date from as early as 5,000 BCE. Indeed, a display on a tourist information board at one of the temple sites, notes that by 4,500 BCE these unknown peoples had developed clear architectural styles that distinguished buildings used for ceremonial and ritual purposes by comparison with that related to purely domestic use.[1]

On the island of Crete in the Mediterranean Sea, within striking distance of the coast of Palestine, there once existed the impressive Minoan culture. This civilisation was reaching the end of its prominence at the time the first Jerusalem Temple was built. Yet, this civilisation had previously flourished for around one thousand years. The reason for its decline centres on a massive volcanic eruption on the nearby island of Santorini. The eruption created tidal waves and earthquakes that demolished many of the prominent Minoan buildings. It is also believed that many Minoans died in the aftermath and that, as a result, the social cohesion of this once prosperous people was seriously undermined. A visit to the remains of the Minoan community at Knossos, a community that existed 3,500 to 4,000 years ago, reveals an impressive understanding of civil works. One can still see the remains of stone ducts used for the distribution of fresh water, and there are separate ducts for carrying away waste. The people of this civilisation were very skilled in the cutting and finishing of stone, achieving remarkably smooth surfaces. Their temples were oriented on an east-west axis; decoration in palaces was colourful and with walls covered in plaster; their handicraft abilities were effective and demonstrated a high degree of skill. This can still be seen in the very large terracotta pots used for the storage of grain and other food products. Ships, delivering and taking a variety of trade goods, were moored in a small natural harbour just below the city. After the Santorini eruption, the earthquakes that followed resulted in a significant lifting in the land so that today the remains of Knossos are some distance inland from the sea that once lapped at its doorstep. It was a civilisation that clearly achieved a high level of sophistication.

In the latter days of the Minoan culture it is highly probable that some of the ships that visited Knossos were owned and operated by a group of traders that later became known as the Phoenicians. Based along a short strip of land that today forms part of the Lebanon, Phoenicia was really a group of individual city-states that operated in alliances with each another. One such city state was Byblos, known to us as Tyre – the domain of Hiram, King of Tyre, who is connected with building the first Jerusalem Temple.

All of the above cultures were based on the shores of, or in close proximity to, the Mediterranean Sea. Little or nothing was known about them amongst the wider public of western society until after the mid-20th century. Such that was known was the domain of those with specialist interest. Changes in education and the availability of mass media entertainment have enabled such discoveries to be brought to the general public in interesting ways. Linked to this has been the progressive development of scientific techniques associated with archaeology, together with a substantial growth in the numbers of people employed in the archaeological discipline. The end result has been new and credible information coming to light which has changed our understanding. And, that change has occurred in a relatively short period of time.

In our western culture of the early 21st century, there are many individuals who are in a position to travel and see for themselves the sites and remains of these ancient cultures. This reinforces the speed with which a change in acceptance of such new discoveries has permeated our society.

Communication, too, has contributed to a changed perspective of the earlier cultures and technologies available to our ancestors. This has come as the result of enabling more and more people to have access to information that, as mentioned above, was previously regarded as the privileged domain of a select few. Television documentaries have helped turn the crusty and musty world of history and archaeology into entertaining education of the masses; well known archaeologists have become the modern treasure seekers and adventurers discovering priceless relics and uncovering secrets of the past. Inevitably, some of those secrets from the past have included information that the governing bodies would rather we had not been made aware of, as such revelations may have a tendency to undermine the authority and credibility of certain long-standing institutions of our civilisation. Communication systems, coupled to information technologies, have also enabled the assembly of many individual pieces of otherwise isolated strands of information into a catalogue. When sorted and compared, the data has sometimes revealed an historical pattern of events with dates that have completely undermined previous estimates of the development of civilisations and their technologies.

In the mid-20th century, I was taught that the boomerang was a hunting implement, evolved over thousands of years, and unique to the aboriginal peoples of Australia. Imagine my surprise then, when on a visit to the Egyptian Museum in Cairo, I found a cabinet displaying boomerangs, dated from around 2,500 BCE and uncovered in archaeological excavations in central Egypt. When I made further enquiries about the origins of the boomerang I found that it was a popular device amongst the aboriginal peoples of Australia, Egypt and the area we now know as California in the United States of America. Looking at a map of the world, one can see that these three locations are very remote from each other. This raises questions about where the device may have originated from, and more to the point, how did the technology of creating it, and making it work aerodynamically, come to be transferred to three different cultures that are very isolated from each other?

Conventional education of the 20th century told us that the Iron Age commenced about 3,000 years ago. Making iron involves collecting and mining iron ore rocks, and then melting them. That is just the start of the technology. Next would have come a whole series of trial and error activities to understand how best to fashion it into the device that was wanted, and for it to be useful. So it was with surprise that an iron hammerhead, complete with the remains of a wooden handle, was discovered in Texas in the 1930s, embedded in a lump of sandstone on a ledge near a waterfall.[2] The implication is that such a hammer must have been made a very long time ago, possibly several thousand years prior to the supposed start of what we are educated to believe was the only Iron Age of civilisation.

These points demonstrate that our ancestors were far more knowledgeable and skilled than they have previously been given credit for. There is also ample evidence that highly sophisticated civilisations existed well before the timelines produced in the mid-20th century might suggest.

These discoveries and changes in our understanding of history are not limited to the science of archaeology. They spill out into the world of religion and theology. They have the ability to change our perceptions about what may have really happened in biblical times together with the chronology and timelines over which those events occurred.

If, therefore, there were far-reaching changes in our understanding of human history over the past 3,000 years, it may also affect the way in which we view certain religious practices. It may change the way we view certain events we read about in the Old Testament. This may place Solomon's Temple, and what it was used for, in a very different context to the one that many people have been encouraged to believe was the reality. A picture in the mind's eye, built up and stored over a prolonged period, could be shattered.

Let the truth come out!!

Our faith in religious events and their meaning

For most people their experience of religion commences at a very early age. Within the Christian Church first exposure may be as a baby through a naming ritual referred to as baptism, a ritual where the parents acknowledge that the child will be brought up within the structure and dogma of the Christian faith. Over the next few years these children may be subjected to attendance at mainstream church services or at Junior Church – where they are given special instruction and introduced to the main biblical characters and events. They may even attend special faith-based schools for their formal education, an environment which reinforces the faith regime. In some cases this process of indoctrination is reinforced by the educational curriculum supported by the State. Thus, by the time the child has completed its first decade of life he or she has been effectively brainwashed and conditioned into a realm of dogma, protocol, bias and superstition. Some people move away from this culture later in life until they totally reject the entire philosophy; some become less active but periodically their subconscious prompts them from the roots of the culture and superstition in which they have been influenced; others remain resolute in their faith with total acceptance of the dogma and adherence to, and belief in, every word that is recorded in the religious scriptures. To this should be added deference to, and acceptance of, those who promulgate the religious message. The same type of process applies to all the main religions of the world, including Christianity, Islam and Judaism.

This strong and unbending adherence by 'the faithful' undoubtedly causes problems of social tension, if or when alternative logical opinions that affect religion are presented based on well-thought-out explanations. There have been certain events that, in biblical terms, were deemed as miracles. In the absence of any logical explanation for the miracle at the time the occurrence was recorded, the event was viewed by the scribes in the context that there must have been some form of divine intervention on the part of the deity. Having been advised of such by priests of earlier generations this idea has subsequently been accepted in every detail, unquestioningly, by 'the faithful'. Archaeological evidence and scientific developments may now enable us to present a logical explanation for such *miraculous* events and, in so doing, undermine the concept of divine intervention. We are only now able to present new interpretations of events seen as miracles in the climate of scientific and academic research and the accumulation of knowledge that exists today. This has enabled certain events previously interpreted as miracles to be explained in a manner that could not have been contemplated, or was even possible, a lifetime ago.

The plagues of Egypt

According to the Old Testament book of Exodus, a series of plagues were visited on Egypt during the period when Moses was seeking to lead his people out of that country. In recent centuries these plagues have been presented by the religious establishment as miracles that were visited on the Egyptians in support of the Israelites, by their deity, to aid their escape from bondage. These plagues included darkness falling over the land, the River Nile seemingly turning to blood, plagues of frogs, flies and locusts, and terrible sores and boils being visited on the people who lived along the banks of this major life source. These visitations can now be explained as a series of concurrent natural events, one being influenced by another, one setting the circumstances from which another was able to develop.

One theory is that the darkness was caused by volcanic ash, perhaps from the eruption on the island of Santorini. The eruption is known to have been extremely violent, blowing the island apart and hurling volcanic dust and debris several miles into the upper atmosphere. This dust and debris would ultimately have been circulated around the world in the upper atmosphere, and caused climatic problems everywhere. In particular it would have created a dark blanket in the geographical region close to the eruption, blotting out the intensity of the Sun, which in turn would have caused a drop in temperature. At the same time there could have been pollution in the River Nile caused by falling volcanic ash. The pollution would have killed the fish which in turn would have further polluted the river. The frogs would have left the river to escape the pollution but being already infected they died on the land. This, together with the dead fish being washed along the shores of the river, could have created conditions for a big increase in flies and lice which transmitted disease to cattle. This caused the cattle to die. The river being so polluted would have resulted in the water being impossible to drink. So, as recorded in Exodus 7:24, the Egyptians dug holes, probably wells, to gain access to drinking water. Those who did drink the polluted water from the River Nile ended up with boils and sores over their body as the bacteria contaminated their bloodstream.

Indeed, there is evidence that similar events have taken place in more recent times. A BBC TV documentary about Moses reported an incident which occurred in 1999 at New Burn, North Carolina, USA. The River Neuse turned a red colour, as if it had become stained with blood. Local people found sores developing on their skin, just as it is reported in the Bible as having happened in Egypt some 3,500 years earlier. The cause of the North Carolina incident was found to have been a mutation of a micro-organism called pfisteria, which in turn had been affected by pollution from a pig farm.[3]

To the Egyptians experiencing the series of plagues which befell them three and a half thousand years ago, and to the scribes who were recording them, such events may well have been interpreted as the gods wreaking vengeance on them for some misdemeanour. It would have been an event which would have caused great concern, and stories that reflected experience from that era would have been retold to subsequent generations and passed into folklore. The Israelites, on the other hand, who may not have been so badly affected, especially if they were not living in close proximity to the River Nile, may well have seen such visitations as a miracle performed in their favour by their protecting deity.

Despite the availability of modern scientific evidence that is able to demonstrate precisely how these events may have occurred, there are those in charge of presenting the religious dogma, such as priests and bishops, who will continue to promote the idea that a miracle had been performed by the deity and instil belief in it by the faithful.

The story of Sodom and Gomorrah

As another example consider the story of Sodom and Gomorrah as told in the Old Testament book of Genesis, chapter 19. In this story, we are told that the inhabitants of these two towns, Sodom and Gomorrah, had become so morally and sexually depraved that the deity had wreaked his vengeance by destroying them with fire and brimstone in a cataclysmic event. Not all the inhabitants of the towns were killed. The hero of the story is a man named Lot, who, together with his wife and two daughters, was given the opportunity to escape, but warned not to look back lest they be turned into pillars of salt. As they made their escape, Lot and his wife could hear the destruction of the towns going on behind them. Lot's wife, unable to contain her fascination for the awesome noise of destruction which was taking place behind her, did the one thing she was told not to – she stopped and looked back, and was immediately turned into a pillar of salt, there to remain for ever.

As such, this story has been presented for hundreds of years with a moral undertone to encourage a chaste and upright existence within the society in which we live, lest the deity might deliver his vengeance on any society which becomes wicked and ungodly. In the absence of any other information, this tale, and the context in which it has been used, would have served a good purpose as a moral lesson for past generations.

Today, however, dedicated research indicates that Sodom and Gomorrah were probably small communities which formed part of a group of five towns that existed on a once fertile plain adjacent to the Dead Sea. The Dead Sea is so called because of its very high salt content resulting in virtually nothing being able to live in it. Sodom and Gomorrah were probably built around 3,000 BCE. It is highly probable that the five towns existed to exploit the gathering of asphalt – found in lumps in cliffs along the edge of the Dead Sea. The asphalt was a trading commodity used for waterproofing boats and fixing stone blocks in the construction of important buildings – such as temples, in the absence of the mortar/cement that we have come to know today.[4]

Current scientific and archaeological investigations suggest that about 2,500 BCE this once fertile plain and the towns that stood on it were subjected to a violent earthquake which caused a massive landslide. During the earthquake a process known as liquefaction occurred, that is, where previous hard ground becomes fluid, rather like water, and the pressures caused by the tremor squeeze moisture out of the soil and create a flow of water where previously none had been seen to exist. It is akin to hard ground suddenly taking on the characteristics of quicksand. Under such circumstances, buildings would have sunk into the ground. The chances of survival of anyone living in the towns immediately affected would have been virtually zero; Sodom and Gomorrah would have slipped into the Dead Sea and any trace would have been lost to the casual observer. Models produced at Cambridge University demonstrated how this could have happened. In addition it has been shown that even today pockets of methane gas can be found just beneath the surface of the countryside close to the Dead Sea. In an earthquake such pockets of gas could escape and ignite, creating a land of fire and brimstone.[5] Brimstone is another word for sulphur, which has a horrid, acrid smell. Satellite surveys, a technology only available to archaeologists since just prior to the end of the last millennium, have enabled the potential remains of the towns to be located beneath the waters of the

Dead Sea, and thus made available for further investigation.⁶ The story of Lot and his two daughters is probably, therefore, a record of the escape of just three survivors from a traumatic earthquake experience that destroyed their homes.

Based on scientific analysis of the event, we can further speculate that this is the story of a family who were in a position to turn and flee towards higher ground as the earthquake started, led by the father of the household. One can imagine that during the pandemonium, Lot could be heard yelling to his family, something like *'Don't stop or pause to look back. Get as far away and as quickly as you can. Keep moving. Just don't stop to look back, every second counts.'* Lot's wife, however, possibly slightly to the rear of the fleeing party, hesitated and looked back to see if any of the people she had known, her friends and relatives, were also fleeing. But, she was on the edge of ground that was affected by the liquefaction. She slid into it and was absorbed as if she had fallen into a pit of quicksand. As the town toppled and slid into the Dead Sea, so she too was carried with it. It could be interpreted that the reference to the *pillar of salt* was a means of conveying that she was absorbed by the Dead Sea, her body to remain encrusted and disintegrated by the high salt content of the waters. Imagine too that, as Lot and his daughters continued their escape, the earthquake enabled columns of methane gas to ignite creating the fire, accompanied by the acrid smell of the escaping sulphur, hence the fire and brimstone. It is easy to comprehend how these events would be immortalised thereafter. Continuing the speculation, let us imagine that, with nothing left but the clothes they stood up in, Lot and his daughters finally reached another nearby town; in the book of Genesis it is named Zoar. Here the escapees would have related their tale and the fate of Lot's wife. It is not difficult to imagine how this story would have become a lasting tale told around the Bedouin camp fires and how it then passed from generation to generation until it was written down, two thousand years after the event, as a point of history by the scribes of the day. It is entirely understandable how people in subsequent epochs, learning of the event but denied the accumulated knowledge that we have at our disposal today, would interpret it as an act of God and have recorded it as such and passed it on to still further generations. It is also understandable how Lot could be set as the 'good guy' character in the story, against the depraved excesses of the two cities of Sodom and Gomorrah. And, because he was the 'good guy' with a sense of moral fortitude he was encouraged by the deity to escape.

The name of Jesus

When it comes to references to Jesus Christ there are many Christians who believe that that there was a person with the forename Jesus and the surname or family name of Christ, who walked the countryside of Israel and Palestine 2,000 years ago. They believe he was named just as today we might refer to somebody named William Smith in our culture – William would be their first name and Smith their surname or family name. The New Testament gospels were originally written in Greek. The name Jesus is derived from the Greek name Jesu, which we might interpret as Joshua. In Hebrew the name Joshua would become Yehoshua.⁷ The word

Christ appears to have several meanings depending on your source. It is the Greek interpretation of the Hebrew word Messiah which has been interpreted as the one to be crowned as King of the Jews. During a visit to Egypt I was advised that word means *the anointed one.* This definition is not too far from the Hebrew interpretation. So, someone who had been appointed as a leader or ruler of a group, and invested with specific powers of authority, a process which may have required a ceremony wherein the selected person was anointed as a means of conferring that authority, could be referred to as *the Christ.* Indeed, the monarchs of England are anointed, signifying a form of tribal leader through what is known as the Coronation. The monarch is anointed with oil as part of the process of conferring authority. Taking it to its logical conclusion, the anointing process is declaring a monarch as a *Christ.* Thus, using the term *Jesus Christ* is really a shortened version of a more proper statement of *Jesus the Christ,* or Yehoshua – the one who was anointed to have the authority as the tribal leader. But that is only the definition in our culture. It has been known for some decades that the person we refer to as Jesus Christ would in his own culture and time have been known as *Yehoshua Ben Joseph* – Yehoshua son of Joseph. This is a revelation that most of the faithful are unaware of, but which many theologians and priests have known of for many years. Indeed, it is such common knowledge that it is presented in the Catholic Encyclopaedia.

This reference to name structure and meaning will be shown to have significance in another context later, directly related to King Solomon.

A conjuring trick with bones

So, against the background outlined by the Sodom and Gomorrah incident and the Christ naming examples, it is hardly surprising that when a senior cleric or academic puts forward a concept which flies in the face of the accepted dogma then that person is likely to be pilloried and held up to contempt by those who constitute 'the faithful' in our community.

Such an event occurred at the start of the last decade of the 20th century when the then Bishop of Durham, the Rt Rev'd David Jenkins, stated that to accept the idea of a supernatural conception of Christ and the subsequent Virgin Birth was not a requirement for being a Christian. Yet both of these concepts have formed a plank of Christian dogma for around 2,000 years. It has been construed as a miracle and promoted as such by religious organisations for centuries. The Bishop of Durham only added to the controversy a while later when the press reported him as suggesting that the resurrection was 'a conjuring trick with bones'. Needless to say, he was criticised by many of his colleagues in the circles of organised religion, derided by 'the faithful' and pilloried by sections of the media. Yet, there were many people who found the comments made by the Bishop of Durham to be of refreshing honesty and realism when considered against the background of our modern understanding of human biology and the associated sciences. This leads one to ask the question – where did the concept of the Virgin Birth come from, and is it really that important?

Virgin Birth – and the Immaculate Conception

The possible origins of terms like *Son of God* and reference to other individuals who had supposedly been delivered of a *virgin birth* is not the real purpose of this book. We will dwell on the subject for a moment only because it sets the scene for accepting what is yet to be presented in respect of Solomon's Temple.

One may have perceptions which have been ingrained by years of religious superstition and conditioning by *faithful* acceptance of the current dogma. Jesus Christ, we are told, was the Son of God. Whilst, after some 2,000 years of systematic indoctrination, we may believe this to be an exceptional statement, in earlier times it was a well established phrase in what today we call the Middle East and Asia Minor. A *Son of God* was one expected to become king. For example, Alexander the Great was also referred to as a *Son of God* in his time; Zoroaster was not only a *Son of God* but was deemed to have been born of a virgin, whilst Mithra was born in a stable on 25th December some 600 years prior to the birth of Jesus Christ. The Greek god, Dionysus, was supposedly born of a virgin, in a stable and also turned water into wine, actions which were later attributed to Jesus Christ.[8]

There may be an alternative credible scenario to the story of the *virgin birth*, as we have come to know it in Christianity, and which has been promulgated over the centuries. I realise that some readers may find some of my forthright views that follow, offensive.

Information about the *virgin birth* is linked with the concept of the *Immaculate Conception* although they are treated as two separate doctrines. They are the cornerstones of Roman Catholic belief which in turn have had a big influence on Christian belief in general. Roman Catholicism is after all, the basis of much of the Christian belief doctrine of Western Europe. The source for most of the Christian understanding relating to the virgin birth and the life of Jesus, is contained in the New Testament *Gospels* – the four books of Matthew, Mark, Luke and John.

The doctrine of the *Virgin Birth* is that Jesus was conceived in the womb of his mother, the Virgin Mary, without the participation of a human father.[9] The Immaculate Conception requires a belief that the Virgin Mary was conceived and born without original sin[10]. Original sin is not an easy subject to get ones mind around. Indeed, the Catholic Encyclopaedia devotes a very large section to the subject but the only meaning that is defined is the sin that Adam first committed – which if one then reads Genesis 3, is related to the incident involving the serpent and an apple which God had told him not to eat or he would die. Both Adam and Eve ate an apple. So, on the face of it Adam and Eve eating an apple which, according to the scriptures, then led to man having a lifespan at the end of which he would die, has little to do with the processes relating to biology, human fertilisation and child birth. It is a concept which implies that Adams sin did not apply to Mary, that she was not stained by the sin he had committed and that she had never committed a sin of any kind – she was without sin.

The term *virgin birth* does not appear anywhere in the biblical texts, but Isaiah 7:14 and Matthew 1:23, both make the same statement:

*"The **virgin** will be with child and will give **birth** to a son...."*[11].

Thus, it is easy to relate this to the words *virgin birth*. However it is in Luke chapter 1 verse 35 that we then find the connection with the idea that Mary conceived without a human father. The concept of the Immaculate Conception is not related to any biblical text except that in referring to a *virgin* and a *Son of God* the doctrine requires Mary to be absolutely blameless, and not tainted or sullied in any way.

The book of Matthew, verses 18 – 20, state that Joseph and Mary were pledged to be married. Before the wedding took place, Joseph discovered that Mary was pregnant, but clearly, he believes, not by him. Quite naturally he considered divorcing her quietly so as not to make a fuss. Divorce in this context clearly means breaking off the marriage agreement. In verses 20-24 we are then told that Joseph had a dream in which he was visited by an angel who intimated that Joseph should stand by Mary, and that her resultant son should be named Jesus. Joseph relented and continued to take Mary as his wife.

Neither the books of Mark or John mention the *virgin birth*. Both start with John the Baptist baptising Jesus in the River Jordan, followed by Jesus gathering together his first disciples. In other words, they start at a point when Jesus was already a fully grown man.

It is only in the book of Luke chapter 1 verses 26-38, that we find any mention of the so called *virgin birth*. Interestingly, in both Luke and Matthew we are told that Jesus was descended from David in a line through his father Joseph. So, even in the chapters that do mention it we are left in no doubt that a *human* father was involved. This is totally at variance with the doctrine of the church. As with the gospel of Matthew, we find that Mary is pledged to marry Joseph, but not yet married. Mary is then visited by an angel who tells her that without any apparent intervention by any man, she is to become pregnant. Mary notes that she is still a virgin and questions how this can happen. In verse 35, the angel answered,

"..The Holy Spirit will come upon you, and the power of the Most High will overshadow you".

The Latin version is,

"et respondens angelus dixit ei Spiritus Sanctus superveniet in te et virtus Altissimi obumbrabit tibi ideoque et quod nascetur sanctum vocabitur Filius Dei".[12]

Put bluntly, it is from this one verse, and a total of seventeen words of modern biblical text[13], thirty five in Latin, that the perception and dogma of the *virgin birth* seems to have been based. It is from these seventeen words that an entire industry of iconography and trinkets has been created. Again, put bluntly, and recognising everything that we know about human biology, two people in the act of sexual contact will inevitably result in one casting a *shadow over* the other. Add to this a mythology which existed two thousand years ago that heaven, the place where the deity dwelt, and where angels came down from, was in or above the sky, then what is suggested here and intimated in the doctrine, is that an unseen spirit zoomed down from the heavens, in a once only event in the entire recorded history of mankind, had some form of sexual encounter with this poor girl, Mary, and zoomed back into the sky, leaving her impregnated and subject to scorn by those who knew her, especially Joseph who was betrothed to her. It has all the hallmarks of Erich Von Daniken's bestselling book from the latter decades of the twentieth century, Chariots of the Gods, in which he suggested that alien life-forms had visited Earth. Newspaper articles at the time used the expression *Was God was an Astronaught?* – an idea widely condemned by the established church. Yet, based on church doctrine, they are implying the same kind of idea. If no human father was involved then who – or what – was? Remember, the doctrine of the *virgin birth* is that no human father was involved. The scriptures go on to make it clear that Mary's offspring entered this world as a baby in the way that all humans are born. There are people I know, very intelligent people, who are perplexed by this doctrine but shrug it off with the suggestion that it was all done with some form of human artificial insemination. That is a technique that it took highly skilled medical scientists, and the development of sophisticated support apparatus, until the closing decades of the twentieth century to achieve for the first time, a time lapse of two thousand years.

So, could there be another explanation? There is.

New Discoveries – New Revelations

Over the past two hundred years or so, tantalising discoveries of small fragments of parchment, believed to have been part of the original texts of the New Testament gospels, and some omitted from the current format but consolidated in the Apocrypha, have come to light and been available for academic scrutiny. In the second half of the 20th century there were two discoveries of quantities of scrolls which, at some time in the past, had been deliberately hidden. These are known as the Nag Hammadi scrolls found in 1945, and the Dead Sea Scrolls which came to light in 1948, the latter having been buried in earthenware jars in caves, probably around two thousand years ago. These two important discoveries have placed archaeologists, historians and theologians in a much better position to understand events which occurred in and around Jerusalem two thousand years ago. Many people have speculated that the revelations they contain could turn our previous religious notions on their head. One such revelation relates to the so-called Virgin Birth.

The Virgin Birth – a revised scenario

Dr Barbara Thiering, a long-standing lecturer in specialised areas of theology at Sydney University, Australia, spent many years researching and studying the texts of the Dead Sea Scrolls. From her position as an eminent researcher and lecturer in theology, she wrote three illuminating and fascinating books, one of which was the best-selling *Jesus the Man*. Based on her research she gives an illuminating background into how we have been left with the notion of the virgin birth. In fact, she devotes a whole chapter to it.

Dr Thiering explains that Mary was a member of a community or sect that was very devout in its religious practices, a community where the men and women spent considerable periods in separation as the men entered a monk-like existence. But, unlike later monks of the medieval period, men in the highest levels of the priesthood were expected to marry and in consequence have families. Marriage was a two-stage process. First there was a betrothal which lasted several years, the sort of 'steady relationship' that might be experienced today by a couple prior to a traditional engagement. At the end of this betrothal period the couple went through a first marriage after which they were entitled to have sexual relations. Until this first marriage, the woman was expected to be a virgin. There then followed a period of up to three years in which the couple lived in a trial marriage. If during the first marriage period, the trial marriage, the woman became pregnant, then when she was at three months the couple would ratify their association by a second and final marriage, beyond which divorce was forbidden. Dr Thiering then states:

'The New Testament, speaking of an ideal like the Essene one, discusses the case of a man who "has a virgin", whose "passions become strong". If it happened that during the betrothal period and before the first wedding, the passions became too strong, and a child was conceived, then it could be said by a play on words that "a Virgin had conceived". The woman was still a Virgin legally, but not physically. It would be just like the case of a couple conceiving a child during their engagement.' [11]

Returning to the biblical text, it is therefore intimated that Mary and Joseph were pledged to each other, that the passions became too strong and that she became pregnant prior to the initial marriage ceremony. Divorce was prohibited after the second wedding which perhaps explains why, in Luke, Joseph contemplates divorce. Because they had not yet had a marriage ceremony, Mary was still legally a virgin, and hence, as noted earlier, a virgin had conceived. The marriage, therefore, had not been fully ratified within the processes normally adopted by the devout community of which Mary was a member. By definition, the legitimacy of a child conceived prior to the initial marriage would also be in doubt, another aspect referred to in *Jesus the Man*.

One can well imagine the difficulty the early Christian church founders would have had in promoting the idea of a *Son of God* being the product of what, if taken at face value, appears to have been an illegitimate birth. Hence, the early church fathers gave Mary and her offspring respectability by creating the notion of the Virgin Birth – divine intervention – coupled with the concept of the *Immaculate Conception*. However, to understand Mary's circumstances and to put them into a realistic context one needs to consider the social structure and practices of the community of which this lady was a member, in the era that the events took place.

The *Jesus the Man* interpretation seems a very acceptable and entirely rational explanation of the background to the concept of the Virgin Birth and provides a logical understanding for notions with which we have been brought up. Needless to say, such an explanation is a bitter pill for 'the faithful' to swallow after nearly two thousand years of institutional indoctrination that promulgates the notion that some form of miraculous and divine intervention had taken place.

This revelation in respect of the Virgin Birth, and others that presented themselves during my research, and which were related to so-called miraculous biblical events, demonstrated to me that in my investigation I could not merely accept the words as printed in the Old Testament at face value as previous generations would have been obliged to do. If the New Testament was subject to interpretation then so too was the Old Testament.

Did Jesus marry Mary Magdalene?

The idea that Jesus and Mary Magdalene were married, and had children, is one which has hovered for many years. In the latter decades of the 20th century what seemed like an an endless stream of materials was produced, advancing the idea. Needless to say, if proven it would substantially undermine a pillar of the Christian faith. This controversial idea has not been conclusively denied, or acknowledged, by the Church authorities, who, in the main, have tended to side-step the issue with statements about *faith*. If, as has already been noted, Jesus was indeed a man with a human mother and father, then it is not difficult to imagine that a human Jesus would have married and had children as a result of it.

This is enlarged on in the book *Jesus the Man* by Dr Barbara Thiering – but, with a difference. Whereas most other writers have drawn on speculative materials and circumstantial evidence, Dr Thiering goes one stage further. In a detailed chronology as support evidence in the book, she cites the following event occurring on Tuesday 6th June AD 30, based on the Julian calendar system, as follows:

'*6.00pm ... Betrothal of Jesus and Mary Magdalene at Ain Feshkha "Cana". "Wedding" under Hellenist rules. Sacred meal 6-10pm precedes ceremony ...*' [12]

Then, on September 23, again at Ain Feshkha, the first wedding ceremony took place with Simon Magus officiating. [13]

Over two years then pass until on Friday December 19th AD 32, Jesus headed for Qumran, a settlement just outside of Jerusalem, to seek final permission from the hierarchy to resume his marriage. [14]

Finally, again at Ain Feshkha, on Thursday March 19th AD 33 we find the '*second wedding of Jesus and Mary Magdalene...*' [15]

To add to the controversy, Dr Thiering, in other works, indicates that Jesus and Mary Magdalene had three children: a daughter named Tamar, a son (who was also the heir to Jesus) named Jesus (Justus), and a second son whose name is not recorded. In addition she states that Jesus had a second wife named Lydia and through this marriage they had a fourth child, also a daughter. So Jesus was the father to four children.

I certainly grew up in an era when, through the doctrine and imagery of the Church, I was encouraged to believe that Jesus was not married, let alone the father of four children.

Things may not be as we were taught.

Things may not be as we were taught

The Bible and attempts at Chronology

As the quest unfolded and I gathered more understanding and data, so I found myself facing what appeared to be an enormous jigsaw puzzle – there were piles of pieces, an overall picture, but the pieces did not fit comfortably together. The dates and events that were recorded in some documents did not seem to correspond with the dates from other sources. The variations in time could represent two hundred years or more. As we will see in a moment, I was not the first person to have encountered a problem with biblical chronology.

It is believed that the early books of the Old Testament were originally written down in their current form around 500 to 600 BCE, by unknown scribes. The widely held view is that prior to that time they were an accumulation of stories that formed part of a verbal tradition which provided a means of conveying information from one generation to the next. But the Bible is not the only source of information. Jewish historians also kept and retained records which passed through the generations and traditions. Much of this material was available to Flavius Josephus, a Roman citizen and a man of the Jewish faith, who recorded much about Jewish history. He clearly had access to certain documents whilst compiling his *Antiquities of the Jews,* documents that, sadly, are not available to us now. The works of Flavius Josephus have helped researchers fill in many of the gaps that are evident if one relies solely on the biblical text.

Throughout the Old Testament there are numerous references to people and their lifespans, to events and their places in the order of occurrence, and to intervals of time between major events. This has led to a number of attempts being made to identify the dates precisely, based on our current calendar structure, as to when certain biblical events occurred, or when characters supposedly lived. One such undertaking was by James Ussher, who added together all the time intervals in the Bible and came to the conclusion that the date of creation, as stated in the opening verses of the Book of Genesis was 23rd October 4004 BCE. James Ussher (1581-1656) was a respected man of his time. He was Archbishop of Armagh, Primate of All Ireland and Vice Chancellor of Trinity College, Dublin. Indeed, his perspective on biblical chronology was so highly regarded that, to quote the Encyclopaedia of Religion,

> '*it was included in an authorised version of the Bible printed in 1701, and thus came to be regarded with almost as much unquestioning reverence as the bible itself'.* [16]

Indeed, the Ussher chronology has been applied to some aspects of Masonic ceremonies where dates and a chronology for the Order are based on Ussher's scheme. With the sum total of the accumulated knowledge that we have at our disposal today, Ussher's idea is patently ludicrous. Yet, based on the knowledge and perceptions of the world as seen through the eyes of such eminent people who lived in the very different world and culture of 300 years ago, together with their interpretation of the religious faith to which they had committed their very being, then such conclusions were a source of encouragement and enlightenment which would have influenced the establishment for several generations to come.

Over the past two hundred years there has been an enormous commitment of time and resources to the archaeological and academic scrutiny of prominent locations that are mentioned in historical records, as well as biblical and other religious sources. As a consequence, our understanding has been placed into a very different context by comparison with that in the era of Bishop Ussher. As time has passed, so the ground-breaking biblical chronology espoused by James Ussher in his capacity as a former Bishop of Armagh has been refined.

By the end of the 20th century, biblical chronology had been the subject of thorough investigation with chronologies developed by eminent historians. Yet, the processes used by archaeologists in developing these chronologies have not been too different from that originally undertaken by the Bishop of Armagh. Through the twentieth century, and by reference to an extensive range of primary sources, researchers compiled lists of kings, rulers and key individuals together with the time period of their rule or influence. By adding together the relevant time periods, making allowance for any gaps in knowledge, then a chronology for certain events could be derived. This approach, of course, presupposes that all the basic criteria and assumptions are correct in the first instance. If the basic assumptions made by the researchers have been incorrect then the resultant chronology will obviously be inaccurate. If an incorrect assumption has been inadvertently built into a reference work such that it has been promulgated to others and used as a definitive document, then any other resultant chronologies will also be adversely affected.

For example, I came across several references stating quite categorically that Moses was in fact the heretical Pharaoh, Akenhaten. These assertions were based on the idea that both individuals had been allocated a time slot in the 13th century BCE. This Pharaoh, famous for what has come to be known as the Amarna Heresy or Akenhaten Heresy, disappeared when a monotheistic religion of Egypt, based on the Sun god Ra, inspired by Akenhaten and established on the banks of the River Nile at Tel-el-Amarna, collapsed. It was a few years following that collapse that the young Prince Tutankhamun became Pharaoh. What happened to Akenhaten and several of his immediate confidants has been the subject of much speculation. It is through this speculation that the connection with Moses appears to have been made.

The changing face of the Old Testament

Changes to the text of the Old Testament could have a profound effect on the possible design of Solomon's Temple by comparison with previous evaluations, no matter how well considered the text may have been in the past.

Scientific analysis of supposed biblical miracles, and archaeological discoveries such as the Dead Sea Scrolls, may change our perceptions of what could have happened in the Holy Land 2,000 years ago. If this is not enough, in the second half of the 20th century there was also a realignment of specific areas of Old Testament text. Some of these text changes can have a profound effect on the way information may be interpreted today by comparison with interpretations made a hundred years ago.

In the United Kingdom, the standard text of the Anglican Bible had been the Authorised King James version. It was first published in 1611 in the reign of King James I of England, James VI of Scotland, son of Mary, Queen of Scots. The majority of original New Testament texts emanated from Antioch around 150 CE. These texts were originally in Greek but were translated into old Latin around 160 CE. As the Roman Church expanded its influence after the Council of Nicaea in 325 CE, at which the contents of the Bible as we now know it were standardised, so these texts became the subject of endless copying by monks and scribes who dedicated their lives to such work. Needless to say, no matter how carefully the texts were transcribed and translated, it was inevitable that some errors would have occurred.

By the 14th century CE there was a move to translate the texts from the Latin version that had become the standard language of the Roman Catholic Church into the languages pertinent to where ordinary people lived. The argument was that very few people outside of the Church, plus a few well-educated souls, understood Latin, so the message contained in the Bible was lost to most people. The belief at the time was that ordinary people should have the opportunity to read, understand and appreciate the text in their own language. Although there were several very early attempts to do this by translating specific texts, it was John Wycliffe (1324-1384) who prepared a most comprehensive and, some would argue, the first translation of the New Testament into English, around 1382. Wycliffe was a teacher at Oxford University. He was a champion of Church reform, critical of the Church hierarchy and felt the Church should give up its possessions. His work incensed the established Catholic Church to the extent that they expelled him from his teaching position following the issue of a Bull by Pope Gregory XI in May 1382. The ramifications of Wycliffe's actions and attitude to the Church rumbled on, such, that some 40 years after his death the then Pope ordered that his bones be dug up and burnt so that no trace of him remained.

The next major step was when William Tyndale (1494-1536) took advantage of a newly developed device called the printing press. Tyndale had also studied at Oxford, as well as at Cambridge. Like Wycliffe before him, he was a champion of Church reform. So much so that he was summoned to appear before the Chancellor of the Diocese of Worcester to answer a charge of heresy. Shortly after this event, he escaped from England under an assumed name and went to Hamburg in Germany. Here, Tyndale completed a translation of the New Testament into English, had copies printed and distributed them in England in 1526. The Catholic Church establishment were outraged. Cardinal Wolsey demanded Tyndale's arrest for heresy. Tyndale was ultimately seized in Antwerp in 1535, tried on a charge of heresy and condemned to be burnt at the stake, a sentence carried out the following year.

With the establishment of the Church of England in the reign of Henry VIII, the dissolution of the monasteries and the effective banishing of the Catholic Church from England, the pressures for having a Bible in English grew and several more versions were started. It was in the reign of King James I that finally a complete translation of the New and Old Testaments was brought together to become the Authorised King James version. It was this version, with its use of prose and older English language styles, which was referenced and used for the next four centuries, and in many instances, still is.

Things changed in the mid-20th century. The English language had moved on over the centuries and there was pressure to produce a version in the plain language of the day. At the same time, academics revisited the text to correct translation and other known errors that had crept in over the centuries.

The Preface to the Holy Bible, New International version of 1978, makes the following observations:

> *The New International Version is a completely new translation of the Holy Bible made by over a hundred scholars working directly from the best available Hebrew, Aramaic and Greek texts. It had its beginning in 1965....*

The text goes on to point out that the work was undertaken with the help of many distinguished scholars from the United States, Great Britain, Canada, Australia, New Zealand, and from across a variety of denominations to safeguard the translation from sectarian bias.

With respect to the Old Testament in particular, the following comments are made in the same Preface:

> *For the Old Testament the standard Hebrew text, the Masoretic Text as published in the latest editions of the* Biblia Hebraica, *was used throughout. The Dead Sea Scrolls contain material bearing on the earlier stage of the Hebrew text. They were consulted, as were the Samaritan Pentateuch and the ancient scribal traditions relating to textual changes.*

What is of note is that the contents of the Dead Sea Scrolls, discovered some thirty years prior to the New International version being released, were deemed to have been of sufficient importance to have been consulted, and, no doubt, had some influence on specific areas of the subsequent text. It is clear from the Preface that considerable effort was exercised to try and ensure a most comprehensive and accurate translation, together with the plain text language of our modern era.

Problems with translations

Whilst most of the descriptions relating to Solomon's Temple are broadly the same as in the previous King James version, there are some changes which create a very different interpretation. Take for example the following text comparisons which relate to the doorway leading into the inner sanctuary:

> *And for the entering of the oracle he made doors of olive tree; the lintel and side posts were the fifth part of the wall.*
>
> 1 Kings 6:31 (King James version, printed circ 1870)

Things may not be as we were taught

*For the entrance of the inner sanctuary he made doors of Olive wood with
five-sided jambs.*

1 Kings 6:31 (New International version, printed 1983)

There is a great deal of difference in the interpretation one can derive from a
statement where the lintel and side posts are the fifth part of the wall, by comparison
with the statement that they were five-sided door jambs. Assuming the length of the
wall had been twenty cubits, then, in the King James version we could interpret the
statement as defining the size of the side posts – four cubits. There would have been
two side posts to the doorway so the total space they would have occupied in the
length of the wall would have been eight cubits. Or, again relating to the King James
version, does the text imply that both side posts were four cubits in total: therefore,
two cubits on either side. When we refer to the text of the New International version,
there is no indication as to the size of the side posts but the text suggests that, being
five-sided, they were pentagonal in shape. We will discuss the implications of this
further in the book.

Did the Exodus cross the Red Sea?
There is even some change relating to the Exodus. Most people with a
Christian upbringing will have been taught that Moses led the Israelites out of Egypt
to the Red Sea. Pharaoh gave chase along with six hundred chariots and his army.
Traditional teaching has been that when the Israelites reached the Red Sea, and
noted that the Pharaoh was in pursuit of them, Moses held out his rod over the
waters and they parted to create a dry passage through which the Israelites could
pass. Pharaoh and his army continued to pursue the Israelites and when the last
Israelite had completed the passage of the Red Sea the waters collapsed on the
Pharaoh and his army, drowning them. In both the King James and New
International versions there is only one reference to the Red Sea. This is in Exodus,
chapter 13 verse 18, where it states:

> *But God led the people about, through the way of the wilderness of the Red
> Sea: and the children of Israel went up harnessed out of the land of Egypt.*
>
> *King James version*

> *So God led the people around by the desert road towards the Red Sea. The
> Israelites went up out of Egypt armed for battle.*
>
> *New International version*

From that verse on, most of the drama associated with the escape of the Israelites
is described in Exodus, chapter 14. There is no further reference to the Red Sea,
merely mention of the words 'sea' and 'water(s)'. So, the text implies that the
Israelites merely set off into the desert regions around the Red Sea, not that they

actually crossed it. Indeed, anyone visiting the Red Sea will be aware that, in general, it is a very deep and very wide waterway. Standing on the Egyptian side one cannot see the opposite banks in Jordan or Arabia, except at the head of the Gulf of Aqaba. What is more, the road towards the Red Sea may have been a reference to a camel trade route. It is now known that the Red Sea provided a number of points where ports were established for the transhipment of silk, ivory and spices which were then carried to cities like Thebes, Memphis and the Mediterranean ports.

The size and depth of the Red Sea, together with an estimation of the massive forces that would have been needed to part and hold back the waters enabling the Israelite crossing, has caused some concern amongst scholars for a long time. Towards the end of the 20th century a new theory presented itself. It was suggested that the Red Sea reference was a misspelling and that it should have been the *Reed Sea*. In Exodus, chapter 15, there are two references to the Red Sea. In the New International version of the text there is a footnote in respect of these two references to the Red Sea as:

Hebrew term is Yam Suph; that is, Sea of Reeds.

The Sea of Reeds is in an area to the east of the Nile Delta – a very different location to the Red Sea. In addition, there are those who have put forward the hypothesis that the Exodus coincided with the eruption of a volcano on the Greek island of Santorini around 1,650 BCE. Based on established chronology it means that this event would have occurred about 100 years before Moses was born. The Santorini event was cataclysmic, blowing the island apart and causing massive tidal waves. The hypothesis is that either during this event, or perhaps later through an earthquake in the same area, a tsunami, a tidal wave, was created just as a group of Israelites reached the banks of a narrow river in the Reed Sea area. The waters were dragged out as the tsunami gathered strength, leaving a path for a group of Israelites to cross. The Pharaoh continued his chase across the same waterway just as the tsunami surged back into the area, sweeping the Pharaoh and his followers away.[17] Whatever actually happened, towards the end of the 20th century the references to the Red Sea in the book of Exodus changed in some Bible editions, to become the *Reed Sea*. This change inevitably means that future generations will probably be taught this new location, as opposed to the scenario presented to previous generations.

It also seemed to me that the emergence of all this new evidence meant that the religious dogma which has existed and been espoused for centuries is questionable. In reality, big holes are blown in it. This must cause the religious establishment some disquiet. They cannot announce and implement wholesale change to dogma overnight. This would undermine confidence and cause considerable anxiety to those who may have invested an enormous portion of their lives and intellect in believing the dogma and rituals that have been presented. There are even ramifications for the political and institutional structures that govern society. Whilst the core belief may remain, changes to the rituals may be a slow process, one step at a time, over several generations, taking maybe a hundred years to fully implement.

In presenting the above, I have not set out to trample on the religious beliefs of anyone. I have merely sought to convey what has become known to me as a consequence of my enquiries. If the changes in our understanding of certain matters biblical, as I have shown above, have currency, then Solomon's Temple and our belief about what it may have been like and used for could also be subject to change.

My enquiries and subsequent investigations revealed a rather different image of Solomon's Temple by comparison with the stereotyped vision that other persons, in previous generations, had created.

Conclusion

Archaeological discoveries, particularly in the lands around the Mediterranean Sea since digging commenced in the mid-Victorian era, coupled with scientific and technological innovation through the 20th century, has resulted in our understanding of certain events in history changing by comparison with the interpretations which existed in the mid- to late-Victorian era when Freemasonry commenced its meteoritic acceptance in society. Much of the foundation literature which existed through the 20th century, and related to Freemasonry and its history, was based on the understanding and scholarly interpretations that existed in the mid-Victorian era. Relying on it and perpetuating it as a source of valid information, especially as it reflects Old Testament and other Biblical sources, must be questioned. The effect on our interpretation of certain events enshrined in religious dogma is also open to question.

After several years of exploring this new evidence, which at times challenged my own religious upbringing and convictions, and realising its implications, it was clear that I needed to proceed with a very open mind. This, I realised, may well set me on a collision course with accepted philosophies and establishment dogma. As time passed and more evidence came to the fore, so a new theory in respect of Solomon's Temple presented itself.

First I needed to understand more about the concepts embedded in Freemasonry, and their possible origins, absorbing knowledge but keeping an open mind.

[1] From information displayed at the Taxien temple.
[2] *Genesis Unveiled; The Lost Wisdom of Our Forgotten Ancestors* – Ian Lawton, 2003, Photograph - Plate 30
[3] A series of Television documentaries have explored options which offer an explanation for these phenomena, based on scientific evidence of the way specific events may have interacted. In particular a BBC-TV program about Moses, first broadcast in December 2002, reported an incident which occurred in New Burn, North Carolina, USA, in 1999, where there were similar parallels to the river turn-

ing to blood, sores developing on the skin, just as reported in the bible to have happened in Egypt. The cause of the North Carolina incident was found to have been a mutation of a micro-organism called pfiesteria caused by pollution from a pig farm.

[4] BBC2 TV Wednesday 4th September 2002, Ancient Apocalypse: The destruction of Sodom and Gomorrah.

[5] This was presented in a BBC TV documentary (broadcast July 2001 and September 2002) entitled Ancient Apocalypse: The destruction of Sodom and Gomorrah, where Graham Harris, a retired geologist presented a theory based on his geological knowledge of the area in which the towns once stood. His theory was investigated by Professor Lynne Frostick, a geologist at Hull University, and Jonathan Tubb from the British Museum. They were supported in their investigation by Dr Gopal Madabhushi at the Centrifuge lab at Cambridge University.

[6] See www.biblemysteries.com/library

[7] See Catholic Encyclopaedia - Jesus and Christ

[8] See The Hiram Key, Lomas and Knight page 58

[9] Wikipaedia - www.wikipedia.org – Virgin Birth

[10] Catholic Encyclopaedia

[11] Holy Bible, New International Version, Matthew 1:23

[12] New International Version and King James Version + Latin version Biblia Sacra Vulgata. www.biblegateway.com

[13] Holy Bible – New International Version, Luke 1:35.

[14] *Jesus the Man*, Dr Barbara Theiring, chapter eight.

[15] *Jesus the Man*, page 299

[16] *Jesus the Man*, page 301

[17] *Jesus the Man*, page 319

[18] *Jesus the Man*, page 322

[19] *A Geological Miscellany* by Craig & Jones, Princeton University Press 1982

[20] Presented in a BBC-TV documentary about Moses, Jeremy Bowen as presenter.

Chapter 9
Moses prepared the foundations
of the Temple

Solomon built the Temple. David designed the temple. But it was Moses who prepared the foundations.

The building of the first Jerusalem Temple was the culmination of a journey lasting nearly 500 years in the efforts of the Israelites to seek and secure their promised land. It brought with it an era of stability, peace and prosperity. The temple was built in a pinnacle era in which the Israelites were confident to display the achievement of the nationhood they so obviously craved. It, thus, became the symbol of that nationhood, the wealth of their collective community and demonstrated a technological understanding and ability that was on a par with, or exceeded, neighbouring cultures. Or at least, that is the impression gained from Kings and Chronicles in the Old Testament.

There are, however, specific aspects of that Israelite journey that seem to provide a key to some of the design aspects of that Temple. And they start with Moses.

The first five books of the Old Testament are the same five books that the Jews refer to as the Torah. For hundreds of years it had been the belief amongst groups of scholars that these five books had actually been written by Moses. Later, it was believed that Moses had access to a range of other scriptures and, whilst he was tending the sheep and goats in Midian, he copied and edited these other scriptures and from them compiled the works which we now know as the five books of the Torah. Modern research, however, suggests that there were a series of scribes who originally wrote down the text in about 500 BCE. Thereafter, the texts were edited and slightly amended by each subsequent generation until around 7 BCE when the Hebrew hierarchy of the day decided that the compilation which then constituted the Torah was the final form – they couldn't go on editing it for fear that they would lose any connection with its origins. So the Torah became a setpiece document around 7 BCE and has not been modified since. It is in the second book of the Torah, Exodus, that we find clues that suggest the influences that later shaped the Temple design.

It seemed obvious to me that the building of any stately edifice by civilisations 3,000 to 4,000 years ago would have been a reflection of the religious beliefs, culture, technology and knowledge that the community undertaking the work had at that time. We only have to look around the towns and cities that have been the basis of our own culture and civilisation to see periodic influences. There are architectural styles, construction principles, materials and designs of façades – all of which are a record in architecture of influences which abounded at the time of construction. Hence, we find throughout Europe: the Gothic style which permeated the era of great cathedral building in the period of 350 years commencing around 1100 CE; styles influenced by the Renaissance, an era of about 200 years through the 15th and 16th centuries; in England we had the Tudor and Elizabethan period, lasting approximately 150 years, also in the 15th and 16th centuries; and the Georgian period, an era of approximately 200 years. What we can see in all these styles is the influence of political, cultural and fashionable attributes pertinent to the era of construction. Such are the affairs of man that such influences are seldom in complete isolation from innovations and fashions transcending other aspects of life.

Solomon's Temple was a major undertaking and important structure for the new nation founded by the Israelites. The design concepts were unlikely to have been a radical departure from the accepted norms of the day. It is more than likely that it incorporated tried and tested concepts, developed by, or in, previous cultures and eras, or familiar to those of their neighbours.

Whilst Masonic ceremonies make reference to the building of Solomon's Temple, we gain very little insight from those same ceremonies to infer what the building may have looked like. Pictorial illustrations used in Masonic lodges, referred to as tracing boards, provide an impression of the potential aesthetic design of certain aspects of the Temple, but they are only artistic impressions. There is not even a consistency in the presentation of these illustrations. There are differing styles depending on the region. Yet, some of these illustrations have been in existence for many years and, if repeatedly seen by Lodge members at meetings, they can create the impression of being based on some documented reality. In short, they are works of imaginative fiction.

The only information we have to go on to obtain clues about what the Temple may have looked like are a combination of the details recorded in the scriptures and archaeological excavations of sites reportedly from the same geographical location and era. Archaeological examination of sites deemed as being of historical or religious significance has only been undertaken for a little over a hundred and fifty years – since the mid-Victorian period. Some of the Masonic tracing board images in use today had their origins some two centuries ago, well before the era of scholarly based archaeology. Furthermore, the comprehensive piecing together of the archaeological evidence from field evidence, and the ability to arrive at sustainable conclusions for the lifestyles and influences of our ancient ancestors, is a relatively new insight, helped by the availability of computer aided design (CAD) and visual reconstruction using computer graphics technology.

It is natural that when one faces a void in knowledge, then that void will automatically be filled with interpretations of the knowledge then existing. Hence, when using the term *Temple,* artists of two hundred years ago would naturally turn to the neo-classical styles of ancient Greece and Rome for inspiration. There are, after all, a number of temple sites still existing and emanating from the Greek and Roman epochs which are available as a point of reference. The Parthenon in Athens, temple ruins at Delphi, and others in Turkey and Cyprus give a guide to architectural styles in use in the era between around 750 BCE and 250 CE. The problem with trying to translate this perspective to Solomon's Temple is that the civilisations of ancient

Moses prepared the foundations of the Temple

Greece and Rome did not have their foundations until long after the first Jerusalem Temple – Solomon's Temple – had been completed.

In Freemasonry, the craft degrees are closely allied to stories which link to Solomon's Temple. There is a point in the proceedings where the candidate is advised that Freemasonry recognises the three noble orders of architecture: namely, Ionic, Doric and Corinthian. In so doing there is an implication that these three classical styles are associated with the Temple. But these three architectural styles are all associated with the Greek and Roman classical periods, which came long after the building of the Jerusalem Temple.

To me it did not seem unreasonable to believe that the influences that ultimately defined the design of Solomon's Temple must have originated from other sources. And a review of some of the political and cultural influences that existed in the epoch leading up to, and during, that in which the Temple was built, show that the leading influence, was most likely to have come from Egypt. Before we explore this specific influence my reasoning will become clear through a brief review of other local cultures in the region.

The influence of the classical Greek and Roman Empires

As already mentioned, the foundations for the Greek and Roman empires, and the classical civilisations they are associated with, only commenced after the first temple in Jerusalem had been built. Their foundations are traced to around 700 BCE by which time the Jerusalem Temple had been standing for some 250 years. So it is impossible for these classical cultures to have had any influence on the design.

The Minoan Civilisation

The Minoans were based on the Mediterranean Island of Crete. Palaces, like the one at Knossos, which archaeologists date to around 1,600 BCE, were built from wood and stone. Where pillars were needed to support a roof or entrance, surviving examples suggest they were made from tree trunks which could be easily shaped, especially at the top, where they might support a wooden roof strut or door lintel. The outer appearance of the buildings was not elaborate, but interior decoration reveals well-developed skills on the part of the craftsmen of the time, with images carefully engraved and set into a plaster finish. The skill and knowledge of the craftsmen is particularly emphasised in the drainage system. There is evidence that Knossos had clean drinking water entering on one side of the site and waste water being carried away in separate ducts from the other side. These ducts were carefully crafted in stone.

At Knossos, the main entrance to the palace / temple was aligned to face the east, so that the first light of the rising Sun would enter the building.

The Minoan civilisation was brought to its knees following the eruption of a volcano on the nearby island of Santorini. It was a devastation which shook the entire region. Crete was, apparently, devastated by earthquakes associated with that eruption. The earthquakes destroyed many of the prominent buildings of the

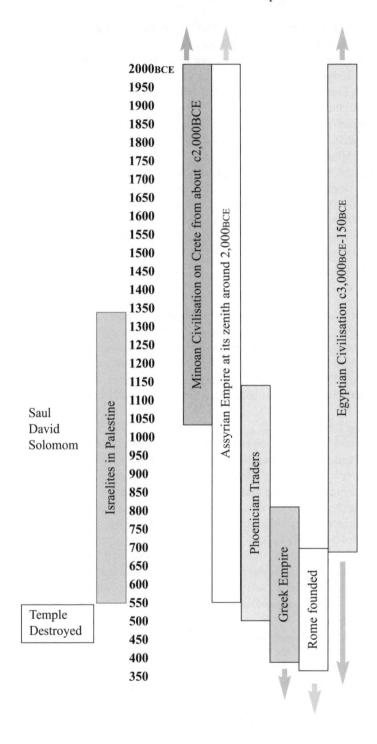

civilisation. Heaving of the Earth's crust resulted in Knossos being cut off from the sea. Tidal waves and subsidence are believed to have destroyed harbours.

As a consequence of the destruction on Crete, the highly developed society that had existed quickly went into decline. By the time the Jerusalem Temple had been built, the influence of the Minoan civilisation was non-existent. It is therefore doubtful that there would have been any influence on the Temple's design from this culture. One cannot, however, dismiss the possibility that, in their heyday, there was a transmission of Minoan influence that permeated the entire Eastern Mediterranean region.

There is, however, one link of similarity between the Minoans and Solomon.

Earlier I mentioned that where there was a need for pillars to support beams in their palaces, the evidence suggests that the Minoans used tree trunks which were round and could be fashioned. In the verses of the Old Testament relating to the building of Solomon's house, we find the following text:

He built the palace.....with four rows of cedar columns supporting trimmed cedar beams....

1 Kings 7: 2

The Assyrians

The Assyrian culture developed in the area which today encompasses the border areas of southern Turkey, Armenia, Syria and northern Iraq. Archaeologists have established that settlements existed in various locations, from as far back as about 5,000 BCE, with at least three major cities and complex societies, having developed by about 2,500 BCE. At various stages of its development Assyria was involved in conflicts in the region, sometimes being usurped by other nations or taking territory from its neighbours. The golden era of the Assyrians lasted from around 2,500 BCE until about 1,400 BCE. From around 1,400 BCE the influence of the Assyrian civilisation went into decline as a consequence of a series of conflicts with the Armenians, so that by about 1,000 BCE, some 50 years prior to the construction of the Jerusalem Temple, Assyrian influence in the area was virtually non-existent. From around 940 BCE the Assyrians again consolidated their territorial influence. A new Assyrian empire rose from the ashes of the old and achieved its peak about 200 years after the Temple was built. It was an empire that extended from Cyprus to the Euphrates. This empire declined around 612 BCE. It was this decline which later provided the opportunity for the rise of the Babylonian independence under their leader Nabopolassar. Such was the independent strength of the Babylonians at that time that it was Nabopolassar's son, Nebuchadnezzar, who led an invasion of Jerusalem and destroyed the Temple, around 550 BCE.

Thus, at the time the Temple in Jerusalem was built, the territorial influence of the Assyrians was very limited and it is difficult to imagine that they could have had any major influence on the temple design. However, accumulated knowledge from previous eras may well have had some influence on basic construction technology.

The Ancient Egyptians and the heretical Pharaoh

The ancient Egyptian civilisation is believed to have evolved from around 3,000 BCE. It was the dominant civilisation in the eastern end of the Mediterranean, and across northern Africa, at the time the Temple was built.

The Old Testament notes that there was a friendly association between King David and Hiram, King of Tyre, suggesting that Tyre, and what today we know as the coastal strip of Lebanon, was a separate country. The reality is that Tyre was one of the city-states that became known as the Phoenician Traders. These city states existed, to a high degree, through Egyptian patronage. The entire region around the fledgling nation of the Israelites was dominated by the Egyptians. It therefore seems logical that the architectural style, and technical knowledge adopted by the Hebrews, would closely mirror that of the Egyptians.

We can gain an interesting insight into the relationship which may have existed around 1,000 BCE between the nation of the Israelites and Egypt, from David Rohl's book, *A Test of Time*. Having been warriors together, the Old Testament tells us how Saul became very jealous of David, and how, although David was married to Saul's daughter, Saul wanted David killed. Saul's son, Jonathan, and his daughter, helped David to escape to the *wilderness*. David had a band of loyal supporters who ultimately joined him. David and his small army became outlaws, and were employed as hired mercenaries by various local war-lords. During this time, David was still being hunted by Saul. Dr Rohl suggests that David's activities were clearly such an irritation to Saul that he wrote to Pharaoh complaining about David's activities and seeking help in dealing with him. From this insight it suggests that Saul was subservient to Pharaoh.

And who was the Pharaoh that David Rohl identifies as ruler of Egypt at that time? None other than Akenhaten, the so-called heretical Pharaoh, who abolished the established religious doctrine then practised in Egypt – the worship of a plethora of gods, but in particular the god Amun – and replaced them with a monotheistic religion which returned to worship of the Aten, the Sun god. Akenhaten, father, so it is believed, of Tutankhamun, built a new capital city dedicated to the Sun God – the Aten, at Tel-el-Amarna, on the banks of the Nile. Although the city was demolished soon after the reign of Akenhaten concluded, archaeological surveys of the site suggest that certain key buildings had an orientation to equate with the various solar progressions.

The chronology set out by Dr Rohl implies that the building of the new Egyptian capital would have been in progress during the reign of David. This being so, it is inconceivable that the activities at Tel-el-Amarna, the influence of Akenhaten's realignment of religious doctrine and the return to worship of the Sun god would have been unknown to the rulers of the new Israelite nation. Saul, David and the heretical Pharaoh Akenhaten were contemporaries.

The Israelites and the land of the Pharaohs

I concluded that the best place to start a review of the background to how and why Solomon's Temple was built, was by starting from the point in biblical history where

Moses prepared the foundations of the Temple

Joseph, famous amongst other reasons for his multi-coloured coat, enters Old Testament texts. We are treated to a gripping story of underhand dealing, resulting in Joseph being sold into slavery. He then has a possible romantic liaison with his master's wife, is imprisoned, and, in the best of Hollywood traditions, he finally breaks free from the yoke of oppression and rises to become the acclaimed hero of the day.

According to the Book of Genesis Joseph was taken prisoner by a group of Midianites. At some stage after their arrival in Egypt, Joseph was sold into slavery. He was probably then in his mid-teenage years, about 16 or 17 years of age. Here he became a servant in the household of an Egyptian army commander, Potiphar. Whilst in this service, Joseph was accused of making sexual overtures to his master's wife, found guilty and imprisoned for several years. He was only released by adequately convincing the Pharaoh that he had the answer to a series of dreams that had been troubling the Egyptian ruler. These interpretations relate to the projection that Egypt was about to enter a period where there would be seven years of plenty followed by seven years of drought and famine. Joseph was clearly an intelligent and resourceful individual with a natural ability in diplomacy, management and organisation because he evidently planned and directed the operations necessary to ensure adequate facilities were available, and then supervised the storage of sufficient grain to help the entire country of Egypt sustain itself through the periods of drought and famine. In this period of about 15 years his abilities became so highly revered that he was literally the power behind the throne, an important right hand of the Pharaoh, and highly respected by the officials responsible for administration at that time.

On completion of this important work a palace was built for him and he retired to a quieter life in the growing city of Avaris, near the Nile Delta. The remains of Avaris are close to a small town which today is known by the local name of Tell ed-Daba.

We are told that Joseph's family joined him in Egypt and as such managed to avoid the worst of the famine. This reference to his 'family' may actually be to note that a section of the surrounding Semitic population moved into Egypt at that time, all attempting to avoid the worst ravages of a famine that had stricken a very large area extending outside of the Egyptian borders. There is certainly archaeological evidence that a large population of people of western Asiatic origins moved into the Nile Delta area around this time, many settling in the area close to Avaris. These people were referred to as the Hibaru, from which it is believed that the term Hebrew may have been derived.

Following the era of the *Joseph famine* there was a period of around two hundred years when clearly the descendants of those Semitic peoples that had moved into Egypt, either voluntarily or as slaves, had prospered and their numbers grown.

> *...the Israelites were so fruitful and prolific, they became so numerous and powerful that eventually the whole land was full of them.*
>
> *Exodus 1:7*

This large contingent of immigrants who had enhanced the overall population of Egypt, was clearly of some concern to the Egyptian authorities because we have the comments:

> *Then there came to power in Egypt, a new king who did not know Joseph. 'Look,' he said to his people, 'the Israelites are now more numerous and stronger than we are. We must take precautions to stop them increasing any further, or, if war should break out, they might join the ranks of our enemies. They might take up arms against us and then escape from the country.' Accordingly they put taskmasters over the Israelites to wear them down by forced labour.*
>
> *Exodus 1:8-10*

The response to the problem was fairly draconian because, in addition to the hard labour of slavery, the Pharaoh issued an instruction that all newborn male children of the Israelites and, we must assume, the male children of other non-Egyptian races and tribes also living in Egypt at that time, were to be killed. Archaeological evidence from some of the cemeteries in the Nile Delta region demonstrates that the population in that area was predominantly female, implying that some intervention had occurred which had indeed affected the male population. The 'immigrant' population was treated very harshly, being given menial tasks like hauling materials and making mud bricks – the standard construction material for most applications at that time. It has been suggested by others that this harsh treatment and genocide were intended as a warning that further migratory incursions into Egypt were unwelcome, whilst also encouraging others to leave.

Moses – educated in the *mysteries*

It is against the background of the persecution and oppression of the Israelites that we read in the Old Testament about an Israelite mother who, having given birth to a male child, and keeping him secretly for three months, placed him in a basket and hid him amongst bulrushes, obviously hoping to avoid the possibility that he would be detected during this period of ruthless purge. We are told that the child was found by an Egyptian Princess. It is believed that the Princess concerned was named Thermuthis. She, unable to have children of her own, adopted the child as a consequence of which he was raised as an Egyptian Prince named Mousos. The Catholic Encyclopaedia suggests that he may have been named Mesh, an Egyptian word meaning 'child'. The encyclopaedia notes that whilst this term is now used widely amongst Egyptologists, no real conclusions have been reached. The names Mousos and Moses, therefore, both still have currency.

Thermuthis is attributed as having selected the name Mousos because the Egyptian word for water was *Mo* whilst someone rescued from it was known as *Usos*.[1]

Moses prepared the foundations of the Temple

During his early years of development the young Mousos would have been raised with an understanding of all the customs and protocols that any other prince in Egypt would have been subjected to. And, if he was to be groomed for higher things, his education would, perhaps, have included exposure to customs and practices not readily available to others.

Philo, a Jewish philosopher who lived about a thousand years after the first Jerusalem Temple was built, suggested that Moses' education included the study of: *'Arithmetic, geometry, the lore of metre, rhythm and harmony'.* [2] These subjects were taught by the Egyptian adepts, members of the highest levels of the priesthood. In addition, Moses was taught the languages of bordering nations and the Chaldean science of the heavenly bodies, what today we call astronomy. To this was added astrology, a highly revered skill of the Egyptian priesthood. Astrology was the process of predicting where the Sun, Moon, certain stars and planets would be on specific days and times. From the astrological results, favourable or unfavourable influence on events would be forecast. It is from this science that we have the astrological predictions that we see regularly in newspapers and magazines today. Whilst some people may mock the concept of astrology, we should remember that it was still the dominant science relating to star and planetary movements until the 18th and 19th centuries, when the more dedicated science of astronomy came to the fore. The Chaldeans are also credited with having determined the twelve segments of the zodiac, or signs of the zodiac, together with an understanding of the process of the rotation and movement of the Earth known as *precession.* What is particularly of interest in Philo's comments, however, is that Moses was apparently taught the concepts of what in the 18th, 19th and 20th centuries were embodied into what became known as the Liberal Arts and Sciences.

Philo also indicates that Moses received from the Egyptian priesthood a thorough understanding of the 'symbols displayed in the holy inscriptions'. This suggests that there was a secret lore that was conveyed in scriptures, a form of allegory, the meaning of which would be totally obscure to, and passed over by, those without the relevant knowledge, yet the meaning or interpretation of which would be clear to those who had been initiated into understanding the message contained in the symbolism.

These symbols displayed in the holy inscriptions, and the other knowledge that was imparted to Moses, seems to have been to good effect. Later in life he appears to have embodied that knowledge in the religious rituals he developed when the Israelites were wandering the desert and he had built the tabernacle. This is expounded on by Josephus in his *Antiquities of the Jews:*[3]

> *consider the fabric of the tabernacle, and take a view of the garments of the high priest, and of those vessels which we make use of in our sacred ministration…. he will find they were every one made in way of imitation and representation of the universe.*

> *when he [Moses] ordered twelve loaves to be set on the table, he denoted the year, as distinguished into so many months*

By branching out the candlestick into seventy parts, he [Moses] secretly intimated the Decani, or seventy divisions of the planets; and as to the seven lamps upon the candlesticks, they referred to the course of the planets, of which that is the number.

The veils, too, which were composed of four things, they declared the four elements ...Earth...Air...Water...Fire

being like lightning in its pomegranates [lightning bolt], and in the noise of the bells resembling thunder

Each of the sardonyxes [onyx in which white layers alternate with sard; yellow or orange cornelian regarded as precious stones] declares to us the Sun and the Moon; those, I mean, that were in the nature of buttons on the high priest's shoulders.

And for the twelve stones, ...we understand the like number of the signs of that circle which the Greeks call the Zodiac, we shall not be mistaken in their meaning.

(Words in brackets [] are the addition of the author.)

Josephus was a Roman citizen and also Jewish. He wrote the above some two thousand years ago. It suggests that he had an intimate knowledge of the hidden symbolism attached to the Jewish religious rituals. It raises an interesting question. This information must have been known to the Pharisees and Sadducees, the senior members of the Jewish priesthood, two thousand years ago. Is it possible that the same symbolism transferred to the Christian religion when it was formalised?

Moses the General – betrayal and escape

In addition to the knowledge imparted to him on science and the mysteries of Egyptian religion, Prince Mousos was clearly an astute military tactician. We are told that he led military campaigns against the Ethiopians and was a very successful general. Josephus makes reference to one particular battle where a Princess named Tharbis, believed to have been the daughter of the king of the Ethiopians, was in a town that was under siege by troops commanded by Prince Mousos. The Ethiopians wouldn't come out and fight so Mousos decided that his army should fight their way in. Princess Tharbis looked over the city walls and noted the actions of the young enemy warrior. Natural instincts prevailed and she fell in love with him – a case of love at first sight. Hostilities were ceased, and Princess Tharbis and Prince Mousos were married. Peace terms were then agreed, after which the marriage was consummated. Prince Mousos then returned to Egypt but, alas, we lose track of knowledge about the fate of his new wife.[4] This is the first marriage recorded for Prince Mousos, which implies that Princess Tharbis was his first wife.

Moses prepared the foundations of the Temple

To have had command of such an army as conveyed in the above story implies that Prince Mousos was a highly respected and competent military leader, and obviously deeply immersed in the Egyptian way of life, its mysteries and its lore.

On his return from his military exploits biblical tradition has it that Mousos was then told about his origins and upbringing. One can well understand the mental confusion that such a revelation would have had on someone, especially a person who was still relatively young. This was a person who, until that time, quite clearly would have had a perception of being someone else, and something else, in terms of the ruling, administration and security of the country. Keeping in mind the bonded status of the Israelite population in Egypt at that time, and the harsh treatment they were experiencing, it is alleged that Prince Mousos observed an Egyptian overseer administering a severe beating on one of the slaves – now, one of his own people. Mousos stepped in, attempting to save his fellow Israelite. He was apparently in such a rage that he killed the Egyptian.

> One day, when Moses had grown up, he went out to his people and looked on their burdens; and he saw an Egyptian beating a Hebrew, one of his people. He looked this way and that, and seeing no one he killed the Egyptian and hid him in the sand.
>
> Exodus 2:11-12

This action, the Old Testament tells us, resulted in his need to flee from Egypt.

Josephus, in his *Antiquities of the Jews*, presents a slightly different perspective on these events:

> Now the Egyptians, after they had been preserved by Moses, entertained a hatred to him, and were very eager in compassing their designs against him, as suspecting that he would take occasion, from his good success, to raise a sedition, and bring innovations into Egypt; and told the king he ought to be slain. The king had also some intentions of himself to the same purpose, and this as well out of envy at his glorious expedition at the head of his army, as out of fear of being brought low by him and being instigated by the sacred scribes, he was ready to undertake to kill Moses: but when he had learned beforehand what plots there were against him, he went away privately; and because the public roads were watched, he took his flight through the deserts, and where his enemies could not suspect he would travel... [5]

The one common theme in these texts is that Moses escaped from Egypt.

Moses finds sanctuary and married for the second time

By all accounts, Moses headed for Arabia and eventually arrived at the city of Midian. Here Moses took rest beside a well. A group of young ladies, daughters of the priest, came to the well to get water for their cattle, only to be chased away by a number of boys. Moses' chivalrous virtues came to the fore and he chastised the boys and helped the young ladies. His reward was to be accepted into the community at Midian, where he married Zipporah, a daughter of the priest. Zipporah was therefore Moses' second wife. Moses appears to have remained in his new home of Arabia for around the next forty years.

The name of the Midian priest is somewhat confusing. In Exodus 2:18 he is referred to as *Reuel*. Nothing more is mentioned about Moses' father-in-law until we get to Exodus 4:18 when he is then introduced as *Jethro*. Josephus gives him the slightly modified name of *Raguel*, but notes that he was also known as *Jethro*. So in subsequent references to either name, the reader must remember that *Jethro* and *Raguel* are one and the same person.

Moses' return to Egypt

The Old Testament text continues that, in his eightieth year, Moses returned to Egypt. He started out on his journey with Zipporah and his family, but he eventually encouraged them to return to Midian.

Moses confronted the new Pharaoh and sought the release of his Israelite brethren from bondage. What is interesting here is that Moses, although he had left the land of Egypt many years previously, still either had connections or access of some kind that enabled him to make an approach directly to the Pharaoh. The Pharaoh refused to let the Israelites go, as a consequence of which a series of plagues were visited on Egypt. After the tenth plague, Moses led the Israelites, en masse, out of Egypt and across the desert towards the Red Sea. Somewhere where there was water (noting earlier comments about the Red & Reed Sea), Moses was aided by a miraculous parting of the waters which enabled them to cross in safety. The Pharaoh and armed followers gave chase to the Israelites, and were hard on their heels by the time the Pharaoh reached the same point. The Pharaoh and his army, whilst attempting to follow the Israelites through the passage miraculously opened in the sea, perished when the wall of water collapsed on them, although it collapsed only after all the Israelites had completed the crossing. (In a footnote to Exodus 15:4, the sea is referenced back to the Hebrew term *Yam Suph; that is, Sea of Reeds.*)[6] The Exodus is estimated to have taken place around 1,400 BCE, about 480 years before the construction of the first Jerusalem Temple.[7]

Moses returns to familiar territory – near the Burning Bush

Having escaped from their Egyptian bondage, the Israelites, we are told, wandered around the desert for the next forty years under the guidance of Moses awaiting their deliverance to a promised land, a land of milk and honey. In other words, a land that was fertile and verdant as opposed to the scant vegetation of the desert. We are further told that the number of Israelites who left Egypt during the Exodus was measured in tens of thousands.

Academics now question whether the tens of thousands mentioned in the Old Testament could have been assembled and led out of Egypt en masse, as suggested. They postulate that there may have been several small groups that left Egypt at different times, perhaps after hearing about an initial departure of a group led by Moses. It is, therefore, not difficult to imagine that a small group initially led by Moses through the Reed Sea grew as more and more Semitic groups fell in behind what must have appeared to them to have been a most dynamic leader. Gradually, these Semitic peoples, sharing a common religion, collected together in one area and eventually the numbers grew to be a significant population that the Old Testament records.

There are a range of Biblical Study guides and dictionaries that include maps intimating the route that Moses and his band of followers may have taken around the deserts. The Old Testament gives clear clues to at least part of that journey.

Exodus, chapter 3, relates the story of the Burning Bush. It states:

Now Moses was tending the flock of Jethro [Raguel] his father-in-law, the priest of Midian, and he led his flock to the far side of the desert and came to Horeb, the mountain of God.

Text in brackets [ ] is my addition

Through Exodus, chapter 16, and the early verses of chapter 17, we read of them wandering from place to place, complaining about being hungry and thirsty. It is then, in Exodus 17:6, that Moses strikes a rock with his staff to reveal a spring of water.

I will stand there before you by the rock at Horeb. Strike the rock, and water will come out of it for the people to drink.

Today, St Catherine's Monastery, first established in the 3rd century CE, stands at the foot of Mount Sinai, or Horeb – Moses' mountain. Within the high walls that enclose the monastery is a wonderful bush which is alleged to be a descendent plant of the Burning Bush, which has erupted from the same roots as the original. A small spring also rises adjacent to it and now fills a well, used by the monks for their drinking water. This spring is alleged to be the one referred to in Exodus 17.

Through the above two verses, several chapters apart, we find that Moses had led the people to a place he knew from having been there whilst tending his sheep. It seems highly likely, therefore, that with all the grumbling about a lack of water, he led them to a place which he knew from his shepherding activity could possibly have water – a natural spring. It was just the sort of place his father-in-law, Raguel, might assume he would find Moses, if he went looking for him.

Raguel brings order – and the seeds of the Commandments?

Having led his people out of the clutches of a country and administration that had been their oppressors and captors for several generations, Moses would have faced new and challenging difficulties on a daily basis. His training and experience as a Prince, Government Official and Army Commander would have provided him with the knowledge, tenacity, skill, determination and ruthlessness that being the uncrowned king would have demanded.

One can only imagine the difficulties this charismatic, though elderly, man must have had trying to exercise authority over the multitude that had gathered about him. What is more, as slaves in Egypt it is most probable that food and drink would have been brought, or rationed, to them. Self-sufficiency was a new lesson they needed to learn. This is adequately demonstrated in Exodus 16 where there are many grumbles about the amount and quality of the food they had in the desert by comparison with the pots of meat they had in Egypt. Moses, however, educated them in the different ways they needed to survive the desert terrain.

So it was that word of Moses' exploits, and the Exodus from Egypt, reached his father-in-law in Midian. Raguel went out into the desert to meet his son-in-law, taking Moses' wife, Zipporah, and their two sons with him. Raguel, it seems, was greatly impressed. However, he noted that Moses was making all the decisions and adjudicating on all disputes. Raguel pointed this out to his son-in-law, noting that if he did not do something about the situation then he was in danger of taking on so much that he would work himself into the ground – the effort of trying to control everything would kill him. In good management tradition, Raguel encouraged Moses to delegate responsibility and deal only with the serious matters. It would also free time to enable Moses to deal with some of the other issues that they may yet face – to take stock of the situation and do some advance planning. Moses acknowledged his father-in-law's observations and implemented them.

Moses listened to his father-in-law and did everything he said.

Exodus 18: 24

One can only speculate that Raguel lent a helping hand, because it was only after a suitable management structure, a structure of delegated authority and justice, had been put in place that Raguel returned home.

And that brings us to the Ten Commandments.

Moses had gathered a considerable community about him. Following Raguel's suggestions, he had put in place a system of authority, administration and justice. But it was still a community without laws against which justice could be administered. In reading the Commandments one can only conclude that they are a set of rules by which a properly ordered society should govern itself; by which the people knew what was expected of them; by which the relationships of one person to another could be established. This was a group of people in need of an identity, to be moulded as one cohesive group, ultimately one nation.

Raguel was a priest. Moses was a warrior. One can well imagine that Raguel had many conversations with Moses during their meeting in the desert and that Raguel had instilled in his son-in-law a need to develop and write down a set of rules by which the multitude could be governed, both then and for the future. One can further imagine that Moses needed to get away somewhere on his own, to think about what was before him and about this mass of people he had taken responsibility for. He needed time and space to set out the laws and processes by which they should be governed. And where better to do that than on Mount Sinai. One can further imagine that Raguel would have instilled in Moses the need to ensure that from the moment he delivered what were to become the Commandments, they had credibility in the eyes of the multitude. Merely sitting down and making a few marks on papyrus was not going to do that. He needed a drama to have impact. What better way to create credibility and impact than if those laws came directly from the hand of their deity – *Yahweh*. Producing something in a single day, or overnight, in the midst of the assembled throng, and claiming it came from the deity, would lack credibility. But on the top of a mountain, closer to Heaven, the domain of the deity, that would have been something different. And, with a suitable lapse of time between ascending the mountain and delivering the result, that would give the entire process a high degree of status.

During his ascent of Mount Sinai, Moses had ensured that he would not be disturbed, by having Aaron, his brother, go part of the way with him and then stop so that Moses went on alone. As Graham Hancock points out in the book *The Sign and the Seal*, that only Moses, therefore, knew what he was up to; Moses was the sole source of detail about what happened on the mount during the time he was there. Nobody else was there to add support or verify events. Moses could have done entirely what he wanted, have said later that any manner of things had happened to him – his was the sole word and record of the events. What better way to introduce the concept of a living and watchful deity, to provide a source of authority for the proclamation of rules, laws and rituals that would be needed to mould an undisciplined and disunited rabble into a cohesive group that would form the basis of a new nation. He had, after all, a precedent to refer to – Horus, the founding god of Egypt, whom he would have revered and understood as the basis and origin for the rules, laws and traditions on which that country was founded. Was Moses attempting to re-create a similar foundation? Instead of producing the Commandments on papyrus, he engraved them on stone. It would be logical that Moses should choose to inscribe them on something more permanent just as he would have seen that in Egypt a record of key events was embossed into the stone of temple walls and pillars. Engraving carefully considered text in stone took time.

It is interesting to note that after the dramatic production of the Commandments by Moses, the social structure, the Tabernacle and its furnishings, the Ark, the garments for the priests, and religious rituals all came into being as recorded in the books of Exodus and Leviticus.

I appreciate that the following comments will not find favour with all my readers. However, after several years of reading and considering the various issues involved, I have come to the conclusion that on Mount Sinai, Moses drew on his education and experience as a Prince and General in Egypt, and the advice he received from his priestly father-in-law. He spent his time compiling a detailed plan of action which brought together the basis of defence, government and religious belief. Where his previous education had conditioned his understanding, he embodied the principles of the *ancient wisdom* as he had been taught them. Hence the reason we find them inculcated in the design of the Ark, the priest's garments and rituals, as outlined by Josephus. And that *ancient wisdom* was then transmitted to later generations to turn up subsequently in Solomon's Temple.

Eventually, Moses delivered his people to the area now known as Palestine and, although he saw the land of his successors, he never set foot in it, dying at this momentous point in time. Based on biblical quotations, Moses (or Mousos) was 120 years old when he died.

The Israelites did not just walk into an open area of land that they claimed as their own, they had to wrest it away from others already living there. One by one they conquered their so-called enemies and absorbed their lands, so that by the time of Solomon their territorial claims ranged from the River Euphrates to the Mediterranean Sea. It is not too far-fetched to say that it all started with Moses.

Nearly 1,500 years after the Exodus, the New Testament book of Acts recorded:

And Moses was educated in all the learning of the Egyptians, and he was a man of power in words and deeds.

Acts 7:22

Moses. What a man – whoever he was!!

The Ark of the Covenant

Having delivered the Commandments, Moses gave the instructions for the building of the Ark of the Covenant, the design for which, the Old Testament records, was also conveyed by *Yahweh* to Moses on Mount Sinai.

The Ark of the Covenant is a key attribute of the first Jerusalem Temple. Indeed, we are told that the Temple was specifically designed to provide a permanent home for it. This implies that there was something special about the Ark if only as the centre piece of the nation. The word 'Ark' is apparently derived from the Hebrew words *'Aron Kodesh'*, which is translated as the *holy cabinet*.

The concept of the Ark was probably not new to Moses. The same type of device, that is to say, an ornate box carried on poles, was a fairly commonplace item used in Egypt by the Pharaoh. In this respect, then, Moses was following an idea he had already seen during his connection with the ruling house of Egypt in which he had once been pleased to be raised and to serve as a Prince.

The Ark has been described as a *strange contraption*. So strange in fact that it, and its uses, have been the subject of considerable speculation. Amongst the more extreme theories is the idea that it was a device for communicating with our alien forefathers who were sitting in space and watching the development of the species they had created, and communicating messages through the cherubim located on the Mercy Seat.[8] (Note that in the King James version of the Old Testament it is called the Mercy Seat. However, it's the atonement cover using the modern translation reflected in the New International Version.) Yet, despite the speculation, one has to conclude that during the period following the Exodus, and until the building of the Temple, it represented a most highly revered item of religious furniture. Therein were deposited at various internals of time:

first, the tablets containing the Commandments
second, Aaron's rod which started to grow when placed on the ground,
and third, the bowl of the Mannah.

Moses prepared the foundations of the Temple

Having deposited the tablets containing the Commandments in the Ark, these important tablets do not seem to have seen the light of day again. Interestingly, in 1 Kings 8:9 we are told that after the Ark was carried into the Jerusalem Temple the only items in it were the stone tablets. This raises an intriguing question – what happened to Aaron's rod and the bowl of the Mannah?

The Ark was then plated with pure gold both inside and outside and decorated with gold moulding. Two rings of gold were then added at each side, probably near or at the corners to aid carrying stability, four rings in all. Two shafts of acacia wood, also plated with gold, were then inserted through the rings with an instruction that the shafts must never be withdrawn from the rings. The length of the poles was about 20 cubits.

To the box was then added a Throne of Mercy, also known as the Mercy Seat. Rendered from pure gold, this item had two cherubim, facing each other, mounted on it. It is obvious that the Throne of Mercy acted as a lid to seal the box, which otherwise would have been open to the elements. The amount of gold used in its manufacture dictates that the weight of this ornate lid would have been considerable, essential for keeping the lid in place whilst the Ark was being carried. It would have swayed and jolted with the movement of those carrying it as they travelled over rough terrain. Anyone with a basic understanding of mechanical engineering principles will quickly realise that the long poles used for carrying the Ark were important for distributing the weight and reducing the load that each carrier had to shoulder. The cherubim would have given the finished article an artistic and distinctive appearance that would have created the aura of something special.

On two separate occasions over two consecutive years, I had the opportunity to visit Egypt and see many of the wonders of the ancient kingdom that I had read about during my research: the pyramids; Karnack Temple at Luxor, the Valley of the Kings; the impressive Cairo Museum; the broken column at Aswan (Syrene) and Abu Simbel. Many books I had read made reference to artefacts that can be seen in collections on display in the Cairo Museum, so it was with something of a burning desire that I was anxious to see them for myself. Amongst the many items of jewellery, for example, were exquisite pieces that any modern craftsman would have been proud to be associated with. The fact that they were made up to 4,500 years ago was even more impressive. I was particularly struck by a folding camp bed, some 4,000 years old, used in hunting expeditions, which demonstrated a remarkable use of hinges. But my family and I were particularly excited to see the exhibition of artefacts that had been removed from the tomb of Tutankhamun. The use of gold for decorative purposes was evident in almost every exhibit. I could not help but note that there had been an opulent use of gold in nearly all the regal funerary exhibits. In this sense, what Moses did with gold when lining the inside and outside of the Ark was again no more than he would have experienced in his association with the ruling elite of Egypt. There was a large sarcophagus, made of several sarcophagi, where one was housed inside the other. They were rather like a Russian doll where multiple dolls are fitted one inside the other, each one smaller than the last. Both the inside and outside of each sarcophagus layer was coated with gold, just as the Ark was finished. I could not help commenting that the Pharaohs clearly used gold in their time as we might use a pot of paint today.

There was one feature on the sarcophagi that I was particularly anxious to see. About two years prior to my visit to the Cairo Museum, I read Graham Hancock's book *The Sign and the Seal*. This is an account of his search for the Ark of the Covenant and a tradition that suggests that it was taken to Ethiopia, where it supposedly resides even today. Hancock had observed the same use of gold in the decorative effect on the sarcophagi that I had seen, but he also noted that on the doors and rear walls of each sarcophagus were images of winged female guardians, with 'their wings spread upwards', and facing each other, just as the cherubim described for the Mercy Seat were fashioned. This is, perhaps, further evidence of the Egyptian influence and tradition that Moses was drawing on, as he developed the basis of the culture that the Israelites were creating.

The Ark, then, was a highly revered object. But, we are told, it had another attribute. It is credited with having developed mystical and perceptive powers. Used in a discriminating manner these powers had sufficient strength to kill those who went near it or touched it when not authorised to do so, or were involved in acts it did not seem to like. It is interesting to note that, with a couple of minor exceptions which can be otherwise explained, the power of the Ark to do harm to others seems only to have been possible when Moses was present. The Ark, it appears, was so revered that it was even carried into battle as a form of protecting mascot. At one stage, to the dismay of the Israelites, it was captured by the Philistines who later returned it when they began to experience the cruel magic of the device. The Ark, it is therefore suggested, was a tool which Moses used periodically to ensure adherence to his leadership and the values that were espoused through the Commandments written on the tablets, to create a climate of fear and respect. One would therefore construe that the victims of the Ark were used as an example in controlling the actions of his followers. This same control strategy was used in the First World War by British Generals. The records show that a number of men, shot at dawn for supposed cowardice, or a minor infringement of army rules or orders during an engagement with the enemy, were noted at their Court Martial hearing as having not committed any serious breach of discipline, but were 'used as an example'. They were shot by a squad of their own countrymen in an effort to engender fear into the troops and keep them in line.[9]

But, there was more to the Ark than is immediately obvious.

The Ark – a cunning device?

Solomon's Temple, we are told, was built to house the Ark of the Covenant.

Bezalel and Oholiab, appointed by Moses as builders of the Ark, were 'cunning' master craftsmen. In text related to the Ark we have further examples of text changes and their implications. As an example we refer to chapter 35 in the book of Exodus, where the details for building the Ark are recorded. It is towards the end of the chapter that we are introduced to Bezalel and Oholiab, two highly skilled craftsmen who are to undertake the construction and are empowered with the ability to teach others. The text reads:

> *Them hath he filled with the wisdom...of the cunning workman....even of them that do cunning work, and those that devise cunning work.*
> *Exodus 35:35   King James version*

> *He has filled them with skill to do all kinds of work as craftsmen....all of them master craftsmen and designers.*
> *Exodus 35:35   New International version*

The impression one gets from the King James text is of a group of individuals who, by dint of being cunning, undertake works in a manner that is perhaps a little underhanded, perhaps with not quite the integrity we might otherwise expect. The Oxford Dictionary defines the word 'cunning' to be:

> *skilled at deception; crafty; ingenious*

What could there possibly be about this gold-encrusted wooden box that was deceptive or even ingenious? We will come to that in due course.

In the second and more recent text, the New International version, the builders of the Ark are given some respectability by being master craftsmen. In reality, both verses make the same point. Imagine someone you know has a need to build a brick wall, is intent on doing it themselves, but it is not their regular profession. The chances are that they would consult a few technical text books on the subject and then commence the task exactly as the experts suggest. A trained bricklayer, on the other hand, might take a lot of apparent short cuts by comparison with the expert opinion. One might look on these short cuts as being *cunning*. The bricklayer, however, could have been merely implementing a few tricks of the trade gained from years of experience. So in the case of the Exodus 35:35 text both versions are saying the same thing – Bezalel and Oholiab were master craftsmen well equipped with knowledge and an understanding of the tricks of the trade. But their tricks of the trade appear to have extended beyond the methods of construction. They included knowledge of the *ancient mysteries*.

When it comes to the presentation of the Ark, religious dogma, explanations, and illustrations designed to support various Old Testament stories have created the impression that it was a highly sophisticated, gold-encrusted ornament, complete with angel-like cherubim sitting on the lid; that this ornament had secret power – a power which some have written of as being akin to a nuclear generator – a power so awesome that it could defeat the enemies of the Israelites virtually on its own. The reality is that the Ark was a relatively small wooden box, 1.5 cubits square and 2.5 cubits long. To get an idea of the size, stand with both arms at your sides. Now raise one arm until it is level with your shoulder. The distance from your armpit to the end of the outstretched arm and fingertips is about 1.5 cubits. The distance across your body to the end of your outstretched arm and fingertips is about 2.5 cubits.

The Ark dimensions

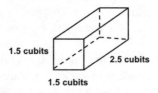

These dimensions appear to have been deliberately chosen and have links with sacred geometry, Divine Proportion, sacred numbers and the value of Phi.

1.5/2.5 = 0.6 the accepted value of Phi.

2.5/1.5 = 1.6 Phi again.

If we now take the square ends

1.5 + 1.5 + 1.5 + 1.5 = 6, a highly revered number meaning harmony. Also the scriptures say that the world and the heavens were created in six days.

There are two ends to the box, so

6 x 2 = 12, the number of months in the year and the number of constellations which make up the zodiac.

Then there are the two ends of the box multiplied by the length.

12 x 2.5 = 30, which relates to the phases of the Moon. The dates for religious festivals were dictated by the lunar calendar, as some, like Easter, still are.

There is yet more. The total length for the sides of the two ends divided by the length of one side of the end;

12 – 1.5 = 8 which reflects the sacred cube.

Of course, a diagonal line drawn between two corners of the square ends will give an angle of 45 degrees, whilst a diagonal line drawn across the face of length will give angles very close to 30 and 60 degrees.

By adding together the four edges which make up the length, we have:

2.5 x 4 = 10. By disregarding the zero, we have 1, unity, the symbol of the deity.

By taking the length of the perimeter of one end and multiplying it by the length of the sides, we have:

(1.5 x 4) x 2.5 = 15 the angular rotation in degrees of the Earth in 1/24th part of a day, what today we call an hour.

Because of its relationship to the value of Phi, 1.6, the area of the side of the length of the box is a visual representation of Divine Proportion as expressed as a ratio of either of the ends.

It is intriguing to note that Bezalel and Oholiab, those *cunning* master craftsmen, were empowered with 'the ability to teach others'. It raises the prospect that what they were teaching was not so much the skill of fashioning pieces of wood into a box, but the secrets of the *ancient mysteries* – the secrets of *ancient wisdom* as it was then perceived. And this is perhaps not surprising for we must remember that their master was Moses. As a prince in Egypt he would have been taught those same mysteries, that same *wisdom*.

From Philo's comments about Moses' education, and his being taught the language of bordering nations and the Chaldean science of the heavenly bodies, we have an indication that Moses would have possessed precisely the type of *ancient wisdom* that would have enabled the building of the Ark to reflect the geometric principles that it appears to display.

Moses. What a man – whoever he was!!

Some five hundred years after the Ark was devised, and then constructed by Bezalel and Oholiab, the first Jerusalem Temple was built. At the consecration of the Temple, the Ark was carried into it and set down. After that it plays no further part in the history of the Israelites.

The Ark and the Queen of Sheba

Quite what happened to the Ark is a mystery of history. Some suggest that it was hidden in a cave close to Jerusalem. Others suggest it was hidden in a secret chamber cut into the rock of Mount Moriah below the Temple and rediscovered 2,000 years later by the Knights Templar. Another suggestion is that it resides today in Ethiopia.

The story goes that the Queen of Sheba visited King Solomon to learn more about his wisdom and to view the Temple. During her stay in Jerusalem a great love affair ensued between them. When the Queen of Sheba returned to Ethiopia, she gave birth to a son, Solomon's son, and named him Menelik. Solomon's son was raised by his mother in Ethiopia but later, when nearing manhood, he visited his father in Jerusalem. At the end of that visit Menelik supposedly returned to Ethiopia, taking the Ark of the Covenant with him. This supposed theft of the Ark is thought to have been instigated by Azarius, son of the High Priest of Israel. Tradition also has it that the Ark continues to reside in Axum, the old capital of Ethiopia, even to this day.[10]

The Tabernacle

The Ark of the Covenant, with its hidden symbolism of ancient wisdom, was set up in a tent referred to as the Tabernacle. There is considerable detail about the Tabernacle in Exodus and from this detail we can identify certain characteristics.

The first is the orientation. It was on an east-west line. We can deduce that by virtue that in Exodus 40:22 & 24:

Moses placed the table in the Tent of the Meeting on the north side of the tabernacle......

He placed the lampstand in the Tent of the Meeting opposite the table on the south side of the tabernacle...

These two references seem to imply that the tent was set up to correspond with the four cardinal points: north, south, east and west. Such an orientation would clearly mean that the first light of day – sunrise – would penetrate the length of the Tabernacle, probably striking the Ark, the only time it would do so each day. In Exodus 38:13 it states:

The east end, towards the sunrise...

Thereafter, the Sun would rise higher in the sky and then move round to the south and west. The interior and the Ark would be shielded from the direct light of the Sun. The text tells us that a curtain was placed at the front entrance of the Tabernacle. This may not have been the thick and heavy curtain material we know from our homes in the western world, but a thin muslin type of material, possibly translucent, used as a veil. Modern translations refer to it as linen.

In addition to the orientation, we find a series of key numbers appearing: 1½ or 1.5, 4, 5, 6, 8, 10, 11, 16, 20, 28, 30 and 50. Keeping in mind what we have already revealed in the Ark, and Moses' apparent familiarity with *ancient wisdom*, these numbers could contain a hidden symbolism.

The number 30 is the number of days in a lunar month. The cycles of the Moon were, and in some instances still are, the basis of the religious calendar. The Moon has a cycle of 27½ days from first appearing as a new Moon to disappearing from view. It therefore disappears on the 28th day. There is then a period of 2 days when it is in darkness before reappearing again. The entire cycle of the Moon takes 29½ days, completed on the 30th day; $28 + 1½ = 29½$, or in the 30th day. It could therefore be that the 1½, 28 and 30 all related to the cycle of the Moon and the establishment of the religious calendar. The 4 possibly relates to the four elements of Earth, Fire, Air and Water or the seasons, as denoted earlier by Josephus. Dropping the zero from the 10 and 20, we have 1 for unity, the deity, and 2 for balance, duality, Heaven and Earth; 5 for the pentagram as a symbol of good luck; 6 because the scriptures say that the process of creation took 6 days; 8 is the symbol of the sacred cube. These insights are too coincidental.

When we come to the courtyard we find another set of numbers:

100, 50, 30, 20, 15, 3, 4

This time there appears to be another hidden factor. We are told that the courtyard surrounding the tent had dimensions of 100 cubits along each of the south and northern edges, and 50 cubits at the eastern and western ends. We are told that there were 20 supporting posts marking the boundary of the longer sides, thereby 10 across the shorter ends. With a length of 100 cubits and 20 posts to support the curtains, it means that the curtains were each 5 cubits long. It also means there was a total of 60 posts. So, we find:

> 60 posts, to support curtains
> 5 cubits long, around a perimeter which is
> 300 cubits long
> =   365 = days in a solar year.

There is also a connection between the 20, 4 and 15. The Earth rotates on its axis 15 degrees in what today we call an hour, and 24 divisions of 15 degrees = 360 degrees, one full rotation.

This type of revelation is difficult to dismiss as being merely coincidence, especially if considered against the possible reference to the lunar cycles above.

Mount Sinai – Moses' Mountain

We had just endured a three-hour drive across the desert in the dead of night. Jostled by the sand-covered and rutted roads, we were weary but filled with excitement and anticipation.

The outline of the old monastery was clearly discernible in the moonlight when we arrived in the early hours of the morning. There was no light or sound from inside. The whiteness of the subdued light emitted by the Moon gave the building an aura of cold stillness as if it had been deserted. We knew it was still inhabited, as it had been since the 3rd century, when it was founded.

It was a wonderfully clear night. The Moon was high in the sky above us, just two days after being full. The white light reflected from the sands of the desert around us, creating a low level of background luminance. Rearing up from behind the monastery was the dark shadow of the mountain, its jagged summit silhouetted against the sky. From somewhere along the valley, hidden by an outcrop of rocks, there was the sound of camels shrieking and the voices of herdsmen encouraging their beasts of burden.

Our guide had suggested we could walk up the mountain or ride on a camel. Filled with bravado, I elected to walk. My wife, who was clearly more aware of her limits than I was of my own, elected to ride on a camel. And so we set off on our three-hour journey to the summit. The ground underfoot was dusty, ragged and uneven. The climb quickly gave way from the gentle incline along the valley floor to become ever steeper as we turned to face the mountain. The pack on my back, which merely contained a couple of bottles of water and had previously provided no discomfort, took on definite weight where there had been little before. Within the first twenty minutes of the climb my legs started to ache, my breathing became heavier and I realised just how unfit I really was. The bravado left me and I, too, climbed aboard a camel to be carried with stately majesty up the mountain. The camels made progress with a steady, sure-footed motion, urged on gently by the camel herder who walked behind shouting occasional instructions that the camel understood but we didn't. I admired the camel herder for his stamina and fitness.

The carefree camel journey provided the opportunity to admire the night sky. The brilliance of the Moon obscured most of the stars, but those that could be seen had a clarity that was awe-inspiring. Living in a western industrial society, with its street lights, tower blocks and flashing neon signs, one seldom sees this beautiful natural backdrop of the canopy of the night sky. I revelled in the knowledge that I was seeing that canopy as countless generations of Bedouin tribes had witnessed it from the earliest periods of antiquity.

At times, the prepared path our camels trod seemed to hang precariously from the side of the mountain. A stumble could lead to a long drop to the valley floor below. I put the prospect out of my mind by relishing the whole experience we had embarked on.

The Moon lit up the sides of the mountain to show that it was devoid of vegetation, and steep. The sides were littered with loose shale, the type you could stand on, slip, and then tumble all the way to the bottom. We were climbing on a carefully chosen route and prepared track which cantilevered its way up the mountain. My mind wondered at the eighty-year-old man, thousands of years previously, who had climbed the same mountain, probably in the heat of the day, carrying the food and water he needed, and without the benefit of this chosen route. I couldn't help thinking he was mad to have even tried it.

Along the valley floor the night air had been still and warm and there was a sweet scent to the air which came from the vegetation grown close to the monastery. As we climbed higher the night air began to chill. There was a slight movement in the air and dust, kicked up by the camels' methodical plodding, billowed upwards and filled the nostrils.

Some two hours after leaving the valley below, the leading camel suddenly swung left into a flat, stone-walled enclosure, and the others in our party trailed after it. Knowing exactly what was expected of them, the camels lowered themselves onto their haunches as an instruction for us to dismount.

Our guide had informed us that this was as far as the camels could go. From here, the remainder of our ascent would take about another hour and would have to be on foot. That meant ascending some 700 stone steps, prepared about 1,000 years earlier, by the monks attached to the monastery below. They were not the type of steps one finds in a modern western building, designed and built to carefully devised building standards which regulated the height, width and depth. These were steps of varying heights ranging from a hands-breadth to knee-high; they were made from pieces of stone laid one on top of the other; there were rounded boulders jammed in position by smaller pieces of rock. Every step was uneven and irregular. It was not an easy climb. I would clamber up perhaps thirty steps at a time and then collapse against the rock face gasping for air and allowing the muscles in my legs to recover before punishing them again. My only relief was to note that I wasn't alone; other members of our party were experiencing the same torture. Eventually we emerged over the final step. We had done it. This was the summit. I found a rocky ledge and sat down, elated at the success of getting there, yet with a feeling of exhaustion. The warm perspiration which had enveloped me during the climb now turned cold in the chill of the early morning air which darted about us in sudden gusts. The Moon still cast its bright aura about us.

Ours was not the only party on the mountain that morning. There must have been a hundred people in total and the variety of languages that were spoken indicated the far-flung places around the globe that they had come from, just to be there to witness the same ancient spectacle that we were – to witness the Sun rise over the desert.

Our climb was well timed. We didn't have to wait long before a glimmer of light appeared on the eastern horizon beyond a distant range of hills. The glimmer gradually became a shaft of light which broadened every few seconds, pressing the darkness of night back against the western horizon.

Then, in the blink of an eye, a thin blood-red line appeared on the horizon. There was an excited chatter amongst the people gathered on the mountain top, a chatter of eager anticipation and the sounds of the clicking of dozens of cameras eager to record the event. With each blink of the eyes, the blood-red line gave way to a progressively emerging ball of fire and, as it silently cleared the top of the distant hills, there was a spontaneous cheer from the assembled throng on the mountain. This was what we had all come for. This is what we had all made the gruelling climb to witness. This was nature's great spectacle – dawn and the rising Sun. A new day in life's cycle had just begun. The whole experience was burnt into my memory to be relived time and time again.

This was the Sinai desert. This was Mount Sinai – Moses' Mountain. This was how Moses must have seen day break during his days on the mountain some 3,500 years ago. And below us was St Catherine's Monastery, denoted as the place of the Burning Bush and the stream that Moses had released by striking a stone with his rod.

Conclusion

It seems clear that whoever Moses/Mousos was, as an Egyptian Prince he was educated in the *ancient wisdom and knowledge* then retained by the Egyptian priesthood. That knowledge included information about the natural world, the macro-cosmos, including the heavens, the Sun and the Moon. It is also clear that he needed to create a set of rules for civilised behaviour that the multitude who ultimately followed him to Sinai could use as the basis of their society. In addition he drew on his knowledge of the macro-cosmos as it had been taught to him, and included elements of it in the religious rituals and furnishings he created. This no doubt included educating the new priesthood in the hidden symbolic meaning of certain characters in the scriptures. He did all of this as part of the process of moulding a disparate rabble into the cohesive body of a new nation.

Amongst the important religious furnishings created by Moses was the Ark of the Covenant. David designed a house for the Ark, so it is to him that we next turn our attention.

[1] Josephus – *Antiquity of the Jews* translated by Winston, W. Book 2 Chapter 9 section 6

[2] *The Sign and the Seal: The Quest for the Lost Ark of the Covenant* – Graham Hancock

[3] Josephus – *Antiquity of the Jews,* Book 3 Chapter 7

[4] This story is attributed to Josephus as recorded in his *Antiquity of the Jews*. It is outlined by David Rohl in *A Test of Time* Chapter 12

[5] Josephus – *Antiquity of the Jews,* Book 2 Chapter 11

[6] Holy Bible, New International Edition

[7] *A Test of Time*, Chapter 12

[8] *Genisis –Tthe First Book of Revelations* by David Wood

[9] A controversial documentary made by Carlton TV in 1998 and subsequently screened on the History Channel, had comments by a military historian, Julian Putkowski. The programme noted that from the time General Haig assumed command of Allied forces in 1915, 306 men were executed at the rate of 3 every two weeks. Executions continued until 2 days prior to the Armistice, even though the Allied Generals knew that a cessation of hostilities was possible. The Australian Government refused to allow their troops to be so treated. No Australians were executed for the same reasons as the British soldiers throughout the First World War

[10] *The Sign and the Seal: The Quest for the Lost Ark of the Covenant* – Graham Hancock

[11] An interesting book on the mystery of what may have happened to the Ark of the Covenant is *The Sign and the Seal: The Quest for the Lost Ark of the Covenant* by Graham Hancock

Chapter 10
David, heresy and chronology

The Old Testament tells us that the design of the first Jerusalem temple, originated with King David.

History tells us that there have been three temples dedicated to the Jewish faith built on Mount Moriah at different periods, in what has come to be known as the city of Jerusalem. The first temple, we are told, was built by Solomon, probably around 950 BCE. After nearly 400 years, this temple was destroyed by an invading army of the Babylonian king, Nebuchadnezzar, around 573 BCE. After this defeat, most of the Israelites were taken into slavery in Babylon, there to remain for 70 years until Babylon was itself conquered by the Persian king, Cyrus, and became part of his Persian empire. On release from their Babylonian captivity, the Israelites returned to Jerusalem and a second temple was built by King Zerubbabel in the 6th century BCE. This second temple may have been based on a vision by the prophet Ezekiel, a vision which had supposedly occurred during his period of Babylonian captivity. It was destroyed and plundered around 170 BCE by the Greeks. Then a third temple was built by King Herod. Construction is believed to have commenced around 20 BCE. The building of this temple was still in progress around the time of Jesus Christ and ultimately became known as the Herodian Temple. This third temple had a short life because it was utterly destroyed by the Romans around 70 CE following the Jewish uprising against the Roman occupation of Palestine and a revolt in Jerusalem which occurred around that time. Today, in the same area of ground where once stood the three temples of the Jewish faith, stands the Al-Aqsa Mosque: the Dome of the Rock, a sacred Islamic structure.

The Al-Aqsa Mosque covers a large area of the original site, and incorporates some of the remaining elements of the Herodian Temple. Detailed archaeological surveys are obviously difficult to instigate, influenced as much by political circumstances as religion.

In-depth modern archaeological exploration of the area that was probably covered by the original Temple building has so far been fraught with difficulty since the advent of progressive scientific approaches. Even so, such surveys can only confirm the outline of any original building and the division of any internal rooms as suggested by the remains of any surviving foundations. It may also confirm the orientation. In all probability it will not tell us what this enigmatic temple finally looked like or how it was used. The only sources we have that give us the clues are a combination of the Old Testament text and the historical setting of the cultures that existed around the time the Temple was built.

Before David designed the Temple

Moses, it seems, prepared the foundations for the temple; Solomon built the Temple but it was his father, David, who, according to the Old Testament, designed the Temple. So, what might the factors have been which influenced that design?

Briefly, we will précis some of the background we can glean from the Old Testament as it relates to the two kings, Saul and David. This sets them in an historical background as well as exploring the influences which existed at that time.

Samuel, David and Saul

We are told that in the era of Samuel the Israelite people made it known that they no longer wanted to be ruled by a collective order known as the Judges, but wanted a king to rule over them.

As a young man, Saul had been out looking for some lost donkeys and decided to go to the town where, by chance, Samuel was based, to enquire if anyone had seen the lost animals. At that time Samuel was obviously conducting an audit of likely candidates for the new position. Saul, by his demeanour, impressed Samuel and so in due course was anointed with oil, and became king. There then followed a period of wars and bloodshed. One draws the conclusion that Samuel was unhappy with the overall performance of Saul as king, or he was playing for time and that Saul had been an opportunistic and interim appointment. Samuel was clearly trying to secure a future succession without it falling automatically to the descendants of Saul. Certainly something was astray because Samuel commenced seeking for Saul's successor, and did so in secret. Although Saul was still king, Samuel went off to Bethlehem taking the Holy Oil used for anointment with him.

Reading the accounts both in the Old Testament and Josephus about the selection process of Saul and David, one has the impression that Samuel realised that he had selected Saul more for his potential to lead an army as a warrior king, rather than a king with the diplomatic abilities that perhaps the position also needed. Being somewhat aged, Samuel was therefore looking for someone else who could be groomed for the position to succeed Saul at the appropriate time – someone who could command stature as a politician, be acceptable to the priestly line, as well as having the ability to be taught how to devise and understand military tactics. By choosing someone quite young it would have provided sufficient time for himself, Samuel, and the ruling hierarchy of the priesthood, to impart all the knowledge they had and which they felt the successor should have: in other words, a solid period of training. This would have included the *priestly secrets* which we will come to later. Their chosen candidate was the youngest son of Jesse – David.

Clearly this entire process was seen as a matter of some delicacy because Josephus comments that Samuel was sufficiently concerned that if he was found out, he might be killed by Saul either publicly or by some more private means.[1]

In Bethlehem Samuel started making enquiries about suitable candidates. It was then that he met Jesse and his sons, all, that is, except David, who had been left to tend the sheep. Clearly Samuel did not see what he was looking for in the sons that Jesse put forward and David was called from his shepherding activity. In this action it is as if Samuel had already had his scouts out looking for a specific type of individual and was aware of how many sons Jesse had because it is he who comments that one son appeared to be missing and had to be summoned from the fields.

> *And he [Samuel] sent, and brought him in. Now he was ruddy, and had beautiful eyes, and was handsome. And the Lord said, 'Arise, anoint him; for this is he'.*   *1 Samuel 16:12*

Josephus records that David appeared to be of:

> *'yellow complexion, of a sharp sight, and a comely person in other respects also'.*

Assuming that Josephus is correct, it seems as though David was suffering from some form of jaundice when he and Samuel first met. David was selected and they all sat down to a feast. After eating, David was anointed.
> *Then Samuel took the horn of oil, and anointed him in the midst of his brothers...*   *1 Samuel 16:13*

There is a very curious passage in Josephus which reads as follows:

> *...So he [Samuel] sat down to the feast and placed the youth under him....after which he took the oil in the presence of David, and anointed him, and whispered in his ear...*[2]

The comment relating to *whispered in his ear* is a quite extraordinary detail to note and one must assume that Josephus recorded it because it was an important part of the anointing ceremony and had a significance that at least some people reading his works would understand. It is as if on being anointed, some secret was passed on to David as part of the king-making ceremony. This being so, it leaves one wondering what that secret was. Indeed, the passing on of highly confidential information – a secret – at the anointment of a king is not unknown. The Egyptians had a king-making ceremony where the secrets of Horus were conveyed. A snippet from a book I discovered when researching this subject, mentioned that even today when a new Pope is appointed at the Vatican, it is alleged that, following his coronation, he retires to a private room where he is presented with a very old but small wooden box and a key. Inside the box is a parchment which the Pope reads, seals and places back in the box which is then returned to a secure location – a secret passed on from one Pope to the next.

David, we must assume, commenced receiving training from Samuel or someone appointed by him in whatever knowledge it was felt was needed. This continued until Saul became unwell and made it known that music eased his condition. The opportunity then presented itself for David to be introduced to Saul and work within his immediate circle, although there is nothing to indicate that Saul had been advised about David's anointment. One can speculate that having received education in other aspects of his required knowledge, perhaps *ancient wisdom*, David has been deliberately planted with Saul to understand more about the tactics of warfare and the use of weapons which, as priests, Samuel and the priestly hierarchy may have had little understanding of. We must assume that David was a good pupil because we find him fighting in future battles.

Initially all was well, but Saul became jealous of David, especially after he killed Goliath, and began to plot his death. David acquitted himself so well in avoiding Saul's scheming that he even married Saul's daughter Michal. The situation between the two men deteriorated, however, and Saul soon returned to his efforts to eliminate the charismatic David. Fortunately, David had a good friend in the person of Jonathan, one of Saul's sons, who warned him about his father's intentions and, with the help of his wife, Michal, David eventually escaped to the desert. A number of other disaffected individuals also defected to David, so that the Old Testament records in Samuel that they were a group six hundred strong.

> *Then David and his men, who were about six hundred, arose and departed from Keilah, and they went wherever they could go…*   *1 Samuel 23:13*

Saul continued to hunt David and his group, who had become outlaws and mercenaries.

> *And David remained in the strongholds in the wilderness, in the hill country of the Wilderness of Ziph. And Saul sought him every day…..*

> *And David was afraid because Saul had come out to seek his life. David was in the Wilderness of Ziph at Horesh.*

> *And Jonathan, Saul's son, rose, and went to David at Horesh, and strengthened his hand in God.*

> *And he said to him, 'Fear not; for the hand of Saul my father shall not find you; you shall be king over Israel, and I shall be next to you; Saul my father also knows this.'*

> *And the two of them made a covenant before the Lord; David remained at Horesh, and Jonathan went home.*

Saul clearly treated David as a 'non-person' and married his daughter, David's wife Michal, off to someone else: Phalti, the son of Laish. Meanwhile, David had an admirer by the name of Abigail who was providing him with supplies. Such was her devotion that David married her.

Twice whilst he was being hunted in the wilderness, David found himself in a position to kill Saul but each time declined to commit the final act on the grounds that Saul was the king and that he, David, had no right to depose him. This, of course, only enhanced David's reputation still further. Saul's sons, including Jonathan, were killed in a battle with the Philistines. Saul, wounded by an arrow from Philistine archers, had no desire to be taken alive and, literally, fell on his sword. Thus, David became king.

Then Saul said to his armor-bearer, 'Draw your sword, and thrust me through with it, lest these uncircumcised come and thrust me through, and make sport of me.' But his armor-bearer would not; for he feared greatly. Therefore Saul took his own sword, and fell upon it.

1 Samuel 31:14

So all the elders of Israel came to the king at Hebron; and King David made a covenant with them at Hebron before the Lord, and they anointed David king over Israel.

2 Samuel 5:3

In the use of the word *covenant* it implies that David was required to agree to meet certain obligations set out by the elders before his kingship was finally agreed. This obligation may well have included the swearing of some form of oath of allegiance. What it also points out is that there was a group of elders who still held overall sway in the affairs of the nation.

The Secret Monitor

In the books of Samuel the friendship between David and Saul's son Jonathan is unmistakable. Jonathan seems aware of David's ultimate destiny and is more loyal to David than he is to his own father.

In English Freemasonry there is a side degree known as The Order of the Secret Monitor. This order is believed to have originated in The Netherlands where it was known as the Order of David and Jonathan. It was apparently introduced to England by a Dr Zacharie in 1875. The object of the Order is described as being to teach the beauties of friendship and fidelity, and is based on incidents in the joint lives of these biblical friends.

A new chronology – a new timeline

In recent years, new light has been shone on this subject of biblical chronology. I have already mentioned the ground-breaking and interesting work undertaken by Dr David Rohl, and published in a book entitled *A Test of Time – the Bible from Myth to History.* Dr Rohl re-examines the subject of biblical and archaeological chronology and redefines the timeline allocation at which certain events probably occurred. From that data the dates of the probable lifespan of key characters and their contemporaries can be derived.

A chronology for biblical events was already well established within the academic community. Against such a background it was clear that the re-evaluation of dates championed by Dr Rohl would be unlikely to gain immediate credibility. So much so, that in the preface to the book, Professor Robert Steven Bianchi makes a plea that the New Chronology espoused by Dr Rohl should receive serious consideration. He says of David Rohl's work:

'He [Dr David Rohl] has been courageous enough to set up a new, revolutionary historical model for critical examination by his colleagues. I trust that they will be prepared to take up his challenge in the true spirit of vigorous and open-minded debate.'

Dr Rohl refers to timelines derived from his work as *The New Chronology.* It is therefore the term I have used.

A new chronology

Dr David Rohl presents a well-founded hypothesis that timelines previously produced by eminent scholars of biblical history are inaccurate in key time zones. These established timelines are used and referenced by a variety of academics in fields of historical research. In the established chronologies certain biblical events and the people associated with them have been allocated specific dates but, because of the inaccuracies, subsequent data produced in the field through archaeology has caused a mismatch with the timelines of previously established biblical history. By definition if archaeologists are using the same established timelines, then they may be attributing strata levels and artefacts to an incorrect biblical era, hence the difficulty of establishing connections with the key events and characters. Using other peripheral information and historical data for which firm dates have been established Dr Rohl claims to demonstrate that specific biblical characters can be identified, along with their connections and contemporaries. Thus, Moses is established as having Pharaoh Khaneferre Sobekhotep IV (1529 BCE -1508 BCE) as his step-father in his youth, Dudimose (who became Pharaoh in 1448 bce) as Pharaoh at the time of the Exodus, and David and Saul as contemporary with the heretical Pharaoh Akhenaten/Amenhotep IV (Pharaoh between 1022 BCE and 1007 BCE). The evidence presented is fascinating, thorough and logical to say the least.

David and the Amarna Heresy

In *A Test of Time,* Dr David Rohl records interesting observations between text of the Old Testament relating to the United Monarchy era of Saul, David and Solomon and certain events that happened in Egypt. These events are recorded in what have become known as the *Amarna Letters.* For expediency I will paraphrase their significance.

In 1887 a number of small clay tablets, used for correspondence 3,000 years ago in much the same way as we might use a letter today, were discovered at a site along the banks of the River Nile, a site which had, for a short period, been the capital of ancient Egypt. The name of the site of this ancient capital is now known as Tel-el-Amarna.

When Amenhotep IV, better known perhaps as Akhenaten, became Pharaoh, he created a monotheistic religion based on a return to the worship of the Sun god – the sun disc – the Aten. For many years prior to that time the centre of power rested at Thebes where a powerful priesthood encouraged worship of the *King of Gods* – Amun. Akhenaten, whose wife was Queen Nefertiti, built the new capital in praise of the Sun god and transferred his royal court and base of power there. As so often happens with the advent of major political change, there were winners and losers. In abandoning worship of the god Amun, he undermined the priesthood of Thebes, and no doubt, much of their wealth. Not only was mention of Amun strictly forbidden, but masons were tasked with travelling throughout Egypt and removing any reference to this former basis of the religion and culture.

According to historical records, the era of Akhenaten was very divisive throughout the land, weakening it economically and militarily, and therefore diminishing the influence of Egypt throughout the region.

There are mysteries surrounding the demise of Amenhotep IV, Akhenaten. Some suggestions are of a military coup funded by disgruntled priests. Whatever happened, Akhenaten was, a few years later, succeeded by Tutankhaten who, shortly afterwards, changed his name to one which was to become, perhaps, the most famous of all the Pharaohs – the boy king, Tutankhamun. The subtle change to the last four letters of his name signal the change of emphasis from *Aten* – the Sun god – to a return to worship of *Amun*, and with that, the revival of Thebes. Tel-el-Amarna, the new capital of the Sun god, was abandoned. This era is now often referred to by historians and archaeologists as the period of the Amarna heresy.

David Rohl points out that there are certain elements of the translated texts from the clay tablets found at Tel-el-Amarna which enable Saul and David to be identified. In short, in the Amarna tablets, reference is made to the *Habiru*. These are identified as the outlawed followers of David, and therefore led by David whilst the latter was in exile and hiding from Saul. There are also some letters written directly for the attention of Pharaoh, from a person known as the Lion Man. He is later named as Labayu – further identified as Saul. Incredibly, in a letter from Labayu (Saul) to Pharaoh, known simply as tablet EA254, David Rohl notes that Labayu's son has been 'implicated in activities of the Habiru'. The Habiru have been identified above as David and his band of outlaws when they were living in exile and keeping away from Saul. The 'son' referred to is probably a reference to Jonathan and the collusion that existed between him and David.

From this splendid piece of detective work by David Rohl we can only conclude that Saul and David were both contemporaries with Akhenaten, and both were well known by name and deed to the Egyptian authorities at that time. Conversely, we can also draw the conclusion that David and Saul must both have been aware of the political change that had occurred in Egypt with the rise of the Sun god – the Aten – and the city of Tel-el-Amarna that was dedicated to him. Such was the power and influence of the Egyptians that David, in particular, could have been influenced by the knowledge of the Sun god as proffered by the Amarna Heresy.

In the Old Testament there is a collection of poems referred to as The Psalms. The Psalms are attributed to David. At the end of the 20th century there was a well-founded suggestion that David was not the author of significant tracts of these poems, with entire sections being attributed to Akhenaten and his praise for the Sun god – the Aten.

Noting the role of the Levite priesthood in their care for the Tabernacle and the Ark, both of which appear to have been designed on the principles of *ancient wisdom,* is it possible that aspects of this wisdom were combined with elements of the new religion attributed to the Sun god as then practised in Egypt, and found their way into the plans and design of the Temple which David later passed on to Solomon?

The result of a comparison with the different chronologies places events as shown in following tables:

As we can see, the time slot allocated to the Exodus varies over a time period of some 200 years. This is critical because the biblical text in relation to the building of the Jerusalem Temple quotes time intervals relative to the Exodus. For example, in 1 Kings 6:1, it states that building the Temple commenced in the fourth year of Solomon's reign and 480 years after the Exodus. In other words, if we take the time intervals as literally stated, then Solomon's reign commenced 476 years after the Exodus. Based on the timelines shown in the table, the Temple would have been built anywhere between about 974 BCE and 775 BCE. This is a huge variance by comparison with the accepted date of around 950 BCE – 960 BCE.

Established biblical chronology puts key events related to this investigation into the following table:

Chronology of key areas of the Old Testament

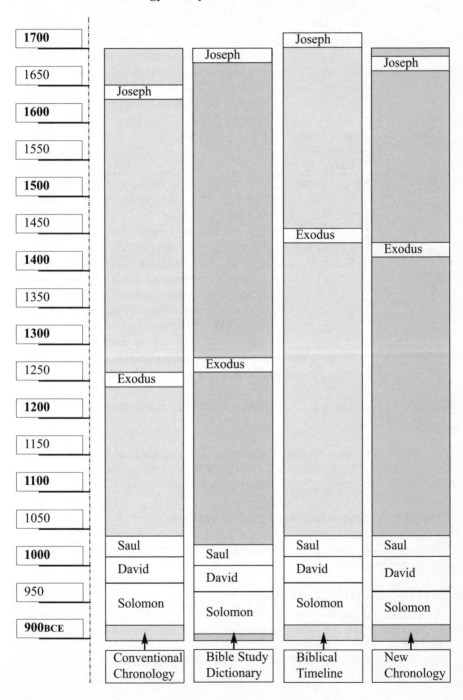

Event	Probable year	Comment
Exodus	1475 BCE	Moses was supposedly 80 years old when the
Moses	1555-1435 BCE	Exodus occurred. With the Exodus based around 1475 BCE, then Moses was born around 1555 BCE. He is recorded as having died after the Israelites had spent 40 years in the wilderness. This implies he was 120 years old when he died, which in turn means he lived until 1435 BCE.
Saul	King of Israel between 1020 BCE -1000 BCE	
David	King of Israel between 1000 BCE- 962 BCE	This means that David achieved the throne of Israel 475 years after the Exodus and reigned as king for 38 years.
Solomon	King of Israel between 962 BCE - 922 BCE	He took around 13 years to build the temple (1 Kings 7:1) 480 years ofter the Exodus (1 Kings 6:1), and the fourth year of Solomon's reign (1 Kings 6:1). This means that the building of the temple was commenced in 958 BCE. Based on the biblical chronology, the Exodus occurred in 480 + 958 = 1438 BCE. Thus, there is a discrepancy of around 40 years between the timescales recorded in the Old Testament Book of Kings and the established chronology used by academics.
Solomon's Temple	958 BCE	Started in 958 BCE and finished (dedicated) in 945 BCE.

The above table is based on information and a timeline published in The Student Bible Dictionary – compiled by K. Dockrey, J. Godwin and P. Godwin.

Chronological comparison with Egyptian Pharaohs

The chronology between key element and the reign of Egyption pharaohs is shown in a table that follows.

David commences the Temple design

It was after his installation as king that David decided to bring the Ark of the Covenant out of storage. It is also the first time that we are introduced to Hiram, King of Tyre.

We then learn that whilst Solomon is credited with building the first Jerusalem Temple, it was to a design created by David. But there is nothing mentioned in either

Chronology comparison with Egyptian Pharaohs

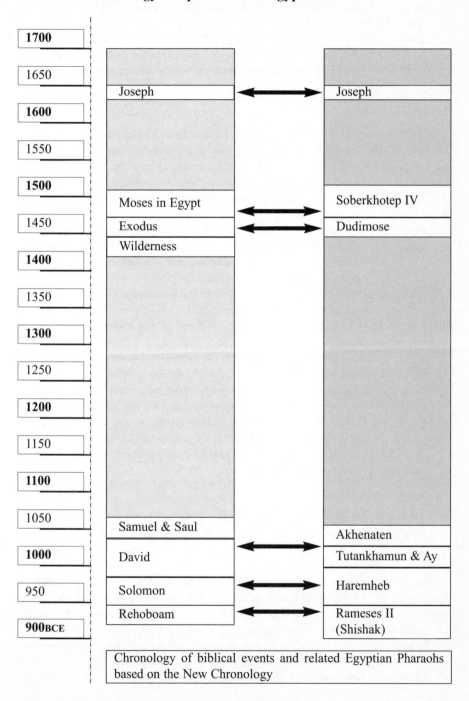

Chronology of biblical events and related Egyptian Pharaohs based on the New Chronology

the book of Samuel or Josephus which outlines how David obtained the knowledge necessary. There are, however, a few clues to where and how such knowledge may have been imparted.

In the first instance we are told that the Temple was primarily built to house the Ark. In 1 Chronicles 13, David seems to suddenly remember that the Ark existed:

Let us bring the ark of our God back to us, for we did not enquire of it during the reign of Saul.

1 Chronicles 13:3

In 1 Chronicles 23 we are told that the Levites had an obligation to take care of the Ark and the Tabernacle. It was their duty to carry them around wherever they were needed. Their duties were to help Aaron's descendants in the administering and care of all the sacred things they possessed. Aaron was Moses' brother and his descendants clearly retained the primary positions of the priestly line as a hereditary responsibility.

Aaron is the first entry in the *Student Bible Dictionary* and is defined as:

Aaron: *Older brother of and early spokesman for Moses....Became Israel's first high priest. The Aaronic priesthood (priests of the tribe of Levi) was named after him.*

It would seem reasonable to assume that with the knowledge that the priesthoods were the custodians of the *ancient wisdom – ancient mysteries,* then the priests of the tribe of Levi would have been the custodians of that knowledge within the Israelite nation. What is more, the Levites still retained the Tabernacle and the Ark, so we may assume, rightly or wrongly, that the symbolism which has already been revealed within both concerning the Sun, the Moon, the geometry and the sacred numbers, was still prominent and well known to those who needed to know.

Through 1 Chronicles 28, David hands over the plans for the Temple to Solomon, along with the details of all the materials, slave labourers and craftsmen he has already marshalled for the task. He encourages Solomon not to flinch from the task.

Then David gave his son Solomon the plans for the portico of the temple, its buildings, its storerooms, its upper parts.....

1 Chronicles 28:11

'All this is in writing,' David said, 'because the hand of the Lord was upon me, and he gave me understanding of all the details of the plan'.

1 Chronicles 28:19

It is the term *understanding of all the details* that is of note as it implies that he understood the elements of the architecture, the concepts and geometry for the setting out of the Temple. There is a specific reference to the portico and its upper parts, implying there was something special in their design.

The amount of gold and precious stones mentioned is staggering. In the footnote to 1 Chronicles 29, there is an approximation of weights of gold and silver. David passed over his personal accumulation which runs into about 110 tons of gold and

260 tons of refined silver. The leaders of the prominent families also made donations which collectively came to some 2 tons of gold and 375 tons of silver. It has been estimated that taking the value of gold and silver as it was around the start of the 21st century, then the total value of these precious metals would have been around £50 billion (US $90Bn).

The Temple was not only a permanent home for the Ark; it also marked the end of the line for the Tabernacle. By this time it was over 450 years old.

Whilst it seems that the architecture devised by David and the priesthood of his day would most probably have embraced the same design knowledge that existed for the Ark and the Tabernacle – *ancient wisdom,* one has to consider if there were any other motivations at that time. And not surprisingly, there were.

The Shechinah

In the King James version of the Old Testament there is a reference to the *Shechinah.* The word appears in the Book of Exodus around the time when the Tabernacle was being constructed and positioned. What was the Shechinah?

There has been the suggestion that it was a reference to the planet Venus, and in particular the 40-year cycle which results in the apparent movement of its orbit to create a pattern of a pentagram progressively described in the sky, and Venus returning to the same point in the sky creating a 40-year precision clock. This was apparently well understood by ancient cultures including the Celts and Druids.[3]

The reference to the Shechinah disappears from the text in the more modern translations – it is replaced by a *glory-cloud.* In Easton's Bible Dictionary we find the Shechinah referred to as follows:

'a Chaldee word meaning resting-place ... used by the later Jews to designate the visible symbol of God's presence in the tabernacle, and afterwards in Solomon's Temple ... It is probable that after the entrance into Canaan this glory-cloud settled upon the ark of the covenant in the most holy place. We have no special reference to it till the consecration of the temple by Solomon when it filled the whole house with its glory, so that the priests could not stand to minister ... Probably it remained in the first temple in the holy of holies as the symbol of Jehovah's presence so long as the temple stood. It afterwards disappeared.'

If, as I have previously indicated, the Tabernacle designed by Moses reflected his knowledge of the macro-cosmos, including the heavenly bodies, then it is also highly likely that he understood the 40-year cycle of Venus as the ancients then understood it, together with the pattern of the pentagram which resulted. If, as some writers suggest, this was a highly revered cycle which was part of their religious beliefs, then it is highly likely that it was known as such by Moses 3,500 years ago. The 40-year cycle would therefore not have been ignored and would have become an important characteristic for inclusion in the rituals of the priests, with that knowledge later being transferred to the first temple in Jerusalem. In particular the ancients are thought to have specifically noted the position of Venus about an hour before sunrise on the day of the equinox as being the start and end of the 40-year cycle. We are told that the tabernacle was oriented so that the first rays of the sun at dawn would shine through the entrance and fall on the Ark. By definition, the same would apply to the light emanating from Venus. This light was highly revered and became known as the *glory-cloud*. Thus, once every 40 years, the light of the planet Venus would fall on the Ark inside the Tabernacle. With the Temple being built to reflect the characteristics of the Tabernacle, the same process would be included. With the destruction of the Temple by the invading Babylonians 400 years later, it is possible that this knowledge was lost or forgotten and when the second temple was built by Zerubbabel, it was omitted, hence the comment in Easton's Dictionary that *'It afterwards disappeared'*. It did not disappear they just lost the knowledge or it was not important any more.

The temple in Jerusalem was built, based on the tables of information given earlier, sometime around 945 BCE to 958 BCE.

Interestingly, on 21st June 945 (Summer Solstice) at 4.00am the Sun-Venus relativity in the sky was almost the same as on the same date in 958 BCE. This was revealed when I used an astronomical software package called *Skyglobe*.

Conclusion

In David's younger years he would undoubtedly have been aware of the influence of the Sun in Egyptian culture through what has become known as the Amana Heresy. It seems most likely that he designed the Temple to reflect the characteristics of the Tabernacle. This was designed by Moses and was also influenced by the rise of the Sun at dawn. It is also possible that another characteristic of the macro-cosmos, the Shechinah/Venus orbit, also played its part.

A pattern is emerging that suggests that the main influences that presented themselves in the design of the Temple relate to the macro-cosmos.

[1] Josepthus *Antiquities of the Jews*, translated by W. Winston Book 6 Chapter 8
[2] Josepthus *Antiquities of the Jews*, translated by W. Winston Book 6 Chapter 8
[3] Lomas and Knight – *Uriel's Machine*

Chapter 11
Solomon and his wisdom – revealed

The Wisdom of Solomon
Having been installed as the king over the Israelites, Solomon delayed building the Temple for some four years, despite having the materials and labour that had already been marshalled by his father, David.

> *In the four hundred and eightieth year after the Israelites had come out of Egypt, in the fourth year of Solomon's reign over Israel ... he began to build the temple ...*

> *1 Kings 6:1*

In that four-year period, Solomon sought wisdom. And such is the perceived breadth of that wisdom, that even today it is not uncommon to hear someone make comments like,

> *'He has the wisdom of Solomon' and 'it would test the wisdom of Solomon' or 'it would take the wisdom of Solomon to solve that'.*

Much credit for this wisdom is attributed to a short sequence mentioned in 1 Kings 3:16-28. Two prostitutes lived in the same house and each gave birth to sons within a few days of each other. One of the babies had died and a dispute arose between the mothers as to which baby had died and who had charge of the one still living. One mother claimed that when she got up in the night to feed her baby she found it dead, but on closer inspection claimed that the one she had been looking at was not her son; the dead child, she claimed, belonged to the other mother. The dispute was taken before Solomon. His judgement was to ask for a sword with which to kill the remaining baby and cut it in two so that both mothers would share a part. The true mother pleaded with Solomon for the baby's life to be spared and the baby given to the other mother. The second mother suggested that cutting the baby in two parts so that both could have a share was the right answer. Solomon ruled that he would give the baby to the first woman as no real mother would sanction seeing her baby killed. This judgement was a clever piece of lateral thinking on the part of Solomon. It is from the 13 verses in the book of Kings which describe these events that the entire scope of Solomon's wisdom is attested and lauded.

There is a second story concerning Solomon's wisdom and often quoted by preachers. This relates to the Queen of Sheba having given flowers to Solomon. Some flowers were real and others were artificial. The artificial flowers were so well crafted that it was virtually impossible to identify them from the real thing and the Queen of Sheba asked him to say which was which. Solomon identified the real flowers by placing them all beside an open window and observing which flowers were visited by bees. The trouble with this story is that it does not appear in any of the defined texts that constitute the Holy Bible. There are, however, stories that have been passed down in Arabia and Ethiopia about the legendary Queen of Sheba. It may be from one of these traditions that the story of the flowers may have later been derived and then passed into our own folklore. But, as it currently stands, we are left with the single story in 1 Kings 3:16-28 as a practical demonstration of lateral thinking to imply Solomon's perceived great wisdom.

In 1 Kings 4:29-34, we are treated to a much broader definition of Solomon's wisdom. It is not of the lateral thinking ability already demonstrated, but wisdom that he has acquired by dedicated study.

> *He described plant life, from the cedar of Lebanon to the hyssop that grows out of the walls. He also taught about animals and birds, reptiles and fish.*
>
> *1 Kings 4:33*

To have had this ability he would have probably been inspired by an interest in the natural world, maybe encouraged and underpinned by the Levite priests. Through reference to the cedar of Lebanon and the hyssop, the scribe is demonstrating an affinity with something large and obvious on the one hand, the cedar trees, whilst at the other end of the scale we have a form of wild mint – the hyssop.

Solomon's wisdom was greater than the wisdom of the men of the East, and greater than all the wisdom of Egypt.

1 Kings 4:30

Could it be that *men of the East* is a reference to the Chaldean science of the heavenly bodies, the zodiac, precession, the orbits of the planets, the principles of astrology and celestial mechanics; the same knowledge, we are told, that was taught to Moses whilst he was a prince in Egypt? It is also the same celestial knowledge that, according to Josephus, Moses used to define certain attributes of the priest's vestments and rituals. This is the same knowledge that was the domain of the priesthoods, the priests from the tribe of Levi. This is the knowledge that constitutes an understanding of the macro-cosmos. It is the same knowledge which constituted *ancient wisdom.*

Could it have been that Solomon deliberately embarked on a course of education into the meaning of *ancient wisdom* so that he had a better understanding of the plans for the Temple, which his father had left for him?

By referring again to Dr David Rohl's New Chronology, it would appear that the reign of the heretical Pharaoh, Akhenaten, was over by the time Solomon came to the throne. Egypt, had the boy-king Tutankhamun as a successor to Akhenaten not long after the latter's demise, closely followed by Haremheb, during whose reign Egypt started to regain its political influence in the region.

David and the Sun god

From this, I came to the conclusion that David had designed the Temple to reflect the influence of the Sun god – the Aten, then prominent in Egypt. David died. Just prior to David's death, there was the demise of his contemporary, Akhenaten, so that both had ceased to hold power within a short period of one another. David Rohl suggests that the Egyptian Princess that Solomon married was Haremheb's daughter, as part of what one might call a peace treaty between the two nations whilst Haremheb re-established control over his own country. Solomon, having been entrusted with building the Temple, and having seen Tutankhamun's demise, waited to see what would happen politically in Egypt. He used his time to gain as much knowledge of the macro-cosmos as he could, being taught by the priests of Levi, and maybe even some from Egypt as a consequence of his marriage to the Pharaoh's daughter. He then modified the plans so that it reflected the design his father had left him, but not so overtly as to cause friction with their powerful neighbour, Egypt.

At the end of the 20th century, members of the academic community suggested that the Book of Psalms, usually attributed to David, may not have been written by him. Several Psalms are now attributed to Akhenaten as poems written in praise and adoration of the Sun god, the Aten.

Conclusion

For nearly two thousand years, text contained in the Holy Bible has been treated as sacrosanct. It is easy to understand how a range of events which were not easy to explain by the leaders of the Church in the distant past were cast into the mould of having been miracles or the consequences of divine intervention. And who knows, maybe they were. However, from the mid-Victorian era archaeological exploration in the area known as the Holy Land, close examination of historical and religious documents, and the application of science based investigation, has placed information before us in a way which enables previously regarded miracles to be seen in the context of natural events which can be explained. Such explanations may be uncomfortable for the millions of individuals who have accepted, unconditionally, the dogma with which they have been educated and inspired to believe.

This same theme can be seen through Solomon's supposed wisdom. He is given credit by preachers in today's church, for the lateral thinking example involving the prostitutes' children, but his wisdom clearly extended beyond that to one of educated knowledge associated with the macro-cosmos, which hardly, if ever, gets a mention.

As the Israelite king it is difficult to imagine that Solomon was not aware of the symbolism attached to the garments of the priests, as noted by Josephus. This symbolism is related to the celestial universe and the primary heavenly bodies of the Sun and Moon. And that has a direct connection with Akhenaten and his worship of the Sun God.

The Secrets of Solomon's Temple

It was time to look more closely at some of the peripheral texts associated with Solomon's Temple.

Chapter 12
Who was Solomon?
What was Moloch?

Solomon was not his name at birth, but a name attributed to him sometime after his death. That is the opinion Dr David Rohl expresses in *A Test of Time*. By virtue that it was a name he acquired, then what was his real name? And, how did he come to acquire this new name?

Looked at another way, was his new name perhaps a function of the Temple, which, as the builder, was then translated to become his name? Or, having acquired the name, was it then reflected back onto the Temple?

The name Solomon is usually cited as having been derived from the Hebrew word *Shalom,* meaning peace. Certainly the Old Testament indicates that the era of Solomon's kingship was an era of relative peace for the Israelites after the bloodshed invoked by Solomon's father, David, and Saul before that. But there is no proof that connects the name of Solomon with the word *Shalom*. It appears to be a fable which started at some point in the past, perhaps as a theory presented by an academic, and has been regularly regurgitated and stated as if it is a fact, proven beyond doubt – which it is not.

David and Bathsheba

We are given an insight into Solomon's real name through the book of Samuel. In chapter 11 we are told how one day David got up and, looking out from his palace, saw a beautiful woman bathing. Her name was Bathsheba. She was summoned to him, and he slept with her. The problem was that she was married – her husband's name was Uriah. David had embarked on an adulterous liaison. Bathsheba returned home only to find that she was pregnant. She wrote to David and explained her situation. David needed to find a solution. He packed her husband, Uriah, off to war and sent instructions to his general, Joab, that Uriah was to be placed in the front line of battle and left to his own defence. Needless to say, Uriah was killed. The way was now clear for David to marry Bathsheba and make the ultimate birth of the child, a son, less contentious. Nathan the prophet then visited David, severely chastised him for the callous action towards Uriah, and told David that he would pay dearly for his actions, maybe even with his own life. In chapter 12 we read how punishment was meted out to him.

Then David said, 'I have sinned against the Lord'. Nathan replied, 'The Lord has taken away your sin. You are not going to die'.

2 Samuel 12:13

But because by doing this you have made the enemies of the Lord show utter contempt, the son born to you will die.

2 Samuel 12:14

After Nathan had gone home, the Lord struck the child that Uriah's wife had borne to David and he became ill.

2 Samuel 12:15

David prayed and fasted in the hope that the child would be spared. Alas, the child died. Bathsheba was distraught. It is against this background that, in verses 24 and 25, we are introduced to Solomon for the first time:

Then David comforted his wife Bathsheba, and he went to her and lay with her. She gave birth to a son, and they named him Solomon. The Lord loved him;

2 Samuel, 12:24

and because the Lord loved him, he sent word through Nathan the prophet to name him Jedidiah.

2 Samuel, 12:25

Keeping in mind the comment by Dr Rohl that the name Solomon was attributed to him sometime after his death, then the above verse 25 suggests a positive action on the part of the scribe who wrote the text, not only to record the known events but to let us know that the person we have subsequently come to recognise as Solomon was originally named Jedidiah, later to become King Jedidiah. It would therefore follow that the first Jerusalem Temple, built by this descendant of David, would have really been known as *Jedidiah's Temple*.

So how did we get from *Jedidiah* to *Solomon*?

What caused this change?

It is Old Testament text that provides a clue when the trappings of dogma are stripped away. This insight comes from looking more closely at the furnishings for the Temple.

Exploring the furnishings

The pillars of Solomon's Temple, as mentioned in the Old Testament, may have had greater significance than has previously been alluded to.

When we use the term pillar, our experience and association with the word may create the impression of a static device, a structure holding up a roof, doorway or canopy covering a doorway. Pillars used in a colonnade usually define a boundary of some kind. In all these cases, such pillars may be decorative and resonate with the classical styles of architecture, yet they are the type of device that most people do not give a second glance to. They are there doing a job which is taken for granted. Suppose then, that there were pillars that did not hold up any roofs or doorways, or anything else, they were just free-standing, they just stood out in the open and did nothing. It would lead us to ask the question – what were they for? – why go to the trouble of building or making them? – and erecting them? Free-standing pillars were built in ancient times but most of those that have survived, like obelisks, have engraved surfaces which record an event of some kind – they are markers.

In the case of Solomon's Temple we are told about two pillars. What we are not told is what they were for, why they were there. Yet they must have had some purpose, otherwise why did these people of ancient times go to the trouble of making them, transporting them many miles, and erecting them. Just for decoration? – that is not likely. These were people who did not have the luxury of decoration for decoration's sake. Everything they built was for a purpose, either practical or symbolic of their culture. A number of scholars assessed the significance of the pillars during the 20th century and variously attributed a range of functions and uses. The two most regularly referenced suggest that they were incense burners or markers for predicting the equinoxes and solstices. But, my enquiries suggest they had other hidden attributes, which we will deal with in due course.

As with other aspects of the Temple I took the view that, by being mentioned in the texts of the Old Testament books of Kings and Chronicles, the pillars had to have had some special significance, otherwise why bother to mention them at all? Furthermore, there is a quite a lot of detail about the size and decoration of the component parts, not perhaps the detail you would expect if they were merely decorative ornaments. As the pillars are recorded with so much detail it must imply that they had a key significance, perhaps ceremonial or for some other major purpose. After all, most of the other furnishings of the Temple are equally detailed, with comments about their functionality.

The Sea, the basins and the implements

The Sea, mentioned in 1 Kings 7 and 2 Chronicles 4, was placed in the southeast corner of the courtyard, or colonnade, in front of the temple. We are told that the Sea was circular in shape, being 10 cubits (15 feet or 4.5M) in diameter. It was 5 cubits (7.5 feet or 2.3M) high, so not the sort of thing you could easily see inside when standing at ground level, thereby providing a degree of privacy for anyone in it. And, the Sea held 3,000 baths, which, the footnotes of the Bible indicate, held the equivalent of some 17,500 gallons (80,000 litres) of water. We are told that it was cast, no doubt of bronze, so it would have been heavy. It would have needed to be strong. The weight of the water would have been around 136,000 lbs (61 tons or 61,690 kg). This would account for the twelve figures of bulls needed to support it. In 1 Kings 7 we are told that the Sea held 2,000 baths, but the footnotes to the biblical text note that 'the Septuagint does not have this sentence' meaning that, for the Book of Kings, it is a sentence added at sometime. The Sea was a very big bath – it was the equivalent of a small swimming pool. No doubt it was used by several priests at the same time, which would account for the need for size. In addition, there was a rim around the top which may have prevented water, displaced by the movement of the priests inside the Sea, from overflowing into the courtyard below.

We are told that the Sea was used by the priests for washing. We are not told whether this washing was before or after the ritual.

Amongst the other furnishings in the courtyard were the basins, ten in total, with five to the north and five to the south. These were for washing the implements used for the burnt offerings. In other words, during the ritual sacrifice. But what was sacrificed?

Could these furnishings have been associated with the festival of Moloch?

Moloch / Molech

Suddenly, a text from 2 Kings, which I had noted several times but dismissed as being irrelevant to my enquiries, took on a whole new dimension. I had previously dismissed its relevance because it was related to the period just before the Temple was finally destroyed by the Babylonians as opposed to its building in the first instance.

The text in question is 2 Kings 23:10 which reads:

'He [Josiah] desecrated Topheth, which was in the Valley of Ben Hinnom, so no one could use it to sacrifice their son or daughter in the fire to Molech.'

It was the latter part of the verse – *to sacrifice their son or daughter in the fire to Molech* – that caught my attention. Were the Israelites actually involved in child sacrifice? – and how long had this been going on?

Josiah was King of Israel about 400 years after the Jerusalem Temple had been built by Solomon. Here was a statement that a group of people, the Israelites, who have been held in the highest esteem and revered by many for generations, were indulging in the grotesque activity of child sacrifice. Human sacrifice is, of course, well recorded as a practice indulged by those cultures branded as heathens, such as the Aztecs and Incas of South America, but not associated with the forerunner of the major western religions. Surely, this could not be right? And what was 'the fire of Moloch'?

Such simple questions sent me stumbling into an arena of an unseemly side of religion in that era. I was somewhat amazed that it was not more widely spoken of. Yet, on reflection, one could understand how the religious authorities of yesteryear would have been keen to mask this grotesque aspect of the practices clearly indulged by high-profile biblical figures revered and worshipped for centuries. It was known as the festival of Moloch, a festival that had even been practised at the time of Solomon, and, it would appear, was an ancient festival even in that time.

According to various encyclopaedia and reference sources, Moloch means 'king' but could also be interpreted to mean 'a god'.[1] In the Old Testament it may also be written as Molech.

The sacrificial altar was apparently a large, hollow statue of a bull, also referred to as a calf. The belief is that children were ritually killed whilst the people danced around the Moloch, making loud music so that they should not hear the screams of children facing the brutality of this abominable ritual. Having been killed, the body of the murdered child would then be placed on the legs of the crouching calf as if it was food, the calf ready to consume the sacrifice – the murdered child. A fire would be built inside the ornamental body of the calf so that its body and eyes glowed red.[2] It is believed that the body of the sacrificed child would then be drawn into the statue of the calf to be consumed by the fire inside. This process is usually described in biblical text as *passing through the fire*.[3] This ritual is believed to have continued until around the 6th century BCE when Josiah finally took measures to stamp it out.

The most prominent evidence quoted to support the child sacrifice association with Moloch is in Genesis 22:2-13. Abraham took his son Isaac to Moriah, later the place where Solomon's Temple was built, to be sacrificed, but at the last minute Abraham was so overcome with remorse that he seized a sheep and sacrificed that instead. It is verse 2 which contains the significant text:

Take your son, your only son Isaac, whom you love, and go to the region of Moriah. Sacrifice him as a burnt offering ...

In Exodus there is the point in the text when Moses is on Mount Sinai receiving the Commandments and, in his absence, disgruntled sections of his followers build a calf to worship. In Acts 7:41-43 there is positive mention of the Israelites indulging in the festival of Moloch, which implies that the memory of such practices was at least still with the scribes.

41...That was the time they made him an idol in the form of a calf. They brought sacrifices to it and held a celebration in honour of what their hands had made.
42...But God turned away and gave them over to the worship of the heavenly bodies ...
43...You have lifted up the shrine of Moloch and the star of Rephan, the idols you made to worship ...

Moloch is not mentioned by name in Exodus 32, merely that the Israelites built a calf whilst Moses was away on the mountain. But the builder of the calf was none other that Moses' brother, Aaron. The text continues:

When Aaron saw this, he built an altar in front of the calf and announced, 'Tomorrow there will be a festival to the Lord'. So the next day the people rose early and sacrificed burnt offerings. Afterwards they sat down to eat and drink and got up to indulge in revelry.

Exodus 32:5 & 6

Moses, we must assume, was appalled by this festival and took steps to stamp it out just as Josiah did 1,000 years later. But it is clear that the legacy remained. In Psalm 106 we are left with no doubt about what was happening. In verse 19 we read:
At Horeb they made a calf and worshipped an idol cast from metal.

Then in verses 37 and 38 it continues:

They sacrificed their sons and daughters to demons. They shed innocent blood, the blood of their sons and daughters to the idols of Canaan, and the land was desecrated by their blood.

By the time that Solomon's Temple was dedicated, Solomon had been king for seventeen or eighteen years; he reigned four years before commencing the construction and was thirteen years building. It is recorded that during that time the worship of Moloch was well established in the hills and valleys around Jerusalem, and in particular in an area known as the Valley of Ben Hinnom. By the time of the Temple dedication, Solomon had acquired a number of wives. And so we read in 1 Kings 11: 7 & 8

On a hill east of Jerusalem, Solomon built a high place for Chemosh the detestable god of Moab, and for Molech the detestable god of the Ammonites. He did the same for all his foreign wives, who burnt incense and offered sacrifices to their gods.

From these verses it is clear that Solomon must have been well acquainted with the sacrificial rituals attached to Moloch, and that it was practised even in the time of David, his father. On the basis that Abraham was alive long before Joseph was taken into captivity in Egypt, then child sacrifice existed amongst the Israelites for around 2,000 years, assuming it did stop in the reign of Josiah.

There is yet another twist in this review of Moloch/Molech which will become more profound later. Moloch was regarded as a Sun god. So, the Israelites and their neighbours who worshipped Moloch were actually worshipping the Sun god. In addition, in Acts 7:42, quoted above, there is a reference to worshipping the *heavenly bodies*. The two most prominent such *heavenly bodies* are the Sun and the Moon. Thus, the implication of the quotation from Acts is that the followers of Moloch/Molech were worshippers of the Sun and the Moon.

In 1 Kings 10, we learn about the visit of the Queen of Sheba. Chronologically within the Book of Kings, she appears after the Temple has been dedicated. There is a tradition that she too worshipped the Sun god. In verses 4 & 5 we are told that she was *overwhelmed* by the knowledge and wisdom of Solomon, including the 'burnt offerings he made at the temple'.[4]

Burnt offerings

At the dedication of the Temple we are told in 2 Chronicles 4:6 that there were *burnt offerings*. What we are not told is what they consisted of. From the text about Abraham and Isaac we learn that, quite possibly, child sacrifice was the meaning. We get a further hint of this later in 2 Chronicles 7. In verse 1 we read:

When Solomon had finished praying, fire came down from heaven and consumed the burnt offerings and the sacrifices ...

This is remarkably close to the practice of Moloch, where the fire inside the calf consumed the body of a sacrificed child.

After this, we are told that the Israelites fell to their knees and prayed. It is only after these two events have taken place, the fire and the prayers, that Solomon offered a sacrifice of 22,000 cattle and 20,000 sheep and goats – 42,000 animals in all. Assuming all of these were killed and butchered at the site of the Temple as part of the dedication ritual, then the precincts of the Temple would have been awash with thousands of gallons of animal blood. From this, we could assume that reference to a sacrifice is probably an indication that it was animal in nature. But, in 2 Chronicles 7:7, two other different types of offerings are also mentioned:

Solomon consecrated the middle part of the courtyard in front of the temple ... and here he offered burnt offerings and the fat of the fellowship offerings.

This implies that the *burnt offerings* and the *fat of the fellowship offerings* were different from the other sacrifice associated with animals. Indeed, in the footnotes to the Biblical text, these are explained away as 'Traditionally peace offerings'. But what did they consist of?

There is, of course, the mention in Genesis that Mount Moriah, the place where Solomon's Temple was built, was the location that Abraham went to conduct his ritualistic human slaughter. It would be natural, therefore, for descendants of Abraham to associate the mountain with such a sacrificial act as part of the dedication ceremony – the first act, as recorded by 2 Chronicles 7:1.

Could it be that Moloch worship was part of the dedication ceremony? – that because of its abhorrent connotations, after the festival was effectively abolished by Josiah in the 6th century BCE, these abominable practices of child sacrifice by their forebears were such an embarrassment to the Israelite rulers and scribes of their day that any reference was deliberately hidden from obvious view in biblical texts by using a guarded reference to *burnt offerings* and the *fellowship offerings* as noted in 2 Chronicles 7:7, with the cover-up being completed by later referring to them simply as '*peace offerings*'? If so, we are considering a dedication ceremony for the Temple which involved the use of children as the sacrificial appeasement. And what is more – the people of Jerusalem were, through that ritual, worshipping the Sun god. No wonder the religious authorities have kept quiet about this aspect of biblical text and swept it under the carpet. Such a revelation would fly in the face of much of what we have been encouraged to believe over many centuries of religious indoctrination.

The use of the furnishings

We know that something, or someone, was expected to be sacrificed, because the books of Kings and Chronicles tell us so. This sacrifice was in such abundance that ten basins were needed for washing the utensils afterwards. There were even shovels, no doubt for removing the sacrificial debris. The Sea was probably used for the priests to wash themselves of the blood, and fats, in which they would undoubtedly have been covered if they had taken an active role in the sacrificial process. It is also interesting to note that the Sea was supported on the images of bulls. Could this also point to a connection with Moloch?

Whatever the ritualistic practice was that was performed, we have, or can deduce, an explanation for the reason why the Sea, basins and utensils were made. Even a massive bronze altar is mentioned as a place on which the sacrifices were presented. The use for the internal furnishings is also made clear: ten lamp-stands, ten tables, one hundred gold sprinkling bowls, plus wick trimmers, ladles, censers and doors.

It is interesting to note the frequency of the use of the number 10 – which has striking connections with the later doctrine of Pythagoras. The one hundred sprinkling bowls is 10 groups of 10.

But what of the two pillars? Despite the fact that they are described as being Temple furnishings, and that a considerable portion of the text of 2 Chronicles 4 and 1 Kings 7 relates to them and their decoration, even down to their names and position outside of the Temple, there does not appear to have been an obvious connection between the use of the other furnishings and the pillars. Or was there?

So, who was Solomon?

We have seen that, according to biblical text, when this son of David and Bathsheba was born he was given the name Jedidiah, which raises the question about how he came to later be called Solomon, the name with which he has passed into biblical history.

We have also seen that the Israelites indulged in child sacrifice through the festival of Moloch. There was not an isolated involvement with this unseemly festival, it had clearly been part of the customs of worship that at least some sections of the Israelite community indulged in for about 1,000 years before the first Jerusalem Temple was built, and a further 400 years after it was completed. In addition, we have seen that Solomon built facilities for his wives to pursue such sacrifices if they chose, and the Queen of Sheba noted the practice of 'burnt offerings at the temple'.

We also know that Moloch was an idol dedicated to the Sun god.

There is a tradition that when the name *Solomon* was first translated it was in an alchemical form.[5] This means it would have been Sol Amon (Omon). What is immediately noticeable is the word Sol – a word for the Sun. The word Amon has several interpretations. One was of the *hidden sun*: the Sun one can no longer see once it has set below the western horizon. It was a word for the Moon, the dominant light in the sky after the Sun has set. Thus, the temple of Sol-Amon would be the temple of the Sun and the Moon. I was very sceptical about this two-word connotation until an acquaintance who had been born and brought up in East Africa, and who followed religious beliefs which were not those of mainstream Western Europe, commented that where he was raised as a child Solomon was always two words. He was amazed when he came to England to find it presented as one word.

Thus, it would seem logical that the term *King Solomon* was a reference to a king who was the son of David and Bathsheba, who we now know was named Jedidiah, and who built a temple in Jerusalem dedicated to the worship of the Sun and the Moon, the Sol and Amon Temple.

Conclusion

The introduction of a new generation of plain text Holy Bibles, based on a re-examination and translation of the best source materials and documents, including recent discoveries such as the Dead Sea Scrolls, places some areas of the text, relevant to my investigation, into a different context by comparison with my earlier education. I realised that I had to look behind the words used in key areas of biblical text and not merely accept them as absolute statements.

Scientific and archaeological evidence and the development of new technologies in the latter part of the 20th century has placed us in a position to be able to re-examine perceptions about Solomon's Temple and identify just who Solomon really was. His original name was, apparently, Jedidiah.

We have discovered how the name Solomon may have been derived. In an earlier chapter we noted that David, who designed the Temple, may have done so against a background of influence involving the Sun god and that in Jedidiah/Solomon's reign the Sun god was connected with the worship of Moloch, which also included child sacrifice. This was not a new practice – there is evidence for such worship having been in place in the times of Abraham and Moses.

Moses also designed the Tabernacle so that the rays of the dawn sun would illuminate the Ark.

The common factors in all of this are the heavenly bodies of the Sun and Moon.

[1] Catholic Encyclopaedia and WebBible Encyclopaedia
[2] MMV Encyclopaedia Mythica
[3] Catholic Encyclopaedia
[4] 1 Kings 10, verses 4 & 5 New International Version at www.Biblegateway.com
[5] David Furlong - *The Keys to the Temple: Unravel the Mysteries of the Ancient World*

Chapter 13
Revealing the design of Solomon's Temple

Before we embark on the step-by-step unveiling of the Temple, it is worth recapping some information discussed earlier:

a. The Sun features extensively in Masonic ceremonies.
b. Solomon's Temple is an attribute of Craft Freemasonry, a Temple we have shown to be the Sol and Amon Temple – a Temple dedicated to the Sun and the Moon.
c. We have looked at some aspects of ancient geometry including the concept of the overlapping circles called Vesica Piscis.
d. From Vesica Piscis we have seen how Solomon's Seal may have been derived and so named.
e. We have noted that the Israelites indulged in the worship of the calf known as Moloch, which in turn was an idol reflecting the Sun god.
f. We have noted that Moses set up the rituals and structure that became the core of the Israelite religion. This included the Ark of the Covenant which was built with great cunning, and appears to embody features associated with ancient wisdom. There was also the tabernacle, which also appears to have dimensional links with the ancient knowledge.
g. We know that when the Sun rose at dawn it illuminated the Ark inside the Tabernacle.
h. We have seen the reference by Bede and Josephus to the fact that at the time of equinox the sun shone between the pillars of the temple, through the porch, the hall and into the Holy of Holies to illuminate the Ark.
i. We have seen that David, who designed the Temple, was a contemporary of the heretical Pharaoh Akhenaten who changed the religion of Egypt, the dominant power in the region at the time the Temple was built, to the monotheistic worship of the Sun god.
j. And it is clear that David designed the Temple to reflect the characteristics of the Tabernacle, and as a house for the Ark.

There was so much I had learned, so much I had seen and read, that I felt I knew enough to apply some of the principles to the Jerusalem Temple. It was all very well having gained a lot of information, but if I was going to succeed in my quest to uncover the reason why Solomon's Temple is regarded with such reverence, I needed to propel myself back into the era of the builders. I needed to think like them. This was easier said than done.

All building starts with the firm foundations. I could not imagine that the Temple builders would have turned up on the site without having an idea of what to build and having undertaken some planning for it. Written plans did indeed exist.

In the Old Testament book of 1 Chronicles 28, it reads:

David summoned all the officials of Israel to assemble at Jerusalem ...

King David rose to his feet and said: 'Listen to me, my brothers and my people. I had it in my heart to build a house as a place of rest for the Ark of the covenant...'

Then David gave his son Solomon the plans for the portico of the Temple, its buildings, its storerooms, its upper parts, its inner rooms and the place of atonement.

'All this,' David said, 'I have in writing from the hand of the LORD upon me, and he gave me understanding in all the details of the plan.'

David also said to Solomon his son, 'Be strong and courageous, and do the work. Do not be afraid or discouraged ... The divisions of the priests and Levites are ready for all the work on the Temple ... and every willing man skilled in any craft will help you in all the work.'

From the above quotation, we know there was a plan. It would follow that the concepts outlined in that plan were based on the ancient knowledge that existed at that time, some of which was under the stewardship of the Levite priests. It would also follow that some details about how it should be built may also have existed. The building methodology would almost certainly have taken account of the geometric principles that we have previously looked at in this book. So, when Hiram, King of Tyre, sent Huram, a skilled craftsman, to take charge of the building work, we can also assume that Huram was equally knowledgeable about geometry and how to use it in construction. In addition, it would also seem to follow that the Israelites based the Temple on the same concepts that had hitherto been employed in the Tabernacle.

When I first embarked on this task I came to a very simple conclusion: that despite the incredible understanding these people had for the natural world around them, they would have used basic and uncomplicated construction methods, based on their knowledge of geometry and the influence of the macro-cosmos. I realised that if I applied that same understanding, I might end up with a structure which did not conform to the stylised architectural interpretations that one can find in a myriad of other books. I needed to make sure that each step was reasoned and justified.

The reign of King Solomon had arrived. It was time to start building. As the building process progresses we will uncover the mysteries of Solomon's Temple, built on Mount Moriah.

Why Mount Moriah? – The significance of the Cube

Archaeologists, historians and theologians who have made a study of the Holy Land and key characters of Biblical times have concluded that in at least the early Israelite religion, considerable emphasis was placed on worshipping celestial objects and high places, with specific high mountains particularly revered as being holy.

We have already seen the influence of the celestial worship through the garments worn by the priests, where the Romano-Jewish historian Josephus tells us that certain attributes were a reflection of the heavens; the Sun, Moon, planets, and constellations of the Great Belt. The garments were designed during the period when Moses and Aaron exerted influence in the days following the Exodus.

We note too that Moses went to the top of a mountain, Mount Sinai, on his own, to receive or construct the Commandments, the laws that would regularise the conduct and relationships within the tribe. It is not difficult to comprehend that in an era when Heaven was seen to be above the sky, then worshipping the deity from a mountain top would have been viewed as being as close as one was likely to be able to get to have direct communication with that deity. So building a Temple, or at least an altar of sacrifice, on the top of a mountain would have been entirely in keeping with the religious principles then in place.

So, why Mount Moriah? The early Israelites saw themselves as descendants of Abraham, and Mount Moriah was the place that Abraham went with his son Isaac for a process of ritual sacrifice. So the early religious traditions would have identified it as a holy place from the earliest days of the Israelite religion.

Mount Moriah is also identified with Abraham for another reason. Tradition has it that Abraham saw an object fall from the sky and land on that mountain. The object was apparently a large black rock. Today we might consider it to be a meteorite turned black as a consequence of the heat created as it fell through the upper atmosphere of the Earth. However, having fallen from the heavens it would be entirely logical that people in that era would have considered it as having originated in God's kingdom, and thereby to be regarded as a most revered and holy object.

In the Islamic tradition we are told that the prophet Mohammed first sought to build the holiest shrine on Mt Moriah – Temple Mount, but later instructed that the holiest shrine be built at Mecca. The shrine, is known as the Kabba (it has several spellings) which Islamic pilgrims travel to see. It is roughly cube shaped and houses a black stone believed, in some quarters, to be the remains of a meteorite. The Kabba is believed to represent the centre of the earth and the point where Adam first performed worship of God, and that the Kabba has a heavenly counterpart. It is also believed to be the place where, under heavenly guidance, a Kabba is said to have first been constructed by Abraham and his son Ishmael when the *sakinah* circled the spot and instructed them to build.

The reference to the *sakinah* seems to have a direct relationship with the *shekinah* noted in the Old Testament Book of Exodus and the building of the Tabernacle by Moses. As previously pointed out, there are those that believe that the *shekinah* is a reference to the planet Venus and a forty year cycle as may have been understood in ancient times. At the time the Islamic religion was evolving, one can well imagine that the same principles of *ancient wisdom* were known, albeit that the Islamic religion evolved some 1,500 years after the building of Solomon's Temple.

The cube, made up of six sides and eight corners was symbolic of heaven. If the same tradition about Abraham building a temple in the shape of a cube existed amongst the Israelites, then it would have been equally important to them. So, it is not surprising to find that it was incorporated into the design of the Jerusalem Temple, created by David.

It would therefore follow that the cube shaped Holy of Holies that formed part of Solomon's Temple was built with the same interpretation in mind. Thus, if the cube represented heaven, then the centre of the cube would have been representative of the centre of heaven, the logical place for the deity to reside.

Setting out the Foundations

In the building of any major structure, the foundations are the most critical element. We are told that the Temple was built on the top of Mount Moriah. We must assume that the ground required some levelling and large stone blocks were needed to provide the level base on which to start the building. Having completed this foundation, the next task would be to mark out the relative positions of the walls.

As discussed earlier, the Tabernacle was originally erected on an east-west axis. The axis centre line needed to be defined because everything else would spring from it.

Setting the orientation was, I suggest, relatively easy. In the centre of the site, a spear, or stick with a pointed end, could be pushed into the ground so that its point was uppermost. At dawn on the day of the Spring Equinox, someone skilled in marking out, like Huram himself, stood on the western edge of the site with another spear. As the first light of day appeared, so the senior surveyor aligned the top of the spear he had in the west with the one in the centre of the site, with both on a line with the point on the horizon where the Sun first appeared. The second spear was then inserted in the ground along that line. A straight line drawn from the base of the second spear, through the base of the first spear, to the point where the senior surveyor stood would provide a perfect east-west axis.

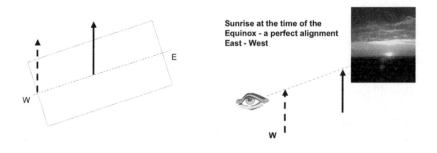

Sunrise at the time of the
Equinox - a perfect alignment
East - West

The Old Testament Book of 1 Kings, chapter 6 tells us that the Temple was 60 cubits long and 20 cubits wide. We are later informed that of the overall 60 cubit length, the Hall was 40 cubits long and the Holy of Holies was 20 cubits. It seems perfectly logical to suggest that these are internal dimensions as nowhere in the Old Testament are we given any exact details about the thickness of the outer walls.

Thus, by describing a circle of 10 cubits radius from the base of the spear at the centre of the site, we would now have a width defined of 20 cubits. By describing two more circles, of the same radius, on either side of the central spear, using the principles of Vesica Piscis, then a total of five circles would exist. The reason for the choice of 5 circles will become clear in due course. The overall length they would create would be 60 cubits and the width would be 20 cubits. In this simple process the width of the Temple is determined and so is its length. Even the two key rooms, the Holy of Holies and the Hall, are also defined. What is more, the setting out is in keeping with *sacred knowledge*.

- The radius of 10, drop the zero = 1 = unity and symbolize the deity.
- The diameter of 20, drop the zero = 2 = duality = Heaven and Earth
- The length of 60 reflects the counting system; drop the zero = 6 = harmony.
- The number 40, drop the zero, = 4 = the four elements: Earth, Wind, Fire, Air.
- Vesica Piscis – the most sacred design in geometry.

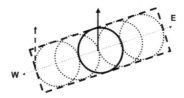

In a very simple process, the basic ground plan outline of the Temple has been defined.

When it comes to the height, the books of Kings and Chronicles state that the Temple was 30 cubits high. This raised a question in my mind about how that dimension was arrived at. We are told that the Holy of Holies was a cube measuring 20 x 20 x 20 cubits. So, the overall height was not dictated by that aspect of the structure. There is, however, one aspect of the Holy of Holies we can look at whilst we are here.

In his philosophical considerations, Pythagoras, attributed certain characteristics to numbers. The sacred cube was defined by the number 8. If we drop the zero from 20, we get 2, and 2 x 2 x 2 = 8 which, in turn, symbolically represents the world.

The height could be determined by two circles, each of 10 cubits radius, in Vesica Piscis. This would result in a simple rectangular building, easy to construct.

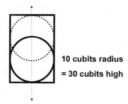

10 cubits radius
= 30 cubits high

The 30 cubit distance would be easy enough to fix, by taking two poles and raising them in the corners at the end of the building, then taking some cord and measuring it to the point where a line drawn at a tangent to the second circle used in the ground-plan for setting out, meets the outer edge of the wall. Thus, the 30 cubit mark would be defined. By rotating the cord vertically, the height would be established.

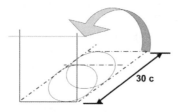

30 c

But this was a building which has been revered as something special, for hundreds of years. The two-circle vesica approach seemed logical, yet it also seemed just too simple. Not that I was seeking to make it any more difficult than it needed to be. The only other route that suggested itself was to use the *Mason's secret square* approach.

Rotating a cord based on just one circle in the ground-plan would result in a height of 20 cubits. Adding half a square on top would give 30 cubits in height.

The Masons Secret   The Masons Secret   Masons Secret = Square
reduced by half

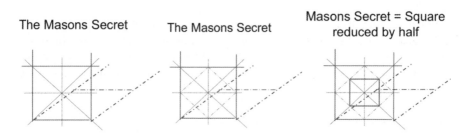

If this square was then added to the top of the square framework already created, it would result in a profile wherein the top portion was exactly half that of the lower. There would be significance to the shape which was not immediately obvious to anyone who was not entitled to know. I decided to run with it as the primary choice.

Possible outline of the Temple

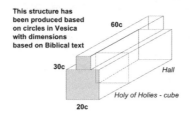

This structure has been produced based on circles in Vesica with dimensions based on Biblical text

60c

30c

Hall

Holy of Holies - cube

20c

Adding the Portico

1 Kings 6:3 states that:

> *The portico at the front of the main hall of the Temple extended the width of the Temple, that is twenty cubits, and projected ten cubits from the front of the Temple.*

From this, it is clear that the portico extended across the width of the building and ten cubits forward, but it does not say how high it was. We will come back to that issue.

What is significant is that the overall length of the Temple can now be based on six circles in Vesica Piscis. Six, the symbolic number of harmony.

Vesica Pisces, the temple + portico

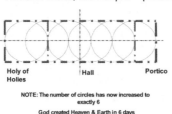

Holy of Holies

Hall

Portico

NOTE: The number of circles has now increased to exactly 6

God created Heaven & Earth in 6 days

It is easy to understand that the design had been based on an overall length dictated by six circles as opposed to five. It would also follow that being as the centre of a circle was regarded as most sacred, then, if the size of the Holy of Holies was defined by one full circle, then the centre of that area would also be the most sacred place in the Temple. We will leave the subject of the portico and structure for while. But, we will return to them.

The position of the Ark

1 Kings 8:6-8 reports the placing of the Ark in the Temple, prior to the Temple being dedicated.

The priests then brought the Ark of the ... covenant to its place in the inner sanctuary of the Temple, the Most Holy Place, and put it beneath the wings of the cherubim.
The cherubim spread their wings over the place of the Ark and overshadowed the Ark and its carrying poles.
These poles were so long that their ends could be seen from the Holy Place in front of the inner sanctuary, but not from outside the Holy Place; and they are still there today.

In the Book of Exodus, it is made clear that when the Ark was built, the carrying poles were to be passed through rings which were part of the design, and that the poles should never be removed. The above text implies that the cherubim were already in place. By virtue that one could see the ends of the carrying poles, the poles must have been aligned in an east-west direction. Thus, the Ark would have been carried into the Holy of Holies and set down on a line directly in front of the door which provided access between the Hall and Holy of Holies.

The Cherubim

The cherubim posed a mystery. Why were they there? They had to have served a purpose. What was that purpose?

Through everything I have read about the Temple, there are numerous references to the existence of these cherubim, but not once have I encountered any attempt to understand what they were for. It was as if these items were identified as religious symbols that writers were prepared to shy away from commenting on.

According to academic sources, the word *cherubim* is derived from Akkadian, and means 'a genie who was the advisor to the great gods and an advocate for the throne of Yahweh'.[1]

Bede attributes another definition. He describes them as being '...filled with the light of heavenly wisdom...'. Bede continues,

'That is why he wanted them called cherub which means in Latin "a great store of knowledge".[2]

What was that *store of knowledge?* What did he mean by *the light of heavenly wisdom?*

I had a vision of them that I later called *Huram's folly*. The picture that formed in my mind was that, during the construction of the Temple, Solomon met with Huram at the doorway leading between the Hall and the Holy of Holies. Solomon looked along the length of the Holy of Holies and all he could see was a dark, grey stone wall at the opposite end. Turning to Huram, he said, 'I do not know what we're going to do about that wall, Huram. It's going to look dark, bleak and horrible as the high priest comes in through this doorway.' 'Do not worry, Solomon,' Huram replied. 'What I've got in mind is to knock up a couple of big bronze cherubim, coated in gold, of course, with wings stretching from one side of the Temple to the other side. They'll cover up that back wall nicely. The priests will forget the wall is there.'

Things did not happen like that. In the era when the Temple was built, everything was done for a purpose, not just for decoration.

The detail about the cherubim is in 2 Chronicles 3:10-13

In the Most Holy Place he made a pair of sculptured cherubim and overlaid them with gold.

The total wingspan of the cherubim was twenty cubits. One wing of the first cherub was five cubits long and touched the Temple wall, while its other wing, also five cubits long, touched the wing of the other cherub.

Similarly one wing of the second cherub was five cubits long and touched the other Temple wall, and its other wing, also five cubits long, touched the wing of the first cherub.

The wings of these cherubim extended twenty cubits. They stood on their feet, facing the main hall.

From this text we learn that the two cherubim each had two wings of five cubits length, they spread across the entire width of the Holy of Holies, just touching the outer walls and just touching in the middle of the chamber. Thus, they met in a position directly above the Ark. As the Ark was placed in the centre of the chamber, beneath the wings of the cherubim, it is obvious that the cherubim were in a position which formed a line across the chamber halfway between the doorway and the rear wall. They also faced towards the Hall, which means they were pointing towards the doorway which connected the two chambers, and thereby facing the rising Sun.

The temple – Holy of Holies

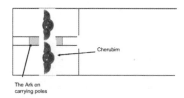

The cherubim were covered in gold, as was the Ark from former times. The inside walls, *the inner parts,* were also overlaid with gold. The notes attached to the biblical text indicate that the weight of gold was some 23 tons. If we assume a value of gold at \$430/oz, then early in this 21st century, the value of the gold used in this one chamber alone would have been worth around \$235,000,000.

We should also remember that gold at that time could also be symbolic of the Sun.

The cube and the centre

We have seen that the Ark was probably positioned in the centre of the Holy of Holies. With their wings outstretched above the Ark, it means that the cherubim too were central above it.

Being a cube 20c x 20c x 20c there was a point directly above the Ark which was the exact centre of the cube. It would be a point from where the distance to the ceiling, the floor and each of the walls was exactly 10 cubits, and by dropping the zero we are left the with number 1, the symbol for the deity. Against such a background it is highly probable that the point at which the wings of the cherubim touched was that point in the exact centre of the Holy of Holies.

The Side Rooms

1 Kings 6:5&6

Against the walls of the main hall and inner sanctuary he built a structure around the building, in which there were side rooms.

The lowest floor was five cubits wide, the middle floor six cubits and the third floor seven. He made offset ledges around the outside of the Temple so that nothing would be inserted into the Temple walls.

In the above verses, we learn that around the outside walls of the Temple a series of rooms were built on three separate levels. Furthermore, the method of construction was such that the integrity of the inside of the Temple was not undermined by protrusions needed to support the external structure.

The above verses also tell us how this was achieved, by the use of a stepped stone structure, offset ledges as part of the external walls.

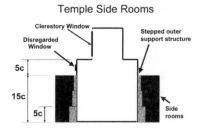

Temple Side Rooms

The stepped stone structure around the outer walls provided a location ledge from which timber beams would rest, thereby creating a floor for the second and third levels, and a roof over the third.

This is reinforced in 1 Kings 6:10

And he built the side rooms all along the Temple. The height of each was five cubits, and they were attached to the Temple by beams of cedar.

With each of the rooms being 5 cubits high, it provided a fourth level of 5 cubits before reaching the 20 cubit height level created by two squares, one on top of the other. Thus, the whole is in balance.

There is, however, something else to draw attention to. The rooms have very specific widths defined, which in turn would have affected the outer support structure. In 1 Kings 6:6 they are described as follows:

The lowest floor was five cubits wide, the middle floor six cubits and the third floor seven.

If we add together the widths we get:
5 + 6 + 7 = 18. In Pythagoras' philosophy 1 + 8 = 9 the symbolic value for Man. There were two sides to the Temple so the total is 36 and 3 + 6 = 9
The same configuration also existed across the rear of the Temple, and three 18s are 54. 5 + 4 = 9.

The Clerestory Windows

1 Kings 6:4 states:
He made narrow clerestory windows in the temple.

By virtue that there is a specific mention that they are *narrow* indicates that the measurement for the width was significantly less than that for the height. Most previous drawings, or attempts to illustrate the Temple, ignore this statement completely and show square windows in the area above the roof over the third level of the side rooms.

Assuming the outline of the Temple was as I have suggested, that is, defined by two squares, one exactly half the size of the other, then the wall area above the side rooms is only 5 cubits high. Making allowance at the top and bottom of the windows of 1 cubit, for structural reasons, then the maximum height of the windows can only have been 3 cubits. To be narrow, they must have had a ratio of something like 3 cubits high x 2 cubits wide. This seems a very small window for the size of the structure.

I decided to investigate the possibility that the windows were placed in the sides of the upper structure. This revealed that it was possible to get 12 windows along the length of the Hall and Holy of Holies, each 6 cubits high, and 3 cubits wide with a gap between each of 2 cubits, and 1 cubit at each end which when added together, also added to 2 cubits.

Windows of the Temple

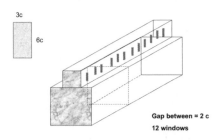

This configuration proved to have another interesting effect related to the Sun.

The Clerestory Windows and the effect of the Sun

Having arrived at what I thought was a logical profile for the windows, I wondered what the effect of the Sun shining through them would be. This I investigated using scale drawings. I chose the three primary elevations of the Sun, namely Equinox, Summer Solstice and Winter Solstice. What became apparent was that as the seasons changed so too did the position of the beam of sunlight entering via the windows on the south side, as it struck the inside of the Temple wall on the north side.

In winter, the position of the beam was naturally high on the wall.

By the time of the equinox in the northern hemisphere, the Sun is higher in the sky and the beam of light would have spread over a larger area of the wall. By the time of the Summer Solstice the light would cover the north wall.

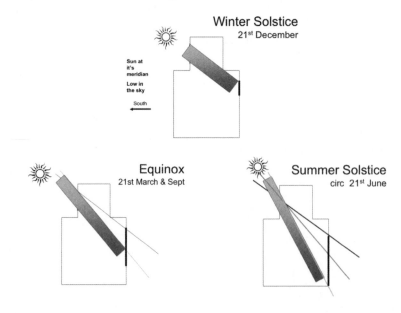

This has other interesting consequences.

In 1 Kings 6 it states that the inside walls of the Temple were decorated with images of cherubim, gourds, palm trees and open flowers. We have already looked at Solomon's apparent wisdom as noted in 1 Kings 4, wherein it states:

He described plant life, from the cedar of Lebanon to the hyssop that grows out of walls. He also taught about animals and birds, reptiles and fish.

The fact that walls were decorated with the *palm trees and open flowers* seems strange for a religious structure, unless it is a reflection of the *wisdom of Solomon*, and his knowledge of the macro-cosmos and its interdependency derived from the earliest days of the creation of the world. Flowers come in many varieties and display their colours at different times of the year. In addition, many plant forms that today we refer to as *vegetables* have flowers associated with them. Peas, for example, produce a flower from which the pod ultimately grows. The same is true of strawberries. Raspberry canes produce a flower before the crop, as do apples and pears. The blackberry in the hedgerows is the same. The word *gourd* means the *fleshy fruit of a climbing plant* which could include blackberries and grapes. So the comment about *gourds and open flowers* may not be a reference to the type of flowers which today we specifically cultivate to provide decorative colour to our gardens and homes, but a comment relating to the flowers which formed what, to the peoples of the Solomonic era, was their source of food.

Solomon's Temple has been handed down to us as a structure of significance, an impressive wonder, which suggests it was more than just a place of worship. It was against that reinforced realisation that the thought hit me that the combined use of the beams of light from the Sun at various seasonal periods and the *gourds and open flowers* decoration could have come together as an almanac for food production.

The inside of the Hall was divided into a series of sections dictated by the placing

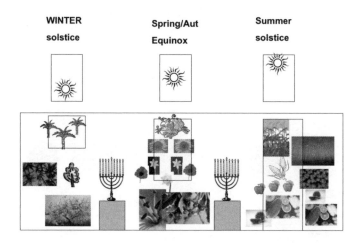

of the candlesticks. I could imagine that each section was decorated with different forms of plant life. As the Sun moved along the horizon, so its elevation above the horizon also changed. As the year progressed, the beams of light through the clerestory windows would highlight certain gourds or flowers to indicate it was time to sow, cultivate or harvest. It would have been a seasonal calendar for cultivation.

The era of Solomon was one of relative peace and prosperity. Both of these attributes may well have been, amongst other factors, the result of plentiful supplies of food. The latter would have been the consequence of a well-structured seasonal calendar for the management of agriculture. That calendar may well have been derived from the beams of light shining through the clerestory windows.

The Door Jambs and Light of the Cherubim

Earlier in the book, I made reference to the changing text between the Kings James version of the 17th century, and the more recent International version. In particular, I drew attention to 1 Kings 6:31 in the New International version, which describes the doorway between the Holy of Holies and the Hall, as follows:

> *For the entrance of the inner sanctuary he made doors of Olive wood with five-sided jambs.*

For many months I pondered on this, noting that in 1 Kings 6:33 there is a description of the entrance into the Hall stating that the doorway was made from four-sided jambs – in other words that the doorway was very conventional. That the door jambs to the Holy of Holies were five-sided implied that they had some special characteristic attached to them. If they were shaped as a regular polygon, then we are considering door jambs which were pentagonal. This did not make sense. As you can see by the diagram below, the shape would result in a pinch-point within the doorway. Neither did it make sense to rotate the shape so that there was a parallel door frame. This could only have led to awkward protrusions inside the chamber. What is more, I could not comprehend why they should decide on such an elaborate and impractical arrangement, although they obviously had all the skills necessary to construct it.

The 5-sided door jams – Holy of Holies

The 5-sided door jams – Holy of Holies

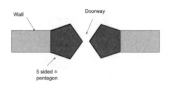

The months passed and this configuration constantly perplexed me. So it was that I found myself on a business trip in the north of England. One evening I was sitting in my hotel room contemplating aspects of the Temple design, when I resolved to find the answer to the door jambs. I tried to cast my mind into the era of the construction and was reflecting on the many Temples of antiquity I had visited in the Mediterranean area, and especially in Egypt, and how they had been relatively simple structures made from square stone blocks. I wondered how one could produce five-sided door jambs using square blocks. I took two square sticky-notes from my briefcase and stuck them on the mirror in the room. I kept telling myself that these were simple people, so they must have had a simple solution. Suddenly, as if by divine inspiration, an answer presented itself. I rotated one of the squares through 45 degrees.

5 sided door jam – possible solution

5 sided door jam – possible solution

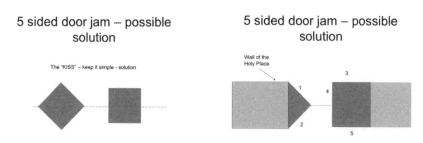

Although the solution was simple, I had doubts. These were dispelled a few months later. On a visit to Egypt to see at first hand the pyramids of Giza and the Sphinx, I also arranged to visit the stepped pyramid at Saqqara and the ancient capital of Memphis. Just on the outskirts of Cairo, close to the ancient centre of Heliopolis, several roads met at a junction formed by a roundabout. As we approached this junction I noted that throughout the surrounding area there were piles of stones, clearly from ancient buildings, remnants of statues and other relics, which, not being attributable to anything in particular, had been marshalled into heaps. In the centre of the roundabout at the road junction, stood two very old stones, each square in shape and about 8 feet (2.5M) tall. They had been deliberately arranged in the configuration I have shown above. It demonstrated to me that someone else saw the beauty of such a simple arrangement.

Now, I had a doorway solution which was simple to construct, but it did not explain why there should still be a sloping side to the door jamb. During the same business trip previously mentioned, I took the opportunity to visit Durham Cathedral. I had visited it twice previously but long before my interest in Solomon's Temple had surfaced. Again, I encountered an effect as if divine inspiration was urging me on. I was admiring some of the stained glass windows when my eye was caught by the shape of the inside face of the walls adjacent to them. They were angled. This was to spread the light. In that moment I realised that the five-sided door jambs could therefore have had an implication for the physics of light and the way it was distributed in the Holy of Holies.

In an earlier chapter, I made reference to the Ark being positioned in the Tabernacle, so that it was illuminated by the Sun at dawn, a function underlined in the translation of Bede's *De Templo:*

> *'... so that the equinoctial sunrise could shed its rays directly on the Ark of the covenant through the three doors, namely the portico, the Temple and the oracle ...'* [3]

If the Temple was built on the same principle, then, with it being on an east-west axis, at the time of the equinox a shaft of sunlight could penetrate through the porch,

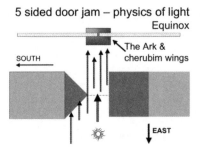

the Hall, the five-sided door jamb, and illuminate the Ark.

In theory, as the Sun moved to the north, through the summer months, to the position at the Summer Solstice, so the inside angle of the left-hand door jamb would permit the beam of light to spread towards the south, whilst the northern half of the temple remained in shadow. Conversely, as the Sun moved south from the equinox, towards the Winter Solstice, then the beam of light would become restricted by the square corner of the other door jamb.

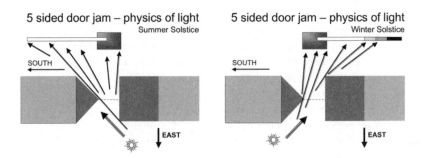

Assuming a doorway of sufficient height, the beam of sunlight at dawn would also progressively illuminate the wings of the cherubim.

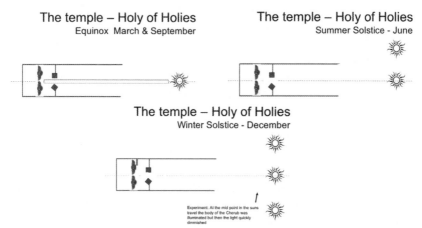

The temple – Holy of Holies
Equinox March & September

The temple – Holy of Holies
Summer Solstice - June

The temple – Holy of Holies
Winter Solstice - December

Experiment. At the mid point in the suns
travel the body of the Cherub was
illuminated but then the light quickly
diminished

From my engineering background, I was aware that sometimes theory and practice do not necessarily support one another. To prove that the principle was sound, I built a scaled replica of the Hall and Holy of Holies out of thick cardboard. I arranged a piece of card across the centre of the Holy of Holies, drawing on it representations of the cherubim and the Ark. I set them up on the centre line of the garage floor, and then marked the angles that represented the position of the solstices. About eight feet back from the model I then positioned a 100-watt spot lamp. As I moved the spot lamp across the span of the solstice angles, so the light inside the replica of the Holy of Holies spread exactly as the theory suggested it should. Furthermore, the point that represented the centre between the solstices and the equinox corresponded exactly with the bodies of the respective cherubim. In many respects, this was characteristic of the origins of the octagram, which I have mentioned earlier in this book, and the Celtic festivals which were held midway between the solstices and equinoxes. As the beam of light moved from the body of the cherub which was positioned in the north of the chamber, so the intensity of the light quickly diminished so that about three-quarters of the way along the northernmost wing, the beam of light was extinguished.

This raised an interesting idea. The cherubim have wings, and wings have feathers. If the wings were suitably arranged so that the feathers at the bottom edge of the wings were clearly defined, and had suitable spacing, then as the Sun moved north and south from the equinox, then the position of the spread of the sunlight would record the passage of the Sun. The cherubim would act as a calendar, and an indicator of the passage of the seasons.

Tradition has it that the High Priest entered the Holy of Holies on one day of the year only. I had wondered what could have been happening and was of such significance for this solitary event. Could it be that the High Priest was observing that sunlight had reappeared on the northern wing of the cherubim signifying an end to winter; that all was well with the macro-cosmos? It would be a slightly different form of observation to watching the Winter Solstice at Stonehenge, but with the same connotations.

As quoted earlier, the Venerable Bede described the cherubim as being *'... filled with the light of heavenly wisdom ... 'a great store of knowledge'.*

The Temple Sun lives on

At Udaipur in Rajasthan, a state in the north of India, there are two magnificent palaces. One palace sits in the centre of a large lake and serves today as a hotel. Its unusual and tranquil setting, together with the romance of the location, results in it being very popular with western tourists. The other and much larger palace, which sits on the banks of the lake, is the home of the Maharanas who are the traditional rulers of that State. The current palace apparently dates back to the 16th century, long before the arrival of British colonial rule.

When I had the good fortune to visit this palace my guide was a man from the Brahmin cast. The Brahmins were similar to a priestly line such as the Levites were in Old Testament Davidic times. As we toured the palace so my guide mentioned that the Maharanas traced their origins and descent back some 5,000 years to the Sun god. Immediately, my interest was aroused. I was struck by the number symbolism which was present and built into the structure; the octagram was particularly visible. I asked if there was any particular reason for these elements being there, and each time any such symbolic existence was denied. Until, that is, we were in what I can only describe as the throne room, where the crowning of a new Maharana was undertaken. My guide mentioned that during the proceedings, which apparently took some hours, the new ruler would have a rosary of twelve beads, which he constantly moved and counted. I questioned the significance of the number twelve. My guide walked away from the group of other tourists that had assembled and beckoned me to follow. He noted my interest in the number symbolism and then went on to point out that $1 + 2 = 3$, and that within the pantheon of Indian gods, the third is the god of creation; that the creation of life as we know it is governed by the light and the warmth of the Sun, and that related back to the Sun god from whom the Maharanas claimed descent.

As we passed through a courtyard at the front of the palace, I noted a large circular golden disc inserted high up on a wall. It stood out against what were otherwise external structural walls that at one time had been coated in a paint that contained a red pigment, a colour that had long since been faded by the intensity of the sun. My guide mentioned that the disc was a symbol of the Sun, again noting the Maharana's descent from the Sun god. As we processed through the palace, I found myself, almost by accident, in a room behind the sun disc I had earlier seen from the courtyard. It was obvious that it had been constructed in a way that enabled it to be removed from the inside. This, my guide told me, was so that on the day when day and night are of equal length, what we call the equinox, at dawn a shaft of light penetrated the length of the room and illuminated a wall on which the image of the Sun god had been mounted. That image has now been moved to a side wall. The guide went on to point out that there were two side windows and when the Sun was at the limits of its travel along the horizon, the solstices, so the beam of light at dawn penetrated into the far corners of the room.

The Sun Disc in the outer wall of the palace, flanked by the two side windows

The "sun penetration" room in the palace, behind the Sun Disc.

The similarity between the solar penetration concept that seemed possible for Solomon's Temple, and what I was able to see in this palace in Rajastan, was startling. And, there was also the link with the Sun god.

The Mystery of the Oracle

> *... and so the total height of the house according to the Book of Paralipomenon amounted to a hundred and twenty cubits ...* [4]

One hundred and twenty cubits high is the equivalent of around 180 feet – 60 yards / 85 metres. What is being suggested is that the height of Solomon's Temple was roughly equivalent to a modern 18-20 floor multi-storey building. It would have been a massive structural undertaking for its day. The weight of the stone alone would have demanded extensive foundations, which have not been identified by archaeologists. The weight could have been reduced by the use of timber from Tyre in Lebanon, but even so, the ultimate weight would still have demanded considerable foundations. An Oracle of such proportions would have been similar to the spires that were added to many of the European cathedrals, pointed towers that reached towards Heaven and provided a commanding view over the surrounding countryside. Even though the construction of spires was substantially based on a wooden framework, such was their weight that many of them collapsed, the thick stone walls on which the structure rested buckling under the weight of these enormous wooden structures. At Chichester Cathedral the spire was added in the 15th century and collapsed about 400 years later in 1861.

Numerous illustrations depicting what the Jerusalem Temple might have looked like have been made since the 18th century. The vast majority of those that I have had the opportunity to inspect do not show any such substantial structure to reflect the height of 120 cubits. The only one I did encounter was that drawn by the Rev

The Secrets of Solomon's Temple

Caldecott, as will be shown later in this book. Even then, for proportional reasons associated with presenting it on a printed page, only part of the overall height is shown.

So, could the reference to the Oracle be a reference to something else other than a massive superstructure? There is a tantalising and surprising answer.

From everything we have noted so far, the Sun at dawn, particularly at the time of the equinox, shone through the portico, the Hall, and the doorway leading to the Holy of Holies, and illuminated the Ark and, it would seem, the cherubim.

The number 15 has already occurred several times and is related to the rotation of the Earth on its axis, where it takes 24 divisions of fifteen degrees to complete one revolution, what we currently define as one hour of time. It is also significant that the Moon is always full on the fifteenth day of its cycle, the mid-point of the lunar calendar used to govern religious affairs.

If Solomon's Temple was based on knowledge of the natural world and the perceived wisdom that existed at that time, then one would expect this reference to 120 cubits to have some link with that understanding. Not surprisingly, there is just such evidence.

It just so happens that all the integers in the range 1 to 15, when added together make a total of 120. What is more, these numbers fit into an arithmetical pattern known as *triangular numbers*.

$$1$$
$$2 \quad 3$$
$$4 \quad 5 \quad 6$$
$$7 \quad 8 \quad 9 \quad 10$$
$$11 \quad 12 \quad 13 \quad 14 \quad 15$$

These integers produce some interesting characteristics. For example, if the all the odd numbers are added together they make 64:

$1 + 3 + 5 + 7 + 9 + 11 + 13 + 15 = 64$ and $6 + 4 = 10$

If we now add them together to produce intervening sub-totals, we get the squares of the consecutive integers:

$1 + 3 = 4 + 5 = 9 + 7 = 16 + 9 = 25 + 11 = 36 + 13 = 49 + 15 = 64$
$2 \times 2 = 4, \quad 3 \times 3 = 9, 4 \times 4 = 16, \quad \text{and so on.}[5]$

So, what could the number 120 relate to? Old Testament text implies the word *Oracle* is associated with the Holy of Holies, which we know is a cube measuring 20 cubits. Inside the room were the two cherubim with their wings outstretched. Each wing was 5 cubits. The nature of two wings about a body is that they form a triangular shape. If the height of the wings at the centre of the body of the cherubim was also 5 cubits, then the three key dimensions for the construction of the wings would be complete by relating them to the wisdom of the number 120 and its relationship to the number 15.

250

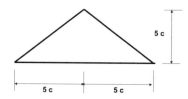

The Churbim wings and the 120 triangle

If the reference to the Oracle being 120 cubits high is actually a reference to a triangular pattern containing numbers that add up to one hundred and twenty, then we are again noting principles of *ancient wisdom*. As the Venerable Bede noted, the Latin translation of the word 'cherub' is 'a great store of knowledge'.

And the Priests stopped

In 1 Kings 8:10 & 11 we find a curious comment. It is related to the dedication of the Temple when the Ark of the Covenant was carried into the Holy of Holies and placed beneath the outstretched wings of the cherubim. The text reads:

> *And it came to pass, when the priests came out of the Holy place, that the cloud filled the house of the LORD, so that the priests could not continue ministering because of the cloud; for the glory of the LORD filled the house of the LORD.*

Some interpretations of this text suggest that the *glory of the Lord* was a bright light signifying the Lord's presence, and was so great that the priests were forced to fall to their knees in the Holy of Holies.

From the design details we have now been able to amass, it would seem that the Ark was carried into the Temple, probably just before dawn on the day of the equinox. No doubt incense was burnt in the gold censer, which in turn provided a slightly smoky atmosphere. Then, at dawn, a shaft of bright sunlight stabbed through the portico, the Hall, the doorway to the Holy of Holies, striking the golden wings of the cherubim reflecting a blast of intense light through the room which in turn reflected off and mingled with the tiny smoke particulates. If the priests had not anticipated such a reaction one can well imagine that they would have been struck with awe, and the intensity of the experience would have been such that they could not administer the ceremonial rites that they had anticipated. Instead, they had stumbled out of the Holy of Holies to seek relief, and this is what the passage above records. If this speculation is correct, then they would have witnessed the glory of the Sun god.

Conclusion

The design and implementation of the Temple appear to reflect the principles of *ancient wisdom* both in the use of geometry and the progress of the Sun along the eastern horizon. This reveals its potential use as a seasonal calendar which a stable and settled society could have used for predicting the seasons and thereby maximising food production. This would have added to the wealth and well-being of the nation.

Is there anything to be learned from the information we are given about the pillars?

[1] Encyclopedia of Religeon
[2] Connolly, S. (1995) with an introduction by Jennifer O'Reilly. Bede: *On the Temple*, section 13.1, footnote
[2] Bede: *On the Temple*, section 13.1
[3] Bede: *On the Temple*, section 13.1
[4] Bede: *On the Temple*, section 6.2
[5] Bede: *On the Temple*, section 8.2
[6] See *Fathers of the Second Century*, from Christian Classics Ethereal Library at http://www.ccel.org/ccel/schaff/anf02.vi.iv.vi.xi.html

Chapter 14
Secrets in the pillars

The pillars prove to be something a little different to the way we may have imagined them in the past.

We have already touched on the pillars in that they are described as being part of the furnishings. They feature prominently in Masonic ceremonies so it seemed logical that I should try and understand them in more detail.

What we are told about the pillars
We get the detail from 1 Kings 7:15-22

> *He cast two bronze pillars, each eighteen cubits high and twelve cubits around, by line.*
>
> *He also made two capitals of cast bronze to set on the tops of the pillars; each capital was five cubits high.*
>
> *A network of interwoven chains festooned the capitals on top of the pillars, seven for each capital.*
>
> *He made pomegranates in two rows encircling each network to decorate the capitals on top of the pillars. He did the same for each capital.*
>
> *The capitals on top of the pillars in the portico were in the shape of lilies, four cubits high.*
>
> *On the capitals of both pillars, above the bowl-shaped part next to the network, were the two hundred pomegranates in rows all around.*
>
> *He erected the pillars at the portico of the temple. The pillar to the south he named Jakin and the one to the north Boaz.*
>
> *The capitals on top were in the shape of lilies. And so the work on the pillars was completed.*

There are some interesting observations here, not least of which is that we are told that the two pillars were on a north-south axis with the pillar named Jakin to the south and the pillar named Boaz to the north.

Whilst in 1 Kings 7:21 it states that:

> *He erected the pillars at the portico of the temple*

in 2 Chronicles 3:15 we get a slightly different perspective:

> *In front of the temple he made two pillars which together measured thirty five cubits long ...*[1]

The two texts combined leave us in no doubt that the pillars were erected at the eastern end of the temple, in front of the portico as opposed to being in the west and behind the Holy of Holies. I make this point because, in many Masonic centres, models of interpretations of the pillars are sometimes added to the Lodge Room decor, and in some lodges they are positioned in the west. There is a perverse logic to this. If one had looked at the pillars from the position of the rising Sun, then by definition they are in the west, relative to it. It is clear, however, that we should not confuse the position – they were at the eastern end of the building, in front of the portico. What the biblical text fails to tell us is how far in front of the portico they were positioned. By chance, modern computer simulation helped me to solve that problem. We will see the results shortly.

According to 1 Kings, each of the pillars was 18 cubits high and 12 cubits in circumference, measured by line. There is a slight variation in the pillar lengths implied by the text of 2 Chronicles 3:15 where it states that 'together they were thirty five cubits long'. This is interpreted in some circles, including certain Masonic ceremonies, that they were perhaps 17.5 cubits each high. The variation is sometimes attributed to a need to have an area around the top of the pillars on which the capitals could be located. Thus, the capitals would cover a length of half a cubit of the full length of the pillars. As we will see later, this may not be the reason for the difference in the two texts, noting there is also a variance in the use of the words, *high* and *long*.

There were, then, the two capitals, also cast in bronze, which were set on the tops of the pillars; each capital was 5 cubits high. Once again we find a slight difference between the texts of Kings and Chronicles. In Kings the capitals have lily-shaped tops, whilst in Chronicles the capitals are described as being bowl shaped. In Kings, there is also mention of a further image of lilies which extended another 4 cubits above the capitals.

Next, we are told that the capitals had engraved on them a network of interwoven chains, seven for each capital.

Finally, we are advised that there were also two rows of pomegranates on each capital, with the total number of pomegranates for both capitals being 400. Thus, assuming they were equally allocated to each row, then there were 100 images of pomegranates in each row. This assumption is confirmed in 2 Chronicles 3.

Thus, the height of the pillars, based on the biblical text, and using the stated 18 cubit height, was

$$18 + 5 + 4 = 27 \text{ cubits.}$$

The capitals – the interwoven chains

He also made two capitals of cast bronze to set on the tops of the pillars; each capital was five cubits high.
A network of interwoven chains festooned the capitals on top of the pillars, seven for each capital.

In Masonic tracing boards and other illustrations of the pillars, the interwoven chains are often depicted as a square mesh. In ancient Egypt a chain was a series of interlocking circles, based on Vesica Piscis and the half radius seen earlier in this work. Such interlocking circles were regarded as having lucky omens. It would therefore seem logical that the reference to the *interwoven chains* would follow the same principle.

If the capitals have a diameter of 5 cubits then the length of the circumference is a little over 15 cubits, two numbers significant with the macro-cosmos. If circles are drawn a little over 2 cubits in diameter, then the result is 7 circles which can surround the rounded capital. In addition, the numerical value would be a reflection of the duality: 2 = Heaven and earth.

Equally interesting is that if 3 rows of such chains are added to the capital, but in Vesica Piscis form the following pattern emerges.

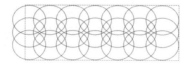

This configuration would therefore result in three rows, representing the three positions of the Sun; 7 circles in each row to represent the 7 days of creation and rest; 21 circles in total resulting in 2 + 1 = 3, plus 3 from the rows and 3 from the total, 3 + 3 = 6 = harmony. Furthermore, the height of the chains would be around 4 cubits, leaving space for other decoration, whilst the number 4 may be an allusion to the four elements of Earth, Wind, Fire and Water.

The capitals – the pomegranates

He made pomegranates in two rows encircling each network to decorate the capitals on top of the pillars. He did the same for each capital.

According to additional text, there were 100 pomegranates in each row, 200 for each capital.

Thus we find the pomegranates sitting above the chains.

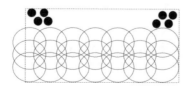

The capitals – the bowl shape and lilies
The capitals on top of the pillars in the portico were in the shape of lilies, four cubits high.

When visiting ancient temples that lined the River Nile in Egypt, I noted that the tops were shaped depending on their function and location. It was an eye-opener to see so many which one could interpret as being *bowl-shaped*. I was struck by those which were clearly meant to imply the underside of a plant, whilst the top edge was fashioned to represent the leaves of a plant. At the temple of Edfu, up stream on the banks of the River Nile from Luxor, there are some wonderful examples which illustrate the bowl shape and leaf patterned tops, and a variety of numbers of petals.

The lily petal shaped tops of the pillars have been fashioned along the lines of Egyptian architecture, such as can be seen at Edfu. Reproduced by kind permission of the Egyptian Government Tourism Department

My conjecture is that this type of arrangement is what was meant. However, I also suggest that the number of petals used in Jerusalem was six. This would again accord with the idea of harmony. But, more importantly the number 6 has a direct relationship to the lily.

We are only told that the representation was of a lily. There are several types, not to mention the hybrids which have been commercially derived in the last century or so. I had not realised it until I started my research on this subject, but the standard lily, which may well have grown in the Middle East during the Solomonic era, has a petal configuration very close to the interlocked triangles of Solomon's Seal. Recalling that the wisdom of Solomon extended to an encyclopaedic knowledge about plants and trees, it is understandable that he should choose such a flower as an emblem of his national identity, in much the same way that the lotus became a symbol in Egypt.

We will leave the subject of the capitals for a while and return to them again after looking at the structure of the pillars in more detail.

Secrets in the pillars

The Lily-like Solomon's seal

The Lily as the shape of the top of the pillars

The Reverend Caldecott's Babylonian Arithmetic

With Solomon's Temple featuring so prominently in Masonic ceremonies, it seemed logical that if there was a single place one could turn to with an expectation of finding information about this structure, it had to be the Global Head Office of Freemasonry, better known as Freemasons' Hall, London. This building also houses a magnificent museum and library, each containing artefacts and documents, some of which are centuries old. Locked away in glass cabinets there are even copies of prominent works about Freemasonry and Solomon's Temple written in languages other than English, notably in Latin, French and German.

It was whilst scanning this array of material that the librarian pointed me in the direction of a book taken from one of the locked glass cabinets. Published early in the 20th century, and written by the Reverend W Shaw Caldecott, it had the simple title of *Solomon's Temple – its history and structure*.

Caldecott was clearly a well-educated man in his time. Like so many of that era, he appears to have had a classical education, giving him a firm grasp of both Latin and Greek. He makes a number of very detailed observations about the Temple structure, including the fact that the base of the Temple would probably have been built up as a raised platform, and suggested that there were 10 steps leading up in front of it.

When it comes to the pillars, Caldecott makes the point of adding the heights recorded of $18 + 5 + 4 = 27$ cubits, as we have previously noted. The 4-cubit area on top of the capitals he refers to as *supra-capitals*. He then goes on to state, quite forcefully, that the pillars had to have been mounted on bases for stability and further suggests that each base was 3 cubits high. Thus, each pillar would have had a total height of 30 cubits. This, he asserts, was to fit with the principles of Babylonian arithmetic which used 60 as the basis of their counting system. Two pillars each of 30 cubits would make a total of 60 cubits.

The Rev Caldecott also makes another assumption: that the capitals were square shaped. This, he argues, was because the pillars fitted inside the porch at the front of the Temple.

Here, I find a weakness in his arguments. The biblical text suggests that the height of the Temple was 30 cubits, but, from the outline design we have already seen, based on geometric understanding, it is probable that the height of the porch was only 20 cubits. So the pillars would not have fitted inside, they would have been too high. If however, the height of the porch was 30 cubits, then the pillars would probably have been structural elements, holding up the roof of the porch. Caldecott seems to overcome this issue by implying that the front tower, the Royal Oratory, had a ceiling which was high enough to accommodate the pillars. If they were structural elements, it is doubtful they would have achieved the acclaim and admiration that is attributed to them, in both Old Testament text and, later, in Masonic ceremonies. What is more, the capitals would have been of a larger diameter, or square sides, than the diameter of the shaft of the pillar. Using the principle that the circumference of a circle was three times the diameter, then with the circumference of the shaft being '12 cubits by line', the diameter was 4 cubits. It would not be unreasonable, I suggest, for the diameter or sides of the capitals to have been 5 cubits. Caldecott shows the capitals in the porch touching, as in the illustration below. By definition, he is implying that the width of the porch was 10 cubits. With the shafts being 4 cubits each, 8 cubits of the 10 cubit width would be taken over by the pillars, leaving 3 gaps, one on each side and one in the middle. Thus, the one in the middle, as shown, would be less than 1 cubit wide to squeeze through to gain access to the Temple. With this conclusion, the pillars would have been effectively acting rather like a fence to deny entry.

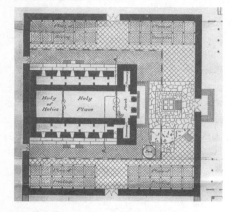

Illustrations copied from originals made by Rev'd W.Shaw Caldecott

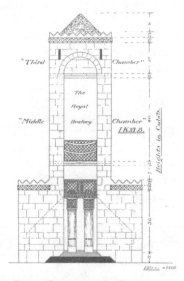

FRONT ELEVATION OF TEMPLE.

Notwithstanding this weakness, Caldecott's review of the structure was the first I had found which suggested that the pillars had been mounted on plinths or bases. Having an engineering background, to me, this simple, yet overlooked, suggestion made complete sense. What I felt uncomfortable with was the height of the bases at

3 cubits. In round terms this is 5 feet (1.5 metres) high, about the average height of a man in more ancient times.

By now I had come to realise that everything that was done in those times featured some reflection of the macro-cosmos. If, indeed, the ceremony for the dedication of the Temple had been in favour of the Sun god and the *heavenly bodies*, then I felt that the height of the pillars had to reflect some aspect of them. In this respect, a 30 cubit measurement fitted exactly because the lunar calendar, which was the basis of the organisation and regulation of religious life in those days, was measured in periods of 30 days. I couldn't help wondering if the Reverend Caldecott was aware of this and how such a revelation on his part would look. Here would have been a man of the cloth, noting the 30-day connection with lunar cycles, and thereby implying that Solomon was associated with what were seen as pagan ideals. The Babylonian arithmetic connection would therefore have been a suitable, and justifiable, alternative.

Notwithstanding this scepticism and cynicism on my part, the point he made about the bases of the pillars stuck with me.

Shortly after encountering Caldecott's work, I made the first of my three visits to Egypt. The first trip took in many of the wonderful sites that I had read about over several years: Luxor, Thebes, the Valley of the Kings, the Temple of Edfu, Aswan and the broken pillar, and the Temple of Abu Simbel. At each temple site the enormity of Caldecott's suggestion was immediately obvious. All the pillars had bases. I measured the height of some of them at each new site I visited. My methodology was simple. I placed my fingertips on the ground and forearm against the base, the distance to my elbow being approx 1 cubit, as with ancient measure. There was a small but notable variation in the heights which, in the main, I put down to the fact that many such sites had been the subject of archaeological restoration and ground heights may therefore have been adjusted in the process. In general, however, I noted that the height of each base was about 1 cubit and that the diameter of the bases was larger than the diameter of the shafts of the pillars, by about half a cubit all around, that is, 1 cubit larger in the total diameter.

The author measuring the height of a pillar base at Petra in Jordan. The height is 1 cubit, based on finger tips to elbow. The base on which it sits measured 2 cubits.

If the bases of the pillars in Solomon's Temple were a reflection of the building principles evolved in Egypt, then, I reasoned, that the bases for the two pillars associated with the Temple may also have been 1 cubit high. This of course would be totally contrary to the Rev Caldecott's suggestion. What did, however, strike me was that the total height of the pillars would now be 28 cubits. This would still fit with aspects of the lunar cycle, the 28 days it takes from new Moon to darkness, and thereby another connection with the religious calendar and the macro-cosmos.

There was something else that struck me about the number 28. In the cubit measuring system there was a smaller division – the digit – which was approximately the width of the index finger. One cubit comprised 28 digits, the number of index finger spans from the tip of the fingers to the elbow. Four digits were equal to one hand's breadth and five digits was a span. With a connection to the natural world by using the human form as a method of measurement, here was yet another association with the macro-cosmos.

Symbolically, too, the number 28 has significance. The number 7 was highly revered because, according to the scriptures, the deity had undertaken all the creation in 6 days, and rested on the seventh, thereby giving 7 days to a week. Adding together the seven numbers from 1 to 7 = 28.

$1 + 2 + 3 + 4 + 5 + 6 + 7 = 28$

I realised that all stately edifices must be built on solid foundations, usually of rock. If rock was not immediately available beneath the position of the foundations, then a solid base would be inserted. In places like Luxor and Thebes, I noted that the pillar bases appeared to be sitting on slabs of stone. It would not have been unreasonable that, if, at the site in Jerusalem where the pillars were to be erected, special foundations would be needed and a stone block might be installed on which the superstructure of the pillars would sit. And such a stone block might easily have been 2 cubits high. And, if it was 2 cubits high, then the overall height would be 30 cubits.

These revelations, inspired by the comments of the Rev Caldecott, provided me with insights which, later, were to unlock what I now believe to have been the secrets of the pillars of Solomon's Temple. They also add strength to Caldecott's arithmetic suggestion, but not quite in the manner he may have had in mind.

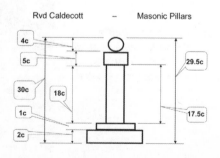

Rvd Caldecott   –   Masonic Pillars

Secrets in the pillars

The shadow of the Pillars

By virtue that the pillars are stated as being on a north-south axis, it is obvious that if the pillars are also in front of the portico, as also stated, then at midday they would have cast a shadow along that axis.

To establish what the seasonal effect would be, I consulted an astronomical simulator. I selected the location as Jerusalem. To take account of the affects of precession, I wound the calendar back to 955 BCE, the epoch in which the Temple was built. It was fascinating to watch the Sun move backwards down the ecliptic out of our current precessional constellation of Pisces into the prominent constellation at the time of Solomon, Aries, at the time of the equinox. I set the dates to equate with the equinox and solstices and recorded the approximate maximum altitude the Sun achieved at that time. On a small home computer simulation, it was not easy to achieve the exact altitude and azimuth, but it did give a very close approximation. The results were was as follows:

Jerusalem	955 BCE Sun at approximate maximum altitude
Equinox	Altitude 54.5 degrees at azimuth 179 degrees
Summer Solstice	81.5 degrees at azimuth 179 degrees
Winter Solstice	35.3 degrees at azimuth 180.5 degrees.

I decided that 2 cubits of the total height would be below ground, therefore leaving 28 cubits above. Some elementary trigonometry produced a simple diagram of the shadow effect. The results were a revelation.

The distance between the pillars
by calculation and using a solar simulator

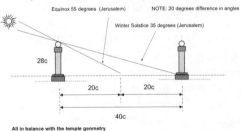

All in balance with the temple geometry

What this produced was exactly the dimensions for the Hall and the Holy of Holies as mentioned in the Old Testament. This means that if seen in plan view, the seasonal shadow effect looks as follows:

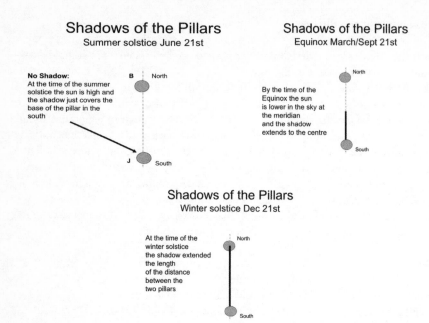

Shadows of the Pillars
Summer solstice June 21st

No Shadow:
At the time of the summer solstice the sun is high and the shadow just covers the base of the pillar in the south

B   North

J   South

Shadows of the Pillars
Equinox March/Sept 21st

North

By the time of the Equinox the sun is lower in the sky at the meridian and the shadow extends to the centre

South

Shadows of the Pillars
Winter solstice Dec 21st

At the time of the winter solstice the shadow extended the length of the distance between the two pillars

North

South

Someone in the priesthood must have had the task of marking the position of the shadow when the Sun was at its meridian. This would have enabled the priests to use the shadow as a calendar and clock. This is an interesting development because in a Freemasons' Lodge, it is the job of the Junior Warden, who is positioned in the south of the Lodge, to 'mark the Sun at its meridian'. Keeping in mind that Solomon's Temple is a feature of Freemasonry, could it be that marking the position of the shadow between the pillars is where this term originated?

The geometry of the pillars was interesting, but I noted that if the pillar in the north, Boaz, had had been placed with its centre line on the end of the Winter Solstice shadow, then the shadow would not have reached the centre of the pillar because of the nature of its construction.

The capitals on the tops of the pillars are quoted as being 5 cubits high. The shafts of the pillars are noted to be 4 cubits in diameter. It seemed logical to me that the capitals would be larger in diameter than the pillars and may well have been the same diameter as the height. In other words the capitals would have been 5 cubits diameter. For the sake of symmetry, I therefore assumed that the exposed area of the base would also be 5 cubits in diameter. Once again, some simple trigonometry showed that if an angle was taken from the centre of the base of the pillar along the line of the Sun at the Winter Solstice, an angle of 35 degrees, the result was a length inside the base of 1.5 cubits. This corresponds with the height of the visible base plus the area between the outer edge of the base and the shaft of the pillar.

Then something else suggested itself. If the visible area of the base was 5 cubits, it was quite possible that the section of base hidden below the surface as a

Secrets in the pillars

Shadows of the Pillars

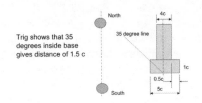

Trig shows that 35 degrees inside base gives distance of 1.5 c

North

35 degree line

4c

1c

0.5c

5c

South

Shadows of the Pillars

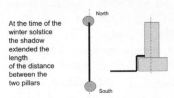

At the time of the winter solstice the shadow extended the length of the distance between the two pillars

North

South

foundation block was probably larger in diameter than the visible base. I decided that it might be 1 cubit larger, similar to the variation between the base and the shaft of one of the pillars. Thus, the foundation block would have been 6 cubits in diameter. If one took the visible base at 5 cubits diameter then it was also 2.5 cubits radius. With two such pillars, it would mean that the centre distance between the centre lines of the bases would reduce by 5 cubits. This produces yet another startling revelation because 40 – 5 = 35. In the Old Testament 2 Chronicles 3:15 it states that:

> *In front of the temple he made two pillars which together were thirty five cubits long each with a capital on top measuring five cubits.*

So, where it mentions that

> *.... he made two pillars which together measured thirty five cubits long.*

this may not be a reference to the height of the pillars as often considered in Freemasonry, but the distance between them measured at the bases.

This all seemed too incredible. Yet everything seemed to fit. For many months after discovering the geometric relationship of the pillars, and the influence of the Sun, I was cautious about the result. It was on a trip to Delhi, India, that any doubts I had were erased.

The distance between the pillars

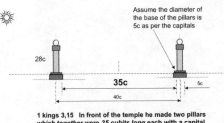

Assume the diameter of the base of the pillars is 5c as per the capitals

28c

35c

5c

40c

1 kings 3,15 In front of the temple he made two pillars *which together* were *35 cubits long* each with a capital on top measuring five cubits

263

The Jantar Mantar

For several years, I had visited Delhi regularly on business. As was so often the case on such trips, I had had barely enough time to see anything of the city as a tourist. At weekends, if I was still in Delhi, I took the tourist bus to places like Agra to see the Taj Mahal, or ordered a new business suit from the tailors in Connaught Place, a major shopping district of New Delhi. I was made aware of a celestial park known as Jantar Mantar, hundreds of years old, in what is now almost the centre of the city, but never visited it. Now, there I was, back in Delhi with an interest in celestial matters and a visit to Jantar Mantar suddenly rated very high on my agenda.

The Jantar Mantar is an observatory built around 1725, some years before the arrival of British colonial rule, by a Maharajah with an interest in solving some of the mysteries of astronomy. In fact, he built two such observatories, which were identical, about 250 miles apart. This enabled his Brahmin priest astronomers to observe the heavens, compare their separate findings and evaluate what they had seen. The site in Delhi contains some wonderful circular buildings, open to the sky but with walls containing dozens of apertures through which the light of the Sun or Moon could penetrate. The inside of the walls are carefully inscribed with angular markings, now much faded but still useful. There is a peculiarly shaped building containing the outline of two hearts, with stone steps which run from the ground to the top. I am told that if one stands at the bottom of the steps at night and looks to the top of the steps, the star above will be the Pole Star. There are cellars carefully designed to monitor the Sun at the key times of the year. The entire observatory is a marvel of construction and I regretted not having visited it years earlier. But, there was an unexpected delight to encounter. My guide led me towards two round pillars, painted red, which stood close to the entrance. I didn't measure them, but they were about 9 feet (3 metres) tall. My guide explained that in high summer at mid day, the shadows were contained within the base diameter of the pillars. By the time of the equinox the shadow from the pillar in the south just touched the base of the other,

The Jantar Mantar New Delhi, India. The two pillars are to the left of the picture.

whilst by the time of the Winter Solstice the shadow from the southern pillar had crept to the top of the pillar in the north. I was ecstatic. This was a virtual re-creation of the shadow movement I had considered for the pillars of Solomon's Temple. All the doubts I had harboured were erased.

The position of the pillars in front of the portico

Somewhat elated that the shadows of the pillars of Solomon's Temple now seemed to have meaning, I wondered how far in front of the portico the pillars might have stood. I already knew that the distance between the pillars was probably 35 cubits, or 40 cubits to their centres. From the biblical text we know that the portico and Hall have a combined depth of 50 cubits, and the depth within the Holy of Holies to the face of the cherubim was probably 10 cubits, a measurement of 60 cubits in all. Incredibly, this is the length stated for the temple in the Book of Kings. Again using the celestial simulator I noted that at sunrise on the day of the Summer Solstice, when viewed from Jerusalem in the era of King Solomon, the sun appeared on the horizon at an azimuth of 62.5 degrees and on the day of the Winter Solstice at 117.5 degrees. This is what one would expect, both being roughly 27.5 degrees either side of the equinox.

The distance from the centre line of the Temple porch to the base of the pillars was 17.5 cubits either side. The angle of the Sun at its rising at the solstices was 27.5 degrees, thus the length from the face of the cherubim to the baseline of the pillars is 17.5 − sin 27.5 degrees = 37.9 cubits. To this must then be added the radius of the pillar base − 2.5 cubits − making 40.34 cubits in total. This can easily be rounded at 40 cubits. Thus 60c + 40c gives 100 cubits as the distance of the pillars from the face of the cherubim. Everything balances perfectly.

The position of the Pillars - proof

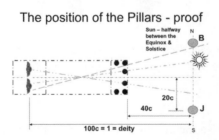

The *supra-capitals*

There is just one element of these structures left to consider − the 4 cubits at the top of the pillar capitals.

In Masonic ceremonies these *supra-capitals* are referred to as being globes on which were delineated maps of the celestial and terrestrial globes, implying the universality of Freemasonry. That they should have had such a connotation in the Solomonic era is highly unlikely. Although historians suggest that the peoples of that time believed the Earth to be flat, we cannot be certain that high-ranking priests, the custodians of ancient knowledge, may not have known otherwise. It just took until several hundred years later, to the era of Eratosthenes, for such a revelation to come into the open. This Masonic reference appears to be derived from these *supra-capitals* being described as *pommels*. For a long time I thought I knew what a pommel was, but to be certain I checked the definition in the Oxford Dictionary. The main meanings cited were that it was the bulbous end of the hilt of a sword, clearly to stop one's hand sliding off at an inopportune time in battle; a raised area at the front of a saddle; the horn of a side saddle; to strike with a sword; to strike with fists. I eliminated the last two definitions as I couldn't envisage how they would have connected to the Temple. A while later I realised that the others could be defined by a single word which would have a connection. The word is *protrusion* – they all stick out from something else. And that would seem to be what was necessary to finish the pillar capitals.

If, as I have so far shown, the shadow cast by the pillars at midday was used to monitor the calendar and the seasons, then one needed to have a pointed structure on top of the pillars to ensure accuracy, rather similar to the triangular shape found on the top of an obelisk. It would be very difficult to get a precise indication of the moment of marking from a shadow created by a rounded top by comparison with a pointed one.

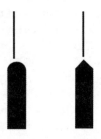

My belief, therefore, is that the *supra-capital* was either a cone or pyramid, finished in gold to represent the Sun, which stood out from the top of the capital to a height of 4 cubits.

The Secret Lozenge

During a visit to Crete and the remains of the ancient Minoan city of Knossos, our guide drew attention to a strange symbol which, she stated, appeared on a number

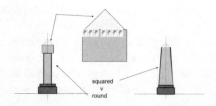

of artefacts recovered by archaeologists. She showed us an example of the symbol engraved into a large piece of stone, which might originally have been used as the base of a pillar. The symbol looked like two triangles, one inverted on top of the other so that their points met. Our guide also mentioned that the origins of the symbol were unknown, but that it was used extensively, even on pots.

Because of the enquiries I had been making about the peoples of ancient times, and their religious connection with the Sun and Moon, the symbol immediately struck me as the pattern one would get from defining the positions of the Sun at sunrise and sunset on the days of the Summer and Winter Solstices. The shadow cast by a single pillar in open space would be similar to the Knossos pattern. By dividing the symbol with a line through the centre of the inverted triangles, I wondered if the resultant angle north and south of the centre line would correspond with the latitude that Knossos was built on. By including the design on components of importance, and on traded goods, it would reinforce the location from which the goods originated – rather like a trade mark.

It was shortly after that visit that I encountered Robert Lomas and Christopher Knight's book titled *Uriel's Machine*. They had made some observations about Newgrange, an historic site in Ireland that is believed to have been constructed around the same time as Stonehenge. Newgrange has certain solar alignments, much the same as can be found at Stonehenge. Lomas and Knight noted that the *Groove Ware people*, who are also associated with the era of Newgrange, frequently used a pattern on pottery which produced a diamond-shaped lozenge. The similarity of the pattern used by the *Groove Ware people*, and that at Knossos, was immediately striking. It was an observation I made and then just stored it away in my memory to reflect on later. It was when I was evaluating Solomon's Temple a few years later that the memory of that observation came flooding back.

Having calculated the possible position for the pillars to be placed in front of the Temple portico, and how the dimensions balanced with the other parts of the structure, it seemed logical to test what shadow patterns would result on the ground at sunrise and sunset on the days of the Summer and Winter Solstices.

Using a software-based solar simulator I turned the sky back to the era in which the Temple was supposedly built, and set the hour to approximately that at which the Sun would have appeared over the horizon at dawn. The azimuth was around 62 degrees for the Summer Solstice and 118 degrees for the winter solstice. This would give an angular variance from an east-west centre line of 28 degrees. The number 28 has lunar religious calendar significance as has already been mentioned. It seemed a perfect balance. However, depending on how robust the code used in the software simulator was, it would, I realised, affect the accuracy of the display result. The azimuth readings were so close to 60 and 120 degrees, giving a 30-degree angular variance, that I wondered if that was not the true intention – 30 degrees would correspond with the 30-cubit height of the pillars. Some basic trigonometry based on these readings showed that the resultant shadows created by the pillars would focus at the centre of the entrance of the Temple. Yet again, everything seems to have been designed to fit harmoniously.

There is another hidden advantage to be gained from this arrangement. It would mean that by measuring the angle of the shadow relative to the centre line of the

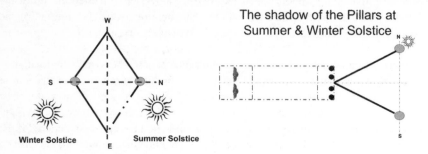

Temple, so the latitude position of Jerusalem, and in particular, the latitudinal position of the Temple on the face of the Earth, would also be recorded. In addition, by marking the angle of sunset on the same days, the lozenge pattern would be completed. Thus, as *sacred knowledge*, it would be realised that by measuring the angles plotted in a lozenge, created by the shadow of the Sun at sunrise and sunset on the days of the solstices, one could determine one's latitude position because the shape of the lozenge would change depending on whether one travelled closer to the equator or away from it.

The hidden square of Rosslyn

During the period I was preparing this book, Robert Lomas, one of the authors mentioned above, wrote a further work with the title *Turning the Hiram Key*. In their previous works, Robert Lomas, and Christopher Knight had drawn attention to the chapel at Rosslyn, just outside of Edinburgh, Scotland – a chapel which contains considerable Masonic symbolism carved into the stone of the structure. Rosslyn was built in the 15th century by William St Clair, the last Norse earl of Orkney, whose family had, for some centuries, provided the Grand Masters of Freemasonry in Scotland. Robert Lomas has argued that the origins of modern Freemasonry can be traced to the building of that chapel.

In a chapter about symbolism in *Turning the Hiram Key*, Robert Lomas visits the subject of the lozenge shape, as it may have been associated with the cult of the Goddess. He also draws attention to the method of using the lozenge shape as a means of determining the latitude of one's position. He goes on to state:

> *At the latitude where William St. Clair built the Temple of Roslin the solstice angles produce a perfect square, and that is where modern Freemasonry began.*

This is an interesting observation because in a Masonic ceremony of initiation, the candidate is admitted '...*on the square*'.

Secrets in the pillars

The pillars – the hidden knowledge

The Temple layout lent itself to the idea of the Sun penetrating the Holy of Holies at dawn, and its design appears to correspond with key solar timings. The clerestory windows would have lent themselves to illuminating a wall calendar for crop production and gathering. The size and location of the pillars appear to have correlated with the altitude of the Sun at midday and the key positions on the horizon. So much lent itself to being designed around the Sun that I wondered if the dimensions of the component parts also added to our knowledge.

After a series of false starts, I decided to create a simple computer spreadsheet that took all the dimensions from the structure of the pillar, and added, multiplied, subtracted and divided them, although I felt that people from the Solomonic era might just have added or multiplied them. Yet again I was staggered by the result. I confess that I had far more data than made sense but when I placed it in a chart, some of it was immediately obvious. The following table is a sample of what some of the numbers revealed. (see the following table).

What particularly struck me were the totals of 27.5 and 29.5 relating to the Moon. Earlier I mentioned that after 27.5 days the illuminated face of the Moon disappears and emerges again two days later as the new Moon. These events happen on the 28th day, which was the basis of the civil solar calendar, whilst the 30th day, the day on which it emerges again, was the basis of the lunar religious calendar. By virtue that 2 cubits of the base of the pillar were underground, and therefore in darkness, it seems that it corresponds with the two days of darkness of the Moon. The Moon also has a grand cycle of 18.6 years, resulting in it returning to exactly the same position in the sky. This corresponds with the height of the shaft of the pillars.

From this, and the other information revealed in the pillar dimensions, plus the location and size of the pillars, I believe that the temple was built to reflect and record the principal information about the movement of the Earth and the effect of, and known information about, the Sun and the Moon.

The Temple – the final solution

To me, it all now fits in place. It was called Solomon's Temple after the death of the builder: Jedidiah, son of David. When it was first built it was known as the Temple of the Sun and the Moon – Sol meaning Sun and Amon meaning Moon.

This would also explain the reason why Solomon's Temple was held in such high esteem for so many centuries – what it was that made it so unique. It would also explain why it is a key feature of Freemasonry in that it may have been information collated by the priests and used by the operative masons of bygone times to help them set out buildings in accordance with the principles of the macro-cosmos which, in turn, was seen to have been planned and governed by the deity. It would also explain why in Freemasonry today reference is made to so many aspects of the Sun, although in the current generation we have not understood what it meant. We have inherited this ancient knowledge but, through the development of science and the processes of systematic education of the masses, we have moved away from understanding how it could be used in our daily lives.

Symbolism	Total	operator	1 or 2 pillars	Diam 4 c	Circumf 12 c	Lilies 4 c	Chapiter 5 c	Pillar 18 c	Pillar 17.5 c	Base 1 c	Base 2 c
12 circ of the pillars/4 diam = 3 = Pi	3	/	1	*	*						
The constellations of zodiac	12		2	*	*						
The number of 15 degree segments (hours) in one revolution of the Earth	24	*	1		*						
The Cardinal points of N,S,E,W +four elements of Earth, Wind, Fire and Water	4		1								
Lunar cycle of 18.6 years	18	+	1								
29.5 = phase of the moon = lunar month 30 days	29.5	+	1			*	*	*		*	*
Days in a Lunar month (religious calendar)	30	+	1			*	*	*		*	*
Pi * 4 (closer to the value of Pi than the value 3	12.5	-	1				*				
nominal angle of the Earth's axis	22.5	+	1				*		*		
angle of inclination + precession at 0.5 degree radius	23.5	+	1			*	*	*		*	*
27.5 = phase of the moon	27.5	+	1			*	*	*	*	*	
29.5 = phase of the moon = lunar month 30 days	29.5	+	1			*	*	*	*		
Precession moves 1 degree in 72 years = degrees of sun on horiz	1		1				*				
Moon orbit circumference x (Millions cubits)	1050	+	1		*		*	*	*		
Earths radius (x 100,000,000 cubits) & moons average days	28		1				*	*			*
Lunar months in a Solar year (religious)	13	-	1				*	*			
4th part of a circle - relates to polar meridian	90	*	1				*	*	*		
relates to circle and polar meridian	180	*	2				*	*	*	*	
Precession axis moves 1 degree in 72 years	72	+	2				*	*			
Precession progresses one constellation in 2,160 years	2160	*	2		*		*	*	*	*	
Venus - 5 cycles each of 8 years makes pentagram + distance of pillars in front of the portico	40	+	1		*	*	*				
Pillar shadow distances & '20/hr/15 degrees = speed of Earths orbit (x 10,000,000 cubits)	20	*	1		*	*					

Furthermore, the pillars were not just token gestures squeezed into the porchway, or metallic incense burners standing just in front of the main door of the Temple, they were huge and magnificent symbols of the nationhood of the Israelites, as tall as the Temple itself. Whilst much of the symbolism and hidden detail was known to but a few, one can imagine these wonderful ornaments standing proudly on the top of Mount Moriah, as beacons that could be seen for miles around, their gold tops glistening in the sunlight.

In Masonic ceremony they are mentioned as follows:

'They were set up at the entrance of the temple....that the Children of Israel might have the happy deliverance of their forefathers continuously before their eyes whilst going to, and coming from, divine worship.'

As the Israelites walked up Mount Moriah, they could not have failed to see the pillars. Being positioned 40 cubits in front of the Temple, they would have stood out, giants standing erect, dominating the landscape. How could the Israelites have forgotten their deliverance?

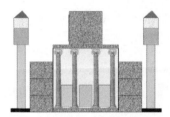

Divine Revelation

Earlier in the book, we looked at examples of *sacred geometry*. In particular we looked at the subject of the Golden Ratio, also known as Divine Proportion, which links with the numbers 1.618 and 0.618. It will therefore not surprise you to know that these numbers now appear in the design of the Temple.

If, as my calculations show, the position of the pillars was 20 cubits north and south of the centre line of the Temple, then they were also 10 cubits outside of the main square structure that represented the main body of the Temple. We are also told that the rooms around the outside walls, used by the priests or for storage, were 5, 6 or 7 cubits wide. So the additional width created by these rooms could not be less than 7 cubits. The position of the pillars means that the diameter of the lower foundation base, being 6 cubits, would mean that it was on the same line as the outer dimension for the walls of the rooms for the priests. The outer wall needed to have a thickness which we will assume was 0.5 cubits so that visually the gap would be closed between the wall and the base of the pillars. This would therefore add 15 cubits to the overall width of the temple, the 15 being in harmony with the 24 time divisions representing the rotation of the Earth in one day. Thus, the bases of the pillars would be seen as being in line with the outer walls of the rooms used by the priests. The bases were 5 cubits in diameter, so the total width at ground level would be increased by a further 2.5 cubits.

The result is as follows:

Temple width	20
Priests' rooms	7
Residual diameter for the foundation base	0.5
Diameter of pillar bases	5
TOTAL	32.5 cubits

Golden Ratio   20 cubits width x 1.618 = 32.36.

The variance between the two numbers is 0.14 cubits, which is roughly 2.5 inches or 600mm based on an 18-inch cubit, or 0.4% of the Golden Ratio calculated width, all of which would be well within an acceptable margin of error.

It is therefore highly possible that a rectangle drawn from the outer edge of the pillar base to encompass the main body of the temple was a hidden reference to the Golden Ratio – Divine Proportion.

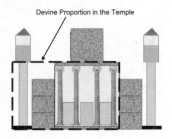

Devine Proportion in the Temple

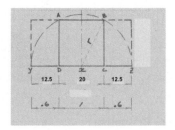

Why has Solomon's Temple been so revered over the centuries?

From my quest, I believe the answer is as follows:

- •–Jedidiah's (Solomon's) Temple was a place of worship. It was also a celestial observatory and a centre of education, with the rooms reserved for the priests, which surrounded the main body of the Temple, being used as the centre for learning. It was a Holy Place because it reflected the true nature of God's creation and how wonderful that seemed as expressed through the pattern of the seasons, predictability of events, resultant geometry, clock and a calendar – a structure in total harmony with the macro-cosmos. It was a demonstration of technology.

- •–The pillars became a repository/record of celestial mechanics, plus geometry, which determined the principles on which the structure was designed. The science provided the influence on customs, regalia, social structure and, ultimately, on nationhood. The pillars were a unique encyclopaedia in stone and bronze, details of which were known to only a few – the dimensions and their significance were hidden from those who did not need to know – a secret and sacred repository of information.

• –In Freemasonry there is an expression used and related to the pillars which states: *'for therein were deposited the constitutional scrolls'*
This sentence creates the impression of a cavity, a hole or a place in which scrolls or other works were hidden, information that was to be known to but a few. The key word, I believe, is *therein*, not *therein* as in some secret cavity but *therein* meaning within the dimensions of the pillars – the data about the Sun, Moon, precession and earth mechanics. This would not have been so different from the Egyptian practice where they engraved information on pillars and obelisks in hieroglyphics, as a record.

• **What was the secret of Solomon's Wisdom?**
  • The Wisdom of Solomon (Jedidiah) was his knowledge and application of the principles of geometry (mathematics) remembering that he sought wisdom (understanding and knowledge) enabling him to reach logical conclusions. He was an expert on flowers, trees and animals. The Old Testament text tells us that *'he was more knowledgeable than the men of the East'*, which is possibly a reference to his understanding of astronomy/astrology (science). He sought this *wisdom* before he started building the Temple. He was educated in the principles of *ancient wisdom*. Reference to his lateral thinking abilities are, perhaps, really a more modern interpretation of what we define as *wisdom*.

• **What is the secret of Solomon's Seal?**
  • I suggest that the geometric shape of the interlocking triangles is derived from the interlocking circles of Vesica Pisces which indicates an understanding of *ancient/sacred geometry;* that Vesica Pisces, being the basis of Solomon's Seal, is the key to the ground-plan and dimensions of the Temple.

• **Why is it called 'Solomon's Temple'?**
  • I suggest that because of its *special features* the temple became known as the 'Temple of Sol and Amon'
Sol meaning *Sun*   Amon meaning *Moon*
  • After his death, Jedidiah was referred to as the man who built the Sol and Amon Temple, which became corrupted over time to *Sol-amon* and then to *Solomon.*
  • The pillar heights were the same but interpreted differently to reflect celestial information. For example, when the shaft is given the dimension of 18 cubits it reflects solar information, whilst when it is referred to as 17.5 cubits it makes allowance for 0.5 cubit to be covered over as a seating boss for the capitals and the resultant dimension reflects information relative to the Moon.

It may even have been that the two pillars were different sizes, reflecting that 0.5 cubit difference and that

Jachin to the South contained information about the Sun
Boaz to the north contained information about the Moon.

In various parts of the United Kingdom, one can find displays of very old Masonic regalia. Thus it was that I noted this freemason's apron from the era 1751. In particular it shows the two pillars with an image of the Sun and Moon over each.

A beautifully embroidered apron dated prior to1800, together with representations of the sun and moon above the pillars.

It is as if this knowledge was well known in Freemasonry at some time in the not too distant past.

Then all was lost

Having devoted considerable time and energy building this unique and stately edifice, things began to go wrong soon after the death of Jedidiah (Solomon). His son, Rehoboam succeeded him as king. Five years into his reign, Jerusalem was attacked by an Egyptian army led by a Pharaoh named Shishak. Pharaoh refrained from razing the city to the ground, but instead took away all the precious jewels and ornaments of gold and silver from the Temple.

Some centuries later, around 570 BCE, Nebuzaradan, commander of the imperial guard of the court of the Babylonian King Nebuchadnezzar, invaded Jerusalem, and took most of the inhabitants into captivity. He burned down every important building in the city including the Temple; the pillars were broken up and the bronze taken away. It is recorded that the fire through the Temple was so fierce that even some of the stone started to melt. The ferocity of the fire is understandable. The interior had been lined with cedar. Protected from the elements, yet in the warm and mild Mediterranean climate, the timber would have been tinder dry after 400 years without exposure to the elements. If, as I suggest, the clerestory windows were high up in the structure and were the only windows in the main part of the Temple, then the result would have been likened to a modern steel-producing blast furnace. Air to fuel the fire would have been dragged in through the Temple portico. As the fire became increasingly fierce and the demand for oxygen increased, so the volume of air passing through the portico would have had the ferocity of a hurricane. The inferno would have had a temperature akin to that of a furnace used for melting iron ore.

Jedidiah's Temple was no more.

Is there a link with the temple of Abu Simbel?

As already mentioned, on one of my trips to Egypt I visited the temple of Abu Simbel. This temple was apparently built by Rameses the Great. With its vast statues guarding the entrance and positioned beside the River Nile and adjacent to ancient trade routes, it is believed to have marked a southern boundary of his kingdom.

In one of the side chambers there are engravings in the stone walls depicting various aspects of Ramesses' life. These include showing his army carrying off the precious materials he had taken from his siege of Jerusalem. Earlier in this book I made reference to Dr David Rohl and his work *A Test of Time* in which he presents a revised chronology of biblical events and identifies certain key characters. He identifies Shishak as Ramesses.

I have noted how the temple of Abu Simbel is arranged so that twice a year a shaft of light penetrates the length of the hall at dawn to illuminate each of three small statues in the Holy of Holies at the rear of the structure. One of those statues represents Ramesses. I wondered where Ramesses got the idea for this arrangement as it is so out of keeping with most of the other temples one can see in Egypt. Could it be that Shishak / Ramesses observed the solar configuration of the Temple of Jerusalem, operating in the manner I have described, and, on his return to Egypt, constructed Abu Simbel to reflect similar characteristics? Could the four statutes in the Holy of Holies at Abu Simbel, three of which are illuminated by the Sun, be suitable replacements for the four wings of the cherubim at Jerusalem? If so, then a visit to Abu Simbel today provides a wonderful memorial for the technology of Solomon's Temple.

The temple design lives on

History tells us that, about three hundred years after the alleged crucifixion of the Christ just outside of Jerusalem, the fledgling Christian religion was used by the Roman Emperor Constantine as a vehicle for uniting a disintegrating Roman Empire, and that the traditions of the faith were regulated by the dictates that originated from the Council of Nicaea in 325 CE. Then, as the religion and its support organisation spread throughout Europe, there followed a period when ancient pagan practices and traditions were regards as heretical, and efforts were made to eliminate them and substitute new rituals. Seven hundred years after the Council of Nicaea, the Order of the Knights Templar began its ascendancy. Shortly after the formalisation of the Order, which in turn followed its earlier encampment in Jerusalem on the site where Solomon's Temple had stood, we find the rise of the Gothic style of architecture, which is reflected in many of the great cathedrals built from the eleventh to the fourteenth centuries. It is interesting to note that on either side of the porchway or entrance to such cathedrals, there are usually two towers that define the outside limits of the width of the building. This appears to be a reflection of the same perspective that one would have seen if approaching Solomon's/Jedidiah's Temple; the body of the temple and the entrance flanked by the two pillars.

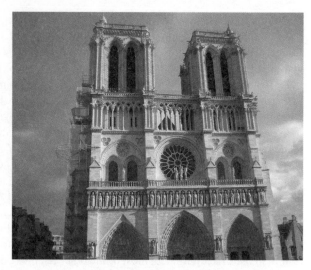

The front façade of the cathedral of St Denis on the northern outskirts of Paris. This is believed to have been one of the earliest cathedrals to experience the gothic style, although it was founded around 500 ce.

This same design philosophy appears in many of the churches dedicated to the Roman Catholic faith, especially in countries where that faith has dominance.

[1] Holy Bible – New International Version

Chapter 15
The Knights Templar legacy
and a new Hiram Abif

Having lived in Cambridge, England, for three years, it had not been unusual to receive and accommodate weekend visitors who wanted to sample the delights of this ancient university town. I soon had a well-planned itinerary for ushering visitors around, giving a commentary packed with historical dates and useless information about the various landmarks we visited.

Adjacent to St John's College, which was founded in 1511 by the mother of King Henry VII, Lady Margaret Beaufort, is a rather unusual small church; unusual in that it is circular. It is referred to in Cambridge as the 'Round Church' but its full name is The Church of the Holy Sepulchre. It is believed to have been built by the Knights Templar around 1130 CE. Its design was intended to complement the Holy Sepulchre in Jerusalem, the city where the Knights Templar then had a secure base.

To put this small church into context, a brief review of the history of the Knights Templar is necessary.

The Knights Templar

There has, for many years, been speculation that Freemasonry was derived from the Knights Templar. In William Preston's *Illustrations of Masonry, Section 4,* published in 1795, a positive statement about the connection exists:

'During the reign of Henry II the Grand Master of the Knights Templar superintended the masons, and employed them in building their Temple in Fleet-street, A. D. 1155. Masonry continued under the patronage of this Order till the year 1199, when John succeeded his brother Richard in the crown of England.' [1]

As a child, I grew up in an area of Kent where there had been a strong Knights Templar connection. Even today a Templar Manor House still stands adjacent to the River Medway, opposite Rochester Castle. Still as a very small child, I once asked my father who the Knights Templar were; he merely described them as 'a dodgy bunch'. So, to me, they were immediately transformed into heroes and remained as such thereafter. Clearly, there was a reputation that went before them. And an interesting reputation, and tale of intrigue, it is.

Jerusalem, a small village which developed into a city, has known little by way of peace in its 3,500 years of history. It is the location of Mount Moriah where Abraham was to take his son Isaac, for sacrifice. It was the town that David made his capital; it was where Solomon/Jedidiah built the first Israelite Temple, and where the events that inspired the Christian religion, two thousand years ago, took place. In the period to two thousand years ago, it was a city that had been invaded by

Egyptians, Babylonians, Assyrians, Persians, Greeks and Romans. When the Romans departed, Jerusalem entered a period of relative peace where the followers of the main religions of Islam, Judaism and Christianity lived side by side without too much difficulty, under the rule of the Empire of Constantinople. Then in the 11th century the city fell again, this time to Seljuk Turks. Christians were not permitted to make pilgrimages to what they regarded as a sacred city. Thus it was that in November 1095, Pope Urban II summoned a council at Clermont, Auvergne, France, at which, it is reported, some 225 bishops and nearly 100 abbots from across Europe, were in attendance.[2] Thousands of noblemen and knights were also present and all agreed that an army should be sent to Jerusalem to free it from the control of the invaders. The crusades were initiated and Jerusalem fell to the crusader army on 15th July 1099.

A monk, later known simply as the Blessed Gerard, founded a hostelry next to the church of St John the Baptist, near Jerusalem, which provided an infirmary to care for sick pilgrims, together with a hostelry. Pilgrims who had taken advantage of the facilities offered would make a donation to the hospital on their departure. The hospital and its organisation gained in stature and reputation. It received papal approval through a bull issued by Pope Paschal II in 1113. Thus, the Sovereign Military Order of St John of Jerusalem was created: better known, perhaps, as the Order of St John, the Knights Hospitallers, or today as the Knights of Malta. Their rule, or uniform, was a black tabard emblazoned with a white cross.

The Order operated on two levels: providing hospitals to care for the sick; and a military wing whose job it was to try to protect pilgrims on the roads to Jerusalem.

Meanwhile, a group of nine Frenchmen set out for Jerusalem, led by Hugues de Payen, a nobleman from the Champagne district. On arrival in Jerusalem, they declared they would also protect the roads used by the pilgrims. They were, it seems, permitted to make an area of the original site of Solomon's Temple as their base, and stayed there for some nine years. They called themselves The Poor Soldiers of Christ and the Temple of Solomon. This Order later passed into history as the Knights Templar.

Whilst the original founding group of nine knights camped in the remains of the Herodian Temple in Jerusalem, remembering that this was the original site of Solomon's Temple, it is believed that they started digging beneath the original Temple site and later discovered something of great value. Over the years, what they discovered has been the subject of much speculation, including the possibility that it was the Ark of the Covenant, or important documents that might have provided a genealogical connection to some of the aristocratic families that existed around 1,000 CE. After nine years, they had not expanded their organisation and were still limited to the original nine knights. Neither is there any evidence that they participated in any activity associated with protecting pilgrims on the roads to Jerusalem which had been their stated intention. After nine years Hugues de Payen left Jerusalem, returned to France and sought help from an abbot who was to pass into history as St Bernard. This abbot was obviously well connected, and after lobbying their case, Hugues de Payen and his other original eight knights received papal support and protection in 1128. Their rule, or uniform, was a white tabard with a red cross emblazoned on it.

The rise of the power and influence exerted by the Templars was meteoric. Commenting on the support that Hugues de Payen received through St Bernard, one writer notes that on the return to Jerusalem, *'They had gone west with nothing and came back with a Papal Rule, money, precious objects, landed wealth and no less than 300 recruited noblemen...'*[3] To this should be added that Hugues de Payen was also recognised as the Grand Master of the Order.

St Bernard, you may recall, is also mentioned in an earlier chapter as having been a prime motivator in the development of the Gothic style of architecture based on information he may have received from the Knights Templar.

All this was happening some 30-50 years after the invasion and conquest of England by William the Conqueror, when Norman influence was still much in evidence. Thus it was that Hugues de Payen married a Scottish woman of Norman descent, Catherine de St Clair, and established the first Templar Preceptory outside of Jerusalem, on the St Clair family lands in Scotland.

The Knights Templar went on to become extremely wealthy, with vast holdings of land across Europe where, on their farms, they produced food and bred horses. They were so wealthy that they loaned money to kings and established what some have referred to as the first European bank, enabling a traveller to deposit money in, say, London and receive a payment against that deposit at his destination, say, Paris.

Although the Templars participated in crusading activity, the indications are that they became progressively distanced from papal governance, becoming very much a law unto themselves. Nevertheless, for two hundred years they prospered.

During the early 14th century, the French king, Philip the Fair, also known as Philip le Bel, had waged a few disastrous wars and was virtually bankrupt. Philip apparently decided to acquire the wealth of the Templars to ease his financial problems. Philip the Fair, in an effort to secure the Templar treasures, is alleged to have murdered two popes and threatened a third, Clement V. At that time, the Grand Master of the Order was James Burg de Molay, more often referred to as Jacques de Molay. He was godfather to one of Philips' sons. Lured to France by Philip le Bel, Molay was arrested along with a large contingent of Knights Templar then in France, through a raid that had been secretly organised by Philip and was instigated on Friday 13th October 1307. In respect of the action taken by Philip le Bel and Pope Clement V, James Orchard Halliwell, in his book *Early History of Masonry in England*, published in 1840, states that:

'There was a convocation at Vienne in Dauphiny, where the extermination was decided upon in 1307.'

It was this action that has ever since rendered any Friday 13th as a day of ill omen.

Despite the efforts by Philip le Bel to arrest the Templars, many of those then in France escaped and apparently made their way to Scotland, Portugal, Sweden to name a few of the destinations. Most of the Templar wealth supposedly eluded

Philip, their property being requisitioned by other monarchs who passed some of it to the care of the Knights Hospitallers at the direction of a papal edict, issued in 1312, whilst some of that property they unquestionably kept for themselves. The bulk of the Templar treasury, however, is believed to have been transferred to Scotland, where Hugues de Payen had established a Preceptory two hundred years earlier.

Denis, King of Portugal, was incensed by the actions of Philip and Clement V. When the edict about transferring the property to the Knights Hospitallers was issued, he took possession of as much as he could for himself with the intention of restoring the Order of the Knights Templar and returning their property to them.

In the following years many accusations were made against the Knights Templar by the Church hierarchy, with charges including heresy, blasphemy and sodomy. These charges are now widely understood to have been false, brought by papal authority at the insistence of Philip the Fair. The power and influence of the Order had, nevertheless, been broken and the Knights Templar was finally dissolved by papal authority in 1314. Jacques de Molay was condemned to death by being roasted alive, not far from the cathedral of Notre Dame in Paris. James Halliwell uses stronger language:

> '... the assassination of the Grand Master, Jacques de Molay, his murderers being Philip le Bel, Pope Clement V and Squin de Florion.'

With the Order officially dissolved, the Templars in Portugal disappeared, but when Clement V died they reappeared, were held in high regard, and received pensions from their estates.

Pope John succeeded Clement V. Denis, King of Portugal, sent ambassadors to him who entered into negotiations with a view to restoring the Order. The negotiations lasted six years and at the end of that period everything that Denis's ambassadors had set out to achieve had been granted, except the restoration of the name, Knights Templar. Instead they became known as the Chevaliers (Knights) of Christ. Despite this effort on their behalf, the new Order failed to regain its former glory.[4]

In England, the residual members of the Order, deprived of their estates and other property, found themselves in a pitiful state. The Bishop of York was so concerned by their circumstances that he took them in and distributed them amongst the monasteries within his jurisdiction.

That, then, is a brief history of the Knights Templar. The other organisation mentioned, The Order of St John of Jerusalem, is still active. It is today based on the Mediterranean island of Malta.

Various writers have pointed out that during the period of the crusades, and their period in the eastern Mediterranean, the Templars came into contact with certain doctrines and culture which they embraced, but which conflicted with those beliefs espoused by Roman Christianity. This is not a place to dwell on that speculation. However, it seems very likely that the organisation did encounter some ideas which may well have resulted in charges of heresy under the philosophy then in place within the Church. This may have resulted from their contact with the sciences understood within the Islamic community that resulted in the development of the Gothic style. And, noting the orientation of Chartres Cathedral, as mentioned earlier, that philosophy may have related to the Sun, geometry, harmony of sound and number, and their links with the macro-cosmos. Science and theology would have been in conflict.

The vast holdings of land and property that the Templars owned throughout Europe resulted in them undertaking some substantial building projects. They built castles and fortresses as protective strongholds, manor houses from which to administer local estates, massive barns for the storage of crops at harvest, churches and bridges. Throughout the territories in which the Templars operated, there are still many wonderful examples of buildings, castles and churches as a testament to their prowess as builders.

Churches in the round were a particular feature of Templar architecture, as was the octagonal shape. Of the many round churches that are believed to have been built in England, only five now survive. The most famous is in London, just back from the banks of the River Thames, in what is today an enclave of the legal establishment. The hub of this centre is known as the *Inner Temple.* The surrounding district is known as *Temple* because it was in that area that the Knights Templar had a major preceptory.

As a consequence of their building prowess, they must have amassed a large contingent of masons within their ranks and with those masons was knowledge of the *ancient wisdoms.* And it is in these *ancient wisdoms*, and one connection in particular, that there may have been a conflict with the religious establishment, leading to charges of heresy and at the same time creating a legendary character of Freemasonry, who relates to the Sun.

First, though, we need to return to Cambridge.

The Templar – Sun Dial church

The Cambridge Round Church has an interior which is rather austere, but such was the mode of the Templars. The church appears to be in fine structural order for its apparent age. After around 300 years of use, in the 15th century it was subject to modification, no doubt coincidental with a need for repairs. After a further 400 years it was the subject of substantial restoration in the Victorian period, 1841-3, by a group known as the Cambridge Camden Society. Documents in the City Library at Cambridge give considerable praise to this restoration work, which included preserving where it was possible and re-creating the 12th century styles where necessary. This restoration work included remodelling some of the windows in keeping with one 12th century window, that had survived.

As the church itself is in the round, it will not be a surprise to learn that the Nave is also in the round at the centre of the building. What is also noticeable is that there are eight pillars which surround the Nave and provide the main structural core. These pillars easily delineate the other Templar feature, the octagon.

*The Round Church
in Cambridge*

On a centre line between each of the pillars are clerestory windows, the bases of which are about 25 feet (18 cubits) above the floor.

*The clerestory windows from
inside the Round Church*

Over a prolonged period, I went to the church as often as possible when I had cause to revisit Cambridge. As my interest in ancient symbolism grew, and I began to appreciate that such symbolism was often incorporated into church designs in the

Medieval and Gothic periods, so I wondered if there was any such hidden treasure to be found in the Round Church. The Nave is given as 19.25 feet/5.86 meters in diameter, which again reflects the standard of Imperial unit measure. In the era when the church was built, no such standard existed. I reasoned that, irrespective of my interest in the *Megalith Yard and Rod* and measurement methods of the masons of old, the Knights Templar would have used the cubit unit of measure, as is referenced in the scriptures. What is more, the 19.25 feet measurement is across the inside face of the Nave, the floor of which is sunken below the level of the ambulatory. I felt that the key dimension at the time when the church was originally built would have been the diameter across the circular centre line on which the main pillars were erected. Each time I visited the church I found it brimming with tourists and other visitors, or the Nave contained exhibition displays, so making detailed measurements was not easy. Nevertheless, I assessed that the diameter of the circular centre-line on which the pillars were constructed was 12 cubits, 6 cubits radius, whilst the overall diameter of the round was 24 cubits. These are symbolic numbers. Encouraged by this unofficial and unsubstantiated realisation, I looked further.

On one visit I took a compass to the church and noted that one of the upper clerestory windows appeared to be on a southern axis. When I stood in the centre of the Nave and looked up at the window, I noted that the sill was angled to permit a spread of light, and appeared to be angled on an invisible line which intersected the centre of the Nave. This implied that on certain days of the year, which I guessed to be the Summer Solstice or Equinox, a beam of light would touch the centre point of the Nave. Thus it was, that noting a favourable weather forecast indicating a sunny day in Cambridge at the time of the Autumn Equinox, I set off to the church once again. We were still operating on daylight saving time with the clocks advanced one hour ahead of solar time. At 12.30pm, I positioned myself diametrically opposite the south-facing clerestory to await the appearance of the Sun. The curator kept a steady eye on me, having noticed my resolute position, but he did not interfere. About 10 minutes before 1.00pm the Sun suddenly burst through the window. A shaft of light penetrated to the point where the floor of the ambulatory and the wall of the round met, on the north side of the church. Unfortunately, some exhibition screens had been positioned in the area, which was not good for photography without disclosing my purpose, but the result was still unmistakable. From this I assessed that at the time of the Summer Solstice the beam of light would be cast to the centre of the Nave and as the year progressed it struck the base of the wall at the time of the equinox, as I had observed it, and then travelled up the wall to the point where the gallery commenced, by the time of the Winter Solstice. If this was indeed what the Knights Templar originally built into the round, then they also built in a solar calendar.

The sun suddenly burst through the south facing clerestory and illuminated the floor - wall connection of the ambulatory.

This was another demonstration of the use of the Sun. It was somewhat unexpected, yet it appears to have been a deliberate design feature. What is more, we see the use of a heavenly body, deemed to be connected with pagan rituals, associated with a building which has strong religious symbolic connections with a temple revered in Christianity – the Holy Sepulchre in Jerusalem. In addition, there is the symbolism of the number 8 and it was built by a group of knights who had in their title the words *Temple of Solomon*, a temple which may well have been the Temple of the Sun and the Moon.

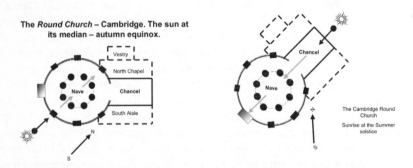

According to documents in Cambridge City Library, the church in the round and the Chancel were built in the 12th century. The South Aisle and North Chapel may have been added in the 15th century whilst the Vestry is a 19th century addition. To add both the South Aisle and North Chapel involved removing part of the walls of the round to create doorways. It may have been that in adding these arched accesses, markings, which would have related to a calendar, were erased.

It is obvious that if the illustration above is rotated through 45 degrees so that the north-south axis is in the traditional vertical alignment, then the axis which runs through the door, centre of the nave and the Chancel, will be on a southwest to northeasterly alignment. This seemed somewhat obscure, so I measured it using a compass and found the alignment corresponded with a bearing of just over 45 degrees. I couldn't help wondering why there had been this orientation. Using celestial simulation software, I decided to check what was happening in the sky in the epoch that the church was built. Several things stood out. First, that the orientation appeared to coincide with the position of the Sun at dawn on the day of the Summer Solstice in the northern hemisphere. As the Sun rose on that day, one can imagine the rays of light penetrating a window in the eastern wall end of the original Chancel, casting a beam of light through the centre of the Nave to the inside of the door. This may have been the celestial marker. Second, in the era of the construction of the church then at the time of the Summer Solstice the Sun rose into the constellation of Gemini – symbolised by the image of the twins, which in turn defines it as a dual sign, the only one in the zodiac. Is it possible that they were alluding to the duality of Heaven and Earth – which would be related to the integer 2 as in the number 20, which we have seen in Solomon's Temple? And part of the name of the Order of Knights was '...*the Temple of Solomon*'.

And then I remembered Chartres Cathedral. The Round Church was built around the same time that the Gothic influence was gathering momentum. By the time the building was supposedly completed, about 1130 CE, the Poor Knights of Christ and the Temple of Solomon, The Knights Templar, had been in the Holy Land for around thirty years, they had their rule, they were officially recognised by papal authority, had hundreds of knights actively participating in the Order, but most significantly, St Bernard, a bishop who had championed their cause, was also the one who had championed the design concepts associated with Gothic design. Chartres has a lunar and solar alignment, with the solar angle directed at the Summer Solstice. The 'Round Church' in Cambridge has a similar solar alignment. The circumstantial evidence and other connections suggest that this is not coincidence.

My observations on this aspect of the Round Church, have since been submitted to the relevant authorities in Cambridge with a suggestion that the church be the subject of further investigations, including perhaps by astro-archaeologists.

The Eight of the Templar Rule and a discovery in Sussex

As mentioned earlier, there was another organisation of knights that was formed just prior to that of the Knights Templar. Both Orders of Knighthood, being under papal protection, had an emblem which was similar, known as a *crux fourchette* or forked cross, which has eight points. In the case of the Hospitallers it was a white cross, whilst that of the Templars was coloured red. The design is symmetrical, which results in each point being an equal distance apart. If a circle, with its centre being in the middle of the cross, would intersect all eight points, then this in turn means that an octagon could be developed from the shape of the cross. And, the Knights Templar did indeed build churches and other structures which reflected the octagon. To the knights, the eight points of the cross symbolised the eight virtues of faith, charity, truth, justice, innocence, humility, sincerity and patience. We should also recall that in Pythagorean philosophy the number 8 signified the *sacred cube* which Bede seemed to define as Heaven. And the *sacred cube* was the Holy of Holies in Solomon's Temple. So, it would seem that the Knights Templar cross, the *crux fourchette*, is also based on the principles of ancient wisdom and geometry. Most of the chivalric orders have, or had, similar crosses. The basic geometric principles appear to have remained the same.

Despite its widespread use I could not find anything in reference books, or anyone, who could tell me how it was constructed. I have to acknowledge, though, that there may have been individuals that knew, but were just not telling. The symmetry made it obvious that it is related to the octagon but for some time, progressing from there, proved to be unproductive. Until that is, I visited a wonderful cathedral built and used by the Order of the Knights of St John.[5] One geometric pattern recurred in the décor: the octagram. At first I was surprised to see it. It is, after all, a symbol revered as a lucky talisman in Islamic countries and linked to the *eight-spoke wheel* of pagan rituals. So finding it emblazoned in a cathedral with a strong Christian connection was rather unexpected. Then it dawned on me that it might hold clues to the construction of the crux fourchette. If it did apply to the Knights Hospitaller and the Order of St John, then, I reasoned, the same principles would have been true for the Knights Templar. From that simple idea the design solution quickly unravelled. And it solved another mystery I had been seeking a solution for.

In an earlier chapter I pointed out the hidden geometric designs included in the Masonic Centre in Sussex. In the centre of the floor are two circles, one being half the diameter of the other, and with the letter 'G' positioned in the centre. Although certain aspects of the design became clear, the reason for the eight black lozenge shapes around the outer edge remained unresolved, as did the reason for the centre circle. I had already identified that the eight points on the outer circle enabled the drawing of an octagon, plus geometry relating to the pentagram, and the *Mason's secret square*, but none of this produced the definite reason for the black lozenges. What I had overlooked was that by producing an octagon, so I could also create an octagram.

Suddenly all became clear.

When the eight points of the outer circle were connected by two squares, a large octagram was revealed; this in turn led to the eight-pointed pattern that resulted in the *Mason's secret square*. This had also produced another smaller octagram towards the centre of the circle. I then drew a circle around the outer points of the inner octagram and found it had produced a circle exactly half the diameter of the outer. This was encouraging because of the obvious link with the pavement. It was then only a short step to reveal a *crux fourchette*, with the black lozenges fitting the pattern perfectly. Needless to say, with this hidden pattern now revealed in Sussex it could also be derived from the eight pillars and the circular nave of the Round Church in Cambridge.

Furthermore, it has long been established through the Old Constitutions of Freemasonry that the letter 'G' stands for Geometry, whilst early Masonic manuscripts are quoted as saying that Geometry and Masonry are the same thing.

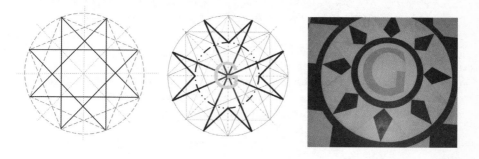

What hitherto had seemed a rather inconspicuous historic little church in Cambridge now appeared to be a seasonal calendar able to monitor the equinox and the solstice, and the harbinger of many of the attributes of *sacred geometry* derived by our ancient ancestors for whom the Sun god was the principal deity.

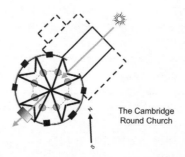

The Cambridge
Round Church

Hiram Abif or Huram-Abi?

One of the key characters in Freemasonry is Hiram Abif, who, according to Masonic legend, was the architect and builder of the first Jerusalem temple. We have already seen that according to Old Testament text, David was the architect and Solomon (Jedidiah) was the builder. If however we take a modern analogy, we might interpret this as being that David oversaw the design and making of the plans, Solomon (Jedidiah) commissioned the works to be done, and Hiram was the person who made it happen – a site project manager or foreman.

In the Old Testament books of Kings and Chronicles we are introduced to Huram-Abi who Hiram, King of Tyre, sent to King Solomon to assist with the building. The relevant texts in Kings and Chronicles are very similar, except that the Chronicles version is more detailed.

> *'I am sending you Huram-Abi, a man of great skill whose mother was from Dan and whose father was from Tyre. He is trained to work in gold and silver, bronze and iron, stone and wood, and with purple and blue and crimson yarn and fine linen. He is experienced in all kinds of engraving and can execute any design given to him.'*
>
> *2 Chronicles 2:13 & 14*

Based on the above text, Huram-Abi was a very skilled craftsman. He was skilled at executing designs given to him as an artisan. That is very different from being an architect. If this person cannot be positively aligned with being the Temple builder, then who was the real Hiram Abif?

Huram the Alchemist

Most people who read the text of Kings and Chronicles may well note the impressive descriptions of the Temple and its lavish furnishings, but few, I venture to suggest, can have any idea of the logistical processes and skills needed to provide such furnishings as the Sea and the pillars especially in the era of 3,000 years ago. These items alone were very substantial metal objects. They had to be cast from molten metal. To do this, Huram needed experience of building and operating a foundry, of identifying and smelting raw ore dug from the ground, and handling very hot molten metals. The size of the Sea and the pillars dictated that the molten materials needed were in relatively large quantities for the era in which the work was undertaken.

We are told in the Old Testament text that the Sea and the pillars were cast in bronze. Bronze is an alloy, that is, a fusion of two or more metals. Bronze is made from copper to which is added zinc and tin. It is a much harder metal than copper alone, and in the era around 1,000 BCE it could be made even harder by the addition of other substances such as arsenic. In the text taken from Chronicles, we also note that Huram was skilled in working with iron. The era when the Temple was built was on the cusp of a change in civilisation and the cultural use of metals – it was the latter Bronze Age and start of the Iron Age. The Bronze Age, as we know it, had origins that can be traced to the third millennium BCE, so it was a well-developed science with a pedigree of some two thousand years by the time Solomon's Temple was built. It is therefore not surprising to find a man who was skilled at smelting copper ore and was also skilled in the use of iron. The techniques of smelting the ore and handling the molten metals would have been very similar.

As stated earlier, the primary material for making bronze is copper, the melting point of which is 1083 degrees centigrade / 1981 degrees Fahrenheit. For this metal to melt and be sufficiently liquid so that it will flow freely for casting purposes dictates that the fire beneath the cauldron holding the raw materials must achieve a temperature greater than that. No doubt the burning medium for the fire would have been wood, or charcoal derived from it. Irrespective of the fuel, good access to plentiful supplies of it, was needed.

Around the era when Solomon's Temple was built, a primary source of tin was from Britain, and in particular, from Cornwall. Traders known to have visited Cornwall to obtain supplies of this tin were the Phoenicians operating from Tyre. So, Huram had a known source of supply of a key metal he needed for producing the alloy, bronze.

If it wasn't for his biblical connection, Huram would have been regarded as an alchemist. Alchemy is usually associated with a quest for turning base metals, such as iron ore, into gold. The mixing of metals, into what we now call alloys, is exactly the type of process indulged in by alchemists as part of their quest. Huram would, no doubt, have been able to identify the base ores of copper, tin, and iron, and been well aware of the consequences of adding substances like arsenic. He was also skilled in working with silver and gold. Such a person, so well versed in the use and manipulation of metals, cannot have done so without being fully acquainted with the alchemist's art.

His knowledge of the fusion of materials follows through to his knowledge about cloth for he clearly had an understanding about how to make and use various dyes. Crimson is mentioned. This is a blood-red colour, the dye for which was derived from worms. But it is the mention of *purple* that is interesting, as it is a colour associated with kingship and royalty – the status attributed to both Hiram, King of Tyre, and Solomon. The basic dye was rare, so materials immersed in that colour were expensive. It is a characteristic of the dye that the colour does not fade. As to its expense, Aristotle is attributed as placing a value on it at ten or twenty times greater than gold[6]. Its rarity was because it was derived from a particular species of sea snails, known as *trunculus murex*, and required the harvesting of over 50,000 such snails to produce 1 pound (450 grams) of the dye. As a result of its expense, the purple dye that was created became known as 'royal' or 'imperial purple'[7]. The reason it is mentioned in the text from Chronicles is significant because it became known as 'Tyrian purple'. This was because it was extracted, processed and sold by Phoenician traders from Tyre[8] – the place from which Huram originated, and the Royal domain of Hiram, King of Tyre.

Huram, it would seem, was no ordinary man. The background to his skill and knowledge was far greater than the text of Kings and Chronicles implies. It is only when one takes a closer look behind his skills that one really appreciates his significance. Although we can now acknowledge and appreciate those skills, it does not necessarily imply that he was the temple architect or builder that is stated in

Masonic ceremonies. The text of Chronicles makes it clear that he was able to take a design which was given to him, and produce it in the material chosen. There is a big difference in that, and being the person responsible for the construction of the temple building. If that is the case, then we again have to ask – who or what was Hiram Abif?

Who was Hiram Abif?

In a Masonic ceremony there is an enactment of a story wherein it is observed that the supposed architect of the Temple, Hiram Abif, was brutally murdered by three ruffians. These murderers were aware that Hiram Abif understood the secrets associated with the building of the Temple and attempted to extort that information from him for their own purposes. When Hiram refused to reveal those secrets he was attacked by each of the ruffians in turn and finally killed. With his death, the ceremony states, the genuine secrets of Masonry were lost and that in their place certain other secrets were substituted until such time that the genuine were restored. It had been the reference to the loss and subsequent restoration of the secrets that I next focused my interest.

The footnotes to the biblical text state that the word Huram is a Hebrew spelling for the name Hiram. So, substituting Hiram for Huram, we have Hiram-Abi which is just one letter short of the Masonic name attributed to the builder. This would rather seem to identify the key character of Masonic ritual. Not necessarily so.

Over the years there has been a great deal written about Hiram Abif in an effort to properly identify him, and a range of allegorical interpretations have been attributed to this name. Some writers suggest that the name is used as an allegorical link in Freemasonry with the death by burning of the Grand Master of the Knights Templar, Jacques de Molay, in Paris on 19th March 1314 at the direction of Pope Clement,[9] as already mentioned. He is also associated with an idea developed by Plato as an *idea* of man.[10] Then there is the suggestion attributed to Elias Ashmole, who was closely connected with Freemasonry in the 17th century, that associated the name with the execution by beheading of the English king, Charles I, in 1649.[11] The name Hiram, in Hebrew, is recorded as meaning 'noble' or 'kingly'[12] whilst the word Abif appears to be old French for 'lost one'.[13] Research by Robert Lomas and Christopher Knight in *The Hiram Key* connects Hiram Abif with a loss of the knowledge of the Egyptian 'king making' ceremony as a consequence of the violent death of the Pharaoh Seqenenre Tao II. It seems that the death of Seqenenre Tao has stark similarities with the Masonic story of the death of Hiram Abif, even down to being able to identify the fatal wounds received by Seqenenre, as revealed by his mummified remains on display in the Egyptian Museum in Cairo. This then raised the question in my mind as to why such an event from Egyptian history should become a key component of Masonic ceremony. The only answer that seemed to make sense was that Huram-Abi and the tale relating to Seqenenre were used as an allegory for pointing out, and at the same time hiding, something else, something that was important, particularly to operative Master Masons. That being so, it implied that whatever it was that was hidden was information being protected for some very special reason.

Musing on this, it was the definition of Hiram as 'noble' and Abif as 'lost one' that attracted my attention. *Noble* and *kingly* refer to high birth and therefore, historically, someone of significance. Something which is *lost* may imply that it is not available at the moment, but that it may in time be found again, recovered.

I rephrased this to be 'Something/someone of significance was not available for use/mention; which one day may be available again and properly restored to its rightful place, but, in the meantime the genuine has been substituted by something else, for convenience'.

So what or who was no longer available so that they or it could have been substituted?

In Masonic ceremony, we learn that the genuine secrets of Masonry have been substituted. A short interchange between the Master of the Lodge and his Wardens, which I will paraphrase, goes as follows:

Q. Where are you going?
A. From the east to the west.
Q. Why are you going there?
A. To seek for that which was lost, which by your instruction and our own industry, we hope to find.
Q. What was it that was lost?
A. The genuine secrets of Masonry.
Q. How came they lost?
A. By the untimely death of our Master, Hiram Abif.
Q. How do you hope to find them?
A. Using the centre of a circle.

There is then another element of ceremony before returning to dialogue again.

Q. Whence come you?
A. The west, where we have been in search of the genuine secrets.
Q. Have you found them?
A. No, but we have certain substituted secrets.
Q. Tell me what they are.

There is then yet another element of ceremony before the interchange resumes.

Master: The substituted secrets have been communicated to me and as the representative of King Solomon, I give approval for them to be represented in Masonry throughout the Universe, until time or circumstances shall restore the genuine.

In this dialogue one thing stands out: the reference to celestial mechanics. The journeymen leave the east, where the Sun rises, to follow the path of the Sun to where it sets in the west. They note that the genuine secret can be recovered using knowledge already available to the Master, by thinking about and working through the problem, which they can do using a circle. So, with the link to celestial mechanics and a circle it could signify the Earth and its orbit. The journeymen then return from the west. The Sun appears to move from east to west, because the Earth rotates from west to east. They make it clear they are imparting substituted information to which the Master notes that all Masons will acknowledge it 'until time or circumstances shall restore the genuine'. It is almost as if he knows what the genuine secrets are but is telling his journeymen to use the substituted knowledge until times change and they can revert to the genuine.

It struck me that there had to have been a pretty serious motivator of some kind to have required such drastic action. And the only motivator that sprang to mind was some form of danger – a risk to life and limb.

So, what was the danger?

Revealing another Hiram Abif

We have already established that at the time that Solomon's Temple was built, it is highly probable that it was known that the Earth revolved on its axis, that it was a big ball and there was a rough idea about how big the ball was, and that the Earth orbited the Sun – the heliocentric concept where the Sun is at the centre of the solar system.

Around the 4th century BCE, the idea that the Earth was at the centre, and the heavens moved around it, came to the fore. This is known as the geocentric system. According to Aristotle (384-322 BCE), who supported the geocentric idea, the Pythagoreans believed that there was a big fire at the centre of the universe and that the Earth orbited this big fire creating night and day.[14] The heliocentric idea came back into fashion about 150 years after Aristotle, when it was supported by Aristarchus, but its return to prominence appears to have been short-lived. It would seem that around 100-150 BCE the concept of heliocentricity was condemned as anti-religious, because the scriptures stated that God had made the world and then the heavens, therefore the Earth had to be centre of the universe. That then became the standing philosophy for nearly 2,000 years and anyone who espoused the heliocentric idea was condemned as a heretic.

Yet, it is the knowledge that the Sun is at the centre of our solar system – the heliocentric concept – that is a key in Masonic ceremonies. Every candidate to be passed to the Second Degree learns and states:

'The Earth, constantly revolving on its axis in its orbit about the Sun, ...'

Just a few hundred years ago, at the time for instance when the Grand Lodge of England was formed in 1717, openly mentioning such a concept was liable to result in an individual being branded a heretic. In the countries dominated by the Holy Roman Empire, that could have resulted in arrest and imprisonment. Just one hundred years prior to the founding of the Grand Lodge of England, a charge of heresy was likely to result in torture and death. Just a few decades before the formation of the Grand Lodge of England, Galileo was tortured in Venice on the orders of the Vatican for suggesting that the heliocentric system was the true science. He escaped death but was placed under house arrest as a form of internal exile. Knowledge about the heliocentric system was therefore not something to shout about. There was a risk to life and limb.

Heliocentricity is the ruling concept which fits entirely with an allegorical definition of Hiram – *noble, kingly* – that is, the ruler, the basis of power. It also fits with the old French translation of *lost one*. In other words the heliocentric system is the ruling/governing concept, the genuine secrets which were temporarily substituted from about 120 BCE because of the risk of being branded anti-religious; the substituted secrets were the geocentric concept; and the restoration of the secrets is the realisation that the heliocentric system, understood even in the times of King Solomon, is the genuine.

Hiram Abif, I submit, is not a reference to a person. It is a reference to the religious conflict that centred around the science of heliocentric and geocentric concepts. To understand how to use the Sun, the shadows created by it, precession and the change of the seasons, one needs to understand the principles of celestial mechanics – the heliocentric system. It was understood by King Jedidiah/Solomon as part of his portfolio of *wisdom*.

The Principles connection

The continuation of the degree of a Master Mason is contained in what is known as Royal Arch Freemasonry – known in Masonic circles simply as Chapter.

There is a point in a Chapter ceremony where it is noted that the building of Solomon's Temple was undertaken by three Principals, namely, Hiram, King of Tyre; Solomon, King of Israel; and Hiram Abif. The implication is that they were three individual people. I suggest this is an allegory for something else:

a. That Hiram, King of Tyre, provided the materials and most of the key manpower, including the skills of Huram-Abi.
b. That the reference to Solomon is a reference to the fact that what they built was the Temple of the Sun and the Moon.
c. That the reference to Hiram Abif and the substituted secrets of masonry, plus the recovery and restoration of the genuine secrets, is a reflection of the fact that at the time the Temple was built in Jerusalem, the concepts of the heliocentric system, the knowledge of which was the basis of building the Temple in Jerusalem, were the genuine secrets, and were fully understood at that time. It was the basic principle that determined how the macro-cosmos worked. This was substituted by the geocentric concept to satisfy the prevailing religious dogma. The recovery of the secrets would be when the heliocentric system was restored to its rightful place – the noble and superior understanding achieved by observation, the application of geometry and logic, by comparison with the substituted philosophy of the geocentric concept dictated by religious faith and dogma.

Thus, I suggest that the genuine secret of Freemasonry has, for many centuries, been an understanding that the Sun was the centre of our solar system, that the Earth and planets orbited around it, and that when that was understood the shadow of the

Sun could be used, together with the basic principles of geometry to aid the design and construction of important buildings.

[1] Preston, W. *Illustrations of Masonry* (online version), Book 4, History of Masonry in England, Sect. 2 - History of Masonry in England under St Austin, King Alfred, and Athelstane; and also under the Knights Templars. – Transcribed by Geraint and Robert Lomas and available on line at http://www.robertlomas.com/preston/padlock/book4/index.html
[2] Catholic encyclopaedia – Pope Urban II
[3] The Hiram Key
[4] See *Early History of Masonry in England*, James Orchard Halliwell.
[5] Co-cathedral, Valletta, Malta
[6] Trunculus Murex. www.wikipedia.org
[7] Wikipedia
[8] Wikipedia
[9] *Early History of Masonry in England*, James Orchard Halliwell, 1840.
[1] *The Secret Teachings of All Ages*, Manly P. Hall p239
[11] *The Secret Teachings of All Ages*, Manly P. Hall p239
[12] *The Hiram Key*, Robert Lomas and Christopher Knight p159
[13] *The Hiram Key*, Robert Lomas and Christopher Knight p159
[14] Wikipedia article about the heliocentric universe attributes this comment to Aristotle in his book *On the Heavens* Chapter 13, Book Two.

Chapter 16
The closing

My quest started with Freemasonry and a Masonic Lodge and that is where it must end. I learned a great deal about many subjects I had not previously taken any great interest in. I had discovered much about Freemasonry, had marvelled at its history and the intricate web of knowledge and connections which traced obvious links back to the earliest understanding about the heavens and world on which we live – the macro-cosmos – that our ancestors had accumulated. I could not help but feel that any brother in Freemasonry could be justly proud of having been permitted to become a member of this august and ancient fraternity.

Before I embarked on my quest,

- I had never stopped to think about who Solomon was. I accepted his position as it was stated in the Old Testament or had been passed on to me by those in positions of religious authority and to whom I was expected to show deference. I discovered a very different character.
- I had never stopped to think about the geometry that may have been deployed in the construction of the great cathedrals I visited in Europe, or the ancient temples of North Africa, the Middle East and surrounding the Mediterranean Sea. I just accepted that they had been built by very skilled masons, without appreciating the enormity of that skill, or the knowledge required in the era in which the construction had taken place.
- Since childhood I had heard about Abraham and Isaac; I had read the passages of the Old Testament about Moses and the calf that the Israelites built whilst he was on the mountain recording the Commandments; the mention of sacrifice, burnt offerings and Moloch, but never once realised that they were all connected by the same theme – that I was reading about child sacrifice. Neither did I realise that such atrocities occurred in the reign of Solomon or that he provided facilities for such events to take place.
- I had little or no comprehension about what Solomon's Temple might have looked like or been used for.

I have no hesitation in acknowledging that many of the conclusions I have reached are my own subjective opinions, but I hope I have demonstrated the processes of evaluation in sufficient depth that they will be seen in a positive light as opposed to being mere fanciful thinking. I also acknowledge that my conclusions and hypothesis, and in some instances, straight forward language, may not sit easily with all readers.

Finding answers to what Solomon's Temple may have actually looked like, and how it and the pillars worked, has been all very well. But, there are still other questions posed at the start of my enquiries that require answers.

It had been a long journey of discovery lasting nearly 15 years. When I set out I had no idea where it was to lead. I had a few questions in mind that I wanted answers to because the people around me who I thought knew the answers, some of the senior officials of Freemasonry, did not seem to know either. To get my answers I travelled to some of the ancient cities and countries of the Middle East, India, parts of Europe and the length and breadth of Britain. I spent many hours in libraries, sitting at home with a calculator, trawling the internet and reading a myriad of books on subjects that would not normally have been on my reading list. I had made discoveries about religion; the way that our ancestors lived and their beliefs, distortions of history, and discovered knowledge of the world in ages past that is rapidly being lost to all but a few dedicated academics. And from all this I have been able to propose an insight into what I believe were the secrets of Solomon's/Jedidiah's Temple, Solomon's/Jedidiah's Wisdom and Solomon's/Jedidiah's Seal.

Most academics start with a theory and look for cohesive evidence to support it. I started from the opposite end of the scale, looking at pieces of information, like pieces of a jigsaw puzzle, and then piece by piece building up a picture that provides what I hope is a credible solution.

I started by asking some basic questions about the Masonic Temple in which my Lodge meets. The answers proved to be tied together with a mixture of celestial information, sacred geometry and ancient wisdom of the type familiar to Pythagoras. And incredibly, until I presented a paper to my fellow masons about my findings, nobody had any idea as to the significance of the hidden knowledge that was present. Some of that original information I have revealed in this book.

I also asked other questions like:

Why in Freemasonry do we mark the Sun at its meridian?

a. By marking the position of the Sun at its highest point in the sky, using a marker stick with a pointed top and the shadow cast by it, at any time of the year one can produce a line of orientation which has a true north-south axis. Then, in bisecting that line at right angles, a second line of orientation can be produced which is an east-west axis. The four cardinal points on the surface of the earth can be determined. This may have been important to an operative Master Mason in times past for setting out the ground-plan of an important building.

b. If one was working on a project which would take years to complete, such as building a cathedral, then marking the position of the shadow at midday provided a calendar for predicting the seasons with a high degree of accuracy.

Why do we mark the setting Sun?

c. The relative angular position of sunset on any given day has the same angular relativity as at dawn on the same day. Just as with marking the rising Sun, it enabled the solstices and equinoxes to be identified. This was not only important for determining the progress of the seasons but may have been significant in re-creating a consistent unit of measure which was transferable from site to site – a unit of measure that Professor Thom called a *Megalithic Yard*.

d. The position of the Sun on the horizon may have been important if a particular structure was to be oriented towards it, such as to mark the feast of a saint, birth of a king, victory over an enemy, or survival of a natural catastrophe.

e. After the setting Sun comes the night and with it an array of new celestial bodies to monitor, including the Moon. There were a series of stars and planets that were recorded and their progress monitored, such as the planets Venus and Saturn, because they held special religious significance.

Why do we note that 'the earth constantly revolves on its axis in its orbit around the Sun'?

f. It was the answer to why the Sun set in the west and rose in the east. It is what creates day and night. It was the basis for defining the week and thereby the Sabbath or day of rest.

g. Reference to the axis is the basis of understanding precession and what the effects of it are.

h. The orbit around the Sun is the way that the seasons are created and follow each other with such regularity and certainty.

Why do we note that 'the Sun rises in the east to open the day ...'

i. It pointed out that the sunrise is an illusion, created by the fact that Earth rotates on its axis from west to east and the Sun is apparently stationary in the universe.

From my enquiries whilst assembling the information for this book I have come to believe that the original three degrees of masonry were, what I call *off-site training in the principles of celestial mechanics*. Someone who was training to be an operative mason would have learned the hard way – on the job, much as the apprentices of the later Guilds system did. Yet, to progress to be a Master Mason required that they had a peculiar understanding, an education, which brought to light much about the world around them and how it worked – the macro-cosmos. Only those who showed signs of possessing a higher intellect were selected to receive this information. That off-site training was given and received in the Mason's Lodge, the place on the construction site where they stored tools and worked on delicate carvings or specially shaped stone. This training was conveyed in secret to the selected adepts who were threatened with draconian penalties for disclosure. As many of these operative masons could neither read nor write, the information was packaged into a series of short plays, or ceremonies, which having been memorised, conveyed all the information they needed to know and how to apply it.

1st degree – taught that the Earth is round – a sphere, that it orbits the Sun; that it rotates on its axis to bring day and night, and the calendar of the year; that the Moon orbits around the Earth together with its cycles.

2nd degree – taught that the axis of the Earth is tilted and that it was because of this we have the seasons; that there is a slow rotation and wobble in the axis that we call precession, and the effect that has.

3rd degree – taught the basic principles of geometry and how, in conjunction with the knowledge already imparted, it could be used to estimate the size of the Earth and even help to pinpoint where one was on the face of the planet.

History of the Arch

I am also convinced that up to around the 16th century, the three Craft degrees of Freemasonry, plus the continuation of the third degree known as Royal Arch Freemasonry, contained the remnants of an historical development of the operative skills of Masonry.

Until the development of Protestant Christianity and the dissolution of the monasteries by King Henry VIII, the Master Masons were also the designers of almost all prominent buildings, and the geometry and symbolic interpretation established by the ecclesiastical connection resulted in such designs following patterns accepted by the Roman Catholic Church. The break from Vatican domination resulted in the need to follow the strict code they had hitherto demanded also diminishing, thereby enabling new design criteria to evolve. It is around that time that the professional architect, separate from the Company/Corporation of Masons, developed. It is also around that time that we find *Speculative Masons* being admitted as members of the fraternity. I am convinced that the history which would then have been contained in ceremonies noted the earliest development of the arch. Up to about the time that the Jerusalem Temple was built, a doorway to, for example, a temple or palace, was likely to comprise three large blocks of stone with an end profile cut roughly as the shape of a square. Two blocks would be placed vertically to provide supports on either side of the door whilst a third would be placed over the top to become what today we call a lintel. This construction method had been in use for several thousand years: it was the building norm in almost all cultures in the Middle East, Mediterranean and Celtic regions.

Then, around the time that the first Jerusalem Temple was built, a new concept evolved – the semi-circular arch which in turn provided the vaulted ceiling that enabled large underground caverns for storage or secret meetings. This was made possible through the realisation that a series of stones, each cut with a slight wedge shaped profile, would make such an arch, and that the most important stone was the one at the top of the curve, the *key stone*. This then enabled large structures of great strength to be built. We can see evidence of this through the aqueducts that the Romans built to transport water, and triumphal gates. The semi-circular arch also featured in Norman architecture prior to the evolution of the Gothic style. Wonderful examples still exist in England, such as the west door of Rochester

Cathedral in Kent, noted as being a fine surviving example of a Norman door. The semi-circular arch then gave way to the slightly pointed arch of the Gothic style, which combined the geometric symbolism of Vesica Piscis with a construction methodology that enabled strong yet efficient structures to be built. This is speculation, but it is hinted at by a few researchers of former times.

Teaching about Celestial Mechanics

In addition to the above, the principal officers in the Lodge, even today, have their positions in the Lodge in the key points of the solar transit. The Master is in the east – the place the Sun rises to bring light and warmth to the day; the Junior Warden is in the south – the position of the Sun at its zenith in the sky; and the Senior Warden is in the west – the place where the Sun sets and enables the glorious canopy of the heavens to be revealed. Because the Sun does not travel through the north whilst giving us daylight, no regular ceremonial officer is stationed there.

There is a point in the initiation ceremony when the new candidate to become a member of a lodge is placed at the northeast corner of the Lodge room. Traditionally, the first foundation stone of a new building was placed at the northeast corner and the superstructure of the building was raised on those resultant firm foundations. The northeast is also the maximum point of travel of the Sun in the northern hemisphere, the point we call the Summer Solstice. So the candidate is placed in the same corner of the Lodge room to symbolically represent the foundation stone, the firm foundation of his first step in his Masonic career. By being at the northeast corner he is also in the east, symbolically starting his Masonic journey; he is still substantially 'in the dark' about Masonic activity, having yet to progress to the point where the Sun rises further along the eastern horizon. In the second degree he progresses to the South side, near the southeast corner, following the passage of the Sun to its daily midpoint, its meridian. Just as the Sun moves from a low point in the sky in winter, to its height at mid-summer, replacing the cold and darkness with warmth and light, so symbolically the 2nd degree mason has moved from the darkness of ignorance into the light of revelation and is encouraged to study those aspects of the natural world and the sciences which would, in times past, have formed the basis of the university Masters degree; the seven liberal arts and sciences of grammar, rhetoric, astronomy/astrology, music, logic, arithmetic, and geometry. Strangely, in the third degree he does not progress towards the west, the place of the setting sun, the point that is at the end of the day. Whilst there is a symbolic substitution, I cannot help but believe that in more ancient times there would have been a progression to the southwest corner of the Lodge, but I can find no trace of it in the documents I have accessed.There is an alternative possibility. The new apprentice starts in the north east because it coincides with furthest northerly position of the sun on the horizon, namely the summer solstice for the northern hemisphere. In the 2nd degree, he moves to the south east corner to symbolise the other extreme – the winter solstice. In the third degree all transactions take place opposite the master, in the centre, the position of the equinox, spring and autumn, the most significant for our ancestors.

There is, however, one remnant of what I believe formed part of the original Masonic ceremonies. It is in the second degree and lasts but a few minutes.

The candidate, because of other aspects of the ceremony, happens to find himself in the west of the Lodge room. He is instructed to proceed to the east, which he can do only by passing the north. All Masonic ceremonial procession rotates round the Lodge from the east, to the south, to the west, and returns to the east through the north. This is of course following the path of the Sun when seen in the northern hemisphere. From the northeast corner the candidate then makes a curved approach towards the Master of the Lodge who is waiting for him, in the east, at the Chair of King Solomon. The curved approach represents about a quarter, or fourth part, of a circle. When the Lodge first starts its proceedings, it is proclaimed that the Master is always placed in the east.

As the Sun rises in the east to open and enliven the day, so the master is placed in the east ...

Symbolically, therefore, the Master is the Sun. The fact that the Sun rises in the east is really an illusion created by the Earth rotating from west to east, whilst the Sun, which is stationary in space, appears to travel from east to west. The candidate therefore starts his journey in the ceremony from the place where the Sun sets – the west, travels round the dark side, symbolised by his parade along the north of the Lodge, and eventually emerges in the curved approach towards the Sun, represented by the Master. In other words, during that short sequence, the Master is the Sun and the candidate is the Earth, rotating towards it. This, I believe, is a remnant from ancient Masonic ritual which explained the processes of celestial mechanics to those who would, at that time, have had no concept as to how the sphere of the world worked.

A loss for the gentleman's club

Over time, it seems obvious that the ceremonies of Freemasonry originally had their roots firmly founded in ancient wisdom and understanding. No doubt, someone in authority, not understanding what the hidden messages were, incorporated changes which eroded the meaning. Then, as others that followed felt that what was left seemed to have no meaning, they termed the fraternity *a gentleman's club* and felt free to make yet further changes. Thus, in the past one hundred years, or more, word and sentence changes, in order to appear more modern or to appease critics, have, in my view, left us with an organisation where even those in the hierarchy have little idea about what the contents and symbolism mean, or from where it came. Yet, if looked at objectively, I believe that Freemasonry provides a connection with our ancestors unequalled by almost any other organisation. It is unique, and long may it continue to be so.

Through the latter years of the 20th century and into the 21st, I have given a number of lectures within lodges. On each occasion I have implored the assembled brethren to take a deeper look at and interest in the history and background to what we are doing and why we are doing it, and to refrain from making any changes, however well-meaning, without understanding what it is they would be changing and the ongoing effects they might have – what might be lost for the future. Freemasonry is an ancient, noble and proud institution. It would be a pity to see it reduced to a series of ceremonies devoid of meaning merely to satisfy a passing fashion of 'political correctness'.

Founded in 1717 – why then?

One of the last questions I had posed was,

'why was the Grand Lodge of England formed in 1717?'.

It is the symmetry of the numbers that originally caught my attention. Was there a specific reason for that symmetry or was it purely by chance? If there was a reason, then what was the reason? Why not form this new body in 1716 or 1718?

The official line is that four lodges existing in London in the early 18th century felt that a single organisation should be created to oversee them. Thus, the Grand Lodge of England was formed.

Other writers have suggested that it had more to do with a desire to distance themselves from the Jacobite rebellion in the 18th century than simply wanting to create a hierarchy of organisation.[1] It is a very plausible argument.

There is some documentary evidence which shows that the moves to create the single governing entity originated in 1716 with 1717 being the year it all finally happened and a Grand Master was installed -1716 was therefore the year of the advance planning. What is particularly interesting to note is that first Grand Master was installed on 24th June 1717, St John the Baptists' Feast Day, which was around the time of the Summer Solstice.

However, it was as I neared the completion of my investigations into Solomon's (Jedidiah's) Temple, that an unexpected solution presented itself.

I was reading about Pythagorean arithmetic when I encountered a table that was comparing various alphabets with those of the Hebrew language.[2] There was also a table of numeral comparisons and I was immediately struck by the similarity between certain Hebrew characters and our western numerals. I was also reminded of a short section at the end of what is known as the description of *The Second Degree Tracing Board*. This piece of Masonic ceremony makes reference to certain ancient military conflicts that occurred before the Temple was built. It also notes the dedication with which the masons involved with building the Temple went about their task and the way in which they were rewarded for their efforts. The section at the end of the ceremony notes that there was a particular room in the temple where the masons went to receive payment for their services, and states that:

Once inside the temple of King Solomon, the operative mason had his attention directed towards certain Hebrew characters ...

As I read through the tables of alphabet comparison so certain of those characters suddenly took on a different characteristic. Looking closer at the number 1717, the 1 & 7 look like Hebrew characters:

being the Hebrew character Vau

and

being the Hebrew character Daleth.

7

At first sight one may agree that they do look similar. However, there the similarity ends because,

Vau is the Hebrew character for the number 4,
Daleth is the Hebrew character for the number 6.

Substituting these two translated numbers for 1717

$$= 4646 \qquad \text{or} \qquad 4 + 6 + 4 + 6 = 20.$$

Twenty cubits was the size of the cube shaped Holy of Holies in Solomon's (Jedidiah's) Temple, it was the length of the equinox shadow created by the pillars, and the Solstice shadow length. The total of 20 cubits + 20 cubits = 40 cubits was the distance between the centre lines of the pillars, and also the distance the pillars stood in front of the Temple porch. 20 cubits + 20 cubits = 40 cubits was also the length of the Temple hall, through which, along with the porch, the Sun shone at its rising to illuminate the Ark of the Covenant that was positioned below the wings of the cherubim and at the exact centre of the cube of the Holy of Holies. And, by ignoring the zero (there is nothing there) we have the number 2, the sign of duality – Heaven and Earth.

Could it have been that a group of Freemasons with more knowledge of the practices of the ancient masons than we have today, who were members of London-based lodges, and who were at the same time seeking to distance themselves from the Jacobites, realised that it was an opportune year, in numerical terms, to record the significance of Freemasonry and the link with Solomon's (Jeddidiah's) Temple?

Is this the real reason for the foundation of the Grand Lodge of England in the year 1717?   Is this the real secret of 1717?

The closing

[1] *The Second Messiah* – Robert Lomas and Christopher Knight
[2] *The Secret Teachings of All Ages* by Manley P. Hall,

Appendix 1
The Mystery of the Megalithic Yard
Revealed

How to create this prehistoric measurement unit for yourself
A guide created by Robert Lomas and Christopher Knight, authors of Uriel's Machine.
This article uses some research data developed in conjunction with Alan Butler. For details see Uriel's Machine.

"And I saw in those days how long cords were given to two angels... 'Why have they taken those cords and gone off?' And he said to me, 'They have gone to measure".

The Book of Enoch

The discovery of the Megalithic Yard
When the late Professor Alexander Thom surveyed over a thousand megalithic structures from Northern Scotland through England, Wales and Western France he was amazed to find that they had all been built using the same unit of measurement. Thom dubbed this unit a Megalithic Yard (MY) because it was very close in size to an imperial yard, being exactly 2 feet 8.64 inches (82.966 cm). As an engineer he could appreciate the fine accuracy inherent in the MY but he was mystified as to how such a primitive people could have consistently reproduced such a unit across a zone spanning several hundreds of miles.

The answer that eluded the late Professor lay not in the rocks, but in the stars.

The MY turns out to be much more than an abstract unit such as the modern metre, it is a highly scientific measure repeatedly constructed by empirical means. It is based upon observation of three fundamental factors:
1.   The orbit of the Earth around the sun
2.   The spin of the Earth on its axis
3.   The mass of the Earth

Making your own Megalithic Yard
These ancient builders marked the year by identifying the two days a year when the shadow cast by the rising sun was perfectly aligned with the shadow of the setting sun. We call these the spring equinox and the autumn equinox that fall around the 21st of March and 21st September respectively. They also knew that there were 366 sunrises from one spring equinox to the next and it appears that they took this as a sacred number.

They then scribed out a large circle on the ground and divided it into 366 parts. All you have to do is copy the process as follows:

Stage one - Find a suitable location

Find a reasonably flat area of land that has open views to the horizon, particularly in the east or the west. You will need an area of around forty feet by forty feet with a reasonably smooth surface of grass, level soil or sand.

Stage two - Prepare your equipment

You will need the following items:

1.   Two stout, smooth rods approximately six feet long and a few inches diameter. One end should be sharpened to a point.

2.   A large mallet or heavy stone.

3.   A short stick with neatly cut ends of approximately 10 inches. To make life easier this should have small cuts made into it to mark out five equal parts.

4.   A cord (a washing line will do) approximately forty feet in length.

5.   A piece of string about five feet long.

6.   A small, symmetrical weight with a hole in its centre (e.g. a heavy washer).

7.   A straight stick about three feet long.

8.   A sharp blade.

Stage three - Constructing a megalithic degree

A megalithic circle was divided into 366 equal parts, which is almost certainly the origin of our modern 360 degree circle. It seems probable that when mathematics came into use in the Middle East they simply discarded 6 units to make the circle divisible by as many numbers as possible. The megalithic degree was 98.36% of a modern degree.

For purposes of creating a Megalithic Yard you only need to measure one six part of a circle, which will contain 61 megalithic degrees. This is easy to do because the radius of a circle always bisects the circumference exactly six times. (Interestingly, the geometrical term for a straight line across a circumference is a 'chord').

So, go to a corner of your chosen area and drive one of the poles vertically into the ground. Then take your cord and create a loop that can be slipped over the rod.

Originally the megalithic builders must have divided the sixth part of the circle into 61 parts through trial and error with small sticks. It is highly probable that they came to realise that a ratio of 175:3 gives a 366th part of a circle without the need to calibrate the circle.

Your next step is to make sure that your cord is a 175 units long from the centre of the first loop to the centre of a second loop that you will need to make (the length of the units does not matter). For convenience use a stick of about 10 inches in length to do this, but to avoid an over-large circle mark the stick into five equal parts (you can cheat and use a ruler for this if you want). Next use the stick to measure out 35 units from loop to loop, which will give you a length of approximately thirty feet.

Now place the first loop over the fixed rod and stretch out the cord to its full length in either a westerly or easterly direction and place the second rod into the loop. You can now scribe out part of a circle in the ground. Because we are using the ratio method there is no need to make out an entire sixth part of a circle; a couple of feet will do.

Next take your piece of string and tie it neatly to the weight to form a plumb line.

Appendix 1

You can then drive the rod into the ground using the plumb line to ensure that it is vertical. Then take your measuring stick and mark out a point on the curve that is three of the units away from the outer edge of the rod. Return to the centre and remove the first rod, marking the hole with a stone or other object to hand. This rod has now to be placed on the spot that you have marked on the circle, making sure that it is vertical and that its outer edge is three units from the corresponding edge of the first rod.

Return to the centre of the circle and look at the two rods. Through them you will be able to see exactly one 366th part of the horizon.

Stage four - Measuring time

You have now split the horizon so that it has the same number of parts as there are sunrises in the course of one orbit of the sun. Now you need to measure the spin of the Earth on its axis.

You will have to wait for a clear night when the stars are clearly visible. Stand behind the centre point and wait for a bright star to pass between the rods. There are twenty stars with an astronomical magnitude of 1.5, which are known as first-magnitude stars.

The apparent movement of stars across the horizon is due to the rotation of the Earth. It follows that the time that it takes a star to travel from the trailing edge of the first rod to that of the second, will take a period of time exactly equal to one three hundred and sixty-sixth part of one rotation (a day).

There are 86400 seconds in a day and therefore a 366th part of the day will be 236 seconds, or 3 minutes 56 seconds. So your two rods have provided you with a highly accurate clock that will work every time.

When you see a first magnitude star approaching the first pole take your plumb line and hold the string at a length of approximately sixteen inches. Swing the weight like a pendulum and as the appears from behind the first rod count the pulses from one extreme to the other.

There are only two factors that effect the swing of a pendulum; the length of the string and gravity - which is determined by the mass of the earth. If you swing a pendulum faster it will move outwards further but it will not change the number of pulses.

Your task now is to count the number of pulses of your pendulum whilst the star moves between the rods. You need to adjust the length until you get exactly 366 beats during this period of 3 minutes 56 seconds. It is likely to take you several attempts to get the length right so be prepared to do quite a bit of star gazing.

Stage five - Making your Megalithic Yard measure

One you have the correct length of pendulum mark the string at the exact point that it leaves your fingers. Next take the straight stick and place the marked part of the string, place it approximately in the centre and pull the line down the stick. Mark the stick at the point in the centre of the weight and then swing the pendulum over to the other side of the stick, ensuring that the marked part of the string stays firmly in place. Then mark the stick again to record the position of the centre of the weight.

Discard the pendulum and cut the stick at the two points that corresponded with the position of the weight.

Congratulations, you now have a stick that is exactly one Megalithic Yard long.

It is interesting to note that the curious British measurement unit known as a 'rod' or a 'pole' is equal to 6 megalithic yards to an accuracy of one percent. There are 4 rods to a chain and 80 chains to a mile. Could it be that the modern mile of 1760 yards is actually based on the prehistoric measure of the Megalithic Yard?

The above has been reproduced by kind permission of Dr Robert Lomas. Further details can be seen at his website : http://www.robertlomas.com.

Appendix 2
The Universe reflected in the details of the Tabernacle and governments of the Priests

Now here one may wonder at the ill-will which men bear to us, and which they profess to bear on account of our despising that Deity which they pretend to honour; for if any one do but consider the fabric of the tabernacle, and take a view of the garments of the high priest, and of those vessels which we make use of in our sacred ministration, he will find that our legislator was a divine man, and that we are unjustly reproached by others; for if any one do without prejudice, and with judgment, look upon these things, he will find they were every one made in way of imitation and representation of the universe. When Moses distinguished the tabernacle into three parts, and allowed two of them to the priests, as a place accessible and common, he denoted the land and the sea, these being of general access to all; but he set apart the third division for God, because heaven is inaccessible to men. And when he ordered twelve loaves to be set on the table, he denoted the year, as distinguished into so many months. By branching out the candlestick into seventy parts, he secretly intimated the Decani, or seventy divisions of the planets; and as to the seven lamps upon the candlesticks, they referred to the course of the planets, of which that is the number. The veils, too, which were composed of four things, they declared the four elements; for the fine linen was proper to signify the earth, because the flax grows out of the earth; the purple signified the sea, because that colour is dyed by the blood of a sea shell-fish; the blue is fit to signify the air; and the scarlet will naturally be an indication of fire. Now the vestment of the high priest being made of linen, signified the earth; the blue denoted the sky, being like lightning in its pomegranates, and in the noise of the bells resembling thunder. And for the ephod, it showed that God had made the universe of four elements; and as for the gold interwoven, I suppose it related to the splendour by which all things are enlightened. He also appointed the breastplate to be placed in the middle of the ephod, to resemble the earth, for that has the very middle place of the world. And the girdle which encompassed the high priest round, signified the ocean, for that goes round about and includes the universe. Each of the sardonyxes *[onyx in which white layers alternate with sard; yellow or orange cornelian'regarded as precious stones]* declares to us the sun and the moon; those, I mean, that were in the nature of buttons on the high priest's shoulders. And for the twelve stones, whether we understand by them the months, or whether we understand the like number of the signs of that circle which the Greeks call the Zodiac, we shall not be mistaken in their meaning. And for the mitre, which was of a blue colour, it seems to me to mean heaven; for how otherwise could the name of God be inscribed upon it? That it was also illustrated with a crown, and that of gold also, is because of that splendour with which God is pleased. Let this explication (16) suffice at present, since the course of my narration will often, and on many occasions, afford me the opportunity of enlarging upon the virtue of our legislator

The above is an extract from Flavius Josephus Antiquities of the Jews, Book 3, Chapter 7, relating to the garments worn by the priests and the high priests.
Translated by William Whiston

Appendix 3
A Speculative Outline Chronology for the History of the Craft

Much has changed. There have been very eminent men of letters and social rank, who have undertaken research into specific aspects of the history of Freemasonry. I do not intend to challenge their independent research and knowledge.

Much of that research was undertaken in the Victorian era of British history between about 1840 – 1910. It reflected the views and opinions then existing and expressed in the context of the background of the social influences of that era. The advent of the Great War 1914 – 1918, the Great Depression of the 1930's and the advent of the Second World War 1939 - 1945, resulted in the pool of Masonic knowledge advancing little.

Archaeology, as an academic discipline, commenced in the mid Victorian era, around 1860. Much digging in the Holy Land and Middle East had taken place in the hundred years leading to the second half of the twentieth century; artifacts had been diligently cleaned, restored and catalogued, but with the exception of a few instances, little analysis had been undertaken.

In the post World War 2 decades, education of the masses was a priority. More people went to university and more engineers, scientists and academics pored out of our colleges than ever before. New technologies were invented and discovered and the combined mass of brain power and science, resulted in in-depth analysis of archaeological artifacts and previously gathered information in a way that was inconceivable fifty years earlier. Our knowledge about almost every aspect of human endeavour grew. Our knowledge of the inter-relationship of what the ancients referred to as the macro-cosmos, became better understood, and adventures in space travel changed forever our perception of heaven and the heavens, by comparison with interpretations by our ancestors.

The sum total was a change in the way we perceived the ancient concepts of the creation of the world and all the things around us. And with that change, came a reinterpretation of our attitudes to religion.

So much, in the last fifty years of the twentieth century, changed. But, it was only in the last two decades of that century that new approaches to evaluating the history of Freemasonry evolved, bringing new and challenging information – and arguments.

At the end of the twentieth century, the official view of the United Grand Lodge of England was that Freemasonry, as we know it, can be traced to 1717. There has been much speculation about the true origins, but the UGL noted, that without document evidence or some other form of clear proof, which they doubted would ever be found even if it had existed in the past, these ideas had to remain just that, speculation. It is, perhaps, an understandable and proper attitude for such a worthy and high profile organization to adopt. But such is the accumulated knowledge of the past, that it is now possible to make a reasoned assessment of the historical path our ancient institution has evolved through.

The following is an assessment based on the information encountered during my enquiry. It starts 12,000 years ago and continues to the present era:

Before 10,000 BCE	Man had taken an interest in the environment that surrounded him as a hunter-gatherer. They had an accumulated knowledge about where to find various types of food, how to track and capture animals; which foods were good, and which were poisonous; how to use bone and skin to make implements and clothing. Shelter was probably still mainly in caves, especially in cooler northern latitudes.
10,000 BCE	Man was still somewhat nomadic, but had taken an interest in the heavens and began to wonder about the sun and moon, what made them work and how they affected the environment and the seasons.
8,000 BCE	Stable communities began to develop, along with crop selection and animal domestication. Inevitably, in any group of people, there will always be a few who will be looked to as the leaders, the tribal elders, and this was no doubt the case then. They collectively structured an orderly aspect to the group, collective hunting and defense, and a few basic rules of tribal governance. As a stable community with structure, the sharing of knowledge would have begun and they started experiments in living. This can be seen through crop selection and cultivation, growing what they wanted where they wanted it; animal husbandry and herding. All this could only have come from a primitive form of experimentation, and learning from the results.
5,000 BCE	The cycles of the sun, moon and seasons were understood and predictable. The pole star was noted along with the stars that moved – the planets. There was an understanding that the sun and moon had an affect of the environment providing periods when food was plentiful and others when survival was hardest. There was organised religion through worship of the Sun God and the fertility Goddess.
4,500 BCE	Early attempts were made to create structures, *scientific apparatus,* for monitoring the cycles of the sun in particular, but may have been temporary and subject to

decay by using porous materials. By about 3,500 BCE, there was a means of making these structures more permanent by prizing large stones from the ground and arranging them in the patterns needed. It also dictated the development of means of transporting those stones; lifting them several feet / metres above the ground; reinforcing supporting stones so that the whole did not collapse. We can see evidence of this in temples on Malta and Gozo.

The art of building a durable and stable *scientific apparatus* had begun. Monitoring the sun was well established as was the religion related to the Goddess of fertility. This dictated an early form of priesthood to administer and devise ceremonial functions.

3,000 BCE – 2,500 BCE   There was a good, but limited, understanding of the macro-cosmos. The tribal elders ruled the communities. Perhaps, a single individual who was a leading warrior or hunter, was elected to adjudicate in disputes. From this, kingship evolved.

The priesthoods became the guardians of knowledge. High Priests were akin to an early form of university professor. They ensured that the cumulative wisdom and knowledge already understood, was passed to succeeding generations. They evolved methods of research and study with junior priests performing the field work, such as observing the night sky, progress of shadows, the numbers of plants with five petals. Such understanding increased their perception of the enormity of the task of creation that had been undertaken by the deity.

Methods of shaping stone had begun, as can be seen in the doorways and roller bearings on Malta. This must have involved developing tools hard enough to cut into the stone and then specific tools for specialized work. No doubt around this time knowledge had been evolved amongst stone workers about what sort of stone was best to use and how it could be cut into manageable blocks. Thus was the stone quarry derived. To cut stone in a quarry would have required the development of yet more specialized tools, lifting devices and methods of working. This, no doubt resulted in the development of metal tools.

Basic geometry and the shape of the circle, triangle and square were defined and there were attempts to understand the arithmetic constants and ratios found in each.

Solar and lunar monitoring was very well established especially in Mesopotamia (Sumer) and Egypt. Elsewhere, and especially in Europe, the creation of stone circles as solar and lunar observatories, commenced, such as at Stonehenge. Different human characteristics, such as intelligence had been noted. There is the possibility that the priesthood selected bright young men and girls to be educated into, and become the custodians of knowledge and wisdom, and encouraged their marriage with a view to their children also being very intelligent. In this way the first dynastic families of priesthood were created. It would also represent the first attempts at cross breeding for a specific purpose other than natural selection - gene manipulation.

Tribes merged or were conquered by larger tribes and what we have come to know as countries, like Egypt, were formed. Large tribes congregated to create the urban environments. Stone walls were built around some such communities for protection and in so doing developed the stonemasons craft further.

2,500 BCE – 2,000 BCE   The macro-cosmos was better understood and very firmly the domain of the priesthoods. The cycle of the sun provided a calendar for civil administration and the lunar cycles for religious festivals.

The cardinal points of the earth had been defined; the first seven planets had names; the concept of precession was understood and the twelve constellations which make up the Great Belt, were mythically represented and their shape noted; the Earth was known to be a ball; seasonal prediction was established.

Building in stone and the craft of the stonemason were well established. There was a quest to build bigger and better structures that were durable and a reflection of the macro-cosmos. Some such structures collapsed during building, others shortly afterwards, but it all provided a learning process. We can see this through the structures of the pyramids both at Giza and those built earlier that extend many miles to the south of the Giza plateau.

Understanding of geometry was reasonably advanced for solving a range of otherwise complex problems.

The significance of proportion and what we know as Phi, had been realized; the circumference of a circle was noted to be three times the length of the diameter. There was an early understanding of the relationships in a triangle and what has passed into history as Pythagoras theorem.

2,000 BCE – 1,500 BCE

Throughout the Middle East, the Eastern Mediterranean, but particularly along the River Nile in Egypt, important buildings, especially temples, were designed to be durable, built from stone and reflected the macro-cosmos by being attuned to solar or lunar cycles, the direction of the prevailing wind, or fertility, but not limited to just these criteria. The development of urban communities increased the power and knowledge of the priesthood. The ability to travel beyond the immediate environment, especially by sea/boat, brought contact with other peoples in other cultures. New knowledge was gained and transferred between communities.

The rate at which knowledge was assembled and understood within the priesthoods, developed. It increased their power still further. Some of that knowledge, particularly that relating to geometry, transferred to the stonemasons who needed to know it in order to be able to both design and construct important buildings, but only the most skilled of those masons were admitted to the secrets of the priesthood where it related to building. They became the designers and overseers.

1,500 BCE – 1,000 BCE

Groups of Semitic peoples, for reasons which are not entirely clear, but possibly influenced by the events resulting from the volcanic explosion of Santorini, subsequent earthquakes and diseases along the River Niles and in the Delta, left the Nile region and congregated in an area of the Sinai near the Red Sea where they could obtain food from the sea. These people have passed into history as the Hebrews. As with all tribes or communities, there will be those that are leaders and those that are followers. The tribes were moulded together and some of the Egyptian customs and knowledge they had acquired became the basis of their own identity and customs. As the tribe of Hebrews grew larger they formed an army and began invading the more fertile lands closer to the Mediterranean. They ultimately secured a large area around which they forged a new nation of the Israelites, but subservient to Egyptian rule. Noting that a country like Egypt had a central town it defined as a capital or centre of administration, the Israelites followed. Egyptian power centred on Thebes where the priesthood was based, and administered from large temple complexes. Then Akhenaten formed his new capital dedicated to the Sun God and broke with Thebes.

1,000 BCE

The Israelites formed a city around a small village called Salem and it became the tribal administration centre that we know as Jerusalem. One tribal leader, from humble beginnings, rose above the others to become a warrior king. We know him as David. The elders decided to build a community as a centre for the priests, like the Egyptians had at Thebes, and thus designed a temple to become the centre for their culture. The prevailing deity was the Sun God, so the temple was built to reflect the solar, lunar and seasonal cycles, whilst embodying the geometric understanding and knowledge of the macro-cosmos as they understood it. It was a centre for learning and transfer of knowledge. The stonemasons that built it were the designers and incorporated the *ancient wisdom* they had then accumulated, but that knowledge was passed on as a verbal tradition. Unlike the Egyptian Temples which were built of large stone blocks, and may have had solar or lunar alignments but did not display specifically dedicated proportional beauty, the first Jerusalem temple, was built on the principles of proportion and beauty, as well as having ceremonial functionality. This made it unique amongst the fraternity of masons.

The knowledge of the macro-cosmos that the masons and priests had, was similar to that known by the Druids, who were the priesthood of the Celts and based in Europe. That knowledge included an understanding about the Earth being a sphere and how big it was, that it rotated on its axis, that the axis had a tilt, that the tilt had a wobble, that the Earth orbited the sun which was a large fiery ball.

750 BCE

The foundations of the later civilizations of Greece and Rome, were formed. The priesthoods became more concerned with religious ceremonial issues; the stonemasons became the harbingers of knowledge about building, about design including proportion and form and the geometry to achieve the end result. The new breed of philosophers developed and consolidated knowledge.

There was the rise of great Greek philosophers and mathematicians, including Euclid, Pythagoras, Plato, Aristotle, to name but a few.

Meanwhile the Egyptians who has recorded their knowledge in hieroglyphic language, gradually used the script which we know as Arabic, and the means of deciphering the hieroglyphics, diminished. The rise of the early Greek philosophers coincided with the ability to travel more widely than the Egyptians had, and new and different knowledge transferred from places such as Persia and India. The mystery schools became a place for developing new ideas and evaluating the old. This enabled them to assemble the accumulated knowledge of the past, assimilate the new knowledge, build on it and record it such that the well known Greek philosophers are seen as having evolved great theories which have been handed down to us.

The stonemasons meanwhile, were pushing the boundaries of elegant design and craftsmanship, embellishing structures with deliberate character, like the Parthenon in Athens. The Ionic, Doric and Corinthian architectural styles began to evolve.

The masons also evolved the means of constructing a semi-circular arch, the secret to which is the keystone, and this they kept as a trade secret.

350 BCE

In the period from about 1,000 BCE the Geocentric versus Heliocentric concepts of celestial mechanics began to be questioned by philosophers and priests, with each concept having merit. Aristotle declared that the geocentric system was the answer. The priests, now more related to matters spiritual and ceremonial endorsed it, and it became the official concept for the next 1,800 years.

The masons knew that the heliocentric concept was correct and kept it as a trade secret pending a re-acknowledgement of it as a scientific fact. This lost knowledge became known later as *Hiram Abif.*

All the information was packaged in a series of short

plays and dialogue which enabled the knowledge to be passed from one generation of masons to another. This was an age old process.

250 BCE

The rise of the Roman Empire resulted in the stonemasons craft and knowledge being in great demand. The trade expanded across Europe, North Africa and the Middle East along with the expansion of the Empire, and the geometric methodology and knowledge of the macro-cosmos, which we have now come to know as the Liberal Arts and Sciences, went with them. The masons built roads, bridges, aqueducts, harbours, cities, warehouses, temples, palaces, domes, majestic houses and fortifications.

The breadth of design, building knowledge and experience went forward in great leaps. The collapse of the Roman Empire resulted in masons being regionally employed, and various new design concepts evolved based on local culture and customs. Chief amongst these was the Arabic affect which passed into the cultural design and patterns associated with the later Islamic communities. In the more remote areas of Northern Europe, including Britain, the skill of building with stone substantially died out when the Roman army withdrew, and building reverted to mainly using wood.

600 CE

The growth of the Roman Church through Europe, replacing much of the authority previously exercised by the Roman Emperors, resulted in a need for the stonemasons craft to again flourish through the building of a newer style of temples, the Christian churches, and housings for the new priesthood - the monasteries. The knowledge of the macro-cosmos prevailed as being related to the concepts of creation as handed down in the scriptures. Many of the new churches were built on alignments that reflected solar and lunar cycles.

The knowledge of the macro-cosmos as it related to creation, and therefore symbolic of the hand of the deity, became knowledge retained within the priesthood.

The geocentric concept of celestial mechanics remained the basis of religious interpretation. The heliocentric concept defined by *Hiram Abif* remained the secret knowledge of masonry.

Appendix 3

Around 700 CE, the era of Bede, masons with the retained knowledge of geometry and celestial mechanics, plus their trade secrets related to design, proportion and building technology, were again introduced into England through the building of substantial religious establishments.

1,000 CE

Jerusalem, Holy to the three main religions of Judaism, Christianity and Islam, was invaded by the Seljuk Turks; Christians were stopped from making pilgrimages to it, leading to the Crusades. The Order of the Knights Templar was formed. They were under papal protection and operated under the authority of the Pope. They were therefore very much part of the religious establishment of the Roman church. During their time in the Holy Land and Middle East, they came into contact with much of the *ancient wisdom* that the church regarded as forbidden knowledge. This included the concept of the heliocentric system, geometry and geometric patterns resulting from it. Building styles evolved from that knowledge. Maybe they also discovered that the religious philosophy being espoused by the church was not entirely in accordance with events that had actually occurred in Jerusalem, 1,000 years earlier. This brought them into conflict with the establishment of the church which used the overtures of Phillip le Bel as an excuse to dissolve this organization.

Meanwhile, captured masons from the Islamic countries, provided design ideas that the Templars included in their own structures. Their benefactor, St Bernard, encouraged these new designs and they became known as the Gothic style. The geometry on which this is based became the design and building principle for almost all the great Cathedrals in Britain and throughout the area of Europe dominated by the Vatican. The design principles also became the specialist and secret knowledge of the masons.

The Guilds and Corporations of the Medieval period became the regulators of the trade, but the knowledge contained in that trade about design and the reflections of celestial mechanics, remained a trade secret.

1,300 CE

Senior figures of the Knights Templar in France were rounded up in 1307 CE. Many others of lesser rank escaped to Scotland where the first Preceptory outside of the Holy Land had been built. The Order of the Knights Templar was finally dissolved by papal bull. The Grand Master, Jacques de Molay, was assassinated in 1314 by being roasted alive on the authority of the Pope. The masons that had been associated with the Order now inherited the residual knowledge they did not already have, especially in relation to the heliocentric system. Many, facing destitution, were absorbed by monasteries across Britain, and probably the rest of Europe. Their knowledge gradually became absorbed into the trade of the stonemason, and as such the esoteric knowledge they had, passed to the more highly skilled practitioners. The retention of that knowledge was still by verbal tradition.

1,400 BCE
Copernicus published a theory which supported the heliocentric system, but was condemned by the Vatican which continued to support the geocentric concept.

In Scotland, the Grand Master of the Masons, and a descendent of the Sinclair family that Hugues de Payen had married into 300 years earlier, built a church on his estate which embodied much of the esoteric knowledge then understood by masons. It was also built at a location which reflected celestial knowledge, the shadow cast by two pillars as had been erected at Solomon's Temple. The shadow at the time of the Solstices, produced the pattern of the square. That church is known as Rosslyn Chapel. It became the spiritual home of masons, especially in Scotland. Because the Chapel built on the land of the Grand Master became the spiritual home of masonry, so being admitted to the fraternity of masons became known as being *admitted on the square*, reflecting the knowledge of the shadows at Rosslyn.

Lodges had previously met only on building sites, but now they began to meet in selected locations. In Scotland, for instance, there are records of special arrangements being made for them to meet in the City Hall at Edinburgh.

1,500 CE
Henry VIII of England broke the dominance of the Roman Church in England, founded the Church of England and dissolved the monasteries, thereby abolishing their power, and that of the Vatican, in the country. A new set of difficulties affected the masons, many of which had been involved in maintaining the

monasteries and churches. Now they were involved in dismantling them. A power struggle between English Kings and Queens, and the Vatican followed, resulting in Elizabeth I upholding the Church of England, and with it, Protestantism.

In this period, with papal authority in England having been eliminated, independent practitioners of building design began to appear – the early development of the profession of the architect. The masons who built their subsequent designs then absorbed some of these architects into the fraternity and referred to them as *Speculative Masons*, as opposed to *operative masons*. This led to the formation of some private lodges as opposed to those dedicated to the operative mason.

Universities began to flourish and the basis of the knowledge imparted to students was the same understanding that had been jealously guarded by masons over the millennia – the *ancient wisdom* of our ancestors – the Liberal Arts and Sciences. These were the basis of the Master of Arts degree.

James VI, son of Mary Queen of Scots, became the King of Scotland. He acknowledged the development of Masonry and regulated it through Shawe Statutes.

1,600 CE

The Stuarts were supporters of Masonry. James VI Scotland became James I of England and the regulation of Masonry he had introduced in Scotland, moved with him. Freemasonry developed and the esoteric knowledge spread in specific realms of society, especially the Architects, certain members of the Aristocracy and those that served them. This continued until Charles I was beheaded and the monarchy in England was abolished.

In Italy, Galileo was tortured on the orders of the Vatican for expressing Copernican (heliocentric) views. The geocentric system was still alive and well in religious circles, so in Masonic connections the heliocentric knowledge was still retained under a reference to Hiram Abif.

The restoration of the English monarchy in 1660 with the coronation (anointing) of Charles II, resulted in Sir Robert Moray, a Scot, supporter of the Stuarts and confident of the Stuart king, establishing the Royal Society along with several other Freemasons. This heralded the open development of science – the era of the Enlightenment – and paved the way for the many discoveries which resulted in the Industrial Revolution and the establishment of branches of science such as Astronomy and Physics which have given us the technology our society knows today.[1]

1,700 CE

Throughout the 16th, 17th and 18th centuries, the esoteric knowledge contained in Freemasonry, was that which was also known as the Seven Liberal Arts and Sciences. It was the starting point for much of the future scientific endeavour.

The Jacobite difficulties of the early eighteenth century caused some embarrassment for members of Lodges based in London and other major provincial towns. They decided to distance themselves from these problems and they set about doing so by creating the Grand Lodge of England. Certain Freemasons, their identity unknown to us but familiar with the esoteric knowledge inherent in Masonic ritual, understood the significance of the number twenty and that certain Hebrew characters could be added together to make that number. They realized that those same Hebrew characters could also represent the year 1717 which they were either in, or was approaching. To distance themselves from their colleagues in Scotland, four Lodges established the Grand Lodge of England in 1717 as a separate administrative body from that based in Edinburgh and in so doing enshrined the number twenty of *ancient wisdom*.

A member of one of those four lodges was Sir Joseph Banks[2], recognized as a leading botanist, and a President of the Royal Society. He sailed with Captain Cook on a voyage to Tahiti to observe the transit of Venus, a planet synonymous with Freemasonry and *ancient wisdom*. They discovered New Zealand and the Eastern coast of Australia. Banks later encouraged the development and settlement of Australia, so that it can rightly be said that Australia as we know it today was colonized from the original encouragement of a Freemason.

1,800 CE

The heliocentric system finally took precedence over the geocentric concept, based on the revelations of the new science of astronomy.

The Liberal Arts and Sciences, the knowledge

inherent in Masonry, remained the basis of study at university for a Master of Arts degree.

As science evolved so more and more questions were raised about the veracity of the history surrounding the Holy Land as espoused by the religious authorities. Archaeological expeditions were organized, and gradually over a period of 150 years, the knowledge base increased. The results did not always support the religious doctrine promoted for the past two thousand years.

With the heliocentric system finally and rightfully re-established, so Freemasonry could become more open, though guarded. Membership was no longer the domain solely of operative and speculative masons. It was open to men who were open minded, had academic ability and were interested in preserving the esoteric knowledge it contained.

From the mid-nineteenth century, the growth of the Industrial Revolution and expansion of the British Empire saw the development of Masonic Lodges in other countries of the Empire. In Britain, there was a massive growth in a social force known as the Middle Class. These were literate men, managers and middle managers in Banks, Insurance companies, Shipping companies, traders in commodities, owners of factories and shops. Many of these substantial institutions, like banks, encouraged managers to ensure that their families regularly went to church, would participate and take an interest in, social and charitable activities. A wide range of social organizations and fraternal benefit societies were created that filled the needs of prospering and diverse communities. Freemasonry in England was one such beneficiary of this new social order. There was a substantial growth in membership, new lodges were formed and special meeting rooms called Masonic Halls, were built in many of the major towns of Britain. In other towns, where this was not easily achieved, specially prepared rooms in hotels and public houses were used as meeting places. Some survive bearing names like, *The Freemasons Arms*.

Then, in the early twentieth century there was a massive improvement in education such that by the mid-twentieth century, most of the knowledge which had hitherto been regarded as the secrets of

Freemasonry were being taught in schools to children who had barely reached their teenage years; geometry, arithmetic, music, logic (reasoning and problem solving), grammar and rhetoric (language and languages), astronomy and science (Celestial Mechanics, the solar system and the universe, Physics, Chemistry, Biology). Much of this is derived from earlier understanding evolved under the headings of alchemy, astrology, ancient wisdom and understanding of the macro-cosmos.

The secret knowledge that had been the domain of Masonry was no longer secret. It was part of the education of the masses - on a global scale.

Thus, when anyone says that there is no secret knowledge or information in Freemasonry, they are correct. It is now common knowledge for anyone who has benefited from a modest education.

So, what of Freemasonry today? I believe that if one cares to look, the knowledge of the *ancient wisdom* is still there embodied in ceremonies and furnishings. Freemasonry still encourages a respectable approach to life based on truth, prudence, charity, justice, modesty and temperance, obedience to law and order. It encourages its members to become upright citizens – pillars of society – in any community in which they live and work. These are all qualities that a properly regulated and upright society needs in its judges, magistrates, doctors, accountants, teachers, public officers and boardrooms. In the early twenty-first century, much Masonic activity has been directed to supporting social needs through its charitable activities. By taking care of the society in which one lives, is the way in which Freemasons look after themselves.

And what of the *ancient wisdom?* It must remain. Who knows when it may be lost to society in general, and needs to be re-discovered. Freemasonry, properly regulated, will remain the custodian.

[1] See *The Invisible College* by Robert Lomas
[2] From information available in the Library, Freemasons Hall, London

Bibliography

For several years I read, noted and copied extracts from many papers and books, viewed many internet websites and other media without recording details, because at that time the information I was gathering was for my own interest – the idea of writing a book was not on the agenda. Needless to say, some of that material influenced my thinking and I may have restated comments by others in innocence. Every effort has been made to track down all copyright holders and obtain copyright clearance but in the event of any omission please contact the author via the Publisher so that any necessary correction can be made in future impressions of the book.

The Encyclopaedia of Religion
The Catholic Encyclopaedia on-line version - New Advent
New Catholic Encyclopaedia, 2nd edition
The New Standard Jewish Encyclopaedia, Edited by G. Wigoden
Encyclopaedia of Creation Myths, David and Margaret Adams Leeming.
Encyclopaedia of Early Christianity
Encyclopaedia of Mythology, Arthur Cotterell
Encyclopaedia Britannica
Encarta Encyclopaedia
Encyclopaedia of Freemasonry
Encyclopaedia Judaica
Holy Bible – King James version
Holy Bible – New King James version
Holy Bible – New International version, Hodder and Stoughton
Macarthur Study Bible – New King James version, World Bibles
Student Bible Dictionary, Karen Dockrey/Johnnie Godwin/ Phyllis Godwin
Cover to Cover, Selwyn Hughes and Trevor J. Partridge
The Temples at Jerusalem and their Masonic Connections, George Farrah
MMV Encyclopaedia Mythica
Wikipedia
Bede: On the Temple, Sean Connolly
Jesus The Man, Dr Barbara Thiering
Jesus of the Apocalypse, Dr Barbara Thiering
The Book of the Dead, E. A Wallis-Budge
The Oxford Bible Commentary, Barton and Muddiman
The Mitre and the Crown, Dominic Aidan Bellenger & Stella Fletcher

The Copper Scroll Decoded, Robert Feather

The Atlas of the Bible, Luc H. Grollenberg

The Templars, Piers Paul Read

The New Knighthood: The History of the Order of the Temple,
    Professor Malcolm Barber

The Yellow Cross, Rene Weis

Legend, Dr David Rohl

A Test of Time, the Bible Myth to History, Dr David Rohl

The Lost Testament, Dr David Rohl

Gothic Cathedrals and Sacred Geometry, George Lesser

Chartres Cathedral, Malcolm Miller – Pitkin Guides

The Geometric Skeleton of Peterborough Cathedral, Frederick Stallard and
    Paul Bush

Solomon's Temple – its history and structure, Rev'd W. Shaw Caldecott

The Hiram Key, Robert Lomas and Christopher Knight

Illustrations of Masonry, William Preston

Ancient Freemasonry, Frank Higgins

Early History of Masonry in England, James Orchard Halliwell

Chartres-Sacred Geometry, Sacred Space, Gordon Strachan

A Geological Miscellany, Craig and Jones

Antiquity of the Jews, Josephus

The Second Messiah, Robert Lomas and Christopher Knight

Uriel's Machine, Robert Lomas and Christopher Knight

The Book of Hiram, Robert Lomas and Christopher Knight

The Invisible College, Robert Lomas

Turning the Hiram Key, Robert Lomas

Templar Gold, Patrick Byrne

The Keys to the Temple, David Furlong

Sacred Geometry, Robert Lawlor

The Holy Kingdom, Adrian Gilbert

The New Jerusalem, Adrian Gilbert

Magi: Quest for the Secret Tradition, Adrian Gilbert

The Mayan Prophecies: Unlocking the Secrets of a Lost Civilization,
    Adrian Gilbert and Maurice Cotterell

Signs in the Sky, Adrian Gilbert

The Holy Blood and the Holy Grail, Henry Lincoln, Michael Baigent,
    Richard Leigh

The Golden Thread of Time, Crichton Miller

The Secret Teachings of All Ages, Manley P. Hall

Genesis Unveiled, Ian Lawton

The Sign and the Seal, Graham Hancock

Fingerprints of the Gods, Graham Hancock

Genisis – The First Book of Revelations, David Wood

Bibliography

The Hole Craft & Fellowship of Masonry, With a Chronicle of the History of the Worshipful Company of Masons of the City of London, Edward Condor
The Antiquities of Freemasonry, Rev'd Dr G. Oliver
The Dead Sea Scrolls Deception, Michael Baigent, Richard Leigh
Freemasonry: A Celebration of the Craft, John Hamill & R. A. Gilbert
History of English Freemasonry, John Hamill
The Temple and the Lodge, Michael Baigent, Richard Leigh
Ancient Traces, Michael Baigent
The Lost Gospel: Book of Q and Christian Origins, Burton L. Mack
The Secret Zodiacs of Washington DC, David Overson

Index

Index

Index

Index